THE POLITICAL
AND SOCIAL THOUGHT OF
CHARLES A. BEARD

THE POLITICAL
AND SOCIAL THOUGHT OF
CHARLES A. BEARD

by

BERNARD C. BORNING

University of Washington Press

Seattle, 1962

Copyright © 1962 by the University of Washington Press
Library of Congress Catalog Card Number 62–12129
Printed in the United States of America

This book is published with the assistance
of a grant from the Ford Foundation.

TO
CORALIE, ALAN,
AND KATHERINE

ACKNOWLEDGMENTS

It is a pleasure to acknowledge my indebtedness to my former teacher, Benjamin E. Lippincott of the University of Minnesota, not only for suggesting this study in the first place but also for his counsel and friendship since undergraduate days so long ago. Although it was never my good fortune to meet Charles A. Beard in person, I must certainly have indirectly felt something of his personality through the kindness and hospitality shown me by members of his family. I am grateful for their help and understanding, and it is my hope that they will feel that this study has treated Beard, the man, as a dignified human being, regardless of how his ideas may have fared. I also wish to thank the many friends and former associates of Beard who have given me the benefit of their impressions and comments. I wish to express my appreciation to the University of Idaho for a semester's sabbatical leave which assisted me in bringing this study to its final stages. I want to record my thanks to my colleague, Robert J. Huckshorn, for his cooperation, and to Miss Rose Renton for her typing assistance.

Numerous publishers of books and journals, as well as other holders of copyrights, have kindly granted me permission to quote passages from the works indicated below, and I wish to thank them for their generosity:

The Academy of Political Science: from *Political Science Quarterly,* review by Charles A. Beard of George B. Adams, *Political History of England.*

The American Academy of Political and Social Science: from *Annals of the American Academy of Political and Social Science,* "Budgetary Provisions of the New York Constitution" and "Training for Efficient Public Service," by Charles A. Beard.

The American Historical Review: "Currents of Thought in Historiography," "Some Economic Origins of Jeffersonian Democracy," "That Noble Dream," and "Written History as an Act of Faith," by Charles A. Beard; reviews by Beard of R. G. Collingwood, *The Idea of History,* and Arthur M. Schlesinger, *The Rise of the City.*

American Mercury: "Bankruptcy Fire-Sale" and "What Is a Statesman?" by Charles A. Beard.

The American Political Science Association: from *American Political Science Review,* "Conditions Favorable to Creative Work in Political Science" and "Time, Technology and the Creative Spirit in

vii

Political Science," by Charles A. Beard; and reviews by Beard of Herbert von Beckerath, *Modern Industrial Organization,* Charles E. Merriam, *The New Democracy and the New Despotism,* and Rexford G. Tugwell, *Industrial Discipline and the Governmental Arts.*

Atlantic Monthly: "Fiction of Majority Rule" and "Historians at Work: Brooks and Henry Adams," by Charles A. Beard.

William Beard and Mrs. Miriam B. Vagts: *The Administration and Politics of Tokyo, Contemporary American History, 1877–1913, Cross Currents in Europe Today, The Devil Theory of War, The Discussion of Human Affairs, Public Policy and the General Welfare,* all by Charles A. Beard; *The American Leviathan,* by Charles A. Beard with William Beard; *History of the United States,* by Charles A. Beard with Mary R. Beard; *The Idea of National Interest* and *The Open Door at Home* by Charles A. Beard with G. H. E. Smith; Foreword by Charles A. Beard to *The New German Constitution,* by René Brunet, copyright 1922 by Alfred A. Knopf, Inc., copyright renewed 1949 by Miriam B. Vagts and William Beard; and a letter from Charles A. Beard to George S. Counts, July 13, 1945.

Columbia University Press: *The Constitution Reconsidered,* edited by Conyers Read; *The Economic Interpretation of History,* by E. R. A. Seligman, and *Politics,* by Charles A. Beard.

Confluence: "Woodrow Wilson, Collective Security, and the Lessons of History," by Robert E. Osgood.

Council on Foreign Relations, Inc.: from *Foreign Affairs,* "Education under the Nazis," by Charles A. Beard.

The Educational Policies Commission, National Educational Association: *The Unique Function of Education in American Democracy,* by Charles A. Beard.

Events Publishing Company: from *Current History,* review by Charles A. Beard of Harry E. Barnes, *The Genesis of the World War;* from *Events,* "The Interpretation of Events," "War with Japan?" and "Will Roosevelt Keep Us Out of War?" all by Charles A. Beard; from *Forum and Century,* "World as I Want It," by Charles A. Beard.

Franklin Watts: *Voices of History: Great Speeches and Papers of the Year 1941,* edited by Franklin Watts with Introduction by Charles A. Beard.

Harper & Brothers: from *Harper's Magazine,* "Bigger and Better

Armaments," "Democracy Holds Its Ground: A European Survey," and "Whom Does Congress Represent?" all by Charles A. Beard.

Holt, Rinehart and Winston: *Public Policy and the General Welfare,* by Charles A. Beard.

Journal of the History of Ideas: "The Skepticism and Historical Faith of Charles Beard," by Whitaker T. Deininger.

Journal of Social Forces: "Municipal Research Abroad and at Home," by Charles A. Beard.

Alfred A. Knopf, Inc.: *The Economic Basis of Politics,* by Charles A. Beard; *Mr. Justice Black: The Man and His Opinions,* by John Paul Frank; Foreword by Beard to *The New German Constitution,* by René Brunet, copyright 1922 by Alfred A. Knopf, Inc., copyright renewed 1949 by Miriam B. Vagts and William Beard.

Longmans, Green & Co.: *Whither Mankind,* edited by Charles A. Beard.

Macmillan Co.: *American Government and Politics, An Economic Interpretation of the Constitution of the United States,* and *Economic Origins of Jeffersonian Democracy,* all by Charles A. Beard; *America in Midpassage, The American Spirit,* and *The Rise of American Civilization,* all by Charles A. Beard with Mary R. Beard; *National Governments and the World War,* by Charles A. Beard with Frederic A. Ogg; *Chief Justice Stone and the Supreme Court,* by Samuel J. Konefsky; *Democracy, Liberty and Property,* edited by Francis W. Coker; *Encyclopedia of the Social Sciences,* edited by Edwin R. A. Seligman and Alvin Johnson; *The Idea of Progress,* by John B. Bury; and *Research in the Social Sciences,* edited by Wilson Gee.

Marshall Jones Co.: *Cross Currents in Europe Today,* by Charles A. Beard.

Maxey, Chester C.: Introduction by Charles A. Beard to *County Administration,* by Chester C. Maxey.

Nation Associates, Inc.: from *Nation,* "Agriculture in the Nation's Economy," "Could Daniel Webster Teach in New York's Schools?" "Count Karolyi and America," "Lo! The Poor Professor," "War with Japan: What Shall We Get Out of It?" all by Charles A. Beard; "What I Expect of Roosevelt," by Charles A. Beard and others; reviews by Beard of Charles G. Fenwick, *Political Systems in Transition: War-Time and After,* George O'Brien, *An Essay on Mediaeval Economic Teaching,* Eden and Cedar Paul, *Creative*

Revolution: A Study in Communist Ergatocracy, and Sidney and Beatrice Webb, *A Constitution for the Socialist Commonwealth of Great Britain.*

National Elementary Principal: "Education Enriched by Living," by Charles A. Beard.

National Municipal League: from *National Municipal Review,* "American Influence on Municipal Government in the Orient," "New York Constitutional Convention," "Our Moot State Constitutional Convention," "Public Employment," and "Political Parties in City Government: A Reconsideration of Old View Points," all by Charles A. Beard; reviews by Beard of Zechariah Chafee, *Freedom of Speech,* and Russell Forbes, *Governmental Purchasing.*

New Republic: "America and the Next War," "Anti-trust Racket," "Big Navy Boys," "Blessed Profit System," "Collective Security," "The Economic Basis of Politics," "Making a Bigger and Better Navy," "Political Science in the Crucible," "What a Budget Should Be," and "The Woman's Party," all by Charles A. Beard; letters from Beard, "Beard on Liberalism" and "An Economic Interpretation of Navies"; reviews by Beard of Viscount Edward Grey, *Twenty-Five Years, 1892–1916,* Harold Loeb and Associates, *The Chart of Plenty,* Hendrick Van Loon, *The Story of Mankind,* and Henri Welschinger, *L'Alliance Franco-Russe.*

Ohio State University: from *Journal of Higher Education,* "Quest for Academic Power," by Charles A. Beard.

Public Administration Service: *The Work Unit in Federal Administration.*

Random House, Inc.: *Capital, The Communist Manifesto and Other Writings,* by Karl Marx, edited by Max Eastman.

Saturday Review, Inc.: from *Saturday Review of Literature,* "Behind the New Deal," by Charles A. Beard; reviews by Beard of Edward C. Kirkland, *A History of American Economic Life,* Eduard C. Lindeman, *Wealth and Culture,* and Otto Neurath, *Modern Man in the Making.*

Charles Scribner's Sons: *The Nature of the Social Sciences in Relation to Objectives of Instruction,* by Charles A. Beard.

Social Research: "Democracy and Education in the United States," by Charles A. Beard.

Social Science Research Council: *Theory and Practice in Historical Study: A Report of the Committee on Historiography,* edited by Merle E. Curti.

Society for the Advancement of Education, Inc.: from *School and Society*, "Methods of Training for Public Service," by Charles A. Beard.

Stevens & Sons, Ltd.: *Political Quarterly*, "Future of Democracy in the United States," by Charles A. Beard.

Teachers College Record: "Politics and Education," by Charles A. Beard.

University of Chicago Press: *The Philosophy and Policies of Woodrow Wilson*, edited by Earl Latham, copyright 1958 by the University of Chicago.

University of Georgia, Institute of Law and Government: *Bulletin of the University of Georgia*.

Vanguard Press, Inc.: *The Devil Theory of War*, by Charles A. Beard.

Viking Press, Inc.: *The Republic*, by Charles A. Beard.

Virginia Quarterly Review: "Constitution and States' Rights" and "Corporations and Natural Rights," by Charles A. Beard.

Yale University Press: *President Roosevelt and the Coming of the War, 1941;* and "Conflicts in City Planning," "Congress under Fire," and "Political Heritage of the Twentieth Century," from *Yale Review*, copyright Yale University Press. All by Charles A. Beard.

CONTENTS

INTRODUCTION

In searching for light on men's thinking it is
fitting and proper, therefore, to inquire into
the circumstances of their individual history
and experience and to examine the great interests which they have been associated with
or espoused. Indeed unless we are to indulge
in idle speculation or in vague psychological
conjectures no other course seems open to us.

Prefatory note, Samuel J. Konefsky,
*Chief Justice Stone and the
Supreme Court* (1945)

There is impressive evidence to indicate that the first half of the
twentieth century has been as rich in social thought as any period in
our history. In the space of scarcely a human life span, our people
have built up giant industrial and financial organizations, acquired
an overseas empire, participated in the Great War of 1914–18, returned to "normalcy," struggled with problems of economic depression, fought World War II, helped launch the United Nations, and
unlocked atomic power. It is small wonder if a great ferment of
ideas has accompanied these developments.

In the present volume we examine the thinking of Charles A.
Beard, whose intellectual career from 1898 to 1948 reflected the major
currents in American thought during this half century.

Beard had the distinction of achieving prominence and wide influence in two fields: political science and history. He attained the
presidency of the national association in each discipline. He wrote
prolifically for fifty years and had a large readership not only in academic circles but throughout the general public. Literally millions
of copies of his writings were published.[1] His ideas were a center of
controversy as early as the progressive era and as late as the year of
his death.

Mere mention of some of his intellectual interests suggests the
broad range of his scholarship and thought. In 1913 his progressive
era view of American politics and history attracted stormy attention

---

[1] Howard K. Beale produces detailed figures showing that sales of Beard's
histories alone, not including studies in government, came to 11,352,163
copies; see Howard K. Beale (ed.), *Charles A. Beard* (Lexington: University
of Kentucky Press, 1954), pp. 310–12.

with the publication of *An Economic Interpretation of the Constitution of the United States.*[2] The work was symptomatic of the anti-formalist temper being displayed in a number of fields of social thought in those years, a temper exemplified not only in Beard's writings but also in those of J. Allen Smith, Carl Becker, and other scholars. Early in the century Beard joined the New History movement then being publicized by James Harvey Robinson. By the 1930's he was arousing the ire of some of his contemporaries by his enchantment with historical relativism. In the later years, too, he qualified his previous economic emphasis to present a considerably broadened explanation of the basic factors in politics.

Beard was active in other areas of social thought as well. From the days of Theodore Roosevelt, through the years of the New Deal, he supported domestic political reform and fought the advocates of laissez faire. In the final period of his life his increasingly isolationist foreign policy views stimulated warm debate and caused many of his former intellectual brothers to part company with him. He was a thinker who for years claimed to disdain theorizing and the power of ideas. Yet throughout his life he valued intellectual freedom, and on numerous occasions eloquently defended it. Regardless of our agreement or disagreement with his ideas or his methodology, we can hardly ignore him.

In order to provide perspective before we examine his ideas and their intellectual environment in further detail, we first briefly sketch his life story.

Charles Beard was born on an Indiana farm November 27, 1874, shortly after American voters, for the first time since the Civil War, had elected a Democratic majority to the House of Representatives. His father, in the years since he had moved to the community from North Carolina, had not only built up substantial holdings of rich farmland and otherwise prospered, but provided his family with a home filled with fine books. Mingled with the generally cherished Federalist-Whig-Republican outlook were certain iconoclastic tendencies in the family's tradition. Thus, on one occasion when it appeared that a visiting colored preacher would have difficulty finding lodgings in the community, he was promptly made an honored guest in the Beard home despite the raised eyebrows of some of the neighbors. Many years earlier Beard's independent-minded Quaker grand-

[2] (New York: Macmillan Co., 1913).

father in North Carolina had married a Methodist girl, and had further dissented from local sentiment by hiding runaway slaves in a trick chimney on his farm. Beyond that, Beard's lineage stretched back to English and Scotch-Irish settlers who had migrated to America nearly two hundred years earlier.

As a boy, Charles trudged to the Quaker academy in nearby Spiceland. On his graduation at eighteen, he joined his older brother Clarence to help run a country weekly which their father had acquired. In the fall of 1895 he enrolled at DePauw University in the neighboring county seat town of Greencastle. Here he continued his journalistic endeavors as a reporter for the Henry County *Republican*. For a time he was active in the local Republican club.

Young Beard's college days opened his eyes to the broader world beyond his rural neighborhood, and to traditions in America's heritage not those of his boyhood. By all accounts, one of the most stimulating influences on his developing mind at this time was his favorite teacher, Colonel James Weaver, Civil War veteran and former American consul in Vienna, a man gifted with a remarkable ability to infect students with his own insatiable intellectual curiosity. Another indelible imprint was left by Beard's visit to Chicago in the summer of 1896 on completion of his freshman year. There he was stirred by the oratory of William Jennings Bryan, and by the unrest, the squalor, the misery, the low wages, the currents of dissent in the throbbing metropolis. Continuing his studies at DePauw, he joined the debating team, arguing the merits of such radical notions as income taxes and legalized labor unions.

At college he had other experiences which were greatly to affect his future. On one occasion, he chanced on the scene just as a boat filled with DePauw students capsized and dumped its occupants unceremoniously into the lake. The dripping coed he helped from the water turned out to be a young lady by the name of Mary Ritter. A few years after this informal meeting she became Mary Ritter Beard. Some of the best things that came his way in life, Beard later joked, had been "pure happenstance."

Just as he was graduating from DePauw in 1898, the war against Spain began. He tried to volunteer his services, but manpower was already overabundant and he was not accepted.

In the fall of 1898 young Beard began study at Oxford, England. France and Britain at the time were on the verge of war over the Fashoda incident, and this further aroused his interest in world affairs. Domestic developments within Britain also fascinated him, and, despite a full study program under Frederick York Powell and other professors at Oxford, he found time outside class to take part in extended student discussions of economic and political problems. The early stirrings of the incipient Labour party attracted his attention, and he felt the influence of such personalities as the Webbs, Keir Hardie, Sidney Ball, and other leaders of dissent.

At the same time he collaborated with Walter Vrooman, a young socialist from Kansas, in working for the establishment of a labor college at the university, a college to train leaders for the unions and cooperative societies. With financial aid from Vrooman's well-to-do wife, and encouragement from certain labor leaders and Oxford professors, the college officially opened in February, 1899. It was named Ruskin Hall in honor of the author of *Unto This Last*. Young Beard himself spoke at the opening ceremonies in the Oxford town hall, helped to secure the first teachers, and energetically solicited support for the new venture. To this day his name appears on a plaque as one of the founders.

Following this first year at Oxford, he returned temporarily to the United States for a semester's study of American history at Cornell University. In March of 1900 he married Mary Ritter, and during that summer the two of them, knapsacks on their backs, bicycled through Europe, sightseeing and visiting among the peasants and villagers. Later that year Beard, now with his wife, returned to England.

Here he applied himself enthusiastically in his new position as extension secretary of Ruskin College. For nearly two years he lectured up and down the industrial regions of England and Wales, set up study groups, and actively encouraged the adult education programs sponsored by the Educational Committee of the Cooperative Society. The "Home and Field Notes" of the *Young Oxford*, early organ of Ruskin College, contain numerous references to his activities. Frequently there are articles by Beard himself, and these reveal the deep imprint made on his developing mind by English reformism during these early years. In 1901 he published his first book, *The Industrial Revolution*.[3] Advertised in the *Young Oxford* as the first of a Ruskin Hall "extension series," the small volume summarized for working people the wider social implications of industrialization, and pointed out its potentialities for future hu-

[3] (London: S. Sonnenschein & Co., 1901).

man welfare. In 1902, after approximately three years of intimate contact with the political and economic problems of Britain, he returned to America to enter graduate school at Columbia University.

Into the ensuing fifteen years at Columbia, Beard packed more activities and accomplishments than most men manage in a lifetime. First the formal educational requirements were met: the M.A. degree was obtained in 1903, and the Ph.D. the following year. Stimulated by such professors as Goodnow, Osgood, Robinson, Burgess, Clark, and Seligman, Beard's keen mind reacted vigorously not only to the world of scholarship but also to the bustling life outside his books.

In the fall of 1904 he himself took a position on the Columbia faculty. Initially he lectured in European and English history and, in something of an intellectual partnership with James Harvey Robinson, became an advocate of the New History. During the absence of Burgess in Germany in 1906–7, Beard was called on to teach his constitutional history course, at that time the only course in government available to undergraduates. This experience apparently whetted his appetite, and in 1907 he joined the Department of Public Law as an adjunct professor of politics. The following February, as a participant in the university's public lecture series on "Science, Philosophy, and Art," he delivered the lecture on *Politics*.[4] From this time on his interest shifted noticeably toward American politics and history. Beard was the father of the undergraduate courses in politics at Columbia, and his 1910 *American Government and Politics*[5] textbook was the virtual trail blazer for the introductory course generally. By 1915 he had advanced to the rank of professor of politics.

To many students who felt his influence in those years, Columbia meant Beard. Later accounts by dozens of former students give ample testimony to his powers as a teacher and to the friendly warmth of his personality. Taking a fresh approach to the study of politics, he fired their imaginations by introducing government as a living process. As one of them has remarked, his lectures frequently induced them to go "legging it to the library" out of sheer curiosity.[6]

[4] (New York: Columbia University Press, 1908).

[5] (New York: Macmillan Co., 1910).

[6] For this and certain other details on Beard's life, the author is indebted to Arthur E. Buck, with whom he spent a pleasant afternoon chatting about "Uncle Charlie" and "the old days," at Norwalk, Connecticut, July 4, 1953.

With a flare for underlining his points deeply, he appeared unaware that even his overstatements were sometimes taken as gospel truth in his crowded classes.

A prodigious stream of writings flowed endlessly from Beard's pen. Almost as soon as he joined Columbia's staff, his textbooks and articles began appearing. For several years he was one of the authors of the semiannual "Record of Political Events" appearing in the *Political Science Quarterly*. Beyond doubt his most notable work during this period, at least in the clamor it aroused, was his *An Economic Interpretation of the Constitution of the United States*. Altogether, during this decade and a half at Columbia, he produced, either alone or in collaboration with others, eleven volumes—not to mention six book-length collections of readings or documents, two revisions, numerous articles, frequent book reviews, and various other writings.

Yet, along with all of these activities, he somehow found time for still others. The New York Bureau of Municipal Research, founded in 1906, attracted his interest, and he quickly became its unofficial consultant. When the bureau in 1911 sponsored a Training School for Public Service, Beard was presently spending two or three afternoons a week supervising its activities. From the earliest days he was active in the National Municipal League, and for many years he served as one of its officers. He was called on repeatedly to address meetings of various kinds. He lent a willing hand to movements for woman suffrage and civic reform.

In 1917 Beard strongly supported America's entry into the first World War, believing our participation necessary in the face of the German militarism which he felt menaced human freedom everywhere. But at the same time he had become increasingly concerned over the growing spirit of conformism which in his judgment endangered intellectual freedom in America. In particular, he was irritated by certain actions within the board of trustees of Columbia University. Ostensibly, limits were being placed on free inquiry on the grounds of wartime emergency, but he suspected that the real reasons behind such maneuvers were the reactionary social and economic views held by certain of the trustees and even their disagreement with his own teachings and writings on the Constitution. When in March of 1917 the trustees resolved to set up a committee to investigate and report on "the conditions of education and administration in the University," [7] Beard spoke for the entire faculty of political science in opposing this step as an unwarranted interference with intellectual freedom.

Although he himself favored America's participation in the war, he stoutly upheld the right of those who thought otherwise to continue to express their views. He strongly disapproved, for example, of the dismissal of two Columbia professors early in the fall of 1917 allegedly for opposing the war. When during the following week the trustees refused to reappoint Leon Fraser, who had been lecturing on international peace in Beard's own department, this was the final straw. He resolved to act. After threshing out the entire situation with Mary Beard in their Connecticut home, he came to Columbia on the morning of October 8, delivered his lecture to a large class, and then announced his decision to resign his position. Mass student protests that followed this dramatic step on behalf of academic freedom clearly indicated the high esteem in which he was held by those who had come to know his work most intimately.

But Beard's departure from the Columbia faculty meant no break with the scholarly world, nor was there any interruption of his numerous other activities. He now devoted himself more fully to directing the Training School for Public Service, and his close association with the parent Bureau of Municipal Research continued for several more years. Largely through his efforts the staff of the bureau was strengthened to include such men as Luther Gulick, Arthur E. Buck, and William A. Bassett. In 1919 he joined with John Dewey, James Harvey Robinson, Alvin Johnson, Herbert Croly, Thorstein Veblen, and others to open the New School for Social Research, where he lectured for a time. He played an important role in other projects as well, such as the Delaware reorganization in 1918, the New York traction report of 1919, and the Newark survey of 1919. In 1921 he had a part in organizing the Workers Education Bureau.

Presently Beard was extending his activities far beyond the New York area. In the summer of 1921 he visited Europe to study the archives in Germany, Russia, and Austria which had been torn open by revolution. In a series of lectures at Dartmouth during the following June, he expounded on what he had learned, and subse-

[7] R. G. Hoxie and Others, *A History of the Faculty of Political Science* (New York: Columbia University Press, 1955), p. 108.

quently he published *Cross Currents in Europe Today* (1922).[8] Later in 1922, on invitation from Viscount Goto, mayor of Tokyo, he crossed the Pacific to make a survey of the problems of that metropolis and to help organize a Bureau of Municipal Research in Japan. His study was published in both Japanese and English. Beard also spent several months exploring other parts of the Orient. He visited Formosa, the great Chinese cities, and the rural countryside of Asia. He boated up the wide rivers, flew over the Great Wall, and traveled through Korea. Everywhere he went he was greeted by former students. He had returned to his home in Connecticut in the fall of 1923 when news came that an earthquake and fire had leveled Tokyo. On urgent summons from Goto, who was now Japanese minister of home affairs, he hastened back to Japan to advise on problems of planning and rebuilding.

In the meantime his writing and other scholarly and public activities continued. When the State Department in 1925, at the request of the Hungarian government, denied permission to Count Karolyi to speak in this country on political subjects, Beard addressed a large meeting held in New York in the Count's honor by the American Civil Liberties Union. At the end of a speech strongly attacking the State Department's action as an encroachment on American rights, Beard was thunderously cheered. In 1926 he served as president of the American Political Science Association. The following year his widely renowned *Rise of American Civilization* appeared.[9] Written in collaboration with Mary Beard, this work perhaps more than any other securely established his reputation as one of America's foremost historians.

Working energetically in his old-fashioned study overlooking the rolling hills at New Milford, surrounded by his thousands of books and his bulging files, Beard was in no sense intellectually isolated but remained in close and constant touch with the outside world. He traveled much inside America as well as outside. He participated in a great many scholarly meetings. To New Milford came a constant stream of visitors from near and far—public officials, professors, writers, politicians, friendly neighbors—to exchange ideas, to discuss controversial issues.

When the directors of the American-Yugoslav Society decided in 1927 to invite some well-known scholar to make a personal study of

[8] (Boston: Marshall Jones Co., 1922).
[9] With Mary R. Beard (New York: Macmillan Co., 1927).

the newly created Kingdom of the Serbs, Croats, and Slovenes, so
that the facts could be presented to the American people, they pre-
vailed on Beard to accept the task. George Radin, executive secretary
of the society, became Beard's guide and interpreter, and the two
met in Europe in December of 1927 to begin their labors. For approximately six months Beard and Radin carried on their investigations in Yugoslavia, studying original documents, observing the
operations of governmental agencies, and consulting numerous officials, scholars, minority leaders, and other individuals in all parts of
the kingdom. The result of their efforts was *The Balkan Pivot:
Yugoslavia,* published in 1929.[10] As an incident of his Yugoslavian
venture, Beard had thus visited a number of European countries for
the second time since the end of World War I. Contrary to a widespread misconception, however, he had not traveled to Yugoslavia
on invitation from the king, nor had he in any sense been an adviser
to the Yugoslavian government.

With the onslaught of the great depression and the advent of the
New Deal, Beard's attention again swung primarily to America.
Private matters as well as public engaged his attention. In 1933, for
example, economic disaster struck the Missouri Pacific Railroad in
which Beard owned stock. When the bankers who were holding the
interest money due stockholders refused to pay, he looked into the
history of the line and helped bring about a Congressional investigation of the corporation's financial affairs. He collected the money
due him. Beard also bought land to see for himself whether or not
a farmer could succeed financially during depressed times. Subsequently he boasted that as a Connecticut dairy farmer he had never
made less than 2 per cent on his investment. That he was no ordinary
farmer, however, was indicated not only by the sizable volume of
milk he sold annually but also by his influence among other Connecticut farmers. On one occasion during the depression when a
crowd of embattled dairy producers had gathered on the Beard
lawn and a statewide milk strike seemed imminent, his skill at
compromise helped settle the controversy. He himself drafted much
of the milk statute subsequently enacted by the state legislature.

Beard's public life, however, leaned toward the scholarly and intellectual rather than toward political leadership. In 1933 he became
president of the American Historical Association. At various times
he led battles for intellectual freedom, as exemplified in 1935 when

[10] (New York: Macmillan Co., 1929).

William Randolph Hearst was seeking the support of the National Education Association for his anti-Red newspaper campaign. Fearful that Hearst might be preparing to move on the schools, the educators called on Beard to address their annual meeting. Unleashing a strong attack on the journalist and his illiberal influence in America, Beard won a resounding ovation from the delegates and blunted the Hearst threat. In 1939, nearly a quarter of a century after he had resigned in protest, Beard returned to the faculty of Columbia University for a year as visiting professor of government. In 1940, although he had frequently declined academic positions, he accepted a year's appointment as professor of American history at Johns Hopkins University.

During all these decades the output of Beard's pen never ceased. But through the 1930's a new emphasis crept into his writings and public utterances. He became increasingly concerned with foreign policy and the danger of American involvement in another world war. Although he had long since become disillusioned about World War I, his disenchantment did not take a noticeably isolationist turn until the early 1930's. Even then, preoccupied with problems of economic recovery, domestic reforms, and planning, he warmly applauded New Deal efforts to realize the "promise of American life." Although such books as *The Idea of National Interest* (1934) and *The Open Door at Home* (1934)[11] revealed his leanings toward "continentalism," his subsequent writings took on a considerably more urgent tone. Convinced that America had been unwittingly drawn into the first World War by economic pressures and diplomatic intrigue, he warned incessantly against repeating the folly. This time America must stand clear of overseas quarrels.

After the Pearl Harbor attack brought the United States fully into the global struggle, the heat in Beard's printed references to foreign policy and military matters appeared to subside. But his deep concern over man's future did not lessen, as the spirited discussions at New Milford and more guarded remarks to personal friends amply demonstrated. His later writings increasingly reflected a somewhat troubled searching for philosophical meaning in human history, as he continued his labors at his home in New Milford or in North Carolina where he spent his winters. With the world conflict drawing to a close, he was still alluding to the merits of an insulated America, and he gave only cautious approval to the newly organized United Nations.

[11] Both with G. H. E. Smith (New York: Macmillan Co., 1934).

Then came his two final volumes: *American Foreign Policy in the Making* (1946) and *President Roosevelt and the Coming of the War, 1941* (1948).[12] Although his books had often created a great stir, these two, accusing the late President of tricking the country into war, produced a bigger storm than ever. There are indications that even many of his friends regretted the tone of the last work. His enemies denounced not only his thesis but even his scholarship.

In September of 1948, while the thunder and lightning he had touched off was still raging, and thus at a moment dramatically fitting for a man who had lived in the thick of intellectual controversy all his life, Beard died. "Beard was like the ocean," reminisced a former student, "sometimes calm, sometimes tempestuous, at times even violent, in his moods." [13] And then, recalling an aptly contrasting image which suggested permanence amid ceaseless change, he added, "There he would sit—on his porch—looking at his everlasting hills."

As a glance at the table of contents will suggest, our strategy in the present study is to divide Beard's adult intellectual development into three major chronological periods. The three parts of this volume deal with these successive periods. Within each part Beard's thought is examined topically.

[12] Both (New Haven, Conn.: Yale University Press).
[13] Arthur E. Buck, personal interview, July 4, 1953.

PART I

STUDENT OF POLITICS

1898–1917

I hold that it is not the function of the
student of politics to praise or condemn
institutions or theories, but to understand and expound them; and thus for
scientific purposes it is separated from
theology, ethics, and patriotism.

Politics (1908)

In 1898 both America and young Charles A. Beard plunged ener-
getically into new ventures in unfamiliar places. For Beard it was
Oxford, and for America, Manila harbor and the heights at San Juan.
In both cases there was a noticeable widening of horizons.

Although it must be acknowledged that some Americans experienced uneasiness over assimilating the concept of imperialism to their
deeply ingrained beliefs concerning freedom of the individual, most
Americans appeared to make the accommodation without undue
difficulty or at least to grow accustomed to the inconsistency. In any
event, with the passing of the Populist decade, America's people in
the progressive era soon became absorbed again in their own domestic concerns. Young Beard, too, after a period overseas, came home
to be swept up in the new currents of science and reform.

It can be argued that beneath the surface churning of progressive
thought was an assumed ethical absolutism not eliminated but only
ignored by impatient reformers. In 1909 John Dewey, politely scoffing at "the sacred ark of absolute permanency" and hailing the revolt
against "the assumption of the superiority of the fixed and final,"
suggested the thesis implicitly embraced by numerous pragmatic
thinkers in the realm of morals and politics.[1] Yet the firm faith in
progress, as well as the tough-minded emphasis on economic "realities," may have represented a species of rationalism as utopian as
that of the eighteenth-century *philosophes* whose outlook the progressive intellectuals scorned.[2] Woodrow Wilson himself, assuming
some kind of invisible guiding hand of unchanging ethical principle,

---

[1] Quoted in Perry Miller (ed.), *American Thought: Civil War to World
War I* (New York: Rinehart & Co., 1954), p. 214.

[2] For elaboration of a similar notion, see Cushing Strout's essay, "The
Twentieth-Century Enlightenment," *American Political Science Review,*
XLIX (June, 1955), 321–39.

declared: "The vision of America will never change. . . . America will move forward, if she moves forward at all, only with her face to that same sun of promise." [3]

But inconsistent or not, the assumptions and attitudes of Beard and his progressivist contemporaries appeared to fit a pattern. There was a certain unity in the disdain first shown by orthodox economists for Veblen's work, the attack on Robinson's New History by traditional historians, the fact that the sociology-based opinions of Justice Holmes were long in the dissent before they became those of the majority, and the shocked disbelief caused by Beard's publication of *An Economic Interpretation of the Constitution of the United States* (1913). Such men formed a brotherhood of heretics. They were united in furthering new trends in economic thought, history, law, and politics. [4]

As America pushed deeper into the twentieth century, and the vigor of progessivism spent itself in Wilsonian reforms, external events once more captured attention. As in 1898, Americans again raised their eyes and looked abroad. Not given to doubts about the inevitable spread of their political way of life or the essentially Christian foundations of international morality, they appeared startled to hear the roar of big guns in western Europe. It was not easy to realize that a new era in world history was opening, and that America would never again be the same. Tenaciously they clung to an increasingly precarious neutrality until, early in 1917, American soldiers, too, were sent into the great crusade.

[3] Quoted in Earl Latham (ed.), *The Philosophy and Policies of Woodrow Wilson* (Chicago: University of Chicago Press, 1958), p. 98.

[4] See also Cushing Strout, *The Pragmatic Revolt in American History: Carl Becker and Charles Beard* (New Haven, Conn.: Yale University Press, 1958), especially his first chapter, "Background to Revolution."

CHAPTER I
POLITICS AND HUMAN NATURE

The "Scientific" View of Human Nature

In 1908, the same year that Graham Wallas first published his pioneering study, *Human Nature in Politics*,[1] Beard declared in his Columbia University lecture, *Politics:*

We are coming to realize that a science dealing with man has no special field of data all to itself, but is rather merely a way of looking at the same thing—a view of a certain aspect of human action. . . . In place of a "natural" man, an "economic" man, a "religious" man, or a "political" man, we now observe the whole man participating in the work of government.[2]

Here Beard was looking to the wisdom of Aristotle, who some twenty-two centuries earlier had likewise examined under the heading of politics various aspects of human life: economics, ethics, education, government, law, and other facets. But Beard was also reflecting his own time, when various of his antiformalist contemporaries were reacting against traditional methodology, which had splintered politics into the autonomous social sciences. Even his former DePauw teacher, Colonel Weaver, it may be remarked, had insisted that the social sciences formed a unity. However, while attempting to paint a more valid picture of man as he actually lived in the real world, Beard in these pre-1918 years also revealed something of the deeper pattern of moral and psychological assumptions that affected his thought. It is this pattern that initially concerns us.

Analysis of Beard's early writings indicates that he consciously

[1] (New York: Alfred A. Knopf, 1908).

[2] (New York: Columbia University Press, 1908), p. 6. Well before Beard delivered his 1908 lecture, a number of American psychologists had begun to study the human individual as an organic whole, criticizing as unrealistic all approaches that narrowly concentrated on a single function. For an account of these and other developments in psychological theory during this period, see Robert S. Woodward, *Contemporary Schools of Psychology* (New York: Ronald Press, 1948).

5

identified himself with the newer empirical tendencies in social thought which, like behaviorism in psychology, were attempting to dispel the fogs of rationalist speculation by concentration on purely objective data. Seeing himself as a scientific-minded student of politics, he reminded his listeners in 1908 of the "ever growing body of sound material, historical on one side, descriptive and statistical on the other," now happily available. Political science, he felt, should aim simply at ascertaining the "truth concerning any set of political facts." Indeed, it was the function of the teacher to enjoin pupils to "observe these facts, consider these varying explanations, ponder upon these theories, study the most impartial records of political operations." [3]

Reflected in this approach was a kind of detached amoralism. In the spirit of some of the younger antitraditionalist psychologists who were declaring their independence of mere philosophical speculation, Beard also believed that it was "not the function of the student of politics to praise or condemn institutions or theories, but to understand and expound them; and thus for scientific purposes it is separated from theology, ethics, and patriotism." [4]

Although it is true that Beard subsequently warned of the danger of speaking of "human life in mathematical terminology," [5] in these earlier years he seemed uninterested in the possibility that rigorous analysis of ethical factors might also be a valid part of the study of politics. He also appeared to be oblivious to the possible defects of a scientific study of the "whole man" participating in politics which so largely took man's nature for granted. Yet the air of amoralism could not veil the moral assumptions actually underlying his thought. Nor did his positivist leanings mean that the largely unexamined psychological foundations of his thought exercised no subtle influence. Vigorously defending the spirit of science, Beard seemed to be attacking the foe out front who, in his words, still wore "the sombre garb of medieval scholasticism." [6] Yet, deceptively garbed ethics and psychology nonetheless crept in through the back door.

---

[3] *Politics*, pp. 7, 14, 34.

[4] *Ibid.*, p. 14.

[5] Review of Bowley, *The Need and the Purpose of Measurement of Social Phenomena, National Municipal Review*, V (July, 1916), 518.

[6] "What Is Worth While in Education," *Young Oxford*, I (December, 1899), 16.

Amoralism and the Moral Worth of Man

A postulate basic to Beard's thinking on politics was his initial assumption concerning the significance and intrinsic worth of human beings. Politics merited study in the first place because its subject, man, was implicitly held in such deep esteem. Although bits of evidence scattered through his subsequent work indicate his firm retention of this basic assumption regarding the dignity of the human individual, the clearest references to the premise occur in his earliest English writings, notably his articles in the *Young Oxford* magazine and his book, *The Industrial Revolution* (1901).[7]

Scoffing slyly at the hopeless confusions of "the metaphysical and theological world" in its attempts to examine the fundamental philosophical bases of man's social problems, Beard proposed that "we merely use common sense." This would avoid fruitless "arguments about materialism or spiritualism." Yet this common-sense approach all but ignored its ethical presuppositions. We had all to agree, for example, that man must have freedom from pain, misery, and anxiety, but Beard failed to explain how common sense alone compelled such unanimity. In like vein, he suggested that it was self-evident to common sense that man had capacity for virtue.[8] However, Beard's urge to help ordinary men to enrich their emotional and intellectual life, an urge he strongly felt as he bustled about as director of the Ruskin Hall Extension Service, was not, of course, simply a matter of empirical evidence. It grew instead out of his own assumed value scheme.

Young Beard's first book, *The Industrial Revolution,* plainly showed his indignation at the wretched treatment men had received during the early factory days in England. As chattel slavery had once offended the humanitarian sensibilities of Beard's paternal ancestors in the New World, so now the wage slavery of the Old filled him with similar revulsion. In devastating terms he attacked the arguments of the laissez-faire economists in their expositions of the benign social results of individual selfishness. His attack seemed to gain special pungency from his concern for the human beings who he felt had been ground under by the laissez-faire system and shrugged off by its apologists. On the other hand, his sympathetic treatment of the humanitarianism of men like Owen, Carlyle,

[7] (London: S. Sonnenschein & Co., 1901).
[8] *Ibid.,* pp. 91 f.

Maurice, Kingsley, and Ruskin was equally revealing. In short, Beard's first book, although it had not explicitly analyzed and clarified the moral and ethical assumptions upon which its argument was based, nevertheless constituted a denial of the contention that man serves a cause higher than man. Implicitly it accepted Kant's dictum that man ought never to be treated merely as a means but always as an end in himself.

Accordingly, as young Beard lectured through Britain at the turn of the century, he enlivened his exposition of the observable features of industrialized society with an ethical fervor not inherent in his data. In the apt phrase of Harlan Phillips, he was "the industrial counterpart of the frontier preacher." [9] Although claiming to avoid metaphysics and theology, he moved in a kind of "theological world" of his own. The yellowing pages of the *Young Oxford* attest not only the keenness of his observations but also the moral message behind them. The problems that really mattered, he informed his readers and listeners, were the problems concerning disease and poverty suffered by fellow men; nothing else in the world was so worthy of our fullest energy. To his humanistic mind "the God who moves in the hearts of men" was the deity to be served, and not some supernatural sovereign who was powerless to relieve pauperism or restrict the wining and dining of opulent nonproducers.[10] At times young Beard's value-loaded phrases seemed almost prayerlike in their intensity:

Greater than all man's victories over nature, greater than the works he has wrought in the material elements, greater than all moulded iron, polished steel, and burnished brass are the world's strong, just, and wise men, whose lives gleam along the line of ages as warning and guiding lights burn along a dark and stormy coast. These products of the ascent reveal, in broken light, mayhap, the characteristics of ultimate man. . . . The world's thinkers, seers, prophets, builders, leaders, and inventors, and their achievements in social advance, in science, and invention are unmistakable evidences of the worth of man. Traditions may fail, creeds may decay, ancient manuscripts may be criticized into nothingness, but man and his work, marred though they may be, stand as an imperishable monument to the divine potentialities of human head and heart. Here in man and his history are prophecy and revelation enough to last until the crack of doom. Here in the work and clay of this earthly

[9] "Charles Beard: The English Lectures, 1899–1901," *Journal of the History of Ideas,* XIV (June, 1953), 451.
[10] "What Is Worth While in Education," p. 16.

existence is enough of the god-like to quicken our energies for endless endeavor.[11]

It seems unlikely that the value pattern here represented should have abruptly disappeared. Despite Beard's later insistence that ethics was alien to the scientific study of politics, he did not thereby escape his own value assumptions. Nevertheless, because of his disinterest in abstract reasoning, he paid little attention to the relationship between the buried foundations and the visible superstructure. But, regardless of his open rejection of eighteenth-century rationalism, his own thought was built on a near-rationalist moral base. He was to continue to rest his politics on the moral worth of man. In 1910, in the first edition of his *American Government and Politics,* he reaffirmed this position: "Man is not made for the state, if we eschew German political science, but the state for man." [12]

Empiricism and an Implicit Psychology

But there were further dimensions in Beard's early picture of human nature in politics. Beyond the moral assumptions there were allusions to various other characteristics. From these notions can be reconstructed the psychological tenets implicitly underlying his political thought.

Why did man behave as he did? Man, it seemed clear, was *moved* to act. Beard's extensive concern with *motives* suggested a picture of man not as an organism that is already in action and manifesting his vital dynamism in numerous ways that can be redirected, but rather as an organism that is quiescent until confronted, like Bentham's man, by a pleasure to seek or a pain to avoid. Admittedly Beard fully appreciated that political activity does not proceed in a vacuum. Nevertheless, his thinking carried hints of Benthamite hedonism and Hobbesian egoism.

When Beard in his Columbia lecture of 1908 indicated that the notion of political man was perhaps an overworked abstraction, he did not deny that man acted upon "vital and powerful motives." When elsewhere in the same lecture he took his listeners behind the ballot box to analyze "the psychological forces controlling the action of the individuals composing the state," he found that many of these

---

[11] "Lessons from Science," *Young Oxford,* II (June, 1901), 340.
[12] (New York: Macmillan Co., 1910), p. 485.

individuals had little "consciousness of the motives" on which they acted. In other words, in these various circumstances, men were *moved* to act. And when Beard decried the inhumane consequences of believing "with the laissez-faire school that the government was a necessary evil and the 'tooth and claw struggle' was decreed for all time from the foundation of the world," he again implied that man, at least in the past, had acted only as a result of inducement.[13]

Given this quietist basis of Beard's implicit psychology, what kind of inducement or stimulus did he believe could move the human organism? Man's nature was such, he suggested, that various stimuli could send men into action. Primarily these motives were economic in nature, but not exclusively so. Since his earliest writings Beard had insisted that "base motives" were not the only inducers of men's actions. Human progress itself, he suggested in the *Young Oxford* in 1901, was a demonstration that moral factors had had much to do with man's ascent from the primitive state, and that selfish and brutish action were no more inevitable than cooperation and kindness.[14] There is not much doubt, however, as to the nature of the motives Beard in those days believed most basic in actuating men. In his first text in American government in 1910, he was speaking unmistakably of the acquisitive urge and other kinds of economic motivation when he glowingly praised the founding fathers for their profound insight "into the springs of human action." [15] And lecturing at Amherst in the summer of 1916,[16] he paraphrased James Madison to show how basic to politics were the economic motives underlying human behavior.

But if man, according to Beard's working psychology, acted from various motives, both egocentric and otherwise, the possibility that man also possessed a degree of free will was not precluded. Although this possibility may have raised doubts in Beard's mind as to the feasibility of a predictive science of politics, which at that time appeared to be his ultimate hope, he nonetheless assumed freedom of moral choice for man. In the *Young Oxford* articles, for example, urging the abandonment of "scholastic" education in favor of education for more clarified purposes, he made it clear that these pur-

---

[13] *Politics,* pp. 6, 19, 25.

[14] "Lessons from Science," pp. 340 f.

[15] *American Government and Politics,* pp. 44 f.

[16] These lectures were later published as *The Economic Basis of Politics* (New York: Alfred A. Knopf, 1922).

poses were alternatives among which men were free to choose. The kind of education a man required, he wrote in 1900, depended on the sort of man he wished to become. "Science and intellect will lead to you to any place . . . you choose. . . . They can flood with light the pathway you choose to take. . . . Science is a mighty but blind giant ready to drag your society in the direction you choose to go." [17]

Discussing in the columns of the *Young Oxford* the great men of the past who had "helped us," Beard pointed out that knowledge was a neutral instrument that did not necessarily carry with it a "will to do." One must desire those things which "ought to be done." Shedding a beam of light on his own view of human nature, he told his readers that "man grows, not by the memorising of facts, but by the formation of habits, the suppression of some tendencies, the liberation of others." [18]

In Beard's psychology, therefore, the motives that initiated human endeavor got themselves translated into action not necessarily according to physical principles like the law of gravity, but through the mechanism of decision-making. Beard's man had come a considerable distance from the Hobbesian brute who, almost like a puppet, had been moved this way and that by a natural law of self-preservation. As time went on, Beard was to become increasingly engaged in the problem of how much free will man in reality has, and to what extent his behavior is strictly determined. In his 1916 Amherst lectures, he toyed with this question without reaching a firm conclusion. Reflection might lead one to decide, he suggested to his listeners on that occasion, that man merely observed rather than helped to make destiny, or one might decide that if man fully understood the forces moving him he could harness them to his will.[19] Beard raised the question but gave no answer.

The hypothetical man Beard saw participating in politics was a creature actually possessing much good at heart. Despite whatever other characteristics his many-sided nature exhibited, he was also blessed with unselfishness, altruism, and love for his fellows. Suggestive of the human nature sketched by Calhoun, he had a sympathetic

[17] "Co-operation and the New Century," *Young Oxford,* II (December, 1900), 99.
[18] "Men Who Have Helped Us: II. Robert Owen," *Young Oxford,* II (March, 1901), 206.
[19] *The Economic Basis of Politics,* p. 44.

side that enabled him to cooperate in good faith with other men. If this benign aspect was accepted by Beard to a considerable extent on faith, his faith appeared to be further strengthened by intellectually convincing evidence. As an observer of human nature in politics, Beard did not doubt that greatness and goodness were emerging as man evolved from barbarism, and that the reform of inhumane criminal codes and the outlawry of the worst abuses of child labor constituted genuine evidence of human virtue.

Beard as a student of politics and history also recognized the evil and malice in human nature, even though it seemed easier for him to slip unconsciously into an emphasis on the brighter side of ultimate man. Consequently the pages of the *Young Oxford* which glowed with his references to the deity in man were also strewn with allusions to the devil residing in the same location. This demon might appear in brutal form in a slave-driving English mill owner, an American "robber baron," or one of history's "glorious" military leaders. When Beard, by the time of his 1908 lecture at Columbia, alluded to the evil side of human nature, he was of course careful to label this as outside the concern of the scientific-minded student of history and politics. Such a student had no business trying to estimate "the exact degree of damnation" due Cesare Borgia and his wicked father, or attempting to judge the possible immorality of men like Cromwell and Napoleon.[20] Beard and some of his contemporaries convinced themselves that it was one thing to recognize that good and evil existed in human nature, but quite another to allow such recognition to mingle with "scientific" matters.

Beard's thinking was profoundly affected by his belief in the vast latent ability that he saw in the human being. Regardless of the irrationality, incompetence, and stupidity that were in evidence in numerous individual members of the species, he believed that humankind as a whole formed an almost bottomless reservoir of potential skill and rationality. The "heart and brain of its common people," he declared to an audience of cooperators at Chadderton in 1900, was the foundation on which a nation's real achievements must finally rest.[21] Human nature, he later explained to readers of the *Young Oxford,* was imbued with ingenuity, curiosity, and a great many talents that could be harnessed for whatever purpose desired.

[20] *Politics,* p. 14.
[21] "Co-operation and the New Century," p. 96.

Humanity had "powers and possibilities running into the infinite." Each of us held within himself "the germs of all the potentialities, one or more of which the genius enlarges abnormally." [22]

Although some of Beard's youthful exuberance presently subsided, he did not alter his basic position. The theme of his earlier years, if more moderately expressed, kept recurring. Discussing in his 1910 American government textbook, for example, the relation of experts and ordinary people, Beard left no doubt of his conviction that if the people were properly alerted and informed they could effectively control the experts. Ordinary Americans, he asserted, had demonstrated both an interest in and "a capacity for" real politics.[23] Where wielders of political power were held strictly accountable, the probable by-product, he suggested in 1911 in urging the merits of the short ballot,[24] would be efficient government rather than the corruption and shoddy politics that skeptics attributed to popular supremacy.

To a great many Americans in the progressive era, democratic self-government undoubtedly seemed not only desirable but also scientifically sound. Beard's pen accurately reflected this hopeful view. In 1916, when the nation was moving closer to military participation in the crusade that was to vindicate man's faith in his own ability to govern himself democratically and competently, Beard declared in the *Annals of the American Academy of Political and Social Science* that efficiency and democracy were fully compatible, provided that a number of administrative reforms were made and that public opinion was "properly educated." [25] Shortly afterward, in the *Teachers College Record,* he echoed the widely accepted notion that popular education was the key that could release vast pent-up human energies and skills. "Complete ignorance," he warned, "is the best safeguard of absolute monarchy." [26] And at the same time he

[22] "Men Who Have Helped Us: I. William Cobbett, Friend of Man," *Young Oxford,* II (February, 1901), 172; "Ruskin Hall and Temperance Reform" (March, 1901), 221; "IV. William Morris" (May, 1901), 290.

[23] *American Government and Politics,* pp. 458, 480.

[24] *Loose Leaf Digest of Short Ballot Charters* (New York: Short Ballot Organization, 1911), p. 10201.

[25] "Training for Efficient Public Service," *Annals of the American Academy of Political and Social Science,* LXIV (March, 1916), 226.

[26] "Politics and Education," *Teachers College Record,* XVII (May, 1916), 217.

proclaimed in the *New Republic:* "Political Tutelage is unnecessary for those to whom the gateways of knowledge are open." [27]

Another aspect of human nature was suggested in Beard's writings in those years by his references to the notion that man did not live alone. Man, although in some respects an individual actor, was primarily and pre-eminently a social being who acted in groups. In this respect, Beard's man differed basically from the self-seeking human atoms of Hobbes. In Beard's view, man derived his nature largely from society, rather than the reverse. Although Beard recognized that human individuals were the elements composing human society, he also sensed that the myriad relationships among these elements helped to make up the real character of the dynamic whole. The individual must fill his role "as a member of a corporate society." [28]

The works of Comte, Mill, Darwin, and Spencer demonstrated the organic nature of society. It is generally recognized that society is more than a mere aggregate of individuals; that the individual is not only a sharer in the life of the organism, but is also capable of modifying by his intersocial activities its structure, function, and lines of development.[29]

In his 1908 Columbia lecture, Beard declared that "society is no more a fortuitous collection of warring individuals than one of Beethoven's symphonies is a mere chance assemblage of individual notes." [30] In his Amherst lectures of 1916, he pointed out the great contrast between the implications of Rousseau's individualist philosophy and the group doctrines of other philosophers. In his various economic interpretation writings, he brought the outlines of his own rudimentary group theory of politics into somewhat sharper focus. Groups of individuals had interests that impelled them to behave in characteristic ways. Groups of individuals contended for the control of government. The group, in short, was the basis of politics.

Human Nature in Politics

Yet the "whole man" whom Beard thus postulated for the student of politics was an ambiguous concept. Despite their scientific intentions, not all observers would "see" the same man. Without considerably more science, they would not necessarily see man as Beard

[27] "The Woman's Party," *New Republic,* VII (July 29, 1916), 330.
[28] *The Industrial Revolution,* pp. 104 f.
[29] *Ibid.,* p. 90.
[30] *Politics,* p. 26.

pictured him: integrated and whole, valued beyond price, aroused
out of quiescence only by inducements, blessed with goodness,
tainted with evil, endowed with reason, gifted with boundless
potential, group-minded and gregarious. A political universe popu-
lated by Beard's kind of man would be vastly different from one
inhabited by some other kind.

Without doubt one of the most striking corollaries of Beard's pre-
1918 psychology was the optimistic idea of progress which then
widely infected American thought. Although Beard, especially after
his earlier English days, did not subscribe to mere utopianism, the
logic of his own assumptions nonetheless led to the idea of progress.
If man were potentially capable of making great changes in his
environment, and if his basic reason and decency impelled him to
apply his talents and science toward improving the world, it seemed
obvious that progress would be inevitable in the long run.

In 1899 Beard told readers of the *Young Oxford* that humanity
had moved forward as it had applied reason and skill to the forces
of nature. Man had drained the streets and set up health boards because he would not believe the superstition that the plagues had
been God's doing. Ahead lay "the triumph over disease, pain, misery,
poverty, wretchedness, and want." The victories already gained
would inspire even greater triumphs in the future, inasmuch as
science was still "in its infancy." [31]

Thus the work of creation is not complete—even scarcely begun. Man,
mental, moral, and social, is yet half-evolved. . . . The work which remains seems almost infinite. But it is the grandest, noblest thing that can
engage our attention and powers. To combat evil and folly is the one
thing worth doing. Where there are wisdom and will spurred by enthusiasm and tempered by judgment, there are powers which can be used
in the advance of man. The hour is rich with opportunities. [32]

How these opportunities could be seized was explained in Beard's
little volume, *The Industrial Revolution*. Technological invention
was to be the "material key to man's spiritual progress." In future
centuries man would finally realize his dream of almost effortless
existence, "leaving all the remainder of his illimitable powers of
heart and brain for the extension, enlargement, and enriching of
life. . . . This is . . . a vision having its foundation on the im-

---

[31] "What Is Worth While in Education," p. 16.
[32] "Lessons from Science," p. 341.

movable, established rock of human achievement in science and mechanics." [33]

When Beard in his 1908 lecture on *Politics* reminded his listeners of the distance man and society had already evolved from crude beginnings, he added a further element to his concept of progress— the growth of democracy. In pointing out the arbitrary nature of absolute monarchy and the inefficiency and irresponsibility of aristocracy, he left no doubt that he considered the majority-ruled democratic state a more advanced type. "This tendency in the evolution of state and government has been fully grasped by many students in the United States," he asserted. "Wilson opened the way." [34] Four years later, when Wilson was about to become president, Beard again echoed the idea of political progress. "The history of the nineteenth century," he claimed, "has been largely a record justifying the extension of popular power." [35]

The belief in the eventual global spread of democracy rested on multiple pillars: that people everywhere had a capacity for popular self-government; that democracy was in fact suitable as a way of life for everyone; that reason and a latent desire for the good as Americans saw it existed universally; that, when awakened to these self-evident truths, men would unhesitatingly take up democracy's banner. Such tenets closely matched Beard's moral and psychological assumptions regarding human nature.

Another political corollary of Beard's concept of human nature was the notion of an expanding role for government. Although it lacked the virtually universal American acceptance that was enjoyed by the idea of progress, nonetheless this belief in the desirability of broadening the scope of government was rapidly gaining adherents in the age of Wilsonian liberalism. It was a belief fully compatible with Beard's psychological assumptions.

Rebelling against the creed of those who assumed a natural harmony in which each man received his just deserts, Beard similarly rejected the idea that the measure of good government was the minuteness of its tasks. According to Beard's implicit psychology, there was no guarantee that competition among self-regarding individuals automatically produced general welfare. To his mind,

[33] *The Industrial Revolution*, pp. 42 f.

[34] *Politics*, p. 21.

[35] *Documents on the State-wide Initiative, Referendum, and Recall*, with Birl E. Shultz (New York: Macmillan Co., 1912), pp. 12 f.

interposition of the state's power into economic and other human affairs seemed therefore necessary. In praising "the revolt against laissez-faire" which had marked the weakening of the philosophy of rugged individualism in Britain in the "wonderful nineteenth century," Beard revealed not only his warm-hearted concern for human welfare but also his conviction that government was the appropriate instrument to advance it.[36]

Finally, an additional notion characterizing Beard's view of human nature was the assumed unity of all mankind. As this involved the question of the scope of the political community to which men belong, it was of some relevance to later developments in his thought. Essentially it was an article of faith centering on the brotherhood of man. Admittedly Beard's early "internationalism" did not depend solely on the proposition that men are spiritual brothers. It rested most noticeably on his recognition of the tightening technological-economic web drawing the world together. But prior commitment to a moral bond reinforced his growing awareness of economic and political interdependence. "Amid all the diversity which various national histories present," he wrote in the Young Oxford, "there is a certain unity." The arena of man's common struggle against ignorance and oppression was world-wide, and "the essential unity of mankind" caused men everywhere to respect human valor wherever it showed itself. "The collective life of humanity," he declared, "is today the one great idea battling for supremacy." [37]

Thus, it is suggested, Beard's pre-1918 assumptions regarding human nature formed a kind of master pattern for the future development of his political thought.

[36] The Industrial Revolution, pp. 84 f.
[37] "Men Who Have Helped Us: VI. Mazzini," Young Oxford, II (July, 1901), 358–60. Writing in the Young Oxford on British imperial policy on another occasion in 1901, young Beard reflected a curiously racist line of thinking which implied that the brotherhood of man might be primarily a white fraternity: "The only sane attitude which statesmen can adopt toward other races is that of non-mixture. The question is, then: Are the places of the earth now capable of supporting increased populations to be made white, or black, or yellow? It is not a question of death; it is a question of birth. The whites are capable of multiplying indefinitely, so are the blacks and the yellow. Some life must be repressed. Which shall it be?" ("A Living Empire, II," Young Oxford, IV [November, 1901], 40.) Two maps of Georgia, showing Negro population by counties, accompanied this essay. Later in the same article young Beard made repeated references to nonwhites as "inferior races." So far as this writer knows, however, these ideas never recurred in Beard's subsequent work.

CHAPTER II
TOOLS OF POLITICS

Beard's political thought in the 1898–1917 period was, of course, more than a mere reflection of his ingrained moral and psychological assumptions. Literally hundreds of his pages were concerned not particularly with "human nature in politics," but with the instruments and techniques man uses to achieve given political ends. Throughout the progressive era his writings were filled with characteristic ideas concerning the institutions, organizational structure, operation, and other instrumental aspects of politics. Without attempting to examine every detail of this massive literature, one may usefully analyze a few of the basic themes.

Means and Ends in Politics

Numerous students of American life in the early part of the twentieth century were especially concerned with means rather than ends. Consequently Beard was not alone in seeking to exclude normative considerations from the study of politics, or in implying that realists concentrate on getting things done and leave moralizing to preachers and poets. He was a part of that tendency in social thought which emphasized the scientific, the realistic, the instrumental, the pragmatic, while correspondingly avoiding the normative, the formalist, the preoccupation with ends, the speculative, and the abstract.

In the study of politics, this emphasis on the instrumental meant a great concern with efficiency, expertness, and "business principles" in government. Improvement was sought in many directions: the civil service, the short ballot, training of professional administrators, the organization of state governments. One of the proudest symbols of progressivist students of politics was the New York Bureau of Municipal Research, established in 1906. In their eyes, here was a trail blazer in the eminently sensible task of discovering by scientific research the uniformities, principles, and techniques applicable to

18

the world of political reality. Beard himself was later to be closely associated with the New York Bureau.

Not surprisingly, Beard's own instrumentalist approach to politics during his years at Columbia University had already been present in germ during his earlier English days. As early as 1899 he had complained in the pages of the *Young Oxford* that political science was "dumb" in the presence of great human problems such as poverty, economic crisis, and disease.[1] It was implied that instruments at hand were lying unused. Two years later in *The Industrial Revolution* (1901), foreseeing the ultimate substitution of organization for the anarchy then existing in society, and showering praise on the nineteenth-century "revolt against laissez-faire,"[2] he implied the efficacy of certain social techniques and means. It is true that in his earliest thinking such vaguely implicit instrumentalism had not seemed to be the central consideration. But, whereas the earlier moralistic strain soon became restrained and submerged, these previously incidental allusions to the means for attaining worthy goals were developed more explicitly.

Thus, in the textbooks and other writings that Beard produced in his years at Columbia, a great many facts concerning political processes and broadened governmental activity were demonstrated and documented at length. The revolution wrought by machinery had transformed the American way of life from a rural existence to an industrialized civilization. It had stimulated the growth of great centers of population and a toolless working class. It had drawn the whole country into a tightly knit web of economic and other social relationships which only the instrument of big government could cope with. In all this, attention centered on the facts.

Aiming thus at realism, Beard, like certain other thinkers of the time, rejected mere formalism in his approach to his subject matter. Yet in a sense he was much concerned with forms. Notwithstanding Pope's couplet ("For forms of government let fools contest;/Whate'er is best administered is best"), to Beard's mind the machinery of politics was a matter of grave importance. The very spirit of science that stimulated Beard and others to aim at realism was closely re-

[1] "What Is Worth While in Education," *Young Oxford,* I (December, 1899), 16.
[2] *The Industrial Revolution* (London: S. Sonnenschein & Co., 1901), pp. 84 f.

lated to the premise that man by using reason could not only understand but also control his environment. Irrational arrangements and
social patterns resting on mere tradition must be sharply questioned.
"Does the present order of society," he asked, "enable its members
to satisfy their needs with the least expenditure of energy, and to
devote the largest possible amount to making the earth a place
beautiful, healthful, and happy?"[3]

This assumed rationalism was one of the unifying threads running
through the thought of various scientific-minded students of the
time, and in some branches of political study it was especially
marked. Thus the area that later came to be known as public administration was early characterized by an air of rationalism, realism,
and science. Beard himself, it may be noted, wrote his master's thesis
in this area under the heading, "The Present Status of Civil Service
Reform in the United States."[4] Years later he praised Frank J.
Goodnow for having been "the first scholar in the United States to
recognize the immense importance of administration in modern
society and to sketch the outlines of the field."[5]

The spirit of rationalism and science among antitraditionalist
intellectuals of the early twentieth century appeared to fit in well
with the democratizing surge in the political sphere. "The great
issue before the American people today is the control of their government," asserted Senator Robert M. LaFollette in 1912,[6] and
numerous researchers and scholars in the field of politics seemed to
be directing their intellectual labors toward making such control
possible. The push for the short ballot, direct primary, and other reforms reflected the urge to remodel political machinery to further
democratic ends. The whole research bureau movement typified
the notion that "experts" in government could serve both efficiency
and democracy. Beard's writings showed his close association with
these developments.

As a young man in England, he had urged "public control over the
means of life" and the weeding out of wasters and parasites.[7] Sub-

[3] *Ibid.*, p. 99.

[4] Unpublished essay, Columbia University Library, 1903.

[5] Statement quoted in Charles G. Haines and Marshall E. Dimock (eds.),
Essays on the Law and Practice of Governmental Administration (Baltimore,
Md.: Johns Hopkins Press, 1935), p. vi.

[6] Quoted in J. Mark Jacobson, *The Development of American Political
Thought* (New York: Appleton-Century-Crofts, 1932), p. 581.

[7] "A Living Empire, II," *Young Oxford,* IV (November, 1901), 39.

sequently there were more discreet phrases about the "problems" connected with overcrowded slums and other aspects of modern industrialism. In both cases the inference was that government must step in to further various human ends and values. In his 1908 Columbia lecture Beard told his audience that the scope of government in practice depended "not upon any theory about its proper functions, but upon the will of the group of persons actually in control at any one time or upon the equilibrium that is established through the conflicts among groups seeking to control the government." [8] By inference, there was virtually no limit to what government could do if only men desired it. To one who assumed the near omnipotence of government, political instruments and their actual operation obviously must have seemed extremely important.

The Actual Political Process

Beard's inclination was to look behind the formal arrangements to the people and forces actually involved in the political process. Rejecting the notion of virtually self-sufficient human atoms, he put heavy stress on the role of groups. Pointing out that individuals were "not all equal in intelligence or influence," he suggested his own group-oriented approach:

This problem has received very little attention from students of politics, but it would seem that the real state is not the juristic state, but is that *group of persons* able to work together effectively for the accomplishment of their joint aims, and overcome all opposition on the particular point at issue at a particular period of time. . . . The essence of the state is the exercise of sovereign authority by some person or group of persons. . . . Changes in the form of the state have been caused primarily by the demand of *groups* for power. . . . The nation as a whole is a high abstraction; it seldom demands remedies; it is *groups* within the state that demand remedies.[9]

This party and pressure group version of politics, although consistent with the antitraditionalist attitude, was somewhat unusual for a student also deeply concerned with "public administration." Except for a few men like Frank Goodnow, whose 1900 work on *Politics and Administration* [10] was notable in that it had linked group dynamics to public administration, the general tendency

[8] *Politics* (New York: Columbia University Press, 1908), p. 26.
[9] *Ibid.*, pp. 19 f., 33 (italics supplied).
[10] (New York: Macmillan Co., 1900).

among scholars primarily interested in the administrative side of government was to neglect parties. Beard in 1908, however, suggested that "the party in general and particular, as a center of powers and a working institution, offers the richest field of investigation now open to the student of politics, and the results of really scientific investigation would have the highest theoretical and practical value." [11] This feeling that the party was close to the real dynamism of politics continued in Beard's writings. Subsequently discussing the various organizational details of government, he stated: "Inevitably those who possess the power of determining these matters, which affect some favorably and others unfavorably, become divided into groups. Thus political parties originate." [12]

Modern students may easily find defects in Beard's early formulation of the group concept of politics. It can be pointed out that individuals possessing similar interests, particularly when such individuals are largely unknown to one another, widely scattered, and unorganized for joint effort, do not automatically become a political action group. The concept of group does not refer to precisely the same entity in all connections. It is all too easy to assume unconsciously that one is meaningfully applying a simple and well-understood concept to new circumstances when it may be that only a familiar label has been transferred. *Group* in sociology, for example, is not necessarily identical with *group* in politics, yet numerous students since Beard have apparently been unaware of this.[13] The point remains that Beard, in his notion of group dynamics, rejected an atomistic psychology and tended to emphasize man's social side.

Beard did not maintain that each individual in society, as a member of some group, was engaging equally in political activity. Rather, it was an "energetic minority" that got things done. This was the basic reality. Regardless of formal arrangements, or rationalizations to the contrary, an energetic minority was the heart and nerve center of the group. "It is apparent to the most casual observer," he noted in 1908, "that not all the persons within any particular group . . .

[11] *Politics,* p. 24.

[12] *American Government and Politics* (New York: Macmillan Co., 1910), p. 100.

[13] For comments on the uncritical borrowing of the group concept by political scientists, see William A. Glaser, Critique of Two Economic Interpretations of Politics: Charles A. Beard and A. M. Simons (unpublished Ph.D. dissertation, Harvard University, 1952), pp. 100, 107, 469, and *passim.*

share in the making of laws or the conduct of government." [14] Two years later in his American government textbook, explaining the transformation of Pennsylvania from colony to state, he indicated that it had been accomplished by "an energetic minority." [15] From this time on, whenever Beard dealt with political dynamics in realistic vein, this same notion was apt to recur. Commenting in 1917 on Michels' "iron law of oligarchy," he remarked, "There is a tendency toward oligarchy in all political organization." [16] In his effort to be realistic, Beard continued to reject the romantic concept of discrete human atoms, all equally active and equally potent.

For similar reasons Beard looked upon the juristic state, whose sovereignty and other legalistic attributes had so engrossed the attention of traditionalist scholars, as largely a meaningless abstraction. Rather, he believed that the state as a variety of human association should be stripped of the metaphysical and mystical aura in which the formalists had draped it, and be scientifically observed.

The spirit of scientific realism which Beard was at that time advocating for students of politics is clearly reflected in his own words later in praising the New York Bureau of Municipal Research:

. . . the first institution in the United States, and for that matter in the world, to introduce into the study of government (at least on any considerable scale) the methods of natural science, namely, the first-hand observation of the primary materials of government, disregard for traditional habits of inquiry, generalization from original data, experimentation with actual installations.[17]

It is noteworthy, also, in this connection, that Beard in 1907 established a somewhat autonomous department of politics within the department of public law at Columbia. This symbolized his attempt to study politics as a complex of real forces and groups, rather than in the legalist tradition suggested by classifying political study as merely an undifferentiated aspect of the study of law in general.

[14] *Politics*, p. 15.

[15] *American Government and Politics*, p. 32.

[16] Review of Michels, *Political Parties: A Sociological Study of the Oligarchical Tendencies of Modern Democracy*, Political Science Quarterly, XXXII (March, 1917), 153.

[17] Introduction, Chester C. Maxey, *County Administration* (New York: Macmillan Co., 1919), pp. ix f.

Indeed, Beard's view of law itself, like his denial of Rousseauan individualism and the juristic state, was also revealing of his version of the actual political process. Catching the spirit of the sociological jurisprudence in revolt against older static concepts, he scoffed at the notion of law as a distillation of "some abstract stuff known as 'justice.'"[18] In tune with the legal realism of men like Holmes, Brandeis, and Pound, Beard saw law as another facet of politics, shaped not so much by eternal principles of morality as by the particular needs of social groups, and resulting not so much in a systematic body of juridical truths as in a temporary truce defining for the moment the lines of battle among contending social forces. Thus law had a highly significant role in society, but it was a tool of politics all the same, and not, as the traditionalists pretended, above and outside of politics. A really practical treatise on government, Beard half-jokingly suggested, would be devoted almost exclusively to party politics and related matters, and would "reduce the formal law to the foot-notes."[19]

Various legal and judicial institutions thus fell into a characteristic pattern of politics in Beard's view. Government, he was fond of reminding his readers, simply did not and could not operate strictly according to the legal formalities, but had to be quickened with the breath of life through the usages, practices, and decisions of judges, legislators, and administrators. Even the law of the Constitution, as well as the regulations presumably growing out of such law, was part and parcel of the political process. Politics, as Beard in reviewing a group of books put it in 1910, was "the very warp" on which constitutional law was woven.[20] A constitution was essentially a balance of interests[21] rather than a set of formal axioms or the fount from which all legal wisdom flowed.

Nor was judicial review a gift from on high, according to Beard, but another facet of politics. In a small volume in 1912 on *The Supreme Court and the Constitution*,[22] he argued that the hard-headed statesmen who had founded the republic had not disfavored

[18] *An Economic Interpretation of the Constitution of the United States* (New York: Macmillan Co., 1913), p. 8.

[19] *Politics*, p. 24.

[20] Review of Errera, *Das Staatsrecht des Königreichs Belgien, et al.*, *Political Science Quarterly*, XXV (September, 1910), 534.

[21] Review of Ripert, *La Présidence des Assemblées Politiques*, *Political Science Quarterly*, XXVI (March, 1911), 145.

[22] (New York: Macmillan Co., 1912).

judicial review. Rather, as he was shortly implying, the practice had resulted "from the practical necessity of creating a foil for the rights of property against belligerent democracy governing through majorities in substantially omnipotent legislatures." [23]

In these attempts to see politics through the eye of scientific realism, Beard was akin to Holmes, who likewise had made clear in numerous decisions from the bench his belief that social forces rather than legalistic syllogisms determined questions of constitutional law. As a progressive-minded citizen of a democracy, Holmes also took the position that legal formalities should not unduly stand in the way of the general welfare, and that the judicial branch ought not to presume to judge the *substantive* merits of the doings of legislators and administrators. Sometimes during these years of the progressive era, when speaking as a citizen rather than as a scientific observer of politics, Beard argued in similar vein. Although Robert E. Thomas in recent years has claimed that Beard "was a consistent and ardent admirer of the Supreme Court," [24] this contention, if it means that Beard never opposed the Supreme Court in his support of progressive measures, cannot be accepted—at least for this period of Beard's life. Both the citizen and the scientist emerged when Beard in 1917 declared in the *New Republic:*

Political science in the United States has always been under bondage to the lawyers. This . . . is mainly due . . . to the nature of our system of government which places constitutionality above all other earthly considerations in the discussion of public measures. In England the first question raised in Parliament during the debates on a bill is not about its constitutionality but its expediency, economy, justice, popular support. . . . The elucidation of our national issues has called for the lawyer's technology and rhetoric although they have been *at bottom matters of politics and public policy.* Moreover, when *powerful economic groups* in the country have sought to block progressive and humane legislation and logic has failed in the forum, the mysteries of constitutional law have been invoked with firm assurance. Pollock *v.* the Farmers Loan and Trust Company and Lochner *v.* New York—there they stand, not for-

[23] Review of McLaughlin, *The Courts, the Constitution, and Parties: Studies in Constitutional History and Politics, American Historical Review,* XVIII (January, 1913), 379. For a vigorous attack on Beard's early contentions regarding American judicial review, see Louis Boudin, *Government by Judiciary* (New York: William Godwin, 1932), pp. 90–91, 104–9, 568–83.

[24] "A Reappraisal of Charles A. Beard's Economic Interpretation of the Constitution of the United States," *American Historical Review,* LVII (January, 1952), 371.

ever, but until political and social forces (not forgetting the grim reaper, Death), change the courts.[25]

In short, despite legalistic forms and language, the courts and the law were an inseparable part of the total political process. Thus when the court under Marshall had vastly extended the scope of the federal powers; when Taney's court had broadened both national and state powers; when, during the rise of American industrialism, the court had permitted the states to engage in a wide variety of activities in the name of the police power; and when the court during Beard's own lifetime had reversed the trend and attempted to read Herbert Spencer's *Social Statics* into the fundamental law—that is, throughout American history—the judiciary had reflected political pressures and philosophical preconceptions "more subtle," in Holmes's famous phrase, "than any articulate major premise." [26]

Reforming the Machinery of Politics

Given the group-structured and minority-energized world of political reality that Beard saw about him, how could the machinery of politics be made more effective as well as more democratically responsive? Here was a continuing challenge not only to Beard but to other progressive-minded thinkers as well.

One point of attack was the doctrine of separation of powers. Swept along in the current of reform, Beard opposed the doctrine as unrealistic, and as questionable even if feasible. Shortly after he drew attention, in 1909, to the fusion of executive and legislative powers in Britain as a "most striking characteristic," [27] various proponents of state reorganization in this country were on the offensive against a rigid dogma of separation. Beard and others called for greatly enhanced executive power and responsibility, the liquidation of boards, and closer cooperation between legislative and administrative branches of the government. Despite traditional American theory on the matter, in Beard's view separation in practice was not only impossible but highly undesirable.[28] In 1911, two years before the city manager plan emerged from the wreckage of the Dayton flood,

[25] "Political Science in the Crucible," *New Republic,* XIII Suppl. (November 17, 1917), 3 (italics supplied).

[26] Quoted in Morton White, *Social Thought in America: The Revolt against Formalism* (New York: Viking Press, 1949), p. 108.

[27] With James Harvey Robinson, *Readings in Modern European History* (2 vols.; Boston: Ginn & Co., 1908–9), II, 258.

[28] *American Government and Politics,* p. 205.

he praised the commission form of municipal government precisely because it eliminated some of the undesirable effect of the separation principle.[29]

The 1915 constitutional convention in New York State represented a milestone in the reorganization movement and a victory for proponents of an integrated executive. Commenting on this achievement in the *National Municipal Review,* Beard hopefully suggested that by

. . . breaking down the rigid separation of the governor and his cabinet from the legislature and admitting them to the floor of the houses, a system of interpellation may be established which will contribute powerfully to efficient and responsible government and will open up undreamtof possibilities in politics.[30]

Thus he considered the separation of powers doctrine, like the formalistic view of law and the static concept of the state, to be not only old-fashioned dogma but also a hindrance to democratic political reform. As the new twentieth century advanced, numbers of progressive-oriented intellectuals became increasingly convinced that it was mainly inertia, lack of imagination, and short-sighted reaction that blocked reform and sustained ritualistic patterns of thinking. Various weapons from the progressivist armory were thrown into the battle against such traditionalism. Sometimes wit or sarcasm seemed to serve as effectively as frontal attacks. "Sacred doctrine of the separation of powers for which our fathers fought and bled!" mocked Beard in the *New Republic* early in 1917. "Treason against our institutions has been committed in Maryland where a constitutional amendment providing for the union of the executive and the legislature in budget-making was adopted last November." [31]

In Beard's view, an obstacle as frustrating to reform as the legal fictions of the traditionalists, and related to these, was the aura of deep mystery often surrounding government in the minds of many people. Consequently he did his best to part the fogs of ignorance. In the first edition of his American government textbook in 1910, he emphasized that government was not some mysterious force virtually beyond the comprehension of ordinary mortals. "Every act

[29] *Loose Leaf Digest of Short Ballot Charters* (New York: Short Ballot Organization, 1911), pp. 30001 f.

[30] "New York Constitutional Convention," *National Municipal Review,* IV (October, 1915), 645.

[31] "What a Budget Should Be," *New Republic,* X (February 17, 1917), 67.

of government," he explained, "is an act of a certain person or of certain groups of persons." Government was "simply an association of men engaged in doing certain things which we separate from the ordinary occupations of life and call 'political.'" Some of these men, he noted, gave their attention "principally to making laws," whereas other men were occupied mainly with "carrying them into execution."[32] This distinction between policy-making and administration was a basic principle in the view of the reorganizers, and one they constantly sought to implement.

Dovetailing with other proposals for reforming the machinery and processes of politics was the short ballot idea. It is not surprising that Beard wrote copiously on this subject, or that he enlisted wholeheartedly in the "short-ballot movement."[33] Radical democratic dogma to the effect that multitudes of offices must be filled by popular election proved in practice to be wholly fallacious, he insisted. The long ballot resulted not in more democracy but merely in more confusion of citizens, as well as in the perversion of politics by hacks and logrollers. Shortening the ballot, he urged, was an indispensable condition of democratic accountability in an industrial age. Furthermore, this shortening must be done not "with a pair of scissors," but discriminatingly in order to keep only the important policy-making positions elective.[34]

There appears to have been scarcely an aspect of "public administration" that Beard in those days was not concerned to improve in some manner. To Beard, as to the other reformers of democracy, the same principles regarding the scientific management of men and materials were to be applied in public affairs as in private. In order to make the managers of any public or private organization "responsive and responsible to the membership and efficient in operation," it was necessary to secure top experts but to limit them, to employ competent personnel, to manage these in a businesslike way, to budget wisely, to plan farsightedly.[35] All aspects of governmental reform

[32] *American Government and Politics*, p. 99.

[33] See *Loose Leaf Digest of Short Ballot Charters*, passim.

[34] "New York Constitutional Convention," p. 640. For other characteristic ideas on governmental reform during this period, see Beard's essay, "Reconstructing State Government," *New Republic*, IV Suppl. (August 21, 1915), 1–16; also his remarks in *Loose Leaf Digest of Short Ballot Charters*, p. 10201; and his discussion of "Popular Control through the Ballot," in *American Government and Politics*, pp. 469–87.

[35] "Reconstructing State Government," p. 5.

were closely interrelated. Running through the complex whole was the unifying thread of finance.

The budget is the very heart of the governing process; it involves fundamental problems in administrative organization, in public policy, in legislative responsibility, and in political leadership. Sound budgetary procedure . . . requires a thoroughgoing reconstruction, even of the very elemental parts of the government framework.[36]

Beard had faith in "the new science of administration." He believed that, by applying intelligence to the actual facts of political life, we could be confident of "the reconciliation of democracy and efficiency." [37]

Theoretical Considerations

If one were to make suitable allowances, it could be said that John Adams in his day had reasoned somewhat as did Beard later regarding the supposed realities of politics. Accepting as realities the baseness of human nature and the opposing drives of "masses" and "classes," Adams had thought that a bicameral scheme of government embodying numerous institutionalized frictions would be the best hope, not precisely for "democracy and efficiency," to be sure, but for freedom and order. Distrusting human frailties, he put confidence in mechanical arrangements.

Beard and his intellectual brothers also placed confidence in the efficacy of political machinery, properly reformed. But as democrats they trusted ultimately in human reason at the controls. If man was somewhat unreliable, he was at least rational enough to insure, by fashioning appropriate machinery, against his own shortcomings. In Beard's mind, although the real political universe was a matter both of laws and of men, fundamentally government was not rules but people. Politics, he observed in his 1908 Columbia lecture, "confronts not axioms of law or polity set like the hills, but complicated social questions to be settled, not in the closet with the philosophers, but amid the multitudinous experiences of the market place where society daily meets the pressing needs of life." [38] In short, politics was a process of endless decision-making and involved the continuous

---

[36] "Budgetary Provisions of the New York Constitution," *Annals of the American Academy of Political and Social Science,* LXII (November, 1915), 64 f.

[37] "Training for Efficient Public Service," *Annals of the American Academy of Political and Social Science,* LXIV (March, 1916), 226.

[38] *Politics,* p. 11.

exercise of human judgment and will. In this situation the mechanical arrangements and channels of action could be extremely important, especially if they hampered the political process. Indeed, as Beard complained in the first edition of his American government textbook, this country wasted "much of its best political energy in overcoming the friction of its governmental machinery." [39]

But beyond the question of reliance on mechanism or men, a further problem arises. Although John Adams, like Beard, meant his theory to include the reality of clashing elements in society, the Adams conception rested also on a basic assumption to the effect that transcending the immediately opposing interests was a more fundamental unity pervading all society. Both classes and masses shared an underlying interest in a kind of general good. Adams, in other words, had not intended his theory to be another version of the "war of every man against every man," or a restatement of the proposition that ultimately might makes right.

Understandably in an age when abstract speculation was out of favor among progressivist intellectuals, Beard's theorizing about politics took little explicit account of any assumed moral unity underlying society. As his English days receded farther into the past and his thinking came increasingly under the influence of American scientific realism, his implicit theory vacillated in a sense between John Adams and Hobbes. Thus, on the one hand, as a sincere democrat, Beard frequently implied a "great society," [40] a kind of moral framework within which democratic politics were presumed to function. Yet, on the other hand, as a realistic student of politics, he sometimes wrote as if the political game rested on no other rules than those of the predominant contending interest.

Beard's implicit "democratic theorizing" was amply demonstrated in his writings by his numerous allusions and hints concerning an idealized American democracy. His writings abounded in criticism of existing defects that prevented the full implementation of the ideal. Under this conception, efficient and rationally organized government was the instrument through which an alert and informed people pursued the general welfare. Such government, "representative, responsible, efficient," was the goal of democratic reformers. [41]

[39] *American Government and Politics*, p. 483.

[40] See, for example, his essay, "Politics and Education," *Teachers College Record*, XVII (May, 1916), 216.

[41] For typical comments, see *American Government and Politics*, pp. 469 ff.

Something of the nature of this ideal was suggested when Beard in 1910 observed:

The fact is, we have tried in the United States almost every scheme known in the history of politics except simple, direct, responsible government. By a strange perversity of fate, the fear of democracy and the passion for democracy have led to the same result—the creation of a heavy and complicated political mechanism, yielding quickly enough to the operations of the political expert and blocking at every turn the attempts of the people to work it honestly and efficiently. Powerful private interests find their best shelter behind a multiplicity of barriers.[42]

It is interesting to notice that these "powerful private interests" who threatened the good of the commonwealth apparently became, when Beard wrote in a different vein, not too unlike the clashing interest groups whose activities featured the real world of politics. In this more "tough-minded" and "realistic" temper, Beard on occasion gave the impression that he viewed social reality, to paraphrase Hobbes, as virtually a "war of every interest against every interest," a kind of repressed anarchy policed by the victor of the day. Attacking the thesis of a book on English political history, Beard in 1906 asserted:

. . . the law is in final analysis the embodiment of concrete interests . . . and . . . however they may be clothed in the garb of "precedent" or of "constitutional" or "natural" law, their assertion constitutes innovation and revolution in so far as it wrests from the sovereign or predominant class a portion of their privileges or prerogatives. The "right" of the English people to coerce their sovereign is in reality nothing more than the "right" which all people have to assert and realize their interest —that is the "right of desire, determination and might." [43]

Thus Beard in these early years of the twentieth century had not faced and resolved a fundamental theoretical problem. His thought contained an ambiguity that allowed him on some occasions to postulate, in terms that Hobbes or Thrasymachus could hardly have rejected, a society ultimately comprising a heterogeneity of self-seeking groups, and on other occasions to assume a society based on a moral unity deeper than any superficial opposition among groups. The one premise was suggestive, too, of Rousseau's notion that despite all seeming diversities and differences men's interests are

[42] Ibid., p. 479.
[43] Review of Adams, Political History of England, Political Science Quarterly, XXI (September, 1906), 535.

"at bottom identical"; the other echoed the Hobbesian concept of nature.

Beard, however, was little concerned with such "metaphysical" matters. Abstract "philosophizing" had too often lost touch with reality. To his mind theories frequently smacked of the moral preachments of a passing order or were only another variety of legal fiction. Instead of bothering with what were looked on as outworn modes of thought, Beard and his antiformalist contemporaries were inclined to study actual institutions, concrete facts, real forces. Yet, interestingly, in so doing they raised further theoretical questions.

To the realist students of government in the first and second decades of this century, nothing seemed plainer than the need for expert administration in the emerging social service state. As early as 1898, the National Municipal League in its model city charter had proclaimed the excellence of concentrating executive-administrative powers. President Taft's Commission on Economy and Efficiency drew further attention to the desirability of professionalizing the executive branch. "Expert, scientific and technical service must be performed by those specially trained," cautioned Beard.[44] And in 1915, speaking of "the recent improvement in public administration," he reflected the new urge to apply science to government when he declared: "It is the function of politics to determine what should be done; it is the function of the trained expert to carry out the public will with all the instruments and methods which modern science—natural and social—can command." [45]

But, beyond the emphasis on the need for experts, a further notion here emerged: that politics and administration were distinct functions. Increasingly this principle of separating policy-making and policy execution became enshrined in the reports—and eventually the textbooks—of public administration scholars.

Here was a new separation of powers doctrine to replace the old. Was it less formalistic than the doctrine Beard and his associates had rejected? How adequately did the newer formulation generalize the political process in modern democracy? Except in a figurative sense, the politics-administration formula quickly lost touch with the actual functioning of leviathan government in the modern age. The progressive era reformers had raised a theoretical and practical

[44] "Training for Efficient Public Service," p. 218.
[45] "Methods of Training for Public Service," *School and Society,* II (December 25, 1915), 906.

problem that is still with us: how to make expert rulership compatible with genuine democratic control.

In 1908 Beard asserted that no student of politics should "attempt to lay down dogmatically what government in all times and places should undertake to do." [46] What was his own theoretical position as to the proper scope of government? Was it Jeffersonian, Hamiltonian, socialist, or some other? In this regard, he has been variously classified.

Certainly in his opposition to laissez faire and the doctrine of the minimal state he was no Jeffersonian, notwithstanding his possible Jeffersonianism in other respects. And, to the extent that the New Freedom retained touches of Jeffersonian laissez faire, he was no Wilsonian. To Beard, both the agrarian democracy of Jefferson and the small business democracy of Wilson were, as he bluntly put it in 1914, "equally unreal and unattainable." [47]

Was Beard therefore a "Hamiltonian"? It is true that Beard, like Hamilton, supported broad national powers. But, unlike Hamilton, he was not inclined to believe that what satisfied the rich and well born necessarily served the general welfare, or that anarchy was invariably worse than tyranny. Beard was Hamiltonian in that he foresaw the coming of an industrialized society in which only strong government could cope with titanic economic power, but he was not Hamiltonian in his rejection of the thesis that only possession of substantial economic power fitted a man to share in exercising political power. If Beard sharply dissented from the Hamiltonian bias toward elitism and aristocracy, he far outdid Hamilton in the tasks he assigned to government. Government, Beard felt, must be empowered to meet its growing responsibilities to all the people—a concept foreign to Hamilton, who thought that putting children to work in factories at an early age would help to develop their own usefulness as well as help to industrialize the country.

Beard continued to call for expanding governmental functions and services as new human needs arose and new technical means were invented. Ever since his Oxford days he had embraced social legislation for the protection of the economically weak and disadvantaged. He continued to applaud efforts to push the "war on poverty." He saw the propriety of using taxes as an instrument to

[46] *Politics,* p. 26.
[47] "Jefferson and the New Freedom," *New Republic,* I (November 14, 1914), 18.

equalize the distribution of wealth and to raise the standards of living. He favored governmental action to alleviate bad housing conditions, equalize opportunity, and regulate business. He endorsed public ownership and operation of certain enterprises. In brief, throughout this period of his life he was a steadfast proponent of social democracy, and of the positive state.[48]

An apt expression of Beard's social democratic principles in the progressive era was a 1912 assertion in which he attempted to steer a middle course between radical extremes:

[The] doctrine that the individual has fundamental personal and property rights which are beyond the reach, not only of the majority but of the state itself, can be sustained on no other theory than that of anarchy. It rests upon a notion as obsolete and indefensible as the doctrine of natural rights, and it is as unacceptable as the opposite conclusion that fundamental rights of person and property should be subject to the will of an incoherent and transient majority.[49]

By comparison, a century earlier John Adams had written to Jefferson:

The fundamental article of my political creed is, that despotism, or unlimited sovereignty, or absolute power, is the same in a majority of a popular assembly, an aristocratical council, an oligarchical junto, and a single emperor. Equally arbitrary, cruel, bloody, and in every respect diabolical.[50]

Beard accepted the Adams creed as far as it went. But it did not go far enough, and it reversed Beard's pre-1918 emphasis. Beard's "political creed" went further in that it included other "fundamentals," such as a passionate Jeffersonian faith in freedom of the human mind. And instead of placing the emphasis on negative restraints it tended, if anything, to glorify man's potentialities.

[48] For example, see his characteristic remarks in: Review of Wilson, *The New Freedom, Political Science Quarterly,* XXIX (September, 1914), 506; Review of Small, *Between Eras from Capitalism to Democracy, National Municipal Review,* II (October, 1913), 772; Review of Walling, *Progressivism and After, National Municipal Review,* IV (January, 1915), 133; *American Government and Politics,* pp. 741 f.; *American City Government* (New York: Century Co., 1912), pp. 6 f., 218–41; *An Economic Interpretation of the Constitution of the United States,* p. 13; *Politics,* pp. 25–29; *Readings in American Government and Politics* (New York: Macmillan Co., 1909), p. 331.

[49] *Documents on the State-wide Initiative, Referendum, and Recall* (New York: Macmillan Co., 1912), p. 68.

[50] Quoted in Alan P. Grimes, *American Political Thought* (New York: Henry Holt & Co., 1955), p. 147.

The sum and substance of the matter is that Beard did not fit neatly into any simple category, whether Hamiltonian, Jeffersonian, or some other. His mind was not simple, but complex.

When writing in a mood of scientific realism, Beard could smile at Jefferson's distinction between the Federalists, who supposedly had operated on the theory of "fear and distrust of the people," and their political opponents, whose ultimate principle supposedly had been "cherishment of the people." [51] Yet with all his passion for realism and despite his urge to lay bare the actual political process, in a fundamental sense Beard himself theorized on the basis of "cherishment of the people." This was the basis on which he could stoutly defend modern democracy:

While no one can be blind to the evils which have been associated with democracy in the United States and in the Old World, no serious student of history, when he compares the long train of abuses, brutalities, and disorders connected with the rule of kings, priests, and nobles, can doubt for an instant that as between democracy and the outworn systems of the past there can be no choice. Every branch of law that has been recast under the influence of popular will has been touched with enlightenment and humanity. Compare the brutal criminal codes of old Europe with the still imperfect but relatively enlightened codes of our own time. Compare the treatment of prisoners, women, and children, the education of the youth, and the public institutions devoted to the general welfare, with those existing before the age of democracy. Mr. Bryce's remark that evidences of philanthropy and humanitarianism are mingled in our state politics with folly and jobbery "like threads of gold and silver woven across a warp of dirty sacking" is true, and yet when one looks for evidences of philanthropy and humanitarianism in the folly and jobbery that characterized aristocratic and monarchical institutions in the old regime, one does not even have the satisfaction of getting the gleam of gold and silver across the dirty sacking. As Desmoulins declared concerning the excesses of the French Revolution, "The blood shed in the cause of liberty was as nothing to that spilt by kings and prelates for maintaining their dominions and satisfying their ambitions." With all its faults, and they need not be glossed over, democracy is justifying itself, and every student of history who devotes himself to the investigation of institutions and social conditions will find encouragement in the record of mankind under democratic government, such as it is.[52]

[51] "Some Economic Origins of Jeffersonian Democracy," *American Historical Review*, XIX (January, 1914), 282.

[52] *Documents on the State-wide Initiative, Referendum, and Recall,* pp. 14 f.

CHAPTER III
ECONOMICS AND POLITICS

By the end of the nineteenth century, when it was again becoming clear to some thinkers that economics and politics were intimately related, traditionalist scholars had grown so accustomed to separating one from the other that they often unconsciously assumed a similar bifurcation in the real world. It was natural, therefore, that this question should have been agitating a number of antitraditionalist writers early in the twentieth century.

"The Fundamental Factors in History"

Not surprisingly, Beard was one of those who saw economics and politics as a seamless web. In his role as scientific observer of human affairs, he called attention to the "whole man," to the unity of the social studies. The barbs and shafts he aimed at the separatists are to be explained, therefore, not merely as the attacks of a progressive-minded citizen against conservative upholders of the political, economic, and intellectual status quo, but also as reflective of the attitude of a scholar moved by the new spirit of science and research.

Beard's writings from the earliest disclose a certain recurrent economic refrain. In this regard, the columns of the *Young Oxford* are revealing. Beard claimed that man's work was a fundamental determinant of his character; that social relationships in modern society were grounded on the industrial revolution; that in this new age "old formulae, maxims, and moralisings" had lost their validity.[1] The title of his first book, *The Industrial Revolution* (1901), was suggestive. In 1906 he told readers of *An Introduction to the English Historians* that it had been this revolution which lay "at the bottom of the great political, reform, imperial, and literary movements of the nineteenth century. To study these without their

[1] *The Industrial Revolution* (London: S. Sonnenschein & Co., 1901), p. 2.

36

economic foundations," he warned, was "to miss the underlying forces in modern history." [2] In the *Political Science Quarterly,* at the same time, he praised the Marxists for helping to divert historians "from purely political and diplomatic affairs to the more permanent and fundamental forces." Although acknowledging that "an economic formula" could not explain all social life, he nevertheless insisted that "the fundamental force in history is economic." [3] He thought that, if ethical judgments were not introduced by the historian, most scholars "who avowedly aim at objectivity" could accept "the economic interpretation of history." [4]

It is useful to remember that Beard was not alone in his anti-traditionalist attitudes in these early years of the twentieth century. A number of other scholars had also taken to questioning the underlying assumptions and first principles of their disciplines. Thorstein Veblen, for example, had already published his *Theory of the Leisure Class* (1899) [5] and his *Theory of Business Enterprise* (1904), [6] maintaining that acquisitive business interests hindered rather than furthered the production of those goods and services which actually advance mankind's material welfare. Permeated by the same pragmatic spirit that infected much of progressive thought, Veblen's theory was as predisposed toward experimentation in the economic realm as the programs of Theodore Roosevelt and Woodrow Wilson were inclined toward political reform.

As a writer and teacher of European history during his first years at Columbia University, Beard also endorsed the newer trends in history. With James Harvey Robinson, he pressed New History's offensive against the sterile institutional history then widely prevalent. In collaboration, Beard and Robinson produced *The Development of Modern Europe* (1907–8) and *Readings in Modern European History* (1908–9), [7] in which they pointed out the great forces that had helped to mold the past, and particularly underlined the basic role of economic factors. At a 1908 history teachers' meeting Beard,

---

[2] *An Introduction to the English Historians* (New York: Macmillan Co., 1906), p. 506.

[3] Review of Jaurès, *Histoire socialiste jusqu'au 9 thermidor, Political Science Quarterly,* XXI (March, 1906), 111.

[4] *Ibid.,* p. 112.

[5] (New York: Viking Press, 1912; originally published in 1899).

[6] (New York: Charles Scribner's Sons, 1904).

[7] Both two-volume works, published by Ginn & Co., Boston.

in urging "greater stress upon the modern period," noted that "our problems are primarily social and economic."[8]

At the same time that Beard was emphasizing the pervasive influence of economic forces, he belittled the role of ideas in history and politics. In his view, theories and philosophical abstractions were for the most part impotent as determinants or deterrents of action. Such mental constructs usually had little relation to the real forces operating in human affairs. Repeatedly Beard returned to this theme. In a 1909 book review he accused an author of ascribing altogether "too much importance to 'ideas' as effective forces."[9] In his own American government textbook in 1910 he suggested that people were actually not much "hampered" by theories in the face of "the concrete interests and problems of our time."[10] Elsewhere he criticized a writer for laying "too much stress on 'ideas' as factors in making institutions."[11] In the *New Republic* he argued that "states of mind" were strictly subsidiary to the concrete factors.[12]

Thus for years Beard's writings asserted his belief that the fundamental factors in history and politics were material, concrete, and economic. When his first interest in history was European, he praised Marxist emphasis while rejecting the dogma. When he turned to American studies, he found Madison's *Federalist* No. 10 a "profound paper." In his 1908 Columbia lecture on *Politics* he maintained that "economic institutions" were the "very basis of all political institutions," and that "a more scientific theory of causation in politics" would have close connections with economic factors.[13] Dismissing "vapid political theorizing," he insisted in his first American government textbook that our republic had originated, not in abstract theories, but in "an expansion of the energy of the ruling agricultural and commercial classes, that burst asunder the bonds with which the competing interests in England sought to restrain

[8] "A Plea for Greater Stress upon the Modern Period," *Minutes of the Sixth Annual Convention of the Association of History Teachers of the Middle States and Maryland* (1908), pp. 12 f.

[9] Review of Zweig, *Die Lehre vom Pouvoir constituant, Political Science Quarterly*, XXIV (September, 1909), 523.

[10] *American Government and Politics* (New York: Macmillan Co., 1910), p. 75.

[11] *American Historical Review*, XVIII (January, 1913), 379.

[12] Review of Channing, *A History of the United States, IV, New Republic*, XI (July 7, 1917), 282.

[13] See *Politics* (New York: Columbia University Press, 1908), pp. 8, 20, 23, 32; also *American Government and Politics*, p. 721.

their growing enterprise." Thereupon he went on to expound on the subsequent realities of American partisan politics "based on economic interests." [14]

Finally, in various writings of 1912, Beard was painting political history in even bolder strokes, referring to the pre-Civil War struggle between slavocracy and its challenger as "the shifting of the balance of political power from the farm to the forge and market place," [15] and to the post-Revolutionary War clash between those who favored state supremacy and those who supported a stronger national government as a "war between business and populism." [16] In short, by 1913 he was prepared to write *An Economic Interpretation of the Constitution of the United States.* [17]

Obviously Beard's 1913 book represented no sudden break in his developing thought, but a continuation of it. In addition, the book reflected the new "scientific temper" then being exhibited by a number of scientists and scholars in their efforts to put aside rationalism and rely increasingly on empirical observation. Although many of Beard's specific conclusions about the Constitution-making period are now shown to have been unwarranted, and much of his evidence inadmissible, the point remains that his "interpretation" revealed much concerning his own political thought in the early twentieth century. [18]

Beard's Thesis Stated

What, exactly, were Beard's contentions in 1913 and the years immediately following? The heart of the matter, according to Beard himself, was simply James Madison brought down to date:

Different degrees and kinds of property inevitably exist in modern society; party doctrines and "principles" originate in the sentiments and views which the possession of various kinds of property creates in the minds of

[14] *American Government and Politics,* pp. 1, 105–8.

[15] *American City Government* (New York: Century Co., 1912), p. 6.

[16] *The Supreme Court and the Constitution* (New York: Macmillan Co., 1912), pp. 80 f.

[17] (New York: Macmillan Co., 1913).

[18] For recent critical scholarship on Beard's 1913 study, see particularly: Cecelia M. Kenyon, "Men of Little Faith: The Anti-Federalists on the Nature of Representative Government," *William and Mary Quarterly,* XII (January, 1955), 3–43; Robert E. Brown, *Charles Beard and the Constitution* (Princeton, N.J.: Princeton University Press, 1956); and Forrest McDonald, *We the People: The Economic Origins of the Constitution* (Chicago: University of Chicago Press, 1958).

the possessors; class and group divisions based on property lie at the basis of modern government; and politics and constitutional law are inevitably a reflex of these contending interests.[19]

Noting that most researchers had not used this approach, Beard suggested that it might be fruitful. "The theory of economic determinism has not been tried out in American history, and until it is tried out, it cannot be found wanting." By economic determinism he meant the "hypothesis that economic elements are the chief factors in the development of political institutions." [20] Among political institutions he included law, which he categorized as being mainly concerned with property relations among men.[21] The whole economic interpretation theory, he explained, was based on the notion that "social progress in general is the result of contending interests in society—some favorable, others opposed, to change." [22]

The formation and adoption of the American Constitution, Beard argued, had illustrated the Madisonian theory of economic determinism in politics. The "sentiments and views" of the possessors of certain kinds of wealth—notably public securities, lands held speculatively, money loaned at interest, manufacturing establishments, and commercial enterprises—had impelled them to favor the establishment of a strong central government. The sentiments of others, principally small farmers and the propertyless, had moved them in an opposite direction. Although Beard maintained that the founding fathers had for the most part represented certain property interests, and knew "the precise results which the new government that they were setting up was designed to attain," his purpose was not to smear the founders or to show that they had drafted the Constitution for their own pecuniary benefit. His point, rather, was: "Did they represent distinct groups whose economic interests they understood and felt in concrete, definite form through their own personal experience with identical property rights, or were they working merely under the guidance of abstract principles of political science?" [23]

Beard tried to show how this question could be answered through the use of an empirical methodology, by scientific research. Taking

[19] *An Economic Interpretation of the Constitution of the United States* (New York: Macmillan Co., 1913), pp. 15 f.

[20] *Ibid.,* pp. 6 f.

[21] *Ibid.,* pp. 7–14.

[22] *Ibid.,* p. 19.

[23] *Ibid.,* p. 73.

up each of the founding fathers in turn, Beard subjected his economic position in society to close scrutiny, recording the amount
of public securities he owned, his calling or occupation, his land-
holdings, his business interests, and other aspects of his social, political, or professional status. The evidence consisted of statements and
writings of the framers themselves, miscellaneous data on their personal lives, information concerning the economic interests of their
fathers, and statistical materials gleaned from old Treasury Department records. This research, claimed Beard, created "a reasonable
presumption" to the effect that the large majority of the Philadelphia delegates had represented distinct economic groups "which
must have expected beneficial results"[24] from the adoption of the
Constitution. Abstract principles, therefore, had had nothing to do
with the matter.

Inasmuch as the framers had been practical men fully aware of
"the stuff of which government is made," they had built on "the
only foundations which could be stable: fundamental economic interest."[25] Accordingly, the new government had been consciously
designed to further and protect substantial property rights, notably
personalty. Its direction was to be entrusted to men sympathetic to
such interests. The founders also included safeguards against undue interference from state legislatures which might be dominated
by men of contrasting sympathies. More precisely, concluded
Beard:

The movement for the Constitution of the United States was originated
and carried through principally by four groups of personalty interests
which had been adversely affected under the Articles of Confederation:
money, public securities, manufactures, and trade and shipping. . . . A
large propertyless mass was, under the prevailing suffrage qualifications,
excluded at the outset from participation (through representatives) in the
work of framing the Constitution. The members . . . were, with a few
exceptions, immediately, directly, and personally interested in, and derived
economic advantages from, the establishment of the new system. The
Constitution was essentially an economic document based upon the concept that the fundamental private rights of property are anterior to government and morally beyond the reach of popular majorities. The major
portion of the members of the Convention are on record as recognizing
the claim of property to a special and defensive position in the Constitution. . . . In the ratification, it became manifest that the line of cleavage
for and against the Constitution was between substantial personalty in-

[24] *Ibid.,* p. 17.
[25] *Ibid.,* p. 151.

terests on the one hand and the small farming and debtor interests on the other. The Constitution was not created by "the whole people" as the jurists have said; neither was it created by "the states" as Southern nullifiers long contended; but it was the work of a consolidated group whose interests knew no state boundaries and were truly national in their scope.[26]

Following publication of this intellectual bombshell, Beard continued refining and developing his thesis, although not at first substantially modifying it. Early in 1914, he argued in the *American Historical Review* that voting in the first Congress had split along economic lines. Not "fear and distrust of the people" on the part of Federalists and "cherishment of the people" on the part of Republicans, but fundamental economic interests, had underlain the partisan battle that had raged over assumption of state debts by the new government. These first legislators, according to Beard, had "represented the dominant economic interests of their respective constituencies rather than their personal interests. . . . It was a clear case of a collision of economic interests: fluid capital versus agrarianism." [27]

In other writings at this time Beard reiterated the notion that solid political power must be based on economic factors. Thus, emancipation of the American Negro, he claimed in his *Contemporary American History* (1914), had come about "without that development of economic interest and of class consciousness that had marked the rise of other social strata to political power. It was fortuitous and had no solid foundation." [28] Similarly the Prohibition party, since it had rested mainly on a moral issue with "no appeal to any fundamental economic divisions," had been built politically on sand.[29] "The industries of a nation and economic groups which they create," he declared in his revised *American Government and Politics* (1914), "determine fundamentally the nature of the government and the issues which the government must consider." [30]

Beard also applied his economic interpretation to Mexico's history. Although rejecting, in a 1914 essay in the *New Review*, a "rigid economic interpretation of the details," he insisted that "the key to

[26] *Ibid.*, pp. 324 f.
[27] "Some Economic Origins of Jeffersonian Democracy," *American Historical Review*, XIX (January, 1914), 282.
[28] (New York: Macmillan Co., 1914), p. 22.
[29] *Ibid.*, p. 145.
[30] (2nd ed.; New York: Macmillan Co., 1914), p. 721.

Mexican history is to be sought in the contest of the peon against feudalism, lay and ecclesiastical, buttressed by foreign capitalism." [31]

In 1915 Beard published *Economic Origins of Jeffersonian Democracy,* companion piece to his earlier volume on the Constitution. Again he stated his thesis that framing and adopting the Constitution had resulted not from abstract principles but from hard economic realities.

This stubbornly fought battle over the Constitution was in the main economic in character, because the scheme of government contemplated was designed to effect, along with a more adequate national defense, several commercial and financial reforms of high significance, and at the same time to afford an efficient check upon state legislatures that had shown themselves prone to assault acquired property rights, particularly of personalty, by means of paper money and other agrarian measures. To speak more precisely, the contest over the Constitution was not primarily a war over abstract political ideas, such as state's rights and centralization, but over concrete economic issues, and the political division which accompanied it was substantially along the lines of the interests affected— the financiers, public creditors, traders, commercial men, manufacturers, and allied groups, centering mainly in the larger seaboard towns, being chief among the advocates of the Constitution, and the debtors being chief among its opponents. That other considerations, such as the necessity for stronger national defense, entered into the campaign is, of course, admitted, but with all due allowances, it may be truly said that the Constitution was a product of a struggle between capitalists and agrarian interests.[32]

Beard then went on to detail how the partisans, after this first battle, had regrouped themselves as Federalists and Republicans, with Hamilton and Jefferson their respective spokesmen. Agrarian interests, now the principal support of the Jeffersonian Democrats, had continued to oppose the centralizing measures which the governing Federalists, in the interests of capitalistic and commercial groups, vigorously pushed. In ten years of persistent attack the Republicans with the aid of small farmers and other anti-Federalist allies were able to wrest control of the government from the hands that had fashioned it and to install themselves as the chief guiders of the nation's destiny. This triumph of Jeffersonian Democracy did not imply, Beard assured his readers, that henceforth American politics had left its economic base or that the national government

[31] "The Key to the Mexican Problem," *New Review,* II (June, 1914), 324.
[32] *Economic Origins of Jeffersonian Democracy* (New York: Macmillan Co., 1915), pp. 2 f.

had suddenly become amenable to the direct control of the mass of the people.[33] The fathers of Jeffersonian Democracy, like the founders of the Constitution, had been moved by economic forces. Here was simply a normal, not ignoble, fact of political life.

Shortly Beard was generalizing even more broadly, in a notable series of lectures delivered at Amherst College in 1916, on "the economic basis of politics." His thought on this subject, he suggested, was not different from that of several great political philosophers through the centuries: Aristotle, Machiavelli, Locke, Madison, Webster, and Calhoun. All of them, Beard maintained, had recognized the economic basis of politics. They had believed that property in all its various forms and degrees, together with the "sentiments and views" arising from its possession, comprised the fundamental factors with which statesmen must deal.[34] As the six great philosophers had also known, there had been throughout history an intimate relationship between the economic composition of society and the structure of the state. That is, the social groupings which arose from economic processes had long been regarded as fundamental units in political structure. For centuries, great nations had deliberately fitted their constitutions to these divisions and groupings of society which revolved around economic interests.

This great fact stands out clearly, that through the centuries—down until our own day—group interests were recognized as forming the very essence of politics both in theory and practice. Statesmen spoke of them, negotiated with them, placated them, legislated for them, and sought sometimes to secure the predominance of one or the other or the balance of several against one or another. At all events, statesmen spoke not of abstract men and abstract rights, but of real men and real rights.[35]

Then onto the stage of history in the eighteenth century, declared Beard, strode a man who threw doubt, confusion, and contradiction into the picture: Jean Jacques Rousseau. Ignoring the connection of politics and economics, Rousseau denied that a man's possessions had any substantial influence on his political sentiments and actions, and failed to recognize that distribution of wealth was fundamentally related to forms of government. Thus he set aside the notion of society as a complex arrangement of interests and

[33] *Ibid.,* pp. 466 f.
[34] *The Economic Basis of Politics* (New York: Alfred A. Knopf, 1922), p. 44.
[35] *Ibid.,* p. 67.

groups. Instead, he substituted an abstractly homogeneous society composed of cosmopolitan or universal individuals. "We are therefore confronted," Beard told his listeners, "by an inherent antagonism between our generally accepted political doctrines, and the actual facts of political life." [36]

Thus Beard, who in these same years was writing fluently on the problem of making democracy and efficiency compatible, who was immersed in the administrative reorganization movement and seemingly a dozen other liberal democratic causes, continued to emphasize that economics and politics in fact were not divorced but eternally wedded. "Disparity in the kinds and distribution of our property, as the father of our constitution, James Madison, said, is the most fundamental cause of parties and factions in all ages and all places." [37] To Beard's mind the implication was clear: political reform must start from political realities. The question arises: had Beard correctly assessed the realities?

A Comparative Analysis

Political society in the actual world, according to Beard's teaching, was neither a homogeneous jumble of discrete human atoms each equally self-propelled into activity, nor a completely solidary mass moved in its entirety to unitary action, but a complex of individuals and groups which responded unevenly to politically energetic minorities. Whatever the field of human activity, it was an energetic minority that was the activator. In the field of politics the energetic minority was found to be primarily *economically* energized.

Investigation of precisely how, in Beard's implicit theory, the economic fuel energized a politically active minority leads quickly to fundamental questions of human psychology. How did his assumptions concerning individual human nature relate to his views on "group nature"? Numerous hints of an implicit theory of "social psychology," however amorphous, appeared in Beard's economic interpretation writings. He was repeatedly referring to groups, interests, divisions, classes, parties, factions.

Madison's factions, the prototype Beard supposed he was borrowing for his own implicit theoretical model, had consisted of "a number of citizens . . . united and actuated by some common impulse

[36] *Ibid.*, p. 87.
[37] "Political Parties in City Government: A Reconsideration of Old View Points," *National Municipal Review*, VI (March, 1917), 203.

of passion, or of interest, adverse to the rights of other citizens, or to the permanent and aggregate interests of the community." A major problem of politics in a republic, Madison had believed, inasmuch as tyranny as a remedy was considered worse than the disease, was to contain the "mischiefs of faction." Short of a liberty-stifling tyranny that would in effect kill rather than cure, there was nothing that could be done about eliminating the virus *causing* the disease because, as Madison pointed out in summing up the basic psychology underlying his theory, "the latent causes of faction are . . . sown in the nature of man." Included among these causes, according to *Federalist* No. 10, were the fallibility of man's reason, the relation between his reason and his self-love, and the fact that men have differing and unequal abilities:

As long as the reason of man continues fallible, and he is at liberty to exercise it, different opinions will be formed. As long as the connection subsists between his reason and his self-love, his opinions and his passions will have a reciprocal influence on each other; and the former will be objects to which the latter will attach themselves. The diversity in the faculties of men, from which the rights of property originate, is not less an insuperable obstacle to a uniformity of interests. The protection of these faculties is the first object of government. From the protection of different and unequal faculties of acquiring property, the possession of different degrees and kinds of property immediately results; and from the influence of these on the sentiments and views of the respective proprietors, ensues a division of the society into different interests and parties.[38]

Individual human nature, according to Madison's exposition, was thus basic to the characteristics and nature of the group. Madison's egoistic psychology assumed that, despite the individual's self-love, he was rational enough to cooperate with other selfish individuals to the degree necessary for furthering the group's immediate interests. He was not, however, rational enough to cooperate with other selfish individuals to the degree necessary to realize the "permanent and aggregate interests" of society as a whole, or, if his reason did reach that far, then his will was not strong enough to withstand the overpowering impulses of his selfish passions. Madison's eighteenth-century psychology thus assumed a compromise between social solidarity and individual egoism, with "factions" the inevitable concomitant. Beard's implicit social psychology and theory of group

[38] Quoted in Francis W. Coker (ed.), *Democracy, Liberty, and Property* (New York: Macmillan Co., 1947), p. 82.

dynamics, to the extent that these were actually Madisonian, had not, in the opening decades of the twentieth century, advanced much beyond this stage.

But study of Beard's earlier work indicates that it was not merely Madison's theory alone which helped shape his ideas regarding economic determinism in politics. Particularly during his younger days, as a student and scholar of European history, he had beyond doubt read more Marx than Madison. If Madison finds no place in his first writings, it was partly because Beard was then working in European, and not American, history. After he had turned to American history and politics, he began including references in his various writings to both the Madisonian and the Marxist emphasis on economic factors. His first American government textbook in 1910, as well as the revision of 1914, alluded to Madison's thesis. Nonetheless, Beard's warm praise of Marx's example in opening men's eyes to the real forces in history suggested something of the inspiration he had received from Marx even while rejecting the Marxist dogma of proletarian dictatorship. Beard also felt the influence of the fundamentally Marxian economic determinism of his former Columbia teacher, E. R. A. Seligman, whose ideas he quoted approvingly in his 1913 book.[39]

What theoretical light, if any, does Marxian economic determinism and the Marxian position on group and class divisions in society throw on Beard's thesis regarding the economic basis of politics? According to Marx:

In the social production of their subsistence men enter into *determined and necessary relations* with each other which . . . *correspond to a definite stage of development* of their material productive forces. The sum of these production-relations forms the economic structure of society, the real basis upon which a juridical and political superstructure arises, and to which *definite social forms* of *consciousness* correspond. . . . It is not the consciousness of men which determines their existence, but on the contrary it is their social existence which determines their consciousness. . . . One must always distinguish between the material transformation in the *economic conditions* essential to production . . . and the . . . *ideological forms,* in which men become conscious of this conflict and fight it out.[40]

[39] *An Economic Interpretation of the Constitution of the United States,* p. 15.
[40] "Critique of Political Economy," quoted in Karl Marx, *Capital, The Communist Manifesto, and Other Writings,* ed. Max Eastman (New York: Modern Library, 1932), pp. 10 f.

Thus in the Marxian view it was a man's relation to the means of production, that is, his relation to the situation existing at a given time in historical evolution, which gave rise to his consciousness of being a member of a certain class. Classes had their basis in economic and social conditions and were not "sown in the nature of man," as Madison had explained it. Men, although possessed of reason to a lesser extent than Madison had indicated, were, according to Marx's version, rational enough to become conscious eventually of where their real interests lay and thus to unite with other individuals of their class, even though in the larger view the great impersonal forces of history were independent of men's individual wills.

Although Beard in his earliest writings had matched this Marxian stress on economic factors as well as the accompanying depreciation of ideas, his position on groups as compared to the Marxian position on classes was less clear. Where Madison had looked upon factions as based on traits inherent in man's nature and hence permanent, Marx's view was that classes were not based on inherent traits of human nature as such but were a function of environment and hence temporary and subject to ultimate elimination from human society. This is a fundamental theoretical difference and has various implications with respect to political programs, governmental forms, and social policy. But here Beard dodged, or else paid little attention to, the basic difference between Marx and Madison on this point. We had the choice of believing, Beard in effect suggested in 1916, either that men could only sit back helplessly and observe the play of "changeless forces," or that men could eventually control social forces and eliminate class struggle. "But here we pause," concluded Beard uncertainly. "Can the spirit of man be permanently enclosed in any system?" [41]

At this point, however, Beard's own group theory, probably without his awareness, appeared in 1913 to lean more heavily on Marx than on Madison. This is suggested by Beard's handling of *Federalist* No. 10 in his 1913 study, in which he omitted from his quotation Madison's most explicit statement to the effect that factions grow out of human nature. Leapfrogging over and hence ignoring or not noticing the implications of Madison's assertion that "the latent causes of faction are thus sown in the nature of man," Beard instead

[41] *The Economic Basis of Politics,* pp. 44 f.

based class and group divisions on property.[42] That is, where Madison had made property merely a link, even if the "most durable" link, between faction and fundamental human nature, Beard made property itself the foundation. Madison, in the lines of *Federalist* No. 10 that Beard skipped, had pointed out that the latent causes of faction were *"everywhere* brought into different degrees of activity, *according to the different circumstances* of civil society," [43] thereby suggesting that social circumstances merely channeled, rather than set into operation, inherent human drives that were basically biological and psychological. Beard, however, asserting simply that "different degrees and kinds of property inevitably exist in modern society," [44] appeared to make property a function of institutional arrangements somewhat after the manner of Marx. This would make Beard's theory imply, unlike Madison's, that class conflict itself could be prevented by appropriate environmental alterations.

Interestingly, Beard treated *Federalist* No. 10 somewhat differently in his 1916 Amherst lectures. On this occasion he quoted a previously omitted portion of Madison concluding with: "The latent causes of faction are thus sown in the nature of man; and we see them everywhere brought into different degrees of activity, according to the different circumstances of civil society." Beard's own comment was: "Thus, in the opinion of the Father of the American Constitution, *politics springs inevitably, relentlessly out of economics."* [45] Yet, notwithstanding Beard's succinct comment, it can be argued that Madison in effect had taken the more subtle position that politics springs fundamentally out of human nature. Later in his lecture Beard quoted Madison's statement that "the causes of faction cannot be removed" and summarized several Madison pronouncements to the effect that, "owing to the nature of man, unequal distribution of property is inavoidable." [46] Nevertheless, the impression remains that Beard still had not actually accepted the Madisonian notion that factions are ineradicable because rooted in unchangeable human

[42] In Beard's words, "class and group divisions based on property lie at the basis of modern government" (*An Economic Interpretation of the Constitution of the United States,* p. 16).

[43] Coker, *Democracy, Liberty, and Property,* p. 82 (italics supplied).

[44] *An Economic Interpretation of the Constitution of the United States,* p. 15.

[45] *The Economic Basis of Politics,* p. 30 (italics supplied).

[46] *Ibid.,* p. 31.

nature, but instead continued to base political classes and groups directly on variable and alterable forms of property. This impression is strengthened by subsequent remarks in the lecture when Beard, after mentioning "the iron necessity of circumstances," declared: "If government here is different from government in other times and places it is mainly because the forms and distribution of property are different." [47]

A further indication that Beard's group theory was not exactly Madisonian in all particulars was Beard's reliance on Seligman's economic interpretation of history. To Beard, Seligman's statement seemed "as nearly axiomatic as any proposition in social sciences can be." The Seligman passage quoted by Beard was, in part, that

. . . individual existence moves within the framework of the social structure and is modified by it. . . . To economic causes . . . must be traced in the last instance those transformations in the structure of society which themselves condition the relations of social classes and the various manifestations of social life.[48]

Seligman, like Marx, based social classes on the economically determined social structure rather than directly on man's nature as such.

We have shown that Beard's thinking, like that of Madison, Marx, and Seligman, closely linked economics and politics, and that he placed much stress on economic factors in his implicit theory of groups. With respect to the second point, however, there appeared to be a noticeably heavier economic emphasis on Beard's part than on the part of either Madison or Seligman. It may be well to point out this contrast in view of the close identification Beard himself made between his own thought and theirs. In essence, Beard made less room for noneconomic factors in history and politics than did either Madison or Seligman. Madison, while indicating that factions were solidly based on human biology and that their causes were not alterable by men's will or by manipulating the environment (even though their effects could be controlled), at the same time pointed out that the ineradicable factious propensity of human nature did not express itself solely in the acquisition of various and unequal amounts of property. Differences over religion, government, rival leaders, and other matters of opinion, passion, and interest likewise

---

[47] *Ibid.*, p. 32.
[48] *An Economic Interpretation of the Constitution of the United States,* p. 15.

reflected men's innate tendency to fall into conflicting factions. Thus various noneconomic consequences of man's quarrelsome nature were also projected into Madison's group dynamics, "according to different circumstances." And Seligman, whose economic interpretation Beard also relied on, had interestingly included in his study a chapter on "The Spiritual Factors in History." Whereas Beard usually took the position that all noneconomic factors were trivial and virtually inconsequential in history, Seligman allowed ethical, religious, and other noneconomic forces a determining place as well, even though these operated within a social framework comprised in large measure of economic factors. "It would . . . be absurd to deny that individual men, like masses of men, are moved by ethical considerations," declared Seligman.[49]

Thus the economic interpretation of history, correctly understood, does not in the least seek to deny or to minimize the importance of ethical and spiritual forces in history. It only emphasizes the domain within which the ethical forces can at any particular time act with success. . . . It endeavors only to show that in the records of the past the moral uplift of humanity has been closely connected with its social and economic progress, and that the ethical ideals of the community, which alone bring any lasting advance in civilization, have been erected on, and rendered possible by, the solid foundation of material prosperity.[50]

Thus upon closer examination Beard's economic interpretation of politics,[51] supported by certain assumptions regarding individual

[49] E. R. A. Seligman, *The Economic Interpretation of History* (New York: Columbia University Press, 1902), p. 126.

[50] *Ibid.*, pp. 130 f., 133 f.

[51] A number of writers in recent years have made theoretical analyses of various aspects of Beard's progressive era "economic interpretation." See, for example, Morton White, *Social Thought in America* (New York: Viking Press, 1949), pp. 123 f., for a related view of Beard's notions on economic classes and human nature. Also cf. the allusions to Beard's implicit theory in Douglas Adair's essay, "The Tenth Federalist Revisited," *William and Mary Quarterly*, VIII (January, 1951), 48–61; Eric F. Goldman, "Origins of Beard's Economic Interpretation of the Constitution," *Journal of the History of Ideas*, XIII (April, 1952), 241–48; Howard K. Beale (ed.), *Charles A. Beard* (Lexington: University of Kentucky Press, 1954), pp. 127–29; as well as George R. Leighton, in *ibid.*, p. 164. For a useful analysis in some particulars different from that here presented, see William A. Williams, "A Note on Charles Austin Beard's Search for a General Theory of Causation," *American Historical Review*, LXII (October, 1956), 59–80. Also see Elias Berg, *The Historical Thinking of Charles A. Beard* (Stockholm: Almqvist & Wiksell, 1957), pp. 18–56; and Cushing Strout, *The Pragmatic Revolt in American History* (New Haven, Conn.: Yale University Press, 1958), pp. 86–111 *passim*.

and group nature, becomes a somewhat unsystematic fusion of ideas from various sources. In a sense this made him a child of his times, an impressionistic thinker reflecting the progressive era aversion to "metaphysics" and doctrinairism. If opponents accused him of sins of material vulgarity, or even Marxism, he could in effect reply that our own American Madison had said it earlier. If it were inferred that Madison's Calvinistic view of human nature merely showed that the poor we have always with us and hence that the politics of laissez faire in the good old days had been realistic after all, he could counter, with Darwinian optimism, to the effect that despite factiousness man was not so stupid as not to try to better his lot. In any event, to Beard's mind reform of specific abuses was more sensible than worrying about the ultimate design of the universe.

Elements of a Theory Reformulated

Strictly speaking, therefore, Beard's pre-1918 thought on "economics and politics" was a theory of politics only implicitly. Some of the dim outlines can, however, be sharpened. Some of the notions operative in his thinking, whether these were stated or assumed, can be brought together and displayed under a brighter lamp.

1. Beard's theory of economic "determinism" (often called "interpretation" by him) was not pushed to the extreme of a mechanistic or logical determinism in which given economic causes invariably result in specified political effects. Neither did he accept a fatalistic view in which predestined political phenomena occur regardless of antecedent economic events or conditions, as in a drama.[52] Instead he inclined toward an empirical-scientific view in which given economic factors or phenomena are probably followed by or found associated with certain political conditions or phenomena.

2. Beard's theory consequently allowed considerable scope to human choice and will. Man could deliberately forestall or affect the

[52] For example, on one occasion Beard says approvingly of an author that he "is writing history—not a drama in which man seems to act automatically and according to approved philosophical forms" (Review of Deville, *Histoire socialiste: Du 9 thermidor au 18 brumaire, Political Science Quarterly*, XXI [March, 1906], 114); and on another occasion Beard refers to "the hasty generalizations of those who have not yet learned, in spite of the warnings of history, how dangerous it is to speak of human life in mathematical terminology" (Review of Bowley, *The Need and the Purpose of Measurement of Social Phenomena, National Municipal Review*, V [July, 1916], 518).

occurrence of the political result that would, if no extraneous factors intervened, probably follow the antecedent economic cause. Man's knowledge of these very principles of causation, for example, or his understanding of "the forces of social evolution," might enable him to interpose his own deliberate will in precisely this way if he did not desire such probable political result. Indeed, knowledge of his own human motives might enable him to choose among conflicting motives and act politically in accordance with some motives and contrary to others. Men's theoretical ability to use their wills thus deliberately and rationally did not mean, however, that they often in fact did so; surrender to passions and lack of understanding frequently stood in the way.

3. In rejecting an inexorably rigid determinism, Beard did not go to the opposite extreme and embrace a theory that man by the exercise of spontaneous will and abstract reason shaped all political institutions, conditions, or phenomena.

What, then, did influence men in those cases in which they actually implemented their "deliberate choices"? Here again economic factors and economic experiences occupied a large place. That is, Beard's theory was broad enough to cover, to some extent at least, the economic determinism of human values.

4. With respect to precisely how economics actually impinged on politics, various possibilities were implied and hinted at in Beard's thought, although not systematically developed. Individuals as more or less rational "economic beings" [53] were influenced by various kinds of "economic interests," a number of which can be identified from Beard's writings: (a) the urge on the part of individuals to acquire wealth,[54] for example, was frequently assumed or suggested, as was (b) the interest in preserving, protecting, and making secure wealth already possessed.[55] (c) A more or less consciously held viewpoint engendered by an individual's particular economic occupation

[53] Thus Beard, in his *An Economic Interpretation of the Constitution of the United States* suggests by implication (p. 253) that in a study of maximum reliability "the people" who had favored or opposed the Constitution would have to be "individualized and studied as economic beings."

[54] As reflected in the statement that "a large group of public creditors were failing to receive the interest due them on government securities" (*American Government and Politics,* p. 36).

[55] As implied, for example, in the claim that "the Federalists had designed [the Constitution] as a foil to the levelling propensities of the masses" (*Economic Origins of Jeffersonian Democracy* [New York: Macmillan Co., 1915], p. 467).

or role in society was likewise indicated.[56] (d) Occasionally there was reference to a kind of general desire for availability of economic opportunities, as manifested for example in demands for governmental paternalism; such demands might imply the existence of various further unspecified economic or other interests.[57] All of these different kinds of "economic interests" then might correspond, implicitly, to as many kinds of economic motive in man's make-up, such as the acquisitive, possessive, role-maintenance, and opportunity motives.

5. The explanation of how these, and doubtless other, economic interests of individuals were translated into political dynamics and institutions was also implied in Beard's economic interpretation writings, although not developed explicitly. The key lay in Beard's concept of energetic minorities [58] or, as they could be called in this connection, political action groups. Individuals whose economic interests were such that numbers of them would cooperate in joint political action comprised an energetic minority. This by no means meant that the individuals thus engaging in joint endeavor necessarily had identical interests or were acting on exactly the same motives. Indeed, hypothetically it was possible that even when exactly the same motive induced political action in large numbers of individuals, these individuals might be acting as members of two or more rival action groups. All that was theoretically necessary to produce an energetic minority was that a degree of joint action must seem to be in the common interest of members, whether for the same or diverse objectives, and that a degree of group solidarity had to be aroused, whether by more or less spontaneous awareness on the part of individuals or by consciously furthered propaganda and "education." Such a situation would be ripe for the play of economic determinism in politics.

In Beard's implicit theoretical model of the political process something like this was going on continuously. It was the stuff of politics.

[56] In *The Economic Basis of Politics,* p. 67, Beard notes, for example, that "the constitutions of government of great nations were, for centuries, deliberately fitted to the division of society in separate orders, groups, and estates, each of which pursued a separate calling and cherished its own sentiments about economic interests."

[57] See, for example, *An Economic Interpretation of the Constitution of the United States,* p. 155.

[58] For related comments on Beard's implicit theory of energetic minorities, see Forrest McDonald, *We the People,* pp. 401–8.

Individuals, often similarly situated in society, comprised the reserves or pools from which energetic minorities could be "recruited." Such reserve strata from which came the potential action groups were referred to variously by Beard under such terms as economic class, estate, order, class in society, social group, and so on. It is true that on occasion it is difficult to judge whether he was referring to a functioning action group or merely intended to denote the social or economic stratum from which such an action group might be forthcoming.

But apart from the foregoing kind of determinism—in which somewhat rationally derived and more or less consciously held economic interests conditioned or caused political phenomena—there crept into Beard's writing at times another type of economic determinism. This was a general intellectual climate or atmosphere that subtly and unconsciously influenced almost everyone's thinking and outlook, regardless of his immediate stake or role in society. This pervasive atmosphere rose from various factors: the state of technology, existent types of economic institutions, physical resources with their resultant occupations, levels of material well-being. Apparently such factors differed, at least in degree, from the more specific individual economic interests tied, for example, to the urge to acquire and preserve wealth. Reminiscent of the "superstructure" in Marx's theory, or the "spiritual forces" in Seligman's theory, this particular strain in Beard's pre-1918 political thought, however, waited more favorable circumstances for fuller development.

A Special Facet

We have not analyzed Beard's pre-1918 ideas on the relation of economics to *international* politics. But in the light of later developments in his thought these earlier views must be put on the record. That this facet was of early concern to Beard is indicated by his inclusion in the 1913 volume of a separate section on "The Economics of International Politics." [59]

As a student of politics in the prewar years, Beard unmistakably saw the growing unity of the world. Near the turn of the century, during his English days, he had noted in his *The Industrial Revolution* how capital—"impersonal and international"—was cutting

[59] *An Economic Interpretation of the Constitution of the United States,* pp. 183–88.

ruthlessly across previous ties of national patriotism and race.[60] Lecturing on politics before the students and faculty of Columbia University in 1908, he paid due attention to world politics, as well.

So far as our political economy is concerned Japan is as much a part of the United States as Oregon; Matabeleland is the next door of Saskatchewan; the spirit of war in the bosom of the Herrero tribesmen makes the issue for an imperial election in Germany. *The shuttle of trade and intercourse flies ever faster and it may be weaving the web for a world state.* It may be that steam and electricity are to achieve what neither the armies, nor the law, nor the faith of Rome could accomplish—that unity of mankind which rests on the expansion of a common consciousness of rights and wrongs through the extension of identical modes of economic activity.[61]

Here Beard, 120 years after Alexander Hamilton had hoped to make the American republic an economic unity on which political unity might be built, was entertaining ideas of a similar development in world politics. "The world," as Beard indicated in 1909, "has become a great economic unity." [62] He fully appreciated that America was included in that unity. He had no doubt that politically, as well, this country was an inseparable part of the world. In 1910, in the first edition of his *American Government and Politics,* Beard again made his position unmistakably clear:

It is apparent that the "splendid isolation" of the United States, as contemplated by many early political theorists, has never been possible in practice. Moreover, no political doctrines with regard to our independence from the rest of the world are strong enough to overcome those material and moral forces which are linking our destinies to those of the world at large.[63]

It was therefore perfectly natural for Beard, a few years later, to insist on the necessity of crushing German militarism. In a world growing smaller, aggression must be forceably put down.

The Validity of Beard's Theory

Taken as a whole, Beard's embryonic theory of politics showed considerable correspondence to aspects of observable reality, but

[60] *The Industrial Revolution,* pp. 51 f.

[61] *Politics* (New York: Columbia University Press, 1908), p. 30 (italics supplied).

[62] Review of Glaser, *Wirtschaftspolitische Annalen, et al., Political Science Quarterly,* XXIV (March, 1909), 165.

[63] *American Government and Politics,* p. 333.

there were defects as well. It was readily observable, for example, that economic factors did after all play a highly significant and basic role in actual politics, a role that had often been slighted in the more legalistic approach. But on the other hand economic self-interest was not the sole ingredient, as observation could also show. In his eagerness to redress the balance, Beard at times came near to implying that it was the only ingredient in politics worth mentioning. Insisting that all motives ultimately come to economic motives is circular. It amounts to saying that human values in general are no broader than preferences about economic objectives, and this is patently false.

Curiously, in view of pragmatism's concern with consequences rather than with ultimate causes, Beard paid so much attention to the motives of political action that he largely lost sight of the consequences of the action. He emphatically reminded readers and listeners of the moving forces in politics and history, but often slighted the lasting achievements of the movement.

Understandably, in terms of psychology Beard's theory was too simple. Tied to the New Psychology of the early twentieth century, it made much of the stimuli behind political phenomena, the hidden springs that make politics "go." Yet, identifying the fuel that powers the vehicle may not tell us why it arrived at one point rather than another. In Beard's case, it appears likely that the social reformer and the scientific student of inexorable laws never quite saw eye to eye. Left hanging was the question of how heavily personal responsibility weighs against the determinism of impersonal forces. Still, Beard did remind his fellows that group dynamics are not simply the play of self-sufficient human atoms, and that if men make society the reverse is also true.

In Beard's thought, realistic insights mingled with a tangle of unresolved problems and more or less conflicting tendencies. In the real world, he pointed out, the human being was a "whole man," and therefore the sciences dealing with him were properly a unity. Yet Beard could also hold that politics "for scientific purposes" had nothing to do with ethics and values. Ideas, Beard often maintained, had slight effect on the hard realities of politics. Yet, strangely, it was the "sentiments" connected with property that were supposedly the real springs of political dynamics. Paradoxically, as a scholar and publicist, Beard was a thinker whose stock in trade was ideas, but one who none the less considered ideas to be only trivial forces in human history.

Beard's thought has often been subjected to critical appraisals and attacks that themselves have been irrelevant. It is easy, for example, to assail a position Beard never took, but this has slight relevance to his actual thought. In 1936 Max Lerner indicated in the *Nation* that Beard "made the members of the Constitutional Convention act— from direct economic pressures and interests," without considering the subtle influence of "the climate of opinion." [64] Yet, as a specific case to the contrary, Beard had plainly noted that Hamilton, "the colossal genius of the new system," had been moved by "large policies" rather than the "personal interests so often attributed to him." [65] Another tactic is to distort Beard's position and then to demolish the monster so created. In this vein Samuel E. Morison in his presidential address before the American Historical Association in 1950 claimed that Beard in his earlier years had usually "dismissed" the *Federalist* papers "as rationalizations of the money-grabbers." [66] Whatever else may be said of Beard's handling of and repeated references to the *Federalist* papers in his earlier years, it can scarcely be contended that he "dismissed" them.

Ever since 1913 Beard's economic thesis has been the object of a great variety of highly critical judgments, some ill-founded, others amply documented. Exemplifying the former category, a recent offering printed by the Sons of the Revolution echoes an ancient refrain in characterizing Beard's initial economic interpretation book as "his attack on the foundations of our form of government." [67] On the other hand, Robert E. Brown in 1956 and Forrest McDonald in 1958 demonstrated through impressive research the deficiencies in Beard's methodology and the flimsiness of his specific contentions. [68] In 1955 Cecelia M. Kenyon argued persuasively that the leading op-

---

[64] "Charles Beard Confronts Himself," *Nation*, CXLII (April 8, 1936), 454.

[65] *An Economic Interpretation of the Constitution of the United States*, p. 114.

[66] "Faith of a Historian," *American Historical Review*, LVI (January, 1951), 266.

[67] Augustin G. Rudd, *Bending the Twig* (New York: New York Chapter, Sons of the Revolution, 1957), p. 42.

[68] Brown, *Charles Beard and the Constitution*, pp. 31, 35, 154, 193; McDonald, *We the People*, pp. 92, 110, 349–99, and *passim*.

ponents of the Constitution had been as antimajoritarian as its warmest supporters.[69]

However, interesting and important as these matters are, it is not our purpose here to ascertain the validity of Beard's thesis as history, or to present a new "interpretation" of the Constitution-making period. Instead, our task centers on Beard's ideas as these have evolved in the twentieth century, implied a theory of politics, and had an impact on recent American social thought.

[69] "Men of Little Faith: The Anti-Federalists on the Nature of Representative Government," pp. 3–43. Cf. also the criticisms of Douglas Adair, "The Tenth Federalist Revisited," pp. 48–67; Eric F. Goldman, "Origins of Beard's Economic Interpretation of the Constitution," pp. 234–49; and William A. Williams, "A Note on Charles Austin Beard's Search for a General Theory of Causation," pp. 59–80. For another recent opinion on Beard and the changing fortunes of his 1913 book, as well as on Brown's and Kenyon's criticisms of it, see Max Beloff's essay, "Another Fallen Idol?" *Encounter,* XII (January, 1959), 73–76; Richard Hofstadter reacts to Beloff's comments in "The Historian's Risk," *Encounter,* XII (February, 1959), 56–58.

PART II

HOPE AT HIGH NOON

1918–32

There was no doubt about the nature of
the future in America. The most common note of assurance was belief in unlimited progress . . . [in] the capacity
of the Power that had summoned into
being all patterns of the past and present, living and dead, to fulfill its endless
destiny. . . . In the high noon of Coolidge prosperity . . . the imagery of the
heavens was altered.

The Rise of American Civilization
(1927)

Despite continuity of most of the dogmas and tenets of the previous age, the world of thought confronting Beard in the decade and a half after his 1917 departure from Columbia University was in some ways strikingly different from that prewar world in which he had grown to intellectual manhood.

Faith in reason appeared to recede. Doubt arose as to man's rational processes in helping to solve social problems. The Great War, which had at first seemed to many Americans to represent a reversion to jungle barbarism among supposedly civilized nations, appeared to have initiated an epoch of violence and irrationalism in the world.

A tendency toward intellectual escapism flourished in some quarters. It was easier to think about a world based on comfortable old beliefs from the past than to face the harsh postwar world. Some Americans shrank from the implications of developing technology. Others refused to admit that aggressive imperialism was still alive in the world, or that it concerned our hemisphere. Social injustices and hard problems of economic maladjustment were often avoided in headlong flight "back to normalcy."

Nonetheless, through the postwar period as a whole, much of the earlier optimism and hope tended to persist. Regardless of disappointments and setbacks, the deep-running American faith in ultimate human progress remained strong.

CHAPTER IV
FREE MAN IN A FREE SOCIETY

Beard's own political ideas during the fifteen years after 1917 were in some respects almost indistinguishable from those of the preceding twenty. Our task at this point is to inquire whether his basic assumptions regarding human nature and its potentialities significantly changed in the postwar era, and, if so, how these changes affected his general political philosophy. We shall conclude that Beard in this golden middle period of his life, although buffeted by strange new winds in a changing world, with minor modifications retained his basic beliefs respecting the free human individual. Despite the tribulation and defeats suffered by liberal democracy over the earth, his faith in human progress persisted.

Psychology and the Study of Politics

With the advent of the postwar period, increasing references to psychological data began to occur in political science literature.[1] There is little indication, however, that Beard was affected by the infusion. His occasional outbursts about human ineptitude and folly were largely what they had always been and signified no fundamental re-examination of long-held conceptions. Doubtless, like American students of politics generally, Beard did not seem particularly impelled to recast his thinking on the subject of human nature in politics.

Nevertheless, human nature had in effect been brought into the laboratory and subjected to quantitative measurement and scientific analysis, however rudimentary. Almost two million men during the war had received the United States Army tests, constructed by psychologists especially for the occasion. Surprisingly, the findings suggested that the human "Intelligence Quotient" was much lower

---

[1] The 1920's experienced the "first wave of enthusiasm" for using knowledge from psychology in political research, according to David Easton, *The Political System* (New York: Alfred A. Knopf, 1953), p. 203 n.

64

than generally supposed, the intelligence of most people not rising beyond fourteen years of age. This problem of scientifically studying human abilities continued to attract attention in psychological circles, even if not among students of politics.[2]

Beard, as always when he addressed himself to the question of human nature, was appreciative of irrationalism and incompetence in man. In the fourth edition of his *American Government and Politics,* which appeared in 1924, he defended the action of the founding fathers in devising limitations on popular government in view of the "lessons of history before them."[3] Speaking of "realities" in 1926, he conceded that "in practice we know that self-interest is not enlightened automatically by the instinct of acquisition."[4] Subsequently discussing the role of experts in government, he admitted that all people were victims of "sentiments, delusions, misinformation, and crass prejudices," and that, since government involved human prejudices which were simply "there," such prejudices had to be "managed just like other phenomena."[5] In short, it was possible to face the facts concerning human nature as realistically as any other aspect of democratic politics. Viewed thus, the actual political process did not merely concern the activities of a multitude of equally endowed individuals, but centered principally on the contests of energetic minorities.

At best it is only a portion of the people who make decisions and display a will of any kind. At the center of every party, group, or faction that

[2] The noted British psychologist, Charles E. Spearman, summed up much of the new knowledge in two works: *The Nature of "Intelligence" and the Principles of Cognition,* (London: Macmillan and Co., 1923) and *Abilities of Man* (New York: Macmillan Co., 1927). Another of Beard's contemporaries, the psychologist John B. Watson, was also attempting in the 1920's to apply the methods of natural science to the study of human nature. Through empirical studies he sought to learn how the human animal responds to various stimuli. Like Beard in political science, Watson in psychology believed that "how people actually behave is a much more reliable way of testing assumptions about human behavior than reliance on introspective evidence" (R. S. Peters [ed.], *History of Psychology* [New York: Macmillan Co., 1953], p. 664). Having already made something of a name for himself before the war by setting forth a number of behaviorist hypotheses, Watson subsequently published his notable *Psychology from the Standpoint of a Behaviorist* (Philadelphia: J. B. Lippincott Co., 1919).

[3] *American Government and Politics* (4th ed.; Macmillan Co., 1924), p. 70.

[4] "Some Regional Realities," *Survey,* LVI (April 15, 1926), 85.

[5] "Life Is Not a Table of Logarithms," *Public Management,* XI (July, 1929), 511.

supports a plan or idea there is a small minority determined in spirit, more or less informed, and bent upon action. From that center outward to the circumference of the group, knowledge, interest, and intensity of feeling diminish. Some are active, creative; others are passive and receptive only. . . . For the present we shall accept *the dictum of Lord Bryce* that the world is governed by active minorities who originate ideas and compel attention of the multitude.[6]

Beard's recognition of human inertia and ineptitude, therefore, did not stem from any newly discovered psychological knowledge. The old wisdom of Bryce was sufficient. Bryce had already taught that the few have ability, the multitude are incompetent. Beard, like others, apparently felt that little could be added to these insights.

It is interesting to notice that at approximately this time the Austrian psychoanalyst Sigmund Freud was publishing *The Ego and the Id* (1923).[7] In Freud's view, the "ego" was the composite of man's instinctive urges as these had been modified by environment and experience to regulate his voluntary actions. On the other hand the "id" consisted of the unmodified biologically conditioned urges. One of the psychological mechanisms by which conflicts between the ego and the id—that is, conflicts between the requirements of the social environment and those of biology—were resolved, according to Freud, was repression of the unacceptable, or keeping it out of the consciousness. In the very year that Beard approvingly paraphrased Lord Bryce's commentary on human nature, Luther L. Bernard published his volume, *Instinct: A Study in Social Psychology* (1924).[8] This work not only emphasized the vital role of the social environment in helping to shape human goals, but had the effect of further developing the field of social psychology which was to attract increasing attention in American social science in future years.

Thus, regardless of whether the psychology of the 1920's found man's actions conditioned primarily by physiology and biology, or coerced and civilized mainly by experience and environment, human nature did not emerge unscathed from the scrutiny. Psychology, while laying the groundwork for more realistic future study

[6] *American Government and Politics* (4th ed.; 1924), p. 19 (italics supplied).

[7] (In English; London: Hogarth Press, 1927). See Peters, *History of Psychology*, pp. 687 ff.

[8] (New York: Henry Holt & Co., 1924).

of politics, was casting a certain amount of doubt on accepted democratic dogma.

Whether or not Beard deliberately took into account the findings of the psychologists of his day, he did not disagree with them in his allusions to the role of force, folly, prejudice, and shortsightedness on the part of unthinking multitudes throughout human history. "A hard head is not necessarily a wise head," he liked to remind his readers.[9] History was full of examples showing man's infinite capacity for irrational action, for adopting means clearly ineffective relative to the ends proclaimed. Sometimes men foolishly took action destructive of the very goals they cherished; at other times they stubbornly resisted an outcome later highly valued.

Did the English ever want a republic? They tried one in Cromwell's day and joyfully crawled back to the throne of the Stuarts, in 1660. Did the French ever want a republic? . . . Only the divisions among the monarchists forced the inescapable republic on the French. . . . War and revolution made America a republic, not a solemn vote of The People.[10]

The point is not, however, that Beard in the postwar years was suddenly emphasizing the defects in human nature. On the contrary, he was mainly continuing his progressive era habit of directing occasional barbs at the foibles of the human species, much as he had always done. If anything, he was increasingly impressed by the complexity of the human being. He appeared to be underlining not the fact that men were incompetent or irrational, but that (1) they were extremely complicated in their make-up, and (2) they differed greatly as individuals.

What adult with any claim to ripeness of spirit would admit belonging merely to one category of history—as warrior, politician, money-getter, novelist, sportsman, mortician, journalist, husband, wife, father, or mother—and aspiring to nothing more? [11]

A highly specialized society [is] composed of engineers, machinists, bacteriologists, electricians, and the masters of a thousand or more professions, crafts, and arts. If all are theoretically equal and alike in the eyes of the state, the members of each group possess capacities, habits, and sentiments peculiar to their occupation. . . . In a machine age, at

[9] For example, see "Democracy Holds Its Ground: A European Survey," *Harper's Magazine,* CLVII (November, 1928), 685.

[10] *Ibid.,* p. 687.

[11] *The Rise of American Civilization,* with Mary R. Beard (1-vol. ed.; New York: Macmillan Co., 1930), p. vii.

least, when informed competence, rather than "native intelligence," is such an important factor, no division of society into the politically wise and foolish is possible.[12]

The Free Mind

Perhaps the most basic and enduring concept in Beard's thinking about human nature was the notion of the free mind. Certainly it was a topic concerning which he could pour out some of his most eloquent and emotion-packed language. For him, freedom of thought, in all its varied ramifications, was both a goal and a method. Lurking behind this position and attitude was the unspoken proposition that the mind is rational, and nature orderly.

This Holmes brand of liberalism was evident on many occasions. Almost as soon as the war ended, Beard vigorously demanded full restoration of all civil rights suspended during the conflict. Political prisoners "whose offense was to retain Mr. Wilson's pacifistic views after he abandoned them" should be released without delay. Postal censorship and all the other restrictions reminiscent of the infamous Alien and Sedition laws should be instantly swept aside. "Is truth so frail and faith so slight that they must be handed over to the police?" thundered Beard, lashing out against the currents of anti-Red hysteria subverting the good sense of numerous otherwise sane Americans in the early 1920's.[13]

In 1921 the New York State Legislature had before it the notorious "Lusk bills" which would have imposed a thinly disguised form of censorship. Beard's pen dripped acid as he addressed readers of the *New Republic* "On the Advantages of Censorship and Espionage." [14] French history, he said, had demonstrated how censorship made radical writers so sharp and clever that the whole regime which supported such stupidities finally fell. As Beard put it later, "Policemen when dealing with ideas are a danger to social stability and orderly progress, while freedom of speech and press offers a safety valve for the escape of noxious and dangerous vapors!" [15]

Frequently Beard turned his guns on attackers of academic and scholarly freedom. "At bottom and forever," he emphasized, "the

[12] *The American Leviathan,* with William Beard (New York: Macmillan Co., 1930), pp. 6, 16.
[13] "The Supreme Issue," letter to the editor, *New Republic,* XVII (January 18, 1919), 343.
[14] XXVII (August 24, 1921), 350 f.
[15] *The Administration and Politics of Tokyo* (New York: Macmillan Co., 1923), p. 159.

question of academic freedom is the question of intellectual and spiritual leadership in American democracy. Those who lead and teach, are they free, fearless, and worthy of trust?"[16] He, himself, believed that the "purveyors of the safe and insignificant" could give little inspiration to the country's future intellectual leaders. "The business of scholarship," he asserted in the *Nation,* "is thinking; not returning to doting parents the undisturbed minds of their off-spring."[17]

One of Beard's most stirring defenses of the free mind was the luncheon speech he delivered at an American Civil Liberties Union gathering in New York City in 1925. The guest of honor for the occasion was the Hungarian Count Karolyi, then seeking haven in America from the vicissitudes of postwar politics in the land of the shattered Austro-Hungarian monarchy. In measured tones, Beard began:

It is not my purpose to answer the critics of our distinguished guest or to pass judgment on the merits of any political controversy in Hungary. I intend merely to consider the American rights involved in the case and to join in the protest against a decision of the State Department that insults our intelligence—a decision to the effect that we are not morally fit to hear anything that our guest may care to say on any subject. I am here to lift up my voice. . . .[18]

A smoking denunciation of the policy of continuing war powers in time of peace followed, accompanied by a devastating barrage on a host of other alleged abuses of the Wilsonian administration. By the time Beard had finished, the electrified audience was on its feet cheering.

In these encounters, Beard was basing his argument on the usual liberal premises, even if unstated. With Mill, he believed that one could defend freedom either as an intrinsic individual right or on the ground of its social consequences. Typically, Beard rested his case by implication on the latter. He showed slight interest, however, in going into the "metaphysics" of the matter. "At bottom everything depends upon the psychology of the people. Do they believe in liberty as a good in itself to which the dignity of human

[16] "The University and Democracy," *Dial,* LXIV (April 11, 1918), 335.
[17] *Nation,* CIX (September 20, 1919), 393; this essay, "Lo! the Poor Professor," is under the pseudonym of "John W. Bradford," but according to Thomas Reed Powell (personal interview, July 2, 1953) it was written by Beard.
[18] "Count Karolyi and America," *Nation,* CXX (April 1, 1925), 347.

nature is entitled?" [19] ". . . And what are rights? Abstract, intangible moral values having neither substance nor form?" [20]

Behind Beard's references to the free mind was the postulate that ordinary man is competent to hold his government under intelligent democratic control. Paper declarations, he knew, had little to do with realizing rights in practice: "It is after all the spirit of a people that gives or withholds liberty." [21] Conceding, too, that freedom of opinion could be abused, he maintained that "far more open to abuse is the right to suppress opinion and far more often in the long history of humanity has it been abused." [22] Ultimately it was "popular criticism" and "democratic pressures and interference" [23] that were the only sure guarantees of intelligence and sane direction in public affairs. "In a democracy," he wrote, "it is the work of unknown hundreds, not the front-page gestures of heroic actors, that accomplishes fundamental results." [24] In *The Rise of American Civilization* (1927), after a glowing account of great accomplishments on every level of government and in every segment of society, the authors proudly asserted: "Such were the processes and products of American democracy when the mind was left free to inquire, to propose, and to champion." [25]

Application of scientific reason to political study itself, as Beard had long deeply felt, depended on the principle of the free mind. "I have definitely cast off all my lingering suspicions about the value of science," he declared in 1925. "I am more convinced than ever that we shall make progress by applying the methods of natural science to the study of government and administration." [26]

Values as Political Facts

Although Beard, some two decades after his first years as a Columbia University professor, thus continued to appeal for a

[19] *The American Leviathan,* p. 59.

[20] *The Rise of American Civilization* (1st ed.; 1927), II, 37.

[21] Review of Chafee, *Freedom of Speech, National Municipal Review,* X (April, 1921), 248.

[22] *American Government and Politics* (4th ed.; 1924), p. 36.

[23] In *Essays in Intellectual History Dedicated to James Harvey Robinson* (New York: Harper & Bros., 1929), p. 117.

[24] Review of Forbes, *Governmental Purchasing, National Municipal Review,* XVIII (September, 1929), 580.

[25] *The Rise of American Civilization* (1st ed.; 1927), II, 589.

[26] "Municipal Research Abroad and at Home," *Journal of Social Forces,* III (March, 1925), 495.

scientific approach to the study of politics, a subtle change nonetheless had crept into his writings. For many years now, little had been heard directly on the point he had stressed in 1908: that politics "for scientific purposes" was to be separated from "ethics." [27] By the 1920's there was tacit recognition that in a sense, even "for scientific purposes," ethics and politics were inseparable. That is, the subjective values held by political actors could be identified and examined just as could the objective processes and institutions, and they constituted part of the relevant data that a realistic student of politics must consider.

Mainly this new point was implicit and not expressly developed. Beard could still complain of the tendency of scholars to confuse "theories and sentiments" with political realities, to permit subjective biases to distort scientific objectivity. In the earlier years it had not always been entirely clear exactly what Beard was attacking. He still showed little interest in stating unambiguously precisely what element or relationship in the ethics-science-politics complex he particularly objected to: (1) permitting subjective biases to distort scientific objectivity, (2) evaluating political machinery and processes according to explicit norms or standards, or (3) analyzing the nature and role of particular values in given political situations.

It seems clear that he opposed as much as ever the mingling of "ethics" with the study of politics in sense (1). In his 1923 study on Tokyo, for example, he pointed out that universal suffrage was "in itself not good or bad," much as in 1908 he had claimed that historians should not "play the moral judge" and students of politics had no business trying "to praise or condemn institutions or theories." [28] In the Tokyo study he stated:

It is sometimes supposed that the suffrage is a matter involving general political theories and sentiments and not a subject to be treated scientifically. . . . In all modern industrial countries which have universal public education, a free press, and the open discussion of public questions the movement toward political democracy is a reality no less tangible and actual than a natural phenomenon.[29]

But in addition Beard could now occasionally allude approvingly, at least by implication, to the relationship of "ethics" and "scientific politics" in senses (2) and (3). Thus, whoever undertook "criticism

---

[27] *Politics* (New York: Columbia University Press, 1908), p. 14.
[28] *Ibid.;* cf. *The Administration and Politics of Tokyo,* p. 154.
[29] *The Administration and Politics of Tokyo,* p. 153.

of any particular administrative system," he claimed, should "present the criteria upon which his judgments are founded," whether these standards comprised "some ideal system evolved by *a priori* reasoning from an abstract concept" or "pragmatic assumptions from practice."[30] And whether the analysis centered on municipal administration, factors favoring democratic government in Yugoslavia, or the effects of suffrage extension in America, the "human choices" and "ideal ends" involved were also admissible as relevant evidence.[31]

These adjustments in Beard's thought appeared to keep pace with the correspondingly greater role he was coming to assign to "ideas" as forces in human affairs (see chapters 6 and 8).

Progress and Democracy

Shortly after the end of the war, Beard and several other scholars published a joint work concerning the tasks now facing the victors, *Democracy in Reconstruction* (1919).[32] Beard's own contribution, an essay on "The Evolution of Democracy," was vibrant with hope for the future. The seed of democracy, he felt, had been planted at the very origin of the state. Although the "progressive democratization of the state" through the ages had not followed an identical pattern everywhere, nonetheless "the general result" had been virtually the same throughout Western civilization. Having already subdued to public purposes a great many institutions during preceding generations, democracy was now relentlessly at work transforming still others, principally economic. Here was a task "magnificent beyond imagination."[33]

In short, the supreme test of the power of the people to conduct government for themselves is now at hand. The achievements of the past, though splendid, throw little light upon the future. Those who work now must work under a sense of responsibility such as never has fallen upon those to whom it is given to teach or lead. The outcome can be seen by the eye of faith alone.[34]

This underlying hope, reflecting a seemingly irrepressible faith in progress, had drawn a unifying thread through much of Beard's

[30] *Ibid.*, p. 19.
[31] *Ibid.*, pp. 53 f.; also cf. "Life Is Not a Table of Logarithms," p. 511.
[32] Ed. Frederick A. Cleveland and Joseph Schafer (Boston: Houghton Mifflin Co., 1919).
[33] *Ibid.*, pp. 486–91.
[34] *Ibid.*, p. 491.

thought from his early English years down to the 1920's. Despite human mistakes and folly, wars, economic dislocations, and other setbacks, the general forward march of mankind had continued— at least up to the present. That Beard believed the general direction of march would not be reversed in the near future was strongly suggested in various of his writings in the afterglow of the Allies' successful defense of democracy against German militarism.

The Beard-Ogg volume, *National Governments and the World War* (1919), which came off the presses shortly after the armistice, raised no doubts as to the near inevitability of human progress, including the progressively wider democratization of mankind. In the authors' discussions of human rights, democracy, and "the progress of enlightened humanity" [35]—the great democratic powers of the world having just brought the forces of autocracy down in ruin—it seemed to be clearly implied that man was basically an enlightened creature whose better nature had lately reasserted itself.

Beard's continuing faith in progress and the ultimate spread of democracy was also interestingly illustrated by the early history of his significant theoretical work, *The Economic Basis of Politics* (1922).[36] Originating as a series of four lectures delivered at Amherst College in the summer of 1916, it was published in book form six years later after the war had been fought and won. As Beard himself explained in the preface, the lectures were reproduced substantially as delivered except for the fourth one, which had now been revised "in the light of recent political experience." This fourth lecture took account of the new developments in Bolshevik Russia. But the first three lectures had *not* been revised or substantially altered "in the light of recent political experience." What Beard had said in these three lectures in 1916 was still what he had to say in 1922: "Long the victim of material forces, man has, by taking thought, made himself master of wind and wave and storm. May he not, by taking thought, lift himself above the social conflicts that destroy civilizations and make himself master of his social destiny?" [37]

This was essentially what Beard as a young man in England had been saying nearly a quarter of a century earlier. Rational men "by

---

[35] With Frederic A. Ogg (New York: Macmillan Co., 1919), p. 143; also see pp. 128 ff.

[36] *The Economic Basis of Politics* (New York: Alfred A. Knopf, 1922).

[37] *Ibid.*, pp. 12 f.

taking thought" could continue to rearrange the world to attain better living, wider democracy, fuller justice. In the 1920's Beard in middle life still retained something of the hopeful faith of the Oxford student who had viewed industrialization and democracy, not as incompatible with each other, but as potential allies. To his mind it was still significant that "the development of political democracy during three revolutionary centuries was accompanied by the rise and growth of science and invention." [38]

A full decade after the guns had cooled in western Europe, Beard published a notable essay in *Harper's Magazine* entitled, "Democracy Holds Its Ground." [39] Written after four extensive postwar trips abroad, including two in Europe where the bloodiest fighting had occurred, and thus taking fullest account of "recent political experience," the essay presumably represented Beard's most informed thinking on the subject up to that date. What was the gist of his thought? Had he been disillusioned by his "European survey"? In glowing terms, he wrote of the marriage of science and democracy. As technology moved forward, so democracy must move forward:

Business enterprise, in seven-league boots and wearing a steel helmet wreathed in smoke, marches across the face of the earth *spreading restless democracy* in its train. A divine monarch, an unquestioned clergy, a ruling landed aristocracy cannot look upon the face of this giant and live. . . . Newspapers, schools, literacy, moving pictures, radios, travel, research, discussion, and endless economic changes make a *restoration of any kind of rigid order so highly improbable as to appear impossible.*[40]

Not pessimism and doubt, but faith and hope, were thus written large. Democracy would continue to spread. The rigid old undemocratic orders were perishing, and their restoration seemed virtually impossible. What of inflation in Germany, power struggles in Russia, the roaring of Il Duce in Italy? Beard apparently was undaunted:

Inevitably, therefore, great masses of untitled people will have a hand in government, democracy will abide and function—in a way. It will pass through dictatorship, perhaps, but dictators are not immortal and divisions will follow their departure. The world cannot go on without masses, and masses are not going on without the instruments and practices that make for democracy.[41]

[38] *The Rise of American Civilization* (1st ed.; 1927), I, 737.
[39] Pp. 680–91.
[40] *Ibid.,* p. 691 (italics supplied).
[41] *Ibid.*

If Beard's faith glowed brightly through the postwar shadows, he was not alone. Justice Holmes, too, with his keen sensitivity to the social consequences of thought and action, was expressing his confidence in the ultimate victory of truth and reason when ideas are left free to grapple. Similarly, John Dewey was continuing to argue persuasively in support of equality, democracy, and the enlightened reason which he himself so admirably exemplified. Despite counter-tendencies, the optimistic, pragmatic strain in American thought was extremely pervasive.

Beard, too, was part of that American tradition of the free individual in the democratically evolving state. Was his "eye of faith," as he peered into the future, telescopic or myopic? Beard himself would have countered: with what other eyes can mortals penetrate the mists?

CHAPTER V
THE ROLE OF GOVERNMENT
IN MODERN LIFE

The Fact of Big Government

The most cursory examination of Beard's writings reveals the persistence of a pervasive concept whose significance, however, it is easy to overlook. Simply stated, it was the notion that the role of government in modern life is and ought to be a great and expanding one. Although certainly present in every period of Beard's intellectual development, this concept reached perhaps its most thoroughgoing articulation during the postwar era. At the beginning of the period he could claim "the most striking feature of modern politics" to be the continuing growth in the scope and functions of government.[1] Toward its close his characteristic reaction to the economic crash and depression was that government was the agency to attack the malaise.

As most literate Americans knew, the expanding role of government had not been a recent mushroom growth, or simply rooted in the late war. It is true that some persons did believe that the "roaring twenties" heralded a New Era in America. To such enthusiasts the New Economic Policy then being launched in Russia only confirmed their convictions regarding the superiority of the American brand of "free enterprise" in hastening the millennium.

Beard himself found the reasons for the striking growth of state functions rather obvious. Not the sudden perversity of human nature, not a decline in the resourcefulness of individuals, not even a conspiracy of politicians, were basic causes. Rather, the root of the matter lay in science and technology. For the most part, increasing governmental activities were simply the product of industrial society.

Despite myth and folklore about individual initiative and the clumsiness of government, the clock could not be turned back. The

[1] "Public Employment," *National Municipal Review,* VIII (January, 1919), 26.

inevitable could be railed against or ignored, but it could not be appreciably postponed. The advent of the new civilization might be dreaded, and the scope of government might even be cut down here and there in minor ways. Yet for practical purposes the great changes were here to stay. Those who thought otherwise apparently also believed it possible to return to "the stage coach and the tallow dip." [2] This was the position of Beard, Republican by tradition, more than a dozen years before the New Deal had been heard of.

In the fourth edition of his *American Government and Politics* (1924), published the year Lenin died and the French began evacuating the Ruhr, Beard told students that in the past "the essence of government" had been *"power."* But in his opinion even a quick inventory of the vast number of functions and services now performed by government showed that it could no longer be explained on the ground of power alone. Government today must be justified on the basis of the services it provided. During times of peace the acts of government were largely acts of service and not of force.[3] In 1927 Beard scoffed at the notion that government paternalism would crush individual initiative and self-reliance. The Republican party, he slyly suggested, had once flung the national domain "to the hungry proletariat as a free gift, more significant than bread and circuses." [4]

Beard believed, in short, that the facts of modern life had conspired to make government the "collective agency for waging war on the five deadly enemies of mankind: ignorance, poverty, disease, waste, and inhumanity." [5] Thus the idea of progress was intimately tied to the concept of expanding government. Furthermore, the same technological factors that had made government big would also enable it to serve as democracy's handmaid. In 1930 Beard emphasized the political effects of the modern technological age, with implications for both progress and democracy, by publishing a book devoted to the subject.[6] This *American Leviathan,* he made plain, was not a Hobbesian Frankenstein who turned on his creators and

[2] *Ibid.,* p. 28.

[3] *American Government and Politics* (4th ed.; New York: Macmillan Co., 1924), pp. 5 f.

[4] *The Rise of American Civilization,* with Mary R. Beard (1st ed.; New York: Macmillan Co., 1927), I, 751.

[5] *American Government and Politics* (4th ed.; 1924), p. 11.

[6] *The American Leviathan,* with William Beard (New York: Macmillan Co., 1930).

enslaved them, but a domesticated giant who served them hand and foot.

A New "Heavenly City"

Beard's concept involved more than a mere factual situation. There was also a value pattern expressed and implicit in it. In his treatment of the modern role of government he indicated not only "what is" but also "what ought to be."

Frequently he drew attention to new fields of activity which he believed it desirable for government to enter. As new social problems rose and demanded solution apparently not forthcoming from other quarters, he felt impelled to urge government intervention. Did the free-enterprise pricing mechanism exhibit certain weaknesses in operation? Then perhaps government ought to enter the picture and make possible the substitution of a "cooperative mediation between producer and consumer for the mediation thus far furnished by business men alone." [7] Did an urban area face growing problems brought on by industrialization? If so, its government ought to be granted powers commensurate with the responsibilities imposed on the community. Government at any level, Beard insisted, was an agent of the community, not an end in itself, and ought therefore to be used to the fullest practicable extent.[8]

Thus implicitly the vague outlines of Beard's "heavenly city" of the 1920's emerged. In his potential philosophy of government functions, he was obviously neither at the totalitarian nor the anarchist extremes. His typical concern, however, was to overcome the predilection toward the minimal state.[9] Repeatedly he urged his fellow Americans to modernize their thinking concerning the role of

[7] "Public Employment," p. 33.

[8] *The Administration and Politics of Tokyo* (New York: Macmillan Co., 1923), pp. 24 f.

[9] At that time, a typical textbook classification of "theories of state functions" might have identified, rather than these extremes, a number of intermediate theoretical positions on this question, such as "individualism," "collectivism," and "socialism" (see, for example, Ford P. Hall, *Government and Business* [New York: McGraw-Hill Book Co., 1934], pp. 1–13). Thus, the position of Herbert Hoover, as expressed in his volumes, *American Individualism* (Garden City, N.Y.: Doubleday & Co., 1922) and *The Challenge to Liberty* (New York: Charles Scribner's Sons, 1934), was farther toward the individualist end of the scale than was Beard's. On this question of the proper tasks of government, Beard was a "collectivist" to perhaps the extent that Stuart Chase was (see Chase's volume, *A New Deal* [New York: Macmillan Co., 1932], published just before Roosevelt's first election).

government. In 1927, two years before the stock market crash of Black October, he complained:

We have no science of social management. Our sociology is, in the main, a collection of special studies and vague abstractions—without practical utility. Our written history is largely fable that does not help to explain the operation of the forces that have made us what we are. Until recently our works on economics have been principally manuals for business or profit-making practitioners, incurably diseased by their neglect of community and political factors—without any concept of national or social grandeur higher than a balance sheet. In short, we are dominated by a generation of leaders brought up in colleges and engineering schools on the philosophy of anarchy plus the police constable.[10]

In his arguments in support of the concept of the modern social-service state, Beard attacked laissez faire on several grounds. In this period at least three may be distinguished. Laissez faire (1) failed on its own merits, (2) had not been the intention of the Constitutional fathers despite claims to the contrary, and (3) showed no positive correlation to meaningful liberty notwithstanding the contentions of writers like Herbert Hoover.

Laissez faire on its own merits, Beard often contended, failed miserably as a guide to policy makers. It was a fallacious bit of ideology from another era, a dogma that had actually never been suitable to any past conditions and was totally unrealistic in the present. In an article in the *National Municipal Review,* he recalled in amusement how in his own youth he, himself, had been subjected to and attracted by the tenets of classical economics: "The grand result of the untrammeled individual quest for success is inevitably the greatest good for the greatest number, perfect liberty, social harmony, universal well-being, utopia." [11] Implicitly he chided all those of his own generation who had not left this dream world of the past:

The only trouble with the splendid scheme of logic lay in the fact that the world persistently refused to walk in the ways prescribed by the doctors of political economy. Capitalists insisted on combining, and laborers insisted on forming unions. . . . Moreover, the government . . . found itself . . . compelled to undertake work which, according to the doctors of political economy, it was physically and mentally unable to do.[12]

---

[10] "Conflicts in City Planning," *Yale Review,* XVII (October, 1927), 74 f.
[11] "Public Employment," p. 26.
[12] *Ibid.*

Beard also assailed the notion that the doctrine of laissez faire was part of America's heritage from the Constitutional fathers. Alexander Hamilton had especially favored harnessing the national government, he pointed out in *The American Leviathan*.[13] The fathers had conceived that the central government should not only protect property interests, but also promote new economic undertakings by means of discriminating measures such as subsidies, tariffs, and bounties. "It was a distinct denial of the axiom that men, if let alone, will make the wisest and best use of their material opportunities and effect a just and beneficial distribution of wealth."

Finally, Beard denied that governmental intervention necessarily cramped human liberty. Those who complained that federal regulation was undemocratic or tyrannical were reminded in *The American Leviathan* of the convenience, protection, and efficiency provided by government rules forcing railroads to follow one standard time, or by the government's confiscation, in pursuance of the interstate commerce power, "of poisons offered as table delicacies." [14] The real significance of government intervention in such situations was that genuine human freedom was not stifled but enlarged. On the eve of the New Deal, Beard in *Harper's Magazine* pointed out, in language reminiscent of his earlier economic interpretation writings, that the chief role of government was still the "regulation of various and interfering economic interests." [15]

In short, throughout the postwar years Beard made plain that his conception of government's role in modern life embraced not only the statement of a verifiable fact but likewise the assertion of an ideal.

Leviathan: Theory and Practice

With the activities of government reaching into so many phases of human existence, Beard and other students of public administration in the 1920's were deeply interested in the methods and techniques used to effect the ends involved. Behind the "acts of service" on the part of the modern Leviathan state was a vast administrative machinery, guided not by an "invisible hand" but by fallible hu-

---

[13] *The American Leviathan*, p. 449.

[14] *Ibid.*, p. 616.

[15] "Whom Does Congress Represent?" *Harper's Magazine*, CLX (January, 1930), 150.

man hands and brains. Although Beard and many of his practical-minded contemporaries overtly shunned "theory" and supposed that "the essence of government" was no longer "power," nevertheless the administrative instruments that concerned them were actually power to effect ends.[16] Their regard for the operating principles and effectiveness of these instruments likewise indicated a fundamental concern with political theory.

During the postwar years the field of public administration was just emerging as a semiautonomous discipline. As such it was finding a place in the curriculum of a number of large universities. Numerous books and articles by students of government indicated a rising scholarly interest in the field. The subject was generally felt to be intensely "practical," with useful applications on every level of government. Finespun abstractions seemed to be out of place in the wholly pragmatic atmosphere surrounding the discipline. Beard, through direct practical involvement as well as through his voluminous writings, was in the thick of "the movement."

In his 1924 American government textbook he pointed out the great importance and complexity of executing and administering the functions of the modern state. "Experts" had become the major reliance of twentieth-century government, and by comparison law-making turned out to be simple. Beard's emphasis on the realistic rather than the legalistic aspects of government continued a tendency already evident earlier and was characteristic of the postwar approach of public administration students. Although warriors and record keepers had been virtually the only kind of "administrators" needed in the dim past, nowadays scientific administration in every phase of social life had become essential for the continued survival of "the great society." In modern times law was merely the beginning, and administration was the heart, of the governing process. Indeed, the conduct of administration had come to determine "the destiny of the state." [17]

How could the new knowledge of "scientific management" accumulating in industry be utilized in the democratic political system? Here was the challenging problem facing Beard and other students in their preoccupation with matters of personnel, organization, and budgeting. "Efficient government," as Beard knew, involved "the

[16] *American Government and Politics* (4th ed.; 1924), pp. 5 f.
[17] *Ibid.*, pp. 38–41.

coordination of many arts and sciences and all sorts and conditions of people." [18] From the literature of public administration the largely implicit theoretical pattern that emerged appeared to hinge unequally on a number of basic questions: (1) What are the ultimate ends? (2) What is available to work with in the way of men and materials, and what are the other realities to be faced? (3) Given the realities and the ends, how can the latter be most effectively realized?

As to ultimate ends, virtually never was the literature expressly concerned with such matters of "metaphysics." The ends were apparently taken for granted, unquestioned, and little thought about. True, here and there passing references were made to undefined concepts such as democracy, the dignity of the individual, freedom, the general welfare, western civilization, and the like. But these occasioned slight pause.

In contrast, some notice was given to the question of the nature of the political reality confronting public administrators. Although "the facts" of nature and human nature were scarcely a center of controversy, the supposed realities of politics sometimes inspired commentary. Here the revulsion against legalism, traditionalism, myth, and theoretical abstraction found release. On the other hand, among the principles accepted as realistic was the fundamental proposition that the political process as a whole comprised two distinct operations: politics and administration. This dichotomy, stated by Beard's teacher Frank Goodnow at the turn of the century, had come to be virtual gospel by the 1920's. Politics was policy making. Administration was policy execution. Policy making could be of various kinds: democratic, autocratic, and perhaps others. Similarly, administration fell into different categories: efficient, inefficient, wasteful, economical, corrupt, honest, and so on. Subsidiary to the primary axiom were two lesser articles of faith: democratic politics was inherently inefficient, and efficient administration was by nature autocratic.

Mainly, however, the attention of public administration scholars appeared to be attracted to the third broad theoretical question, the many-sided problem of how most effectively to realize assumed political and social ends. Both from a priori reasoning and from practice, a number of "laws" emerged. Arthur E. Buck, for example, who himself was greatly influenced by Beard and his "criteria of

[18] "Life Is Not a Table of Logarithms," *Public Management*, XI (July, 1929), 511.

municipal science," [19] was prominent among those enunciating such principles, and textbooks a generation later continued to quote his canons as these were hammered out in successive versions. One of the principles was that the administrative work of government should be confined to "experts." A corollary rule was the need of a merit system for personnel. Another principle required proper departmentalization, that is, administrative structure organized according to function. High in the list of standards was the concentration of responsibility and authority. Supporting this broad concept were several others: the short ballot, the power of hiring and firing in the hands of the top man, the rejection of boards for administrative (i.e., "nonpolitical") functions, the provision of adequate staff aids for key administrators. Finally, and related intimately to all the others, was the necessity of coordinated planning, including budgets, work loads, long-range operations, and so on. Such canons were driven home to a generation of practitioners and scholars in textbooks, journals, lectures, and forums until they approached the finality of physical law.

The paramount point in all this was how to reconcile democracy and efficiency. The desirability of democratic politics was given, and the advantages of efficient administration were granted. Yet the stark facts appeared to be that democratic politics was essentially inefficient, and efficient administration was by nature undemocratic. Reams were written on all phases of the subject. Beard contributed his share.

As he realized, "this halting, stumbling democracy of ours" [20] was confronted with mountainous tasks. It was vital, he wrote in 1918, that "the requirements of our very human American democracy" be reconciled with "efficient and expert technical service." Whereas the expert was "mechanistic and impersonal," politics was "intensely personal." [21] The many bureaucrats and administrators in various levels and sectors of government were like "privates in a great army," he told students in his 1924 textbook on American government. In 1925, again comparing administrators to those "who work on the firing line of the advancing army," he suggested by contrast that demo-

---

[19] See Luther Gulick's discussion in Howard K. Beale (ed.), *Charles A. Beard* (Lexington: University of Kentucky Press, 1954), pp. 55–60.

[20] "Municipal Research Abroad and at Home," *Journal of Social Forces*, III (March, 1925), 497.

[21] "Human Nature and Administration," *Nation*, CVI (April 25, 1918), 502.

cratic politics tended to drift.[22] Democracy lacked military precision and efficiency because many of its institutions had originated in an age when such traits were not essential for its survival. In 1932, on the eve of the New Deal, he declared that the institution of representation which had arisen in a simpler agricultural era failed to "function efficiently in a closely meshed technological society."[23] From outward appearances, Beard seemed to accept the view that perfected administration was somewhat autocratic and democratic politics was naturally inefficient.

To his mind, accordingly, the main task appeared to center on making administration effective and scientific. "The hope of the future," he exclaimed, "lies not in tinkering up assemblies but in the development of the ideal and technique of public service."[24] The research bureau movement, with its application of "the methods of natural science" to the study of government, won his warm praise.[25] Through careful research applied to actual practice, the "businesslike management" of the public business could be furthered, including the "elimination of petty wastes at a thousand points, the selection of able people to discharge even the smallest duties, the persistent watchfulness at the points far and wide."[26]

Yet Beard did not concede that the "nonadministrative" apparatus of the democratic Leviathan—the naturally clumsy devices and institutions of popular policy making—were hopelessly beyond remodeling. Although he might smile at those who would "tinker up assemblies," he himself continued strong in his prewar belief that democratic political machinery must be made as simple as possible. Indeed, he was convinced that, unless the political linkage between citizens and their government in a complex industrial society could be streamlined, meaningful democratic direction of the modern state was in danger of extinction. As a firm democrat, he felt impelled to bend every effort to preserve ultimate popular control.

Consequently, Beard also continued to devote much attention to the possibility of modernizing traditional democratic institutions.

---

[22] "World Bureau of Municipal Research," *National Municipal Review*, XIV (January, 1925), 1.

[23] "Congress under Fire," *Yale Review*, XXII (September, 1932), 42.

[24] Review of Webb, *A Constitution for the Socialist Commonwealth of Great Britain*, *Nation*, CXI (December 8, 1920), 666.

[25] Introduction, Chester C. Maxey, *County Administration* (New York: Macmillan Co., 1919), p. ix.

[26] "John Purroy Mitchel," *Survey*, XL (July 13, 1918), 437.

One line of attack was concentrated, as in the earlier years, on relieving the political parts of government of administrative tasks for which they were clearly not fitted.[27] Petty matters should be delegated to administrative agencies, even though according to the outworn "scheme of tripartite negation" [28] they might theoretically seem to be legislative in nature. Interestingly, as in the prewar years (see chapter 2), Beard in effect demolished the old separation of powers doctrine with one hand while setting up a new politics-administration dichotomy with the other. In essence, however, he was simply arguing for modernization of institutions and concepts originating in an earlier society: "Systems of checks and balances and the dispersion of power designed to prevent action now stand in the way of the kind of planned and concerted action necessary in a civilization founded on machinery, specialization,—industrial and geographical—and long-haul transportation." [29]

Another line of attack centered on the problem of representation itself. The so-called "failure of representative government," Beard believed, stemmed from the fallacious "head-counting theory," that is, from the Rousseauan abstraction concerning equality, and this theory neglected to take adequate account of group sentiments and interests.[30] Yet he felt that representation of economic groups as such was not the whole answer, inasmuch as men were not merely bankers, farmers, or any other single economic category. At least, lobbies should be openly recognized but more strictly regulated. Perhaps an "economic council" could be set up to hear lobbyists from the different interests, and a "grand committee" established to handle affairs during recesses of the legislature.[31]

Both avenues of democratic reform—that is, separating policy making from administration, and revising the instruments of popular representation—were pursued when the National Municipal League in 1919 created its "model state constitution." Beard was a central participant. The old files of the *National Municipal Review* reveal how he left his indelible imprint on the annual meeting that gave birth to the model constitution. "Dr. Beard opposed the ma-

---

[27] "Congress under Fire," p. 46.
[28] Review of Seymour, *The Intimate Papers of Colonel House, I–II,* New *Republic,* XLVI (March 17, 1926), 109.
[29] "Congress under Fire," p. 42.
[30] *The Economic Basis of Politics* (New York: Alfred A. Knopf, 1922), pp. 90–94.
[31] "Congress under Fire," pp. 44 ff.

jority report with such effect," ran the account, "that the convention, which on Monday leaned toward the adoption of the majority report, was swung back." [32] Apparently disapproving an outright parliamentary form, he favored the combination of a strong executive with a small legislature elected according to proportional representation:

Under Dr. Beard's plan the governor would be elected by the people, with absolute power to appoint and remove heads of departments, would prepare the budget, which the legislature might reduce but not increase; and would have the power to dissolve the legislature when it defeats any of his measures. The legislature, organized with one committee on appropriations and revenues and one standing committee for each of the major branches of state administration, might, on the other hand, call a general election to support it in any break with the governor. There would also be introduced the recall principle.[33]

Efficiency, Accountability, and Planning

Beard's position throughout the postwar era, then, in effect came down to the pragmatic contention that democratic politics and efficient administration were not incompatible, but actually indispensable to each other. If the Leviathan state were to provide the services and steer the general course people wanted, the service providers would have to be expert and the pilots responsive. Like all viable human contrivances, representative government must change to meet new tasks presented by changing times.[34] Perhaps no clearer statement of Beard's continuing belief in the dependence of democratic accountability on structural simplicity can be found than the 1919 report he, himself, wrote regarding the proposed reconstruction of New York State government:

The only serious argument advanced against such a proposed reorganization and budget system is that it makes the Governor a czar. The President of the United States has administrative powers far greater than those here proposed to be given to the Governor. The Mayor of the City of New York appoints and removes all of the important department heads, and the citizens know whom to hold accountable. The Governor does not hold office by hereditary right. He is elected for a fixed term by universal suffrage. He is controlled in all minor appointments by the

---

[32] *National Municipal Review*, IX (February, 1920), 67.

[33] *Ibid.*, pp. 67 f.

[34] See, for example, "World Bureau of Municipal Research," p. 1; "John Purroy Mitchel," p. 437; "Representative Government in Evolution," with J. D. Lewis, *American Political Science Review*, XXVI (April, 1932), 224.

civil service law. He cannot spend a dollar of the public money which is not authorized by the Legislature of the State. He is subject to removal by impeachment. If he were given the powers here proposed he would stand out in the limelight of public opinion and scrutiny. Economy in administration, if accomplished, would redound to his credit. Waste and extravagance could be laid at his door. Those who cannot endure the medicine because it seems too strong must be content with waste, inefficiency and bungling—steadily rising cost of government. The system here proposed is more democratic, not more "royal" than that now in existence. Democracy does not merely mean periodical elections. It means a government held accountable to the people between elections. In order that the people may hold their government to account they must have a government that they can understand. No citizen can hope to understand the present collections of departments, offices, boards and commissions, or the present methods of appropriating money. A Governor with a Cabinet of reasonable size, responsible for proposing a program in the annual budget and for the administering the program as modified by the Legislature may be brought daily under public scrutiny, held accountable to the Legislature and public opinion, and be turned out of office if he fails to measure up to public requirements. If this is not democracy then it is difficult to imagine what it is.[35]

As in the simple theory of "radical democracy," the contention was that what the people want, the people should have. Structural complexities and operational frictions should therefore be eliminated. Nothing must stand in the way of desired human ends. Yet the haunting theoretical possibility remained: might not the means used be in some degree incompatible with the ends sought? If a coldly efficient administrative structure was necessarily as mechanical and autocratic as typically assumed, what of the myriads of public servants in Leviathan who were human beings as well as instruments? Like politics-administration, was the ends-means complex a dichotomy, or a continuum? [36]

Overtly Beard's aim was to avoid dogma. In the 1920's he rejected the Marxism of the Russian Revolution as he had rejected the fruits of laissez faire most of his life.[37] The logic of his own position inclined him toward social democracy, toward a modified form of "capitalist democracy." He was not moved to dispute those who con-

---

[35] Quoted by Gulick in Beale, *Charles A. Beard,* pp. 54 f.

[36] Cf. Dwight Waldo, *The Administrative State* (New York: Ronald Press, 1948), pp. 74 f.

[37] *Cross Currents in Europe Today* (Boston: Marshall Jones Co., 1922), pp. 206–8.

tended that Karl Marx was dead, except to rejoin that "Cobden and Bright are dead also." [38]

Accordingly, in the early 1930's, as depression came on, Beard boldly advocated general planning of the nation's economic life. To his mind the only alternative to drift or dictatorship was planned democracy. Indeed, he now squarely emphasized what he had formerly suggested only speculatively: that even economic class strife might be outmoded by planning.

Science and machinery have made crude class fights archaic. . . . Hence a mere balance of powers is not enough. The necessary rediscovery of the Fathers means a new Science of Political Economy that transcends the everlasting battle of capitalism and agriculture for advantage—a science that has its points of reference or bench marks, not in the bald interests of cotton spinners or wheat raisers, but in the very center of Planned National Economy.[39]

If this sounded like Utopia, the tone was a measure of Beard's concern over the danger of supine surrender in the face of economic chaos. Vigorously attacking "the myth of rugged American individualism" in 1931, he charged that the distress in which Western civilization found itself was principally due to the outworn dogma of individualism and laissez faire.[40] The following year, as economic stagnation deepened, he warned that our political leaders must make a choice, one road "leading in the direction of planned economy and the other backward to an outworn individualism." [41] With America facing issues as fundamental as those once confronting the fathers of the republic, heroic action was again demanded.[42] Simply put, the task was "to discover how much planning is necessary, by whom it can best be done, and what limitations must be imposed on the historic doctrine of Manchesterism." [43]

Beard was clearly in a receptive mood for the New Deal which lay just ahead. His concept of the expanding role of government in modern life had reached its most advanced stage.

[38] *Ibid.*, p. 235.

[39] "Whom Does Congress Represent?" p. 152.

[40] "The Myth of Rugged American Individualism," *Harper's Magazine,* CLXIV (December, 1931), 22.

[41] *America Faces the Future* (Boston: Houghton Mifflin Co., 1932), p. 195.

[42] *Ibid.*, p. 409.

[43] "Myth of Rugged American Individualism," p. 22.

CHAPTER VI
BROADENING BASES OF POLITICS

Beard entered the postwar period firm in his belief that economics was the basis of politics. Keenly interested during his Columbia University days in the real political forces and the actual functioning of government (see chapter 3), he had produced voluminous writings advancing his economic interpretation ideas, incidentally supplying the fragments of an implicit theory of politics.

Energetic minorities, he had pointed out, were the initiators of action in politics as in other aspects of human existence, and these groups, as he had shown at great length, were economically energized. In effect building on his assumptions and views concerning individual human nature, he had expounded "group nature" and behavior. He had further contended that man's social and physical environment also conditioned group dynamics. Partly influenced by Madison's concepts, partly based on certain Marxist assumptions, and drawn from other thinkers as well, Beard's thought regarding individuals and groups in politics had been an unsystematic fusion derived from various sources.

In abbreviated form, his implicit theory as it had developed by 1917 embraced the following. (1) Economic phenomena are found empirically associated with political phenomena; the explanation of "how" economics affects politics is that persons similarly situated economically comprise a reservoir or stratum in society from which political action groups may be drawn on occasion when such persons are sufficiently aroused. (2) Scope for human choice exists, however, and through foreknowledge of how economics affects politics men can forestall unwanted results by the deliberate exercise of their wills. (3) Economic factors also influence and condition men's values and thus may underlie even their choices.

In the present chapter we shall show how the economic emphasis and implicit theory continued in Beard's writings during the initial postwar years. Subsequently our purpose will be to present evidences of change in his views, indicating what points in his prewar thesis are affected. Finally we shall notice the revised position Beard had reached on the eve of the New Deal.

The Economic Basis

The end of the war did not end Beard's time-honored habit of praising writers who in his opinion paid due attention to the "real stuff" of politics and of assailing those who showed undue neglect. When Arthur M. Schlesinger's *Colonial Merchants and the American Revolution* appeared in 1918, for example, it won Beard's ready acclaim. Evincing satisfaction that "science" was at last advancing into "the domain of mythology," Beard gleefully announced that the book had disposed of "the fiction writers who make the American revolution a quarrel over legal theories." [1] Similarly, Carl Becker's work on *The United States: An Experiment in Democracy* was applauded in 1920 for its attention to "the real instead of the mythical" and because it found "the secret of American democracy in the conditions of American life." [2]

Beard was in finest form when on the attack. Of Laski's *Political Thought in England from Locke to Bentham* in 1920 he asserted that "economics receives scant consideration," a neglect that seemed "fatal." Caustically he demanded to know what "ethics, metaphysics, Freud, the psychology new or old, or any other emotional or intellectual coloration" had to offer that compared with the economic hypothesis as to the origin of the Tory and Whig parties. To Beard the "aroma of tea-cups" was no substitute for "the rough stuff of reality." [3] Subsequently, he could not understand why Laski was so easy on political philosophers who did not know "what it was all about" and who skipped so lightly over "the real stuff of politics." [4]

Beard's sharpest gibes were reserved for those who maintained that politics rested on ideological or spiritual factors. In a *New Republic* review of late 1920, for example, he hooted when Carlton J. H. Hayes suggested in his *Brief History of the Great War* that "spiritualism" was now triumphing over "materialism and determinism." Acidly Beard remarked that he was "not aware that the Ouija board had made any serious inroads upon excess profits since

[1] *New Republic*, XIV (April 6, 1918), 304.

[2] *Nation*, CXI (October 13, 1920), 416.

[3] *New Republic*, XXIV (November 17, 1920), 303.

[4] Review of Laski, *The Foundations of Sovereignty and Other Essays*, *Nation*, CXIII (October 26, 1921), 483.

the war broke out."[5] Nor did he believe, as he commented in the *Nation*, that "the fall of man" had had much to do with the institution of private property. "Religion controlled economic life in the Middle Ages," he contended, "about as much as it did slavery in America."[6]

If anything, Beard appeared bent on sharpening his economic stress in the immediate postwar years. At least there was no retreating from it initially. Approvingly he quoted Daniel Webster for his "unqualified exposition of the principle of economic determinism." To Beard, certain aspects of Webster's thesis especially stood out:

Our ancestors . . . were forced to parcel out the lands, and this *"necessary act* fixed the future frame and form of government." The character of their political institutions was *determined* by the necessary laws respecting property. . . . Most "economic interpreters," including Professor Seligman, leave a margin for "other factors." Even the Marxians, like the Utopian dreamers, will have it that man shall in time transcend the thraldom of economic laws. Daniel Webster did not palter with "other factors." "Fixed" and "determine" are his words.[7]

If Beard's postwar admiration for the economic interpretation of politics was not stronger than previously, at least it had few bounds. "The state," he declared in 1920, "originated in economics and has gone into economic matters just to the extent which the classes dominating it have desired—no more and no less."[8] Nor was this solely an American political phenomenon. The new postwar constitution of Weimar Germany demonstrated economic characteristics similar to those of the United States Constitution. In a foreword, he warmly greeted René Brunet's volume on *The New German Constitution*:

There is no doubt that the new German constitution is the product of a sharp and determined conflict of classes. M. Brunet records the fact and gives the alignment of parties. No sophisticated person will ever imagine (whatever he may say) that the German fundamental law was drawn from abstract political thinking, theories about the rights of states, or reflections on the fate of Greek democracies and ancient Rome. The pressure

[5] *New Republic*, XXV (December 22, 1920), 115.

[6] Review of O'Brien, *An Essay on Mediaeval Economic Teaching, Nation*, CXI (October 27, 1920), 480.

[7] *Nation*, CIX (August 2, 1919), 147; this essay, "Could Daniel Webster Teach in New York's Schools?" is under the pseudonym of "John W. Bradford," but according to Thomas Reed Powell (personal interview, July 2, 1953) it was written by Beard.

[8] Review of Webb, *A Constitution for the Socialist Commonwealth of Great Britain, Nation*, CXI (December 8, 1920), 666.

of class interests is evident in almost every line. . . . Having recovered from the shock of learning that the Fathers of our Constitution were made of mortal clay, [American scholars] . . . are prepared to receive M. Brunet's book with open minds.[9]

Nevertheless, in his quest for scientific realism, Beard shunned formulations that to his mind spelled doctrinairism. Bolshevist ideology, even if based on economic factors, he held to be as unrealistic as socialism.[10] Whether men's "eternal systems" faced backward or forward to a millennium, and whether they rested on rigid determinism or on great men, Beard rejected them all. Summing up his antidoctrinairism in the *American Mercury,* which H. L. Mencken and George J. Nathan had just founded, Beard in 1924 observed:

Carlyle . . . stormed a great deal on the subject and ended with the general conclusion that the statesman is a genius, a hero, a sort of divine messenger sent now and then to set the weary world aright. The Marxians at the other end of the pole dismiss the statesman with a scoff as a mere automaton produced by a complex of economic forces. But neither of these answers is an answer. . . . Neither satisfies the requirements of the scientific spirit.[11]

As in the case of his prewar thesis, Beard's postwar economic interpretation implied a vague group theory of politics. As formerly, the notion that general political power shifts are based on broad economic strata in society recurred frequently in his writings. So did the idea of energetic minorities. Sometimes it is difficult to know whether Beard was talking about organized pressure groups or merely similarly situated elements of society. Apparently he paid little notice to such distinctions. When, for example, he considered whether "plantation logic" and "factory logic" were merely "defense mechanisms for what Madison called the sentiments arising from the possession of different degrees and kinds of property,"[12] was he assuming that Madison's factions were parties, pressure groups, or broad economic strata?

Beard's postwar economic interpretation writings exhibit at least

[9] (New York: Alfred A. Knopf, 1922), p. viii.

[10] See review of Paul, *Creative Revolution: A Study in Communist Ergatocracy, Nation,* CXII (March 2, 1921), 342; cf. review of Penty, *A Guildsman's Interpretation of History, Nation,* CXI (December 29, 1920), 783.

[11] "What Is a Statesman?" *American Mercury,* I (April, 1924), 394.

[12] Review of Channing, *A History of the United States, 1815–1846,* Vol. V, *New Republic,* XXIX (January 4, 1922), 161.

three more or less identifiable levels of specificity in their references to economic groups: (1) broad economic strata in society which under-lie general political movements, (2) somewhat more specific economic groupings which have an interest in the pursuit of certain policies by government and the avoidance of others, (3) actually functioning political action groups composed of elements drawn from the more general groupings and strata.

In part, Beard's treatment of the Civil War in *The Rise of American Civilization* (1927) illustrated his contention that fundamental power shifts must be based on broadly extended societal elements having roughly similar economic interests. Looking back into the previous century of American history, he noted that in the decades before Lincoln became president industrial wealth had overtaken and passed the total of agricultural wealth in the country.

By the middle of the century, the balance of power in the United States had already been shifted. . . . King Cotton had lost his scepter and nothing but a severe jar was necessary to overturn his throne. The supreme question to be debated, if contemporaries had only known it, was whether the political revolution foreshadowed by the economic flux was to proceed peacefully or by violence.[13]

Thus Beard believed that "the second American Revolution" was largely a conflict between rival economic imperialisms. Elsewhere in *The Rise of American Civilization* the Civil War was further described as "the social cataclysm in which the capitalists, laborers, and farmers of the North and West drove from power in the national government the planting aristocracy of the South."[14] Although this "economic interpretation" was reminiscent of Beard's 1913 thesis, here sectionalism as well as class conflict seemed to be an important determinant.

In other writings of the 1920's Beard made reference to more specific economic groupings whose activities appeared to be tied in more directly to the regular political process. Political parties were often treated as groups held together largely by economic factors, although it was recognized that they were not necessarily tightly knit economic interest groups. As Beard told students in his 1924 American government textbook, "every party is a more or less mis-cellaneous aggregation with a conservative right and a radical left

---

[13] *The Rise of American Civilization,* with Mary R. Beard (1st ed.; New York: Macmillan Co., 1927), I, 636.
[14] *Ibid.,* II, 54 ff.

shading off into each other by imperceptible degrees," and the party's candidates and platform "usually represent the middle average."[15] Describing political developments during the first decades of the Republic, Beard indicated that "the political forces of agriculture" had driven "Hamilton's party of finance, commerce, and industry" from power in 1800.[16] Subsequently the southern leaders with "their economic and political power" had in turn been overwhelmed by "the dominion of the northern capitalists."[17] The implication in all this appeared to be that a relatively more closely knit economic grouping of leaders at times formed the vanguard of a broader and less sharply defined economic stratum.

The most specific group in Beard's implicit theory of politics appeared to be the "energetic minority." This was also the group most immediately involved in political activity, whether such activity consisted of constitution making or of more routine matters. References to this concept recurred with considerable frequency. At the close of World War I, Beard pointed out that constitutions were "often made by minorities and imposed on majorities."[18] In 1922, after having visited Europe where he had studied the new German constitution, he drew attention to the "hair-trigger" character of the democracy it provided for, suggesting that this feature would shock "conservative circles" if proposed in the United States, and once more reminding his readers that "it is minorities not majorities that are radical."[19] Again, writing of politics on his return from Japan in 1923, he pointed out that not "the whole people" but *"groups* of citizens" accomplish results. Of the first elections under the new United States Constitution, he commented in 1927: "As many times before in history, an informed and active minority managed the play."[20] Indeed, majority rule was a "fiction," he argued in the *Atlantic Monthly:*

All the great lunges forward along the path from barbarism to civilization have been forced by energetic minorities, against the indifference or the

---

[15] *American Government and Politics* (4th ed.; New York: Macmillan Co., 1924), p. 141.

[16] *The Rise of American Civilization* (1st ed.; 1927), I, 508.

[17] *Ibid.,* II, 57.

[18] Review of Taft, *Popular Government, Political Science Quarterly,* XXXIII (December, 1918), 595.

[19] *Cross Currents in Europe Today* (Boston: Marshall Jones Co., 1922), p. 153.

[20] *The Rise of American Civilization* (1st ed.; 1927), I, 336.

opposition of majorities, using those terms in the correct mathematical sense. With equal justice also it may be said that the backward lunges have been made in the same manner. . . . The crucial decisions of American politics . . . have been the work of minorities.[21]

Related to Beard's postwar economic interpretation and implicit group theory of politics was his continued insistence that law and judicial actions were in essence part of the general political process. In the fourth edition of *American Government and Politics* (1924) he reiterated the views expressed in earlier editions on this point, namely, that the courts are not simply passive arbiters but in reality make law and policy. With respect to constitutional interpretation, he argued that reversals of earlier decisions verified his contention as to judicial policy making inasmuch as "either in one case or the other the Court had read into the document ideas which it did not contain." [22] Even the Constitution itself, he pointed out in *The American Leviathan* (1930), was the "product of social conflict." Moreover, it established the legal rules and the arena for the continuation of the struggle. Judicial controversies, in brief, were "among the staple issues of politics," [23] and the judiciary was naturally and normally in the thick of political strife.

Similarly, international politics, in Beard's view, was firmly based on economics. This notion, too, was not new, but a continuation of his former progressive era thought. As before, he did not hesitate to set straight an author who in his opinion had neglected this base. In 1922, for example, he wrote a blistering review of a group of books on international relations and diplomacy. "In spite of Professor Laughlin's statement that foreign relations are probably eight-tenths economics," he exclaimed, "this book is about ninety-nine one-hundredths formality and ancient history." [24] Four years later he applauded Louis Fischer's *Oil Imperialism* because the author had made clear that international relations did not consist of "metaphysical conversations between angels representing abstract entities known to jurists as sovereignties," but instead were concerned with "the jurisprudence of kerosene, oil and markets, economic reali-

---

[21] "Fiction of Majority Rule," *Atlantic Monthly,* CXL (December, 1927), 834 f.

[22] *American Government and Politics* (4th ed.; 1924), p. 98.

[23] *The American Leviathan,* with William Beard (New York: Macmillan Co., 1930), pp. 82, 135.

[24] Review of Walsh, *The History and Nature of International Relations, et al., New Republic,* XXX (March 29, 1922), 144.

ties." [25] The American Revolution from Britain's viewpoint, Beard wrote, had been an event in international politics, and British soldiers had been recruited for the purpose of "saving America for the land-lords and merchants of England." [26] Despite Anglo-Saxon traditions about empires resulting from "accidents of history," imperial politics, like domestic politics, rested primarily on an economic foundation.[27]

An Evolving Thesis

One of the most significant intellectual events in the development of Beard's postwar economic interpretation was the 1922 publication in book form of the series of four lectures he had delivered in 1916 at Amherst College concerning the "economic basis of politics." [28] This postwar publication would seem to suggest that Beard's views on the relation of economics and politics had remained constant during the intervening years. Repeating them in book form might even indicate that he had come to hold the views more firmly by 1922. On the other hand, it should be noticed that only the first three of the lectures had been repeated and that *the fourth lecture had been revised* "in the light of recent political experience." Subsequently in a footnote he repeated that the fourth lecture had been rewritten since the World War, "but the main conclusions have not been al-tered." [29] The revised lecture must therefore be carefully examined for possible deviations from Beard's prewar economic thesis.

At the very outset of the fourth lecture Beard conveniently summed up the ideas developed in the first three. Thus, the first lec-ture pointed out how the great philosophers of the past—Aristotle, Machiavelli, Locke, Madison, Webster, Calhoun—had clearly recog-nized the close relationship between "the forms of state and the dis-tribution of property." The second lecture dwelt on the fact that centuries of political evolution had demonstrated a similar recogni-tion of "economic classes in the creation of political organisms." The third lecture explained how, starting with Rousseau, "modern equalitarian democracy" had come to ignore "economic classes" and to consider "all heads as equal and alike," thus cutting "sharply

[25] *New Republic*, XLIX (December 8, 1926), 82.
[26] *The Rise of American Civilization* (1st ed.; 1927), I, 276.
[27] *The American Leviathan*, p. 690.
[28] *The Economic Basis of Politics* (New York: Alfred A. Knopf, 1922).
[29] *Ibid.*, p. 90.

athwart the philosophy and practice of the past centuries." [30] In short, the first three lectures appeared to be fully compatible with Beard's thesis as he had developed it in numerous other prewar writings. There was the same emphasis on economic factors in politics, and the same allusion to "economic classes."

Beard went on, in the revised fourth lecture, to draw attention to the various attempts and proposals that had been made to resolve the "contradiction between political theory and economic facts." But neither minority representation in parliament, functional representation, nor social ownership had succeeded in resolving the contradiction. Even nationalization in Bolshevik Russia, because of "one powerful propertied class," had failed to "abolish class antagonism." [31] All attempts had been in vain, he maintained, because all had in essence ignored hard economic realities.

In short a great society, whether capitalist or communist, must possess different kinds and grades of skill and talent and carry on widely diversified industries. There must be miners, machinists, electricians, engineers, accountants, transport workers, draftsmen, managers, and a hundred other kinds of specialists. They may be temporarily welded together in a conflict with the capitalist employers, but they will be divided over the distribution of wealth among themselves after the capitalists have been disposed of. [32]

A considerable, if subtle, change had crept into Beard's formulation. Where Madison had talked of various interfering economic interests that "grow up of necessity in civilized nations, and divide them into different classes actuated by different sentiments and views," Beard was now suggesting that "a great society . . . must possess different kinds and grades of skill and talent and carry on widely diversified industries." But it is doubtful that technical specialists would have qualified as Madisonian economic classes involving "the spirit of party and faction." The previous Beard thesis to the effect that clashing economic interest groups comprise the real stuff of politics had here apparently become diluted into the notion that various skilled technicians and specialists, although sometimes allied, are usually in economic rivalry with one another. They might temporarily combine against their employers for economic advan-

[30] *Ibid.*, p. 89.
[31] *Ibid.*, pp. 90 ff.
[32] *Ibid.*, p. 98.

tage, but, even if the capitalist employers are "disposed of," the employees will fall out among themselves over distribution of "wealth." Beard, however, did not make clear whether they would then clash as diverse specialists or as a new set of capitalists.

At the end of the revised fourth lecture Beard purported to come to "exactly" the grand conclusion reached by Madison. It should be recalled that Madison had been concerned with the "distribution of property" and had stressed the divergences between "those who hold and those who are without property." Similarly Webster, whom Beard had quoted approvingly in 1919, had contended "that in the absence of military force, political power naturally and necessarily goes into the hands which hold the property." [33] Beard, however, now took the position that the ownership of property was irrelevant to possession of political power.

> The grand conclusion, therefore, seems to be exactly that advanced by our own James Madison in the Tenth Number of the Federalist. To express his thought in modern terms: a landed interest, a transport interest, a railway interest, a shipping interest, an engineering interest, a manufacturing interest, a public-official interest, with many lesser interests, grow up of necessity in all great societies and divide them into different classes actuated by different sentiments and views. The regulation of these various and interfering interests, *whatever may be the formula for ownership of property,* constitutes the principal task of modern statesmen and involves the spirit of party in the necessary and ordinary operations of government.[34]

Beard's 1922 volume, like his earlier economic interpretation books, almost immediately became the object of searching attention by scholars and critics. For the most part, as earlier, he allowed the commentary to pass by, formally unnoticed. But there was at least one notable exception. This was in the case of Walter Lippmann's review of his book, and the subsequent skirmish with Lippmann appeared to mark a turning point in Beard's evolving thesis, the beginning of an extended rethinking of his prewar ideas on the subject.

In a vigorous letter to the *New Republic,* he bluntly rejected Lippmann's charge that he was trying to revive "the economic man" in refurbished guise. He had always believed the dogma of the economic man to be utterly fallacious, he thundered. Furthermore, "economic classes contending for what they feel to be their interests are more likely to destroy civilization than to realize anything approaching

---

[33] "Could Daniel Webster Teach in New York's Schools?" p. 147.
[34] *The Economic Basis of Politics,* p. 99 (italics supplied).

their 'interests'—whatever that may mean." [35] Was Beard here unwittingly equating the egoistic *individual* with the selfish interest *group?* Self-seeking individuals guided by an "invisible hand" would imply underlying social harmony and laissez faire, whereas interfering interest groups would imply social conflict and the necessity for government regulation. Ignoring or unaware of any inconsistency, and in any event not interested in theoretical hair-splitting, Beard undoubtedly intended to emphasize (1) that there was a place for human choice in history, and that all was not rigidly determined; (2) that human beings did not necessarily possess enough intelligence to know their long-range welfare or enough will power to pursue it if they could know it; and (3) that he was unalterably opposed to laissez faire.

Aside from this tangle over the economic man doctrine, another theoretically interesting point in the Lippmann encounter of 1922 concerned "the metaphysics of the relations between economics and politics." Agreeing that he had not gone into this phase of the matter, Beard claimed that he had been "more busily engaged in the analysis of concrete historical and economic situations." The implication appeared to be that speculative intellectual operations were of no use to the scientific student of politics.

Mr. Lippmann asks me to explain "how" economics "determines" politics. . . . As to "how" economics even influences politics, I cannot make answer, any more than the physicist can explain "how" a dynamo explains electricity. . . . Metaphysically speaking, so-called economic interpretation . . . cannot answer any of the important questions about "how" and "why." I do not think that economics determines or even explains politics in the philosophic sense. Neither does anything else. [36]

Beard's contention that "in the philosophic sense" nothing explained politics was hardly crystal clear. It suggested, at least, that he did not feel at home in philosophic discourse. Yet, despite his inference that his economic thesis was based on empirical investigation with no trace of a priori speculation, and regardless of his apparent uneasiness in the face of philosophical attack, from approximately this time on he was to engage increasingly in speculation as to the bases of politics. Whether or not the Lippmann incident was the

[35] "The Economic Basis of Politics," letter to the editor, *New Republic,* XXXII (September 27, 1922), 128.
[36] *Ibid.,* p. 129.

precise turning point, Beard's subsequent writings on the relation of economics and politics were frequently more defensive than previously and offered numerous clues suggesting that his former thesis was being gradually modified.

Henceforth, for example, noneconomic factors received increasingly greater emphasis in his running commentary on the actual stuff of politics. In the 1924 edition of *American Government and Politics* he acknowledged that "Madison's explanation does not explain everything. . . . Solidarity of interest . . . cuts across party lines . . . but it does not account for everything in the course of political evolution." [37] In *The Rise of American Civilization* in 1927 he indicated that various noneconomic motives had influenced human migration, and that the political aspects of any civilization were intricately interwoven with many other facets.[38] Two years later, after coming back from Yugoslavia, he again reminded readers that a considerable number of factors, both economic and noneconomic, affected and helped determine the politics and form of government in any country.[39] In a volume devoted specifically to American political parties, he admitted in 1928 that "if two people of the same economic class, seeking the same economic advantage, disagree on methods, evidently in this case the theory of economic interpretation breaks down." [40] By 1930 Beard could quite reverse his earlier emphasis and assert that "Madison's explanation" had been "too simple and open to many exceptions." [41]

Aside from general suggestions that politics comprised various basic elements, Beard at times also drew attention to the relevance of specific noneconomic factors. He indicated, for example, that great men helped make political reality and history, and that behind this greatness were such factors as brains, morals, ideals, and good luck,

---

[37] *American Government and Politics* (4th ed.; 1924), pp. 21 f.

[38] *The Rise of American Civilization* (1st ed.; 1927), I, 8 f., 124.

[39] *The Balkan Pivot: Yugoslavia,* with George Radin (New York: Macmillan Co., 1929), pp. 1 f.

[40] *The American Party Battle* (New York: Macmillan Co., 1928), p. 11.

[41] *The American Leviathan,* p. 84. See also Beard's essay, "Method in the Study of Political Science as an Aspect of Social Science," in Brookings Institution Committee on Training, *Essays on Research in the Social Sciences* (Washington, D.C.: Brookings Institution, 1931), pp. 51–63, in which he indicated not only his concern with explanations that appear "too simple" but also an apparently increasing preoccupation with the nature of social reality and the methodological barriers hindering man's understanding of it. Cf. also chapters 9 and 10, below.

among others.[42] In addition, great ideas likewise had an impact on politics, as for example "the great concepts of human rights and human equality" which would have profoundly affected American history without economic changes, new social forces, or the influence of Europe.[43] Nationalism, too, was a factor to be reckoned with, as Beard pointed out in a paper at the 1929 meeting of the American Historical Association.[44] Politics, he inferred in a 1927 book review, would have little meaning if "divorced from economics *and ethics.*"[45]

Perhaps the single noneconomic factor that by the end of the 1920's came to receive the greatest special emphasis in Beard's writings was military force. Although in 1927 he mentioned in passing that military force was indispensable to the state,[46] he soon went much further than this. Attacking an economic history book for omitting politics just as he had often attacked books on politics for omitting economics, he declared that wealth was not distributed merely by natural economic processes but had often been "distributed by the sword —in the American Revolution and the Civil War—and on numerous occasions by the exercise of governmental power."[47] In the *Yale Review,* discussing the evolution of the European nation-state, he maintained that "iron and blood" and not economics or ideas had been the basic factors:

The substance of the consolidating business remained much the same to the end—iron and blood as in the beginning. If James Watt had never invented the steam engine, if Rousseau had never proclaimed the Social Contract, if Darwin had never written the "Origin of Species," the process of unifying feudal chaos would have gone forward to its logical conclusion. The outstanding political achievements of the nineteenth century were not vitally dependent on factories and railways; Germany and Italy would have been unified, it seems safe to say, if George Stephenson had not brought the locomotive to a high state of practical perfection.[48]

[42] "What Is a Statesman?" p. 396. The fact that Beard wrote the introduction to a biography a few years after this suggests his increasing emphasis on the role of "great men" in history (Paxton Hibben, *The Peerless Leader: William Jennings Bryan* [New York: Farrar & Rinehart, 1929]).

[43] *The Rise of American Civilization* (1st ed.; 1927), I, 725.

[44] *American Historical Review,* XXXV (April, 1930), 490.

[45] Review of Catlin, *The Science and Method of Politics, American Political Science Review,* XXI (August, 1927), 653 (italics supplied).

[46] *The Rise of American Civilization* (1st ed.; 1927), I, 31 f.

[47] Review of Kirkland, *A History of American Economic Life, Saturday Review of Literature,* IX (August 13, 1932), 42.

[48] "Political Heritage of the Twentieth Century," *Yale Review,* XVIII (March, 1929), 457.

But perhaps more significant theoretically than his growing recognition of noneconomic factors was Beard's occasional hint that he was changing his ideas as to how economics actually impinged on the processes of politics. Thus, at one point in the 1929 American Historical Association meeting, on being invited to participate in the discussion, Beard denied that he believed in the doctrine of the economic man although, he insisted, he did believe that "all men, women, and children, all the time, must have food, clothing, and shelter, and that the ways in which they acquire these necessities have a profound, constant, and inescapable influence on all departments of their life, political, moral, and religious." [49]

Whereas in 1913 he had stressed the notion that clashing economic interest groups form the real stuff of politics, and in 1922 the idea that modern society gives rise to a great many divisions based on technical skills, by 1929 his thesis had evolved into the more diluted double proposition that people must have the basic essentials of life and that the methods of making a living deeply influence human existence.

Beard's political thought in this middle period of his intellectual development displayed other modifications and refinements, as well. His earlier concept of energetic minorities, for example, appeared to be extended, in *The American Party Battle* (1928), to cover an additional kind of political phenomenon. Explaining how the bulk of twentieth-century social legislation had come to be enacted, he "confessed that it sprang from movements of opinion quite outside the range of political orthodoxy, that is, from the agitations of minorities winning concessions from the major parties." [50] This suggested a variation on his usual theme that energetic minorities themselves headed movements. Likewise his thought concerning the nature and characteristics of groups was further refined in his discussion of political parties in the fourth edition of *American Government and Politics*. Here he pointed out that, regardless of the economic origins of a political group, its continued existence might have quite other bases. "The political party itself," he noted, "tends to become an institution apart from its origins and purposes." [51] His notion that organizations possess an inner tendency toward autonomy was somewhat reminiscent of Robert Michels' "iron law of

[49] As quoted in *American Historical Review*, XXXV (April, 1930), 485.
[50] *The American Party Battle*, p. 144.
[51] *American Government and Politics* (4th ed.; 1924), p. 22.

oligarchy." According to Beard, "All organizations controlling sources of money and power tend to perpetuate themselves and to become institutions after their original purposes have been realized." [52]

By the latter years of the 1920's Beard appears to have acquired a more defensive attitude than formerly regarding his economic interpretation thesis, a new sensitivity as to possible misunderstanding of his precise position. Did this reflect a subconscious realization that his thesis had actually changed, a sublimated attack on his own former contentions? In any event, some years after he had replied to Lippmann that he had not thought it necessary to put his readers on guard against the preposterous dogma of the economic man, he could introduce even an essay on city planning with words of caution:

By way of preliminary warning, I want to say flatly that I never did and do not now hold that man is an economic automaton capable of discovering and pursuing his interests with unerring accuracy. . . . Individuals and whole classes, nay even great states, have been destroyed while striving to realize what they imagined to be their interests.[53]

If Beard had become more inclined to put his readers on guard against presupposing an economic man, he was still apparently making no distinction between applying the doctrine to "individuals" and applying it to "whole classes." Yet such indiscriminate application implied that an individual's independent self-seeking was identical with his cooperative behavior as a member of a group. Undoubtedly all Beard meant to say, without going into the "metaphysics" of the matter, was that human beings, whether singly or in droves, are neither ominscient nor entirely altruistic.

Broadened Bases

By the end of the postwar era Beard's implicit theory of politics had, in a number of respects, come to depend on considerably broader bases than previously. In his view, the "economic basis" had apparently become too narrow. He appeared to be rethinking his earlier conceptions respecting human nature, interest groups, determinism, and other matters. In effect he admitted that he no longer subscribed wholly, if he had ever done so, to the economic interpretation advanced by a number of eminent political philosophers of the past. Man by nature, as he pointed out in 1924, was not simply a gre-

[52] *Ibid.,* p. 156.
[53] "Conflicts in City Planning," *Yale Review,* XVII (October, 1927), 66 f.

garious animal whose group interests centered solely around economics.

Moreover people of widely different interests who live side by side in a district have many things in common, such as police and fire protection, the maintenance of public health, the suppression of contagious diseases. They are united by religious, racial, and patriotic ties. So after all there is good reason for the representation of heads as well as economic interests. Besides it is difficult, nay impossible, to classify people today into rigid classes.[54]

In the early 1930's Beard hinted that he had been overemphasizing the economic basis of politics in order to redress its previous underemphasis in political literature. Almost apologetically he admitted, in a typically critical book review: "Perhaps I bear down too heavily on one side. If so it is in the interest of the even balance." [55]

On occasion he could argue with as much vigor against economic determinism as he had once displayed in praising the determinists for opening men's eyes to the "real forces." In a 1931 letter to the *New Republic* he replied to an attack on him by Karl Gerber for his alleged betrayal of the doctrine of economic determinism as applied to German navalism. Although Germany had had a smaller overseas empire and less trade than France, she had built a bigger navy than had France.

But French statesmen had insight enough to avoid a battleship rivalry with Great Britain. German statesmen did not have that insight and were blown up for their pains. Mr. Gerber evidently thinks there are no choices in the world. Philosophically speaking, he may be right, but nobody operates on that theory. If I were compelled by necessity to write as I did, how then could I be downright dishonest? Water is not dishonest when it runs downhill. Mr. Gerber is not a true Marxian when he allows for moral choice.[56]

Here Beard was suggesting the possibility that, "philosophically speaking," economics might determine politics as strictly as gravity pulls water downhill, whereas at an earlier date he had answered Lippmann by saying that "in the philosophic sense" he did not think economics or anything else determined politics.[57]

On the whole, it must be concluded that on the eve of the New

[54] *American Government and Politics* (4th ed.; 1924), p. 27.
[55] Review of Kirkland, *A History of American Economic Life,* p. 42.
[56] "An Economic Interpretation of Navies," letter to the editor, *New Republic,* LXIX (November 25, 1931), 47.
[57] "The Economic Basis of Politics," p. 129.

Deal Beard's once emergent theory of politics had become vaguer, less certain. In a sense the embryonic prewar theory had failed to mature in the twenties. The elements of economic determinism once potentially present in it had greatly receded. No longer was economics considered virtually the only basis of politics worth mentioning. Not only were economic factors in general now assigned less influence over human sentiments, views, choices, and values, but in his mind property ownership in particular had virtually ceased to have any correlation with possession of political power.

CHAPTER VII

AMERICA AND THE WORLD

In 1917 Beard had strongly favored America's participation in the Great War, and for a time after the war's end he continued to believe that our participation had been necessary and beneficial. But as the years passed his ideas and mood changed.[1] The change was exhibited not only in his attitude toward the late war as it receded into the distance, but also in his way of looking at international relations in general.

Looking Backward

Beard's early postwar idealism as to the Great War and his exuberant optimism respecting its result were admirably illustrated in *National Governments and the World War,* written in collaboration with Frederick A. Ogg in 1919.[2] Beard himself wrote the lines that presented a justification for America's entry into the conflict:

To say that the outcome of the war in Europe was of no concern to the United States was to ignore forty years of German history. Thousands

[1] It is interesting to note that there is an apparently widely held belief that Beard's isolationist ideas originated during the depression or the early New Deal. "Early in the 1930's," states one writer, "Beard came forth as an advocate of national isolation" (Lewis Mumford, letter to the editor, *Saturday Review of Literature,* XXVII [December 2, 1944], 27). Says another: "But just at this time [around 1930] Beard was hit, as we all were, by two discoveries—disillusionment with the war of 1917–18 and the depression" (Perry Miller, "Charles A. Beard," *Nation,* CLXVII [September 25, 1948], 345). Even the Secretary of Agriculture, Henry A. Wallace, confessed uneasiness in December of 1934 when several of his friends told him that Beard in his latest book had "gone isolationist" (*New Republic,* LXXXI [January 2, 1935], 225). By hindsight, however, it is now evident (as the present chapter indicates) that Beard's isolationist views were in full process of formation from the early 1920's. Somewhat in contrast to the view developed here, Cushing Strout (*The Pragmatic Revolt in American History* [New Haven, Conn.: Yale University Press, 1958], pp. 137 ff.) takes the position that Beard was slow in becoming disillusioned with United States participation in World War I.

[2] (New York: Macmillan Co., 1919).

of peaceful citizens, though looking with horror upon the thought of war, were slowly and reluctantly driven by events to the conclusion that a German victory in Europe would imperil democracy in the United States in coming years. They realized that with Great Britain beaten and her colonies annexed by Germany, America would not be spared by a power founded on the sword.

They remembered the hundred years of peace which we had maintained with the British Empire; they recalled the three thousand miles of border between this country and Canada, without a fort or battleship or patrol; and they could not bring themselves to believe that with the Hohenzollerns entrenched anywhere in the New World the United States could go on her way undisturbed by German intrigues, spies, and military ambitions. To them the triumph of the German war machine, dominating all Europe, would make vain and foolish two centuries of struggle for popular government, for popular control over the power of kings and aristocracies, for the extension of the suffrage and the advancement of democracy. Accordingly they took up arms to aid in overthrowing militarism and imperialism and in preventing their return to plague the earth's weary multitudes.[3]

In a subsequent chapter Beard ventured the hope that the ideals for which America had fought would make a profound imprint on history and on future relations among the states of the earth. Wilson's fourteen points, he felt, would eventually come to voice "the slowly maturing opinion of the masses of the people everywhere in the earth." In effect comparing Wilson's pronouncements with the Declaration of the Rights of Man and the Declaration of Independence, he expressed confidence that men of faith and vision would in time realize that the years of 1917–18 had marked a notable change in the world's long history, "the opening of a new epoch in the rise of government by the people and in the growth of a concert among the nations."[4]

It is impossible to know all the complex stimuli that may have acted on Beard in the following months. His postwar visit to Europe to inspect the uncovered archives no doubt had a considerable effect on him. But in any event, whereas at first he had looked back at the Great War and America's relation to it and seen a vision of hope, from about 1921 or 1922 the picture steadily darkened. Before long, hints of doubt and skepticism gave way to caustic criticism, and by the early thirties he was virtually waging war on the late war.

As early as February, 1921, Beard in the *Nation* displayed some

[3] *Ibid.*, pp. 13 f.
[4] *Ibid.*, p. 570.

doubt as to his previous position, especially as regards Wilson. "Reflecting" on the strange things that could happen as a result of the dynamic relationships between the American democratic system and military affairs, he pointed out how a minority president as commander-in-chief might conceivably maneuver the country into war. Thereafter practically any action necessary to victory would be constitutional. Even appeals to the voters to discharge the administration and elect a new one might become treason. "So distinguished a jurist as Charles E. Hughes," noted Beard significantly, "is reported to have expressed doubts whether the republic could survive a long war conducted along the lines followed by Mr. Wilson's administration." [5]

Beard was not long in revealing reasons for his growing disillusionment with "the recent unpleasantness." "Slowly the official myth about the war and its origins is being dissolved by sunlight," he wrote in the *New Republic* early in 1922. "The catastrophes in Germany, Russia, and Austria brought into open day thousands of documents that were not intended for the general public." [6] This unexpected uncovering of secret archives gave Beard a glimpse of the wily diplomatic maneuvering that had gone on behind the scenes in prewar Europe. Beyond doubt he was greatly impressed by the scholarly significance of these newly discovered data. But at the same time his idealistic image of "the war for democracy" had suffered irreparable damage.

In addition to disenchantment as to the origins of the war, Beard was soon showing impatience with the proposed peace settlements. Even if America had been drawn into a bloody European war by the intrigues and selfish designs of imperialists abroad, he felt that matters should not be made worse by shortsighted diplomacy following the disaster. Lecturing in the summer of 1922 at Dartmouth, he critically examined various "cross currents" of Europe and the world, particularly those growing out of the war. To his mind it appeared that two different objectives were being mixed up in the European peace settlements: punishment and restoration. The arrangements having as their objective punishment of the vanquished had pro-

[5] Review of Fenwick, *Political Systems in Transition: War-Time and After, Nation,* CXII (February 23, 1921), 298.

[6] Review of Welschinger, *L'Alliance Franco-Russe, New Republic,* XXIX (February 22, 1922), 375; cf. review of Commons, *Industrial Government, Nation,* CXIII (November 9, 1921), 543.

duced great economic upsets and had obstructed measures aimed at restoration. In like manner, the reparation plan had reflected a "clash over ethics and economics." [7] .Unfortunately, the measures so far implemented had taken cognizance only of the ethical aspect of the situation. The motive to date had been solely to punish the criminal nation bearing the war guilt. But what if it turned out that both sides had been equally guilty? In that case, he contended, the peace settlements would stand doubly condemned: disruptive of economic restoration as well as morally unjust.

When Beard, after his first visit to the Orient in 1922–23, published the third edition of his junior high school text, *The History of the American People* (1923), some interesting changes had crept into it. For example, the Allied intervention in Russia during the war was no longer treated as it had been in the previous second edition of 1920. Immediately after the event Beard had apparently accepted the intervention as simply to "protect supplies," but with the passage of time he became more critical of the operation, claiming in 1923 that the protracted stay of American soldiers in Russia was "never made entirely clear." [8] He also felt impelled to make certain alterations in his previous description of America's entry into the Great War. It is true that he had not expurgated the suggestion that it may have been "an economy of time, blood, and treasure to crush Prussian militarism, while so many other nations were ready to help." But he had noticeably toned down and abbreviated his former version of the idealistic aims of the war. He had entirely eliminated the statement that the majority of the American people had believed that President Wilson "had seen a true vision and made a call which could not be denied." [9]

In various unobtrusive ways Beard's language concerning the late war steadily changed. His 1924 textbook on *American Government and Politics* still discounted the American tradition of "isolation" running back to the beginning of our history and pointed out that this country had participated in world affairs before the Spanish-American War as well as after. But, when Beard in the same volume discussed foreign relations in Wilson's administration, a new note

[7] *Cross Currents in Europe Today* (Boston: Marshall Jones Co., 1922), p. 92.

[8] *The History of the American People,* with William C. Bagley (3rd ed.; New York: Macmillan Co., 1923), p. 640; cf. 2nd ed. (1920), p. 634.

[9] *Ibid.* (2nd ed.; 1920), p. 626; but cf. 3rd ed. (1923), pp. 623 f.

entered. Detailing how the management of foreign policy had passed from the State Department to the President, Beard claimed that "by his notes directed to foreign governments, especially the Central Powers, President Wilson announced American foreign policies and steered the Government in a course which inevitably led to war." [10] Thus by 1924 Beard was hinting that America's entry into the war might have been largely the work of Wilson.

After Beard's second trip to Asia in 1923-24, his writings reflected a new interest in America's relations with the Far East. In a critical essay in the *Nation* early in 1925, for example, he castigated United States Far Eastern policy past and present. Despite American pretensions of lofty motives, the real basis of our quarrel with Japan had long been "trade and profits" in Asia and not, as he acidly put it, the "promotion of Christian virtues with bayonets, bombs, and gases." Beard's postwar travels and investigations thus seemed to reveal successively more damning implications of the secret papers. Our statesmen could get "terribly shocked" at Japanese behavior, he noted sarcastically, and yet blink at the equally greedy actions of the English, French, and Italians. Even Americans who considered themselves liberals could get worked up over the actions of the Japanese "imperialists" in far-off Shantung. Fortunately, that crisis had been headed off late in 1921 "when Senator Borah forced the calling of the Washington conference." [11]

The opened-archives theme occurred intermittently in Beard's writings for some time. Publication of Viscount Grey's memoirs prompted Beard late in 1925 to expound again on the theme that by now had become familiar:

As everyone knows, the devastating revolutions that accompanied the close of the World War tore open the secret archives of Germany, Austria, and Russia, and let a flood of dazzling light in upon the hidden sources of the great armed conflict. For seven long years, scholars have been at work with microscopes and x-rays examining, comparing, tabulating, and commenting. Propagandists have likewise been busy using the findings for political ends. Though the cautious will shrink from conclusions too sharp and dogmatic, all must admit that one thing has been established beyond question, namely, that responsibility for the War

---

[10] *American Government and Politics* (4th ed.; New York: Macmillan Co., 1924), pp. 325, 341–44.

[11] "War with Japan: What Shall We Get Out of It?" *Nation*, CXX (March 25, 1925), 312.

must be distributed among all the participants, with Russia and France each bearing a Titan's share.[12]

Beard's backward glances were soon arousing even warmer suspicions on his part and casting further reflections on the supposedly lofty motives of the Entente Allies in the struggle. Discussing "Heroes and Villains of the World War" in *Current History* in 1926, he pointedly reminded readers that, although revolutions had revealed the foreign office secrets of prewar Russia, Germany, and Austria, "the archives of Great Britain, France, Italy, and the United States are still intact." [13] He suggested that the materials recently made available had already put "a new face" on the official pronouncements put forth by the Allies. Clearly he did not accept the proposition that only the defeated powers had been guilty of starting the war. To his mind "the Sunday-school theory" of its origins had been wholly discredited.

According to that theory, three pure and innocent boys—Russia, France, and England—without military guile in their hearts, were suddenly assailed while on the way to Sunday school by two deep-dyed villains— Germany and Austria—who had long been plotting cruel deeds in the dark.[14]

Not only could Beard now claim that the punitive measures incorporated into the peace settlements were interfering with economic restoration, but he could further maintain that the notion of punishment itself was invalid, since some of the Allies had shared in the guilt. Although he apparently could not bring himself to believe that the United States should be counted among the culprits, by the midtwenties he had begun to pay exceedingly close attention to President Wilson's role. More than a slight trace of innuendo seemed present in his statement that "there is not now available any conclusive evidence to show that President Wilson was cleverly engaged all along in working up the war spirit." Although Beard stated explicitly in his *Current History* article of 1926 that Wilson had remained cold to the entreaties of both sides in the early stages of the European conflict, he also emphasized the importance of examining "with un-

[12] Review of Grey, *Twenty-five Years, 1892–1916, New Republic*, XLIV (October 7, 1925), 172.

[13] "Heroes and Villains of the World War," *Current History*, XXIV (August, 1926), 730.

[14] *Ibid.*, p. 733.

remitting zeal everything that throws light upon the statecraft which precipitated that crisis." [15]

Again, in *The Rise of American Civilization* (1927), he reiterated in moving language the story of the secret archives that had revealed the "sordid and grimy diplomacy" eventuating in the bloody conflict.[16] Thus despite Beard's feeling, expressed as late as 1927, that Wilson had had no other course than the one he had chosen once Europe's sordid diplomacy had started the war,[17] there is no doubt that by the latter part of the postwar decade Beard, in looking back, had departed drastically from the Wilsonian idealism infecting him a few years earlier.

The Perilous World of Political Reality

The real point of Beard's preoccupation with America's role in World War I was his concern for the future. Dread of a new general war and apprehension that the United States might again be drawn in haunted his thinking. Perplexed by America's existence in an interdependent world, a reality he, himself, had long stressed, yet fearing that another great war would endanger democracy and even the existence of the republic in the form Americans had known, Beard appeared to face a serious dilemma.

Moreover, he did not pause to work out certain other apparently contradictory tendencies in his thought. Discernible in his writings, for example, was vacillation between an assumption that statesmen have it within their power to bring on or prevent wars, and a belief in the inevitability of another war inasmuch as wars are caused by impersonal forces.

Reflecting the former assumption, Beard complained in the *National Municipal Review* that "our secretary of the navy walks down to the shores of the Pacific and shakes cold steel under the noses of our neighbors. Admirals of the navy, active and retired, periodically ring the alarm bell and warn us to be prepared for the coming crisis." [18] In his 1924 American government textbook he put great emphasis on the efficacy of diplomacy. Diplomacy, he pointed out, could help bring on war or peace. If America avoided the world wars

[15] *Ibid.*, pp. 730 ff.

[16] *The Rise of American Civilization*, with Mary R. Beard (1st ed.; New York: Macmillan Co., 1927), II, 673.

[17] "Bankruptcy Fire-Sale," *American Mercury*, XI (July, 1927), 286.

[18] "American Influence on Municipal Government in the Orient," *National Municipal Review*, XIV (January, 1925), 11.

of the future, diplomacy could be credited with that happy result. If, on the other hand, "in the long flow of time, America becomes involved in a terrible conflict with a combination of foreign foes and is brought face to face with ruin on land and sea, that circumstance, too, will be laid at the door of diplomacy." [19]

On the other hand, in the *American Mercury* he predicted that:

. . . another storm is brewing. . . . Nobody pretends that the United States will benefit from the next calamity any more than it did from the last, and it is highly probable that, given the same dangers to the balance of power, America will be drawn into the new bloody shambles as into the latest adventure in madness.[20]

When the note of inevitability crept into Beard's writings, he usually implied that the impersonal forces were economic, but when he dwelt on the role of leaders, he portrayed them variously as military, economic, or political.

In 1929 Beard asserted that "one thing seems clear: international bankers can stop war. . . . Europe cannot fight long without American credit; it saved the Allies in 1917, and saved Germany later." Although he noted that enlightened self-interest on the part of the bankers would make them see peace as the best policy in the long run, he also added that there was an "almost dead certainty that the United States, with respect to substantial things, will throw her sword into the scales if hostilities open again." [21]

Aside from his apparent uncertainty as to whether leaders or impersonal forces ultimately create wars, Beard also wavered between optimism and pessimism as to the fate of democracy in a war-threatened world. It should be recalled that in 1921 he implied that our republic might not be able to survive another long war such as World War I. Yet, typically, his basic optimism about the future of democracy reasserted itself. As late as 1928, after his Yugoslavian venture, he reached optimistic conclusions about the prospects for democracy in Europe. "No country with a literate population," he wrote, "imitates Italy . . . Russia is declining, not increasing in influence. . . . No other country has imitated the Bolshevik political

[19] *American Government and Politics* (4th ed.; 1924), p. 323; cf. Beard's essay, "The Inside of Germany's War Politics," in *Essays in Intellectual History Dedicated to James Harvey Robinson* (New York: Harper & Bros., 1929), pp. 109 f.

[20] "Bankruptcy Fire-Sale," p. 286.

[21] "Forces Making for Peace," *Bulletin of the University of Georgia: Institute of Public Affairs and International Relations,* XXX (November, 1929), 83.

design." [22] In short, as Beard saw it, democracy was not giving way before the threat of dictatorship, either proletarian or fascist.

Still, at least so far as the United States was concerned, Beard could issue dire warnings about the fate of civil liberties and democracy should another war occur. In 1925 he forecast in the *Nation:*

There would be "cost plus" once more, labor boards, and committees on public information. There would be created a few thousand additional millionaires. The Hon. Charles E. Hughes has soberly said that in view of the precedents already set, constitutional government as we now know it would hardly survive a long war even if victoriously waged. So there would be sedition and espionage acts. Professors would be expelled for expressing doubts about the infallibility of Congress and the President. The jails would be filled with American citizens unable to believe what their conscience forbid [*sic*]. Aliens would be deported by the ship load. The Department of Justice would let loose a million spies to stir up suspicion and hatred.[23]

It is hard to say with certainty what perils Beard most feared. Variously he referred to the risk of human bloodshed, the danger to American freedom and democracy, the hazards for democracy in the world at large, the crass glorification of economic greed, and other evils. For a time his misgivings appeared to center on possible American involvement in Asiatic affairs. The consequences of a United States war with Japan, he complained in bitter sarcasm, would be our seizure of Formosa and other islands, the Manchurian railroads, and similar spoils. We would assume "moral responsibility" for Manchuria, Mongolia, and Korea and would easily convince ourselves that "Christian ethics did not require us to follow the example of Japan in the case of Shantung and return Manchuria to China." American civilization and imperialism would spread along the Chinese Eastern Railway into Siberia. The "benevolent administration of the Philippines" would be repeated in Korea.[24] He was also alarmed at the possibility that such an Oriental conflict might explode into general war.

Would it be possible to isolate the burning house? What if the conflagration started on the Yangtze or on the Inland Sea spread to Europe? It is easier to start a war than to stop it or to divine its outcome. Would the spoils and the fun then balance the blood, treasure, frenzy,

[22] "Democracy Holds Its Ground: A European Survey," *Harper's Magazine,* CLVII (November, 1928), 683 f.
[23] "War with Japan: What Shall We Get Out of It?" p. 312.
[24] *Ibid.*

and hysterics? Who would hold the bonds, gather the profits, reap the dividends? Who would give their lives and pay the taxes? Would the loot be worth the pain? For a little while the sun shines and it is constitutionally permissible to ask these questions.[25]

In 1929 Beard not only expressed doubt as to the effectiveness of the recently signed Kellogg-Briand antiwar treaty, but also took the occasion to suggest a number of possible causes for war. He was convinced that one of the "causes of the World War" had been the discontent of minorities. Among the "disturbing factors" of the future he included increasing armaments, sharpening commercial rivalries, and the foisting of war guilt on the Central Powers. "If state support for commerce was a powerful cause of the World War," he warned, "then according to all signs, we are headed for a bigger and better conflict, in spite of ourselves, perhaps against our hearts' desire." [26]

What doubtless intensified Beard's dilemma concerning international relations and attendant United States foreign policy was his own long-standing appreciation of certain of the hard realities of the actual political world. Long before the Great War, he himself had taught not only the basic importance of economic elements in world politics, but also the fact of the ever tightening interdependency of all the earth. After the war, as in his Dartmouth lectures of 1922, he continued pointing out these same realities:

There is now a web of international relations—trade, finance, and intercourse—so fine in mesh and so tough in fibre that no sword can cut it. The East and the West have met, and they are one. The world is an economic unit and the United States is being woven into the very fabric of that unity.[27]

The factual aspects of such propositions were not repudiated by Beard, although modifications occurred in his writings as the 1920's wore on. In his 1924 edition of *American Government and Politics,* for example, although he noted that the "economic ties binding America to the world" had grown stronger and more numerous than ever,[28] he significantly omitted the bold lines that had stood in the 1910 edition:

It is apparent that the "splendid isolation" of the United States, as contemplated by many early political theorists, has never been possible in

[25] *Ibid.,* p. 313.

[26] "Bigger and Better Armaments," *Harper's Magazine,* CLVIII (January, 1929), 139.

[27] *Cross Currents in Europe Today,* p. 2.

[28] *American Government and Politics* (4th ed.; 1924), p. 344.

practice. Moreover, no political doctrines with regard to our independence from the rest of the world are strong enough to overcome those material and moral forces which are linking our destinies to those of the world at large.[29]

And, although in his early postwar view of world politics Beard saw "the roots of imperialism, armaments, and warfare" in commerce, industry, and various other economic realities, he could subsequently suggest that "the towering rise of international capitalism" might be the best hope for peace.[30]

The Road Ahead

Given the political realities and the perils, what courses were open to America? As we now know through hindsight, Beard in the 1920's was groping for some form of American insulation from outside troubles, some form of insurance against war that would not, however, cut off the economic and cultural benefits stemming from world ties. It was a kind of isolationist ideal, even if dim in initial outline.

Although it is impossible to say exactly when this inchoate image first began forming, there were hints of it soon after the war's end. Perhaps Beard's first postwar trip to Europe in the summer of 1921 started him on the isolationist path. At any rate, after he had returned from this journey, he told the students at Amherst in the following summer that, although a new cooperation among European nations seemed to be the only way to forestall a more terrible war than the one just ended, it was "another thing to say that the United States, enjoying the comparative security of this hemisphere, should attempt to take part in the conduct of a cooperative system for all the nations of the earth." [31] Already Beard was tentatively suggesting policy alternatives:

At this fateful juncture in American history, there are three courses open to those who fain would mould the world to their hearts' desires. There is first the policy of positive imperialism, naked and unashamed. . . . There is before us, possibly, a second policy. It is covered by that term of opprobrium hurled at it by the devotees of imperialism, namely, "Little Americanism." . . . It would bend all national energies and all national genius upon the creation of a civilization which, in power and glory and

[29] *Ibid.* (1st ed.; 1910), p. 333.
[30] "Prospects for Peace," *Harper's Magazine,* CLVIII (February, 1929), 320; but cf. *Cross Currents in Europe Today,* p. 242.
[31] *Cross Currents in Europe Today,* p. 139.

noble living, would rise above all the achievements of the past. . . . There is finally another alternative, that of no policy at all, save the policy of drift and muddle.[32]

From this, one easily guesses that Beard in 1922 inclined toward the policy of "Little Americanism."

Beard was not alone in either his dilemma or his inclination toward an insulationist "solution." He reflected as well as helped influence a more widespread "liberal dilemma" of the 1920's.[33] A number of thinkers, such as Veblen, Beard, Dewey, and others, came to share a common hatred of the war and distaste for the peace settlements that followed it. Disappointed that the war had not safeguarded democracy in the world, that the Russian Revolution was betraying the democratic socialist cause, that Italy had bowed to a demagogue, that international relations appeared to be shaped more by sordid diplomacy and economic greed than by Wilsonian idealism, that Weimar Germany was in danger of slipping from her democratic moorings, and that the foreign policies and domestic politics of France, the United States, and the other former Allies seemed to point toward another world catastrophe, numerous American intellectuals were beginning to turn inward and to recommend that America henceforth mind her own business.

It was against this background that Beard sketched his ideal for America, an ideal whose pattern became clearer as the years passed. In 1927 he began a public address by confessing

. . . a prejudice for the land of my birth and for the ideals that were professed before we began, under the thoughtful patronage of our mother, England, to acquire dependencies, protectorates, moral obligations, and mandates in the interest of humanity, to administer water-cure and Krag-rifle medicines, to shoot, bayonet, gas, bomb, and eviscerate backward peoples in the name of the higher good and profitable investments.[34]

Nostalgically, Beard apparently envisaged the "good old days" prior to the Spanish-American War, during the years of his own

[32] Ibid., pp. 267, 269 f.
[33] See Morton G. White, Social Thought in America: The Revolt against Formalism (New York: Viking Press, 1949), pp. 199 f.; Bruce Bliven, "The Hang-Back Boys," New Republic, CX (March 6, 1944), 305–7; Hans J. Morgenthau, In Defense of the National Interest (New York: Alfred A. Knopf, 1951), pp. 28 f.
[34] "Agriculture in the Nation's Economy," Nation, CXXV (August 17, 1927), 150.

youth. It was a picture of pre-1898 America scarcely implied in his numerous previous assertions to the effect that America had been as fully engaged in world politics before 1898 as afterward. In any event, regardless of what America may or may not have been in the past, Beard clearly indicated what he hoped she would become in the future.

I conjure up in my mind the kind of land that I would have my country become. We have here the most magnificent material endowment ever given to any people, with diversities of climate, soil, and vegetation sufficient to make us in the main self-contained. By developing our economy intelligently with reference to that independence, we can escape the huge burdens of military and naval expenditures necessary to defend trade and investments in all parts of the globe. At a relatively slight cost we can protect our own shores effectively against all foreign foes. Relying upon an economy primarily self-supporting, we cannot be shaken by the disasters of war or the coming revolt of the subject people of the earth against the arrogance of imperialists. . . . Such is the prejudice from which I start.[35]

This vision was closely related to a concept Beard called "nation-planning." [36] Later, when the depression gave renewed urgency to his plea for national economic planning, the isolationist overtones likewise heightened. Sometimes Beard's logic in linking insulationism with ideal ends was not impressive, as when he painted his picture of "the good life" in a *Scribner's* essay in the early thirties. "The ethics of the good life," he argued, "though universal in its implications, is perforce national in application. It must have a geographical location, and most geographical locations are within national states." [37]

To Beard's mind, given the hard realities, the problem of what foreign policy to pursue in order to realize his American ideal bristled with uncertainties. Though he could picture an idealized America, insulated from the storms across the seas, he could not be sure in his own mind that the dream was possible of realization. "It is decidedly to the interest of the United States," he wrote in 1926, "to help prevent the rise of any single European power to a dominant position." And yet he was careful to add the warning that we should not be "bamboozled by the racial and national hatreds of Europe" or get emotionally aroused over "all the quarrels of Europe." [38] He vac-

[35] *Ibid.*
[36] *Ibid.*, p. 151.
[37] "Search for the Centre," *Scribner's Magazine*, XCI (January, 1932), 5.
[38] "Heroes and Villains of the World War," p. 735.

illated between the assumption that America could insulate herself from a future war and the assumption that she could not. In *The American Leviathan* (1930) he indicated that the historic "creed of isolation which once seemed convincing, *unless wisely interpreted*, may be employed to defeat . . . national security." [39] Although America's own interests prevented her from refusing all participation in world affairs, America must at least not pursue a policy of trying to dominate the world. "Strict and adequate national defense," which meant "defense of the land and people of the United States," [40] was virtually the extent of Beard's prescription for American foreign policy in a difficult world.

In his view, the difficulties and uncertainties were not lessened by the activities and pronouncements of people he regarded as military-minded or otherwise misguided. In early 1932, in a series of three articles in the *New Republic*, he sharply attacked "the big navy boys." [41] He feared that undercover plotting by interests favoring a bigger navy would appreciably increase the probability of war. Left to make policy themselves, the militarists would soon be extending "strategic frontiers" to the moon unless overruled.[42] Not "brag and bluster," but a foreign policy free of military and other unwanted pressures had become a supremely important concern for Beard on the eve of the New Deal. "Upon the correct answers to these questions," he declared, "hangs the long fate of American civilization." [43] His ideas and his mood had changed considerably in a decade.

[39] *The American Leviathan*, with William Beard (New York: Macmillan Co., 1930), p. 736 (italics supplied).

[40] "Five-Year Plan for America," *Forum and Century*, LXXXVI (July, 1931), 10.

[41] "Big Navy Boys," *New Republic*, LXIX (January 20–February 3, 1932) 258–62, 287–91, 314–18.

[42] In a letter, *New Republic*, LXIX (December 16, 1931), 137.

[43] *Ibid.*, p. 258.

CHAPTER VIII
THE SEARCH FOR A SOCIAL PHILOSOPHY

From Beard's first postwar years around New York City, until the early thirties—after he had journeyed extensively over the face of the globe both in Asia and Europe and had returned to his house at New Milford to continue to write and to reflect on human affairs—only a little more than a decade in time had transpired. Yet that brief span represented not only thousands of miles of travel and voluminous writings, but also an evolution in ideas and outlook in some respects considerable, even if negligible in other respects, as previous chapters have shown. In this chapter it is our task to view his developing concepts during this middle period in a somewhat different light —as the gradually intensifying search for the elements of a more comprehensive social philosophy.

Since the beginning of the century, Beard had been fascinated by the problem of causative patterns in human affairs. Although he had toyed only briefly with the notion of a predictive "science of politics," he had found economic determinism suggestive. Madisonian ideas, especially, seemingly impressed him deeply for a number of years. But successively he broadened his theoretical bases of politics until, by the late twenties, his groping had in effect been transformed into a quest for a general theory of historical causation.

The Substance of Human Affairs

As we have seen, Beard had long considered reality in human society to consist of rough stuff, mainly economic and material in nature. In his view, legalistic, ideological, and philosophical matters were largely myth and rationalization, or at most something for preachers and poets to worry about. His attacks on other writers and thinkers whose approach to reality he considered faulty were skillful and numerous. Political scientists, lawyers, economists, and social thinkers of various descriptions came under his guns, but he seemed to derive extra delight from intellectually drawing and quartering

120

traditionalist historians. Special censure went to those who slurred over the economic, social democratic, and labor developments. He liked to allude sarcastically to "the elder statesmen of the American Historical Association." [1]

Beard appeared to feel about ideas in general much as he did about art and literature when he wrote in the *New Republic* that "it must be remembered that in art as in literature we see what is behind our eyes." [2] Thus the upbringing and presuppositions of a judge had much to do with his interpretation and finding of the law. Written history reflected the historian. An ideology could be found to justify any "system."

Political philosophy, to Beard, was "a great armory of logic, history, sociology, economics, theology, law, biology, and what not." From this armory one could select whatever sword or shield best fitted his particular needs. Although political concepts might on occasion, therefore, be useful as weapons or in some other instrumental capacity, he felt that in the abstract they were a poor policy guide. Reviewing Charles E. Merriam's volume on *American Political Ideas* in 1921, Beard seemed unable to take the ideas seriously. [3] The real substance consisted of bankers and finance, Standard Oil, labor organizing, farmer discontent, excess profits taxes, and the threat of war in the Pacific. The ideas or philosophy appeared to be merely "a great deal of talk." The amount of it since the Civil War, asserted Beard with tongue in cheek, "is dreadful to contemplate." The author, he acknowledged, had analyzed all this talk "carefully and given us a fair and balanced digest of it. That is a real service, but it adds to the confusion by showing us how great the confusion always has been." [4] As Beard mockingly admitted in another connection:

The wild welter of kingdoms, empires, republics, democracies, and city states stretching across the centuries from Sargon the Great to Warren Gamaliel Harding has been accompanied by an equally wild welter of political philosophies. Every little system must have its reason for existence founded in the very nature of things. [5]

[1] See, for example, review of Haworth, *The United States in Our Own Times, 1865–1920, Nation*, CXI (October 13, 1920), 417.

[2] Review of Van Loon, *The Story of Mankind, New Republic*, XXIX (December 21, 1921), 105.

[3] *New Republic*, XXV (January 19, 1921), 235 f.

[4] *Ibid.*, p. 236.

[5] Review of Paul, *Creative Revolution: A Study in Communist Ergatocracy, Nation*, CXII (March 2, 1921), 342.

Beard's early postwar travels in Europe only confirmed his belief that ideas were not the real substance of politics and history. In his judgment "the wordy creeds of mankind have little effect upon the main course of things." [6] It was not their philosophy that had brought the Russian Bolsheviks to power, for example, but such realistic factors as "world war, a bankrupt Tsardom, a revolt started, it seems, by allied forces, a discontented peasantry, and a war-weary nation." Beard's conception of hard reality, as well as his disdain for theorizing, was amply displayed in his *Cross Currents in Europe Today* (1922), written on his return from the Old World:

It is not what we say about the sea that counts; it is what our sailors do upon the seas. It is not our academic theories about finance that carry weight in the councils of nations; it is our dollars and our cents that imperatively command the attention and wholesome respect of those engaged in the counting houses of the earth's great cities. It is not what President Harding thinks about China or what John Hay has written about China that will shape the coming fateful years in the Pacific; it is what our merchants, our capitalists, our railway builders, and our money lenders do in China that will set the problem for the rising generation.[7]

When Beard wrote a lengthy review of S. G. Hobson's *National Guilds and the State* in 1920, he took the occasion to make his own analysis of two centuries of political thought.[8] The record of political ideas in the past two hundred years, claimed Beard, vividly demonstrated how oblivious to mere ideas the actual political, economic, and other social realities had been. Thus, despite ideological attacks on the state, numerous proposals for minimizing or eliminating it, and various philosophies such as guild socialism, the state had continued on through the ages, anchored securely to its substantial foundations. Quickly dismissing the notion that the state was destined to assume "the spiritual leadership of the nation," Beard derisively wondered who or what was to "conquer territory or defend oil wells." Hobson and others who thought like him deluded themselves in seeking "finality." They continued doing this, added Beard in feigned disbelief, "two thousand years after the Greeks and fifty years after Darwin."

[6] "Potency of Labor Education," *American Federationist*, XXIX (July, 1922), 501.

[7] *Cross Currents in Europe Today* (Boston: Marshall Jones Co., 1922), pp. 239 f.

[8] *New Republic*, XXV (December 8, 1920), 50 f.

Reality as Movement

Beard's reference to Darwin was more than incidental. If the substance of human affairs was economic and material, the events and accidents of history showed that the mode was movement, evolution, change. The reality that many people could not face, Beard contended, was the bitter truth that "the world is process not system, movement not finality." [9] Although the Darwinian concept of ceaseless change had long found a secure place among Beard's most basic assumptions, it was only late in the postwar era that it was in effect to become an element in his implicitly forming social philosophy. Though his continuing re-examination of the *substance* of human affairs led him to modify his earlier economic emphasis, his further reflections only strengthened his conviction that the world was eternal *movement*. Whatever else reality might comprise, it was not static finality.

Repeatedly, in various connections, Beard stated or implied that students of human affairs, if they would see their subject matter with realism, must acquire a mental grasp of this inherent state of motion, this unfolding in time. Historians, for example, were performing their true function in the grand manner when they sensed the "master current" of an age and expressed it.[10] Philosophers had as their main task trying to see things as "they really are and are becoming." [11]

When Beard discussed the "three systems of thought" available to nineteenth-century thinkers, he similarly made an assumption of never-ending movement in history, even though he regarded all three ideologies as mainly "defense mechanisms." According to Beard, one of the systems had been "a new philosophy," presently taken up by Hegel, which itself "conceived of the world as endless change." The two older systems—the scholastic "fixed order of God" and the later "fixed order of nature"—had both conceived of reality as basically static. But, interestingly, Beard himself, in portraying these two static systems as weapons used by a *defending* status quo, was implying

[9] *Ibid.*, p. 51. Also cf. Beard's discussion in "Democracy Holds Its Ground: A European Survey," *Harper's Magazine*, CLVII (November, 1928), 680 ff., for implied movement.

[10] Review of Rhodes, *History of the United States, 1877–1896, New Republic,* XXI (December 17, 1919), 83.

[11] Review of Laski, *Political Thought in England from Locke to Bentham, New Republic,* XXIV (November 17, 1920), 303.

that the defenders had nonetheless been confronted by irresistible forces of change.[12]

As he had long recognized, "the mutability of human affairs" gave just cause for skepticism as to the permanence of any status or condition in society.[13] His chief quarrel with "utopians" of various categories was their futile hope of altering or stopping the dynamic course of history. Whether they saw their golden ideal in a past system of "anarchy and the police constable," in a lush status quo of the present, or in a future classless millennium, their static utopias would be shattered by relentless change. Socialism, guild socialism, individualism, direct actionism, or communism were all equally powerless to defeat or paralyze restless reality.[14] Neither could Mussolini do it in Fascist Italy where Beard saw "destiny riding without saddle and bridle across the historic peninsula that bridges the world of antiquity and our modern world." [15]

Is the capitalist dictatorship the real answer? . . . The transitory character of other dictatorships and tyrannies suggests caution at least. . . . If Italy moves, Mussolini will move with her or be unhorsed. If he keeps in the saddle to the end, it will be because he commands political, economic, and moral wisdom and modifies his scheme until it has become something else. . . . So the dictatorship of Fascism, like all other tyrannies, must always tremble on the brink of uncertainty, for it does not automatically generate its own life insurance.[16]

It can be said with much truth that the idea of progress never lost its hold on Beard's mind. In 1932 he himself wrote the introduction for John B. Bury's volume, *The Idea of Progress.*[17] Despite his knowledge that dictatorship was flexing its muscles in Italy and Manchuria and that economic depression in America was deepening, Beard in the early thirties was still in a sense the convert of hopeful Darwinism. As such, he conceived of reality as progressive movement:

[12] "Political Heritage of the Twentieth Century," *Yale Review*, XVIII (March, 1929), 463 ff.

[13] Cf. *The Administration and Politics of Tokyo* (New York: Macmillan Co., 1923), p. 158.

[14] See review of Hobson, *National Guilds and the State*, pp. 50 f.; cf. review of O'Brien, *An Essay on Mediaeval Economic Teaching, Nation*, CXI (October 27, 1920), 480.

[15] Review of Schneider, *Making the Fascist State, New Republic*, LVII (January 23, 1929), 278.

[16] "Rushlights in Darkness," *Scribner's Magazine*, XC (December, 1931), 576 f.

[17] (New York: Macmillan Co., 1932).

Whether the evolution of mankind is at bottom a progressive revelation of the spirit of God, an unfolding of the Idea, as Hegel taught, or a continuous adaptation to changing material circumstances, as Marx emphasized, it is essentially movement. . . . Conceding for the sake of argument that the past has been chaos, without order or design, we are still haunted by the shadowing thought that by immense efforts of will and intelligence, employing natural science as the supreme instrumentality of power, mankind may rise above necessity into the kingdom of freedom, subduing material things to humane and rational purposes.[18]

Ideas and Reality

Although no clean break is discernible in Beard's thinking, his writings toward the end of the postwar decade tended less and less to treat ideas as insignificant factors in social life. With increasing frequency he attributed to ideas additional roles and uses. In brief, reality was being taken to comprise not only oil wells and labor unions and clashing economic forces, but also the conceptions existing in men's minds. As Beard's search for an adequate social philosophy went on, ideas steadily became more important to him. Yet, at the same time, his old aversion to theoretical abstractions kept reasserting itself. Like a man purporting to despise the nourishment he actually hungers for, Beard continued probing for the deeper meanings in human existence.

In *The Rise of American Civilization* (1927), for example, mental constructs were both glorified and gently discounted. Thus Otis, Dickinson, Hamilton, and Jefferson had easily found ready-made before them "all the theories and dogmas which their cause required." [19] Beard made it sound almost as if a workman had happily stumbled on a tool just when he needed it. In somewhat similar vein, wage earners in America, like other economic classes, had evolved "ideas of defense and aggression." [20] On the other hand, the idea of progress had been "the most dynamic social theory ever shaped in the history of thought." [21] The power of ideology to influence human affairs was implied, too, when Beard quoted Oliver Wendell Holmes's statement: "Not by aggression but by the naked fact of existence we are an eternal danger and an unsleeping threat to every government

[18] Introduction, Bury, *The Idea of Progress*, p. xi.
[19] *The Rise of American Civilization*, with Mary R. Beard (1st ed.; New York: Macmillan Co., 1927), I, 188.
[20] *Ibid.*, p. 643.
[21] *Ibid.*, p. 443.

that founds itself on anything but the will of the governed." [22]

Writing toward the end of 1927 on the "Recent Gains in Government," Beard attributed the advance not only to political action and economic pressure but also to "the spread of ideas." [23] Indeed, for Beard, ideas appeared to have attained front rank among the "real forces."

These gains have been made by the insistence of agitators, the endless discussions of fireside, forum, shop, and office, the pressure of citizens' committees, the writings of critics, the logical and sentimental appeal of constructive proposals, in short, by the activities of millions of men and women, most of them unknown to the pages of written history, who have thought, written, spoken, and dared. A word, an article, a pamphlet, a speech, or a book may set in train forces of incalculable moment. Such is the mystery of the life in which we work—the unforeseen potentialities of what men and women think and do. [24]

If Beard, in *The American Party Battle* (1928), could claim that certain constitutional theorizing looked "more akin to protective coloration than to causation," [25] he could also write in *Whither Mankind* (1928), at virtually the same time, in a vein sounding strangely unlike the man who had often discounted mere "metaphysics." In a concluding statement in the latter work he asserted:

In a way, all divisions of this book are but departments of philosophy, truly considered, and it would seem not too much to say that strength will come to modern civilization just in proportion as philosophy attends to the business of living under the necessities imposed by technology, and the business of living itself is inspired by an effort to see things whole and steadily, relating means to the highest imaginable ends, making use of reality rather than attempting to escape from it. [26]

Contributing the essay on "Political Science" to Wilson Gee's joint compilation on *Research in the Social Sciences* (1929), [27] Beard had occasion to reformulate his views concerning political writings and the ideas they convey. Treatises on politics, he explained, fell into two main classifications: those which aimed at "describing some phase of statecraft with exactness" and those designed "to attack or defend

[22] *Ibid.*, p. 824.
[23] *World Tomorrow*, X (November, 1927), 439.
[24] *Ibid.*, p. 442.
[25] *The American Party Battle* (New York: Macmillan Co., 1928), p. 139.
[26] *Whither Mankind* (New York: Longmans, Green, 1928), p. 408.
[27] Wilson Gee (ed.) (New York: Macmillan Co., 1929).

some order of political affairs." [28] He appeared to be suggesting a distinction between causal theorizing and value theorizing. He was careful to indicate, however, that "the greatest works" were to be found in the latter category. Thus he pointed out, for example, that with respect to the noted political philosophers of the past—Locke, Hobbes, Rousseau, Jefferson, Madison, Hamilton, and Calhoun—none could be strictly considered a "scientist."

Comparison of Beard's 1929 exposition on "Political Science" with his Columbia University lecture on *Politics* twenty-one years earlier reveals that he not only had long abandoned his former hope of an eventual "science of politics," but by the latter date had also come to assign a vastly greater role to men's ideas in a nondeterministic frame of reference. If scientific predictions could be made in politics, Beard now explained, the future "trajectory" that could be plotted would be "inexorable." But such scientifically discovered foresight would be useless knowledge, he felt, because men could do nothing to change the outcome. "If we could get enough knowledge to make a science of politics, we should imprison ourselves in an iron web of our own making." [29]

Fallaciously, however, he was equating scientific prediction with predestination. With respect to actual scientific prediction an outcome becomes *probable* and *conditional,* not absolutely certain or fated as Beard implied. The empirical relationship is: if this, then probably that. Scientifically based knowledge that falling trees kill a certain percentage of the people they hit does not "imprison us in an iron web" but warns us to jump clear. [30]

Although Beard late in the 1920's was thus granting that ideas had greater influence in history than he had formerly admitted, neither his facility in manipulating theoretical concepts nor his urge to assimilate them into a systematic political philosophy had correspondingly strengthened. His apparent classification of political treatises into scientific-descriptive and ethical-valuational seemed less than profound when he concluded: "There is no valid distinction between descriptive politics, political science, political theory, or politi-

[28] *Ibid.,* p. 270.

[29] *Ibid.,* pp. 273–75.

[30] On this point, also see Sidney Hook's exposition, "Destiny, Fate, Predestination" in Merle E. Curti (ed.), *Theory and Practice in Historical Study: A Report of the Committee on Historiography* (Social Science Research Council Bulletin, No. 54, 1946), pp. 119 f.; cf. David Easton, *The Political System* (New York: Alfred A. Knopf, 1953), pp. 24 ff.

cal philosophy. They all represent more or less serious efforts to think about a phase of life called political." [31]

There were indications, however, that Beard was continuing to re-examine the theoretical relationship between ideas and objective reality. "In some mysterious way," he remarked, "thought and the materials of life evolve together." [32] Discussing "The Development of Social Thought and Institutions" in the *Encyclopedia of the Social Sciences* in 1930, he further elucidated the formula he attributed to William James:

There are times in the history of the world when facts almost stand still, when ways of living, working, traveling, and fighting change so slowly that thought more than catches up with them—seems in reality to control, rather than to reflect, them. Broadly speaking, such a period was the Middle Ages. Then again there are periods when new facts come pell-mell upon the world, devastating wars and revolutions, epoch-making inventions, defying old systems of thought, making them appear incongruous with the world of reality and compelling a revision of logical patterns once satisfactory to their possessors. Sometimes these new facts come so swiftly and spread so widely that thought is apparently incapable of reducing them to a system, to say nothing of controlling them in relation to ideas, inherited or novel.[33]

Applying this notion to the rise of capitalism, he rejected the Marxian version of the development as well as the explanation that "capitalism sprang from the soil of Calvinism." Both fact and idea were the parents of capitalism, he insisted. "A certain intellectual climate, as well as technological conditions," was necessary. He was ready to admit the efficacy of ideas—conceptions existing in men's minds—whether these stemmed from sensuous apprehension of external reality or from more subjective mental activity. "Movements in ideas, either as a result of abstract speculation and dialectical processes or as the reflection of novel changes in material circumstances, must be taken into account in explaining the rise and development of capitalism." [34]

Beard at this time was also becoming increasingly fascinated by the methodological and epistemological problems involved in the

[31] "Political Science," p. 286; cf. Beard's similar description of political treatises in his *A Charter for the Social Sciences in the Schools* (New York: Charles Scribner's Sons, 1932), pp. 14–16.

[32] *The Rise of American Civilization* (1-vol. ed.; 1930), p. xi.

[33] E. R. A. Seligman and Alvin Johnson (eds.), I (New York: Macmillan Co., 1930), 145.

[34] *Ibid.*, pp. 147 f.

scholar's attempt to comprehend and explain *past* reality. Since the earliest years of the century, of course, he had been deeply interested in the methods and techniques of the historian's craft. With James Harvey Robinson he had supported the New History, in opposition to the traditionalists with their emphasis on "barren" political history. Now in the twenties, in his attacks on the "objective" historians who worshiped at the shrine of Ranke, he frequently implied that written history reflected the ideas and assumptions of the historian and his time as much as it did the past reality it purported to explain.

Beard's historiography of the 1920's was closely tied to his general viewpoint on the relationship of ideas and reality, but it also foreshadowed the "newer history" he was to espouse—to the consternation of many of his less venturesome colleagues—in the final fifteen years of his life. In his presidential address before the American Political Science Association at the close of 1926, he made clear his own contention that historians could set before their readers not past reality itself but only their ideas about it:

The historian proudly tells us that he has nothing to do with interpretation, that he deals only with indubitable facts, with things as they actually were. . . . The historian himself knows, on sober thought, that with reference to any theme of importance, he does not present all the facts, no matter how minute his analysis, but in truth selects a few from the multitudes that have by chance merely found a pale record on the pages of the books and manuscripts and papers that have escaped the ravages of time. And any selection, except one made by lot, is an interpretation, no matter how vehemently the historian protests his innocence of ideas. More than that, the very denial of any desire to interpret is perhaps the most profound interpretation of all—namely, a confession that there is not even a discoverable fringe of order in the universe, that anarchy is the name for the chaos.[35]

In his 1932 introduction to Bury's *Idea of Progress,* Beard went so far as to exclaim that "the world is largely ruled by ideas, true and false. . . . It is not only in politics that ideas are important. They are regnant in every department of civilized life." [36] Although he could still speak disparagingly, in the *New Republic,* of "the theorists who

[35] "Time, Technology, and the Creative Spirit in Political Science," *American Political Science Review,* XXI (February, 1927), 6 f.; see also Beard's subsequent address at a history teachers' meeting in which he discussed various concepts of history and to a considerable extent foreshadowed his later historical relativism ("A Historian's Quest for Light," *Proceedings of the Association of History Teachers of the Middle States and Maryland,* XXIX [1931], 12–21).

[36] Introduction, Bury, *The Idea of Progress,* pp. ix f.

imagine that the world can be ruled by ideas without reference to realities," he was equally critical of "those Marxians who think that ideas automatically arise from given economic conditions." [37] As he declared in the *Yale Review,* in analyzing the "Political Heritage of the Twentieth Century," [38] "new facts do not automatically bring their appropriate ideas. On the contrary, new facts must be considered at first in the light of existing ideas." He could hardly have taken a more un-Marxian position.

The Ethical Center

Another element of the social philosophy Beard seemed to be piecing together in the postwar era was ethics. Ethics not only received greater consideration but soon became the nucleus around which all else clustered.

It is true that Beard had previously recognized ethics. In his 1916 lectures at Amherst he had complained of the modern practice of dividing the social sciences among specialists in contrast to the wisdom of Aristotle, who had combined "economics, politics, and ethics." [39] In 1923 he had claimed that it was "impossible for the coldest 'efficiency expert' in administration to stop with a study of 'what is.' He must inevitably ask: 'what ought to be.' " [40] Beard had appeared to agree vaguely with Aristotle that governments are "an approximation to an ideal of some kind." But such "ethical" considerations had given Beard slight pause. He had usually moved quickly on to the more central aspects of the "tough web of politics." [41]

By 1929 and the early thirties, however, his treatment of ethics had changed. Remarking that "mankind lives not by politics alone nor by bread alone but also by things of the spirit which form ideals, inspire love of beauty, and ennoble action," [42] he became increasingly concerned with the role of ethics, ideals, and values. "There can be no

[37] "Making a Bigger and Better Navy," *New Republic,* LXVIII (October 14, 1931), 223.

[38] P. 463.

[39] *The Economic Basis of Politics* (New York: Alfred A. Knopf, 1922), p. 15.

[40] *The Administration and Politics of Tokyo,* p. 163.

[41] Cf. his attitude, for example, in *American Government and Politics* (4th ed.; New York: Macmillan Co., 1924), pp. 58 f.

[42] *History of the United States,* with Mary R. Beard (rev. ed.; New York: Macmillan Co., 1929), pp. v f.

creative work in political science without ethics," he declared in 1930 in the *American Political Science Review*.[43]

Presently he was proclaiming that ethics would have to be central in the new social philosophy needed by the twentieth century. Thinkers would have to recant their former neglect. "The supreme cause of our confusion," he alleged, "is our contemptuous dismissal of ethics."[44] Complaining that "our best thinkers have turned their backs on it," he claimed to see a "philosophy of ethical reconciliation" on the way.

It will not take aboard any of the epic theologies. . . . It will take the good life as its centre, for the plain reason that there is no other immovable bench mark in the universal flux. It will proceed from that inescapable assertion of value. . . . In sum, it will return after two thousand years to the beginning made by Aristotle, who in moments of doubts and despair continued to proclaim himself a disciple of Plato, and it will make use of science as its weapon of conquest.[45]

Beard made clear that the study of politics as well as the social sciences generally must center around this ethical core. Discussing "Conditions Favorable to Creative Work in Political Science," he warned that political science, to be fruitful, could no longer ignore ethics.

Science never tells anyone what to do in any large human situation, what is most valuable, what is most worth doing. It never commands anyone to do anything. A light and superficial skepticism respecting all values is easy; perhaps it is the prevailing temper; if nothing is worth doing, then certainly nothing is worth doing well. Now the ethics of which I am speaking here is not the ethics of convenience and utility; it is the ethics of the effort that transcends the immediately useful and proper and relates itself to that which is simple, humane, and sacrificial. Without ethics, political science can have no more vital connection with life than have the tables of an adding machine.[46]

However, once Beard had enthroned ethics, he found himself face to face with a dilemma. Would the newly found ethics that was to be central in the coming social philosophy be absolute or relative? In his introduction to Bury's *The Idea of Progress* he sensed the diffi-

[43] "Conditions Favorable to Creative Work in Political Science," *American Political Science Review*, XXIV Suppl. (February, 1930), 29.
[44] "Rushlights in Darkness," p. 578.
[45] *Ibid.*
[46] "Conditions Favorable to Creative Work in Political Science," p. 29.

culty but avoided taking a clear stand. The idea of progress itself contained an element of ethics, he suggested, for it implied a "fixed point of reference" or some "bench mark" by which one could judge whether history was moving in a desirable direction or not. This "bench mark" could also guide one in making choices appropriate to that desired direction. Although, as Beard admitted, Bury himself had not attempted to solve the problem of absolute versus relative ethics, "those who seek to pass judgment on his book must face the issues involved." Whereas absolute ethics, according to Beard, assumed values with the same status philosophically as "mathematical and logical truths," relative ethics rested on "the equilibration of interests and their rational adjustment to environment." The whole subject, he acknowledged, was fraught with "immense difficulties." [47]

Having posed the dilemma, Beard pressed his "Search for the Centre" in *Scribner's Magazine* in 1932. On the one hand, he rejected the "ethics of absolutism" with its notion of the good "outside of the human mind." The absolutist in actual practice, he felt, got tangled up in his theory. Yet Beard also refused to accept an ethics that would be too relativistic and too devoid of landmarks for guidance. Suggesting the need of "a moral standard to which all mankind may repair," he hastened to qualify his remarks as mere "guesses and assertions." Not wishing to be tied down too rigidly by absolute ethics, he appeared to have some yearning for the freedom of relativism. But he did not wish to go all the way with relativism because he feared that relativism carried too far would destroy human society. In any event, he hoped that "in due course the philosophy of the twentieth century will be written by some one competent to do it." It was a task that required "prodigious thinking." [48]

Finding serious defects in both absolutist and relativist ethics, and still somewhat distrustful of "metaphysics," Beard nevertheless decided that the "search for a scheme of ethics" must go on until some kind of "reconciliation" could be reached. Moreover, the "assertions" on which the scheme would be based had to appeal to "reason and the noblest impulses of mankind."

What, then, is the immovable base, the fixed bench mark, from which to survey the land of values? Since all ethical systems and all philosophies start with assumptions, the problem is to find one which makes the least strain on credulity and knowledge, which commands the widest assent,

[47] Introduction, Bury, *The Idea of Progress*, pp. xxix f.
[48] *Scribner's Magazine*, XCI (January, 1932), 2 f.

which seems most congruous with the world of fact and potentiality. The assumption which appears to offer the best clew is this: We are here in the world of external phenomena. We live. The most desirable, the firmest, foundation for a system of ethics is the good life for as many people as possible.[49]

As if feeling a twinge of guilt at his own words—"metaphysics" from the mouth of a "realist"—Beard quickly threw up a defense against the "hard-minded reader." What if the formulation were called utopian? "In the true sense of the word, every system of ethics is utopian, for it mingles with known realities dreams of what is possible." But if the hard-minded reader meant to charge him with proposing "a system of reasoned perfection to be discovered, imposed, and maintained forever," then Beard flatly denied that this was his intention. Such a scheme of ethics would be "destined to defeat by the changeful nature of things, by the mutability of human affairs, by the fallibility of the human mind." He appeared to want at all cost to avoid "that dread spectre" which Bury had called "the illusion of finality."[50]

Beard's scheme of ethics, he insisted, did not rest on theology. A theological system would be "challenged by countless millions" and would tend to divide rather than unify mankind. He explained that "it may as well be frankly confessed that the scheme of ethics here advocated is telluric. It avoids ultimates."[51]

Elements of a Philosophy

From the early 1920's to the early 1930's, Beard's "search" had thus taken him a long way. From an economic interpretation of politics and history, he had moved to a broad and indefinite conception of human affairs. From an earlier tendency to discount ideas as unreliable abstractions, he had developed the habit of looking on idea patterns as mainly rationalizations, and finally he had come full circle to hint that thought might be the prime determinant in human affairs. In his thinking, ethics had shifted from a marginal location to a central position. But, floundering among the pitfalls of philosophical speculation, he appeared to be unwilling or unable to put the elements of a philosophy together into a system that satisfied him.

As to the study of politics, he gave little evidence of comprehending

[49] *Ibid.*, pp. 3 f.
[50] *Ibid.*, p. 7.
[51] *Ibid.*

the possibility of any "theory" except that found in the classics advocating "what ought to be." When he associated in his mind politics and causal theory as found in the physical sciences, his thinking seemed to leave the world of empirical science and leap to the realm of fate and predetermination.

Regarding history writing, he often implied that it reflected the historian more than it did actual history. It is hard to say whether he considered the discipline on balance to be predominantly scientific-descriptive or subjective-interpretative.

Still, at the end of the postwar period Beard did explicitly, if tentatively, state his social philosophy. As American voters flocked to the polls in early November of 1932 to elect Roosevelt, Beard published a thumbnail philosophy. In answer to the *Literary Digest*'s query, "What keeps you going, what help—if any—[does] religion [give] you, what are the sources of your inspiration and your energy?" he replied:

As I look over the grand drama of history, I find (or seem to find) amid the apparent chaos and tragedy, evidence of law and plan and immense achievement of the human spirit in spite of disasters. . . . Something magnificent is taking place here amid the cruelties and tragedies. . . . If there was no grand design in the beginning of the universe, fragments of one are evident, and mankind can complete the picture. A knowledge of the good life is our certain philosophic heritage, and technology has given us a power over nature which enables us to provide the conditions of the good life for all the earth's multitudes. That seems to me to be the most engaging possibility of the drama, and faith in its potentialities keeps me working at it even in the worst hours of disillusionment. The good life—an end in itself to be loved and enjoyed; and intelligent labor directed to the task of making the good life prevail. There is the little philosophy, the circle of thought within which I keep my little mill turning.[52]

Shortly afterward, in the *Journal of Higher Education,* Beard added: "Science is neutral with respect to the choices of the human race. When it ceases to be neutral, it ceases to be science and becomes something else. Science can serve purposes. Thought, will, desire, dreams, and hopes must discover and affirm them." [53]

But it must be emphasized that Beard was not satisfied with his

---

[52] "What Is the Meaning of Life?" with Others, *Literary Digest,* CXIV (November 5, 1932), 20.

[53] "Quest for Academic Power," *Journal of Higher Education,* III (December 1932), 469.

social philosophizing. Too many perplexing problems remained unsolved. How could the tragedy of another war be avoided? How
could democracy and humane progress be safeguarded? In what
direction must one turn for the most realistic understanding of
human affairs? The actual result of Beard's searching, as of the early
1930's at least, was uncertainty. He must continue to search.

PART III

DOUBT AT DUSK

1933-48

_____

The exponents of all systems of thought, including under that head all social philosophies, are now troubled by doubts. If they are still convinced that they have the truth, they nowhere find practice conforming to their theory with pleasing exactitude.

"Twilight of Social Systems" (1940)

In 1933 the Western world appeared to be entering a new era. Americans, after months of disheartening uncertainty, looked hopefully to Franklin D. Roosevelt to lead them forward. In mid-Europe, deadlocks and discouragement seemed about to vanish under the bold touch of the new German *Führer*. But it quickly became evident that the millennium was not at hand. Perplexities, fears, and mounting emergencies continued to plague the world of action and thought in which Beard lived out his last years.

American intellectuals reacted in diverse ways to the turbulent times. For a time a rekindled interest in reform glowed brightly on the national horizon. Small extremist movements and a minor flurry of Marxism soon were apparently submerged in the generally moderate wave of early New Dealism. Casehardened liberals once inclined to look with critical eye at America's past now took a kindlier view of their country and its problems. In some quarters this neonationalism developed into a defensive isolationist temper which became more unyielding with each new disturbance on the international scene. When global war overshadowed all else, apparently few Americans imagined that the world was to be made finally "safe for democracy."

The final sixteen years of Beard's life fell in the initial decades of this modern era of virtually permanent crisis. In some ways these last years constitute the most fascinating period of his intellectual development.

CHAPTER IX
THE NATURE OF SOCIAL REALITY

Two years before the 1929 stock market crash, Beard had intimated that, although American civilization had already marched on through many generations, it was still "the dawn, not the dusk, of the Gods." [1] But by 1933 this hopeful view of the future had been revised. In place of this terse ending, *The Rise of American Civilization* now concluded with a broad discussion of the world economic depression and its impact on education, literature, and various sectors of the social order. A new chapter entitled "The Mirage Dissolves" had been added. Apparently Beard, like numerous other thinkers during these years, felt intellectually adrift, perplexed as familiar old landmarks seemed to melt away.

Methodological Barriers to Understanding

As he continued to reflect and write on human affairs in this last period of his life, Beard became more than ever convinced that there were fundamental defects in men's approach to social reality. Thus handicapped, they could acquire no genuine grasp of the problems of society. "The new generation," he observed, "may not know where it is going; neither did the old, for that matter." [2] In his view it was clear that, without full understanding, social scientists could give no real guidance in a troubled age. Students of politics, for example, long preoccupied with the state in its historic role, had little to offer now that the state was rapidly taking up a great many new tasks. From their studies came largely trivia rather than "essays on statecraft in the grand manner." [3]

[1] *The Rise of American Civilization*, with Mary R. Beard (1st ed.; New York: Macmillan Co., 1927), II, 800; (new ed.; 1933), pp. 713–43.

[2] Review of Beckerath, *Modern Industrial Organization, American Political Science Review*, XXVII (October, 1933), 833 f.

[3] *The Rise of American Civilization* (new ed.; 1933), II, 835.

140

One of the methodological barriers Beard believed to be blocking true insight into social reality was the intensive specialization among students of human affairs. Undue specialization not only failed to capture the essential "unity of the human spirit" but also tended to divorce thought and practical action.[4] As late as 1946 he contended that "all the humanistic sciences, such as economics and politics," being selected abstractions from a vastly wider range of knowledge, could in no respect be "independent, free-moving sciences."[5] Thus, many years after he had made a similar complaint in his 1908 lecture on *Politics* before the faculty and students of Columbia University, he was continuing to insist that modern thinkers had falsely separated the social sciences.

Beard in the later years of his life emphasized, however, that the social sciences were quite unlike the physical sciences. He believed that failure to appreciate the differences led to serious methodological error. Despite the need for fullest possible use of available verification procedures in the "humanistic sciences," the "exactness of physics and chemistry" could not be expected.[6] Historical methodology, he particularly felt, suffered from the illusion of some historians that their discipline closely resembled the natural sciences. Yet the matters with which historians dealt were "not identical in nature with the data in physics." Meaningful values could not be assigned to the "imponderables, immeasurables, and contingencies."[7]

For similar reasons he attacked the "Unity of Science Movement." In Beard's view it was based on the faulty concept that all fields of knowledge—physical, biological, social, and psychological—were one, and that all could be reduced to quantitative methods and statistical measurement. He appeared to delight in directing shafts at the "obvious limitations" of this approach. As he wrote in 1939:

A mother's love for her child exists; it can be measured; let us say that it is 1.23456789 per pound of her weight. My query is: How much do we

[4] "Sign of the Times," *National Municipal Review*, XXII (December, 1933), 583.

[5] "Grounds for a Reconsideration of Historiography," in Merle E. Curti (ed.), *Theory and Practice in Historical Study: A Report of the Committee on Historiography* (Social Science Research Council Bulletin, No. 54, 1946), p. 10.

[6] *Ibid.*

[7] "Written History as an Act of Faith," *American Historical Review*, XXXIX (January, 1934), 224 f.

know and what, when we have arrived at this result? And I have no more use for metaphysics and theology than the Unified Science Movement has.[8]

Beard's basic objection to treating the social and physical sciences as a unified whole consequently went beyond the matter of mere exactness. Instead, he was concerned with the limitations of facts in themselves, regardless of whether these could be "measured" or not. All students of human affairs, he urged, should rid themselves of the false notion that fact hunting alone could solve social problems and furnish guidance for the future. It was a delusion, he claimed, which had been fostered by experts.

Facts do not ask or answer any questions. Facts never tell anybody to do or to refrain from doing anything. Furthermore, among the billions of facts that might be assembled by the new investigators only a few thousands or millions will be unearthed. The amount and character of facts dug up will depend upon the ideas which the investigators already have in their heads. What is to be done, if anything, about the facts will depend upon sources of conviction, prejudice, and opinion which lie in part, if not wholly, outside the facts that are excavated.[9]

It was this infinite vastness of the potential data which was the source of many of the methodological difficulties that engaged Beard, and which led to much of the perplexity in his own thinking during the last decade and a half of his life. If potentially the data were limitless, in reality because of the loss of evidence through the ages only a part was actually available, and of this part only a minute fragment could be included in even the profoundest expositions of scholars. Beyond question some kind of selectivity principle operated, either implicitly or openly. Yet how could familiarity with a minute fragment of the totality—even if this represented a lifetime of knowledge —possibly provide full understanding of the whole of social reality? Obviously, believed Beard, it could not. Full understanding was beyond the reach of the human mind.

But recognition of these limitations and handicaps facing the thinker in itself constituted the beginning of greater comprehension, Beard maintained. Conversely, denial or ignorance of the fact that inevitably only a relatively tiny portion of the data could be selected from the infinitely larger total meant not only shrunken under-

[8] Review of Neurath, *Modern Man in the Making, Saturday Review of Literature,* XX (September 30, 1939), 11.

[9] "Anti-trust Racket," *New Republic,* XCVI (September 21, 1938), 183.

standing but, what was worse, also self-deception. A firm grasp, as well as frank acknowledgment, of the selectivity principle—or "frame of reference"—operating in the human intellectual process became an increasingly crucial methodological and epistemological matter from Beard's point of view.

Accordingly, from the early 1930's, Beard never tired of reminding his readers and listeners of the assumptions and frames of reference controlling the thought of scholars and scientists and, indeed, every conscious human being. It was totally irrelevant to the actual presence of such a frame of reference whether its existence was fully recognized or not even suspected. The fact that the student of human affairs could not possibly present all of the data respecting his subject but had to engage in selecting proved beyond all doubt that he operated on the basis of a frame of reference. It implied an interpretation of some kind. The very denial of interpretation was itself a profound interpretation, Beard claimed. "We may shut our eyes to the abyss of thought that yawns devouringly at our feet, so perilous; the abyss remains. . . ." [10] "If the fact be denied, if a large, clarified, and informed frame of purposes is rejected, is deliberately and ostentatiously put out at the front door of the mind, then small, provincial, local, class, group, or personal prejudices will come in at the rear door, occupy the background of the mind, and constitute the frame." [11] There was absolutely no escape from "the intellectual presuppositions" of a writer or thinker. [12]

Beard's concern with the ramifications of the selectivity principle operative in the mind of the thinker seeking to understand social reality brought him to a kind of impasse. On the one hand, if facts did not automatically "answer questions," then value judgments must be the ultimate source of the answers. This seemed to imply that men could more confidently rely on values than on facts, or at least that they must do so. On the other hand, as Beard also indicated, one could not hope to comprehend the whole of anything without complete facts, and hence the process of selecting contributed to lack of full understanding. But this implied that value-guided selections were unreliable. As time went on, Beard appeared

[10] Review of Schlesinger, *The Rise of the City, American Historical Review,* XXXVIII (July, 1933), 780.

[11] *The Nature of the Social Sciences in Relation to Objectives of Instruction* (New York: Charles Scribner's Sons, 1934), p. 181.

[12] Review of Toynbee, *A Study of History,* I–III, *American Historical Review,* XL (January, 1935), 309.

to become increasingly engrossed in the question of whether value judgments were reliable or not, and in the possibility that trustworthy knowledge of social reality might ultimately be wholly beyond man's reach.

Related to these difficulties was another methodological device that, as Beard was fond of warning, often became a pitfall in practice. This was the use of fictions and abstractions in the social sciences. The economic man, the political man, and similar constructs sometimes incorporated into the theoretical models invented by students were examples of this device. When judiciously employed, such fictions could be highly useful. Thinkers in "analyzing, selecting, and organizing their data," as Beard acknowledged in 1946, made "these abstractions serve their purposes as constructs or fictions based on emphasized particularities" and thus were enabled to "advance their respective sciences." [13] But these fictions should not be carried to such lengths as to obstruct realistic thinking. They could lead to serious deception if regarded as literally true.[14]

The fiction of the economic man was highly useful for many purposes in examining and predicting the behavior of human beings in relation to the production and distribution of wealth. It is still highly useful. Without it we should know a great deal less than we do about the nature of human affairs and we should not be as well equipped to deal with many situations of life, large and small. But as Adam Smith proceeded he almost became a victim of his own fiction. When he confronted the issue of justifying his emphasis on the economic man and explaining how it came about that general good resulted from the avid pursuit of material interests by acquisitive individuals, Smith lamely referred to the "invisible hand," to some mysterious providence which turns individual greed into collective beneficence. Here he introduced something besides the economic man and sought to escape the moral question that he himself had raised.[15]

Beard recognized that vague analogies and semantic inaccuracies likewise beclouded the study and understanding of human affairs. As he grew older he appeared to become more conscious of such traps for the unwary. In a 1938 essay entitled "The Word-Revolution Begins," he admitted, half-facetiously, that when he first "ran into" semantics he "received a horrible shock." [16] Subsequently he stressed

[13] "Grounds for a Reconsideration of Historiography," pp. 7 f.
[14] Cf. *ibid.*, pp. 9 f., and *Public Policy and the General Welfare* (New York: Farrar & Rinehart, 1941), p. 143.
[15] "Grounds for a Reconsideration of Historiography," p. 8.
[16] *Events,* III (January, 1938), 25.

the need for greater precision in the terminology of historians, carefully pointing out that he himself was employing the term "history-as-actuality" to mean "all that has been felt, thought, imagined, said, and done by human beings as such and in relation to one another and to their environment since the beginning of mankind's operations on this planet." [17] The word "cause" also seemed to trouble Beard. Physicists, he claimed, had grown reticent about using the term "even in connection with sequences recognized as deterministic in nature." [18] The implication was that use of such terminology was still less appropriate for social scientists. In 1946 he warned of the ambiguity and confusion created by social scientists who uncritically borrowed analogies from other fields. Too often the use of highly figurative expressions meant that the idea was "not clear enough to be directly formulated." [19]

In all this Beard's underlying point was that social scientists must constantly strive to free themselves of the defects and limitations of their methodology. It was necessary to subject all phases of the approach to knowledge to the most searching scrutiny, to uncover the shortcomings, eliminate the barriers. Habitual thought patterns must be carefully studied and questioned so as to minimize "the tyranny they may exercise over the human mind." [20] Only in these ways lay the hope of attaining the most valid knowledge and the clearest understanding.

Search for a Formula

At the same time that Beard was thus finding fault with the methodology of the social sciences, he engaged in what is perhaps a characteristic mental activity of the troubled intellectual, namely, "formula-searching." He seemed to be probing and hunting for some key to unlock the mysteries that perplexed him, some formula to enhance his grasp of the universe and the human drama it embraced. At the end of 1933, for example, he told his assembled colleagues of the American Historical Association that the totality of actual historical reality fell into one of three possible frameworks:

[17] "Grounds for a Reconsideration of Historiography," p. 5.
[18] Review of Toynbee, *A Study of History,* IV–VI, *American Historical Review,* XLV (April, 1940), 594.
[19] "Grounds for a Reconsideration of Historiography," p. 12.
[20] *The Nature of the Social Sciences in Relation to Objectives of Instruction,* p. 20.

Only three broad conceptions of all history as actuality are possible. History is chaos and every attempt to interpret it otherwise is an illusion. History moves around in a kind of circle. History moves in a line, straight or spiral, and in some direction. The historian may seek to escape these issues by silence or by a confession of avoidance or he may face them boldly, aware of the intellectual and moral perils inherent in any decision —in his act of faith.[21]

Thus, according to Beard, the whole of unfolding social reality was either meaningless chaos, cyclical change, or directional development. There is little doubt that his own choice, resting on the faith of a lifetime despite moments of pessimism and wavering, was the third conception. Moreover, in his mind this general current, although complicated by reversals and countertendencies, was one of progress rather than retrogression.

This contention that the historian could not escape making an interpretation according to some more or less clearly defined formula was applied by Beard to all social thinkers and scholars, and not merely to historians. Writing of "all the humanistic sciences—that is, organized bodies of knowledge and thought pertaining to human affairs," he insisted that they all rested on comparable assumptions as to the nature and movement of social reality:

Such assumptions, for example, presuppose that things will continue very much as they are, that some former state of affairs will be more or less restored, or that one or more of certain current tendencies will become dominant through change. In any case here appears a theory of a continuum of some kind, a rejection of the idea that history-as-actuality is a senseless chaos of unrelated events, and a penchant for the old or the new which enters into the selection and ordering of "facts" and "dicta" for presentation as economics, sociology, political science, etc.[22]

Some months after his address to the American Historical Association, Beard in *The Open Door at Home* (1934) unveiled another formula apparently suggested to him by his reading of Machiavelli. "We are driven to a formula which seems to strike bottom: in human affairs are to be found *necessity* or things inescapable, *fortune* or the appearance of choice, and *virtue* or the capacity for choice and action."[23] To Beard's mind this was apparently an abbreviated description of social reality. Within this

[21] "Written History as an Act of Faith," pp. 228 f.
[22] "Grounds for a Reconsideration of Historiography," p. 7.
[23] *The Open Door at Home,* with G. H. E. Smith (New York: Macmillan Co., 1934), p. 34.

complex, some of the necessities presented to an American statesman, for example, were the English language, natural resources and territory, and a particular cultural heritage. The statesman was also faced with the possibility of choices as to the use of these things. Finally there was the problem of actually making the choices, and this introduced "ethical and esthetic values—one possible choice is more desirable than another with reference to some posited canon of evaluation." Having expounded this threefold formula, Beard added the strange proviso that "no other operating hypothesis of life is possible, whatever pure contemplation may have to say in the case." [24]

In *The Nature of the Social Sciences* (1934), Beard applied this formula to the frame of reference inevitably present in the mind of every human being, "a more or less definite pattern of things deemed *necessary,* things deemed *possible,* and things deemed *desirable;* and to this frame or pattern, his thought and action will be more or less consciously referred." [25] Here, it should be pointed out, Beard was clearly treating his threefold formulation as descriptive of a construct within a person's mind, whereas in *The Open Door at Home* he also seemed to be applying it to objective reality. In the one case the formula concerned things the individual *deemed* necessary, possible, or desirable, whereas in the other case it concerned things *to be found in* human affairs. It was therefore not entirely clear whether Beard believed that the frame of reference within the mind was a threefold affair, or whether he believed that only the "things deemed desirable" comprised the mental frame. [26]

In any event, his groping for formulas persisted. At the same time, he successively modified his own previous ideas and tried to fit them into revised formulas. In 1936, in *The Discussion of Human Affairs,* he formulated a broad conception called "realistic dialectics" which he attempted to stretch to cover "the totality of culture in its time unfolding." The formula for realistic dialectics, however, seemed to be more revealing of Beard's state of mind than of the social reality the formula was supposed to describe. Contrasting the approach taken in realistic dialectics with the method of the physical sciences, he explained that realistic dialectics was not concerned

---

[24] *Ibid.*

[25] *The Nature of the Social Sciences in Relation to Objectives of Instruction,* p. 181.

[26] Cf. *The Open Door at Home,* pp. 31, 34.

with trying to arrange particulars into causal chains. Rather, it took into account all "congeries of facts and uniformities" in the total span of time. It dealt with no less than "the enveloping totality."

Conflicts appear also in human affairs. Ideas and interests are found to be in opposition. Sometimes one set of ideas and interests appears to triumph over another. For example, liberalism and the middle class in France became predominant over the feudal conception and the landed aristocracy. Antagonisms between nations in time of peace often break out into armed warfare, and one contestant or the other is accounted victorious. A contradiction appears in things and is resolved for the time being.

But the victory of a class, an interest, or a nation over another seldom, if ever . . . completely extinguishes the ideas and interests of the vanquished. . . . This adjustment, compromise, or merging of survivals with victories is in substance neither the one nor the other of the conflicting sets of ideas and interests. It is in some measure a reconciliation of contradictions, a synthesis embracing both.

Under this conception, history is viewed as assertion of ideas and interests, antagonism to ideas and interests thus asserted, and resolution of the conflict by victory and adjustment. Hence the formula: thesis, antithesis, and synthesis.[27]

Careful examination of Beard's exposition of realistic dialectics results in something less than total clarity. Ideas, nations, classes, and interests were apparently all the same type of "things" among which antagonisms and contradictions appeared. Did ideas as such conflict? Did the warfare of ideas occur in individual minds, or were two or more persons or groups of persons necessarily involved? Was it, then, actually persons rather than ideas that were in conflict? Such matters were not elucidated. Nonetheless, Beard felt that his dialectical conception was the "only tenable method for taking in all relevancies." It was scientific, he thought, because it avoided making value judgments. Yet it was not confined to segregating and arranging any particular sets of facts, whether these were political, religious, military, or economic. It made an effort to confront the whole. "That this conclusion is bewildering and startling," he declared, "is no ground for rejecting it." [28]

But he had not abandoned his previously stated threefold Machia-

[27] *The Discussion of Human Affairs* (New York: Macmillan Co., 1936), pp. 115 f.

[28] *Ibid.*, pp. 116 f.; for a related criticism of Beard's "realistic dialectics," see Lloyd R. Sorenson's useful essay, "Charles A. Beard and German Historiographical Thought," *Mississippi Valley Historical Review*, XLII (September, 1955), 284 f.

vellian formula. At a 1939 gathering honoring John Dewey's eightieth birthday, Beard again discoursed on Machiavelli's notions regarding *necessità, fortuna,* and *virtù.* "The older I grow," claimed Beard, "the more inclined I am to accept the interpretation." As he explained it, *necessità* meant "the inexorable that will happen no matter what we wish or declare or assert or desire." *Fortuna* embraced "contingencies in human affairs . . . oases of freedom . . . in the great universe of necessity." *Virtù* was "not virtue in our sense, but all the force of a human personality working in contingencies amid necessity." In these words, Beard felt, Machiavelli had "described to us the nature of our world and our history. If you have a better formula, all right." [29]

A few years after this occasion Beard, in *The American Spirit* (1942), presented another tripartite formula. It was intended to classify the three possible kinds of reference frames, or "world-views," which different people carried around in their heads. Although Beard did not explicitly say so, presumably this notion of world-view was closely identified with the notion of "things deemed desirable" which he had previously expounded in *The Nature of the Social Sciences.* In any event, he now asserted:

Broadly speaking, there are three sets of world-views—contradictory in nature. One set includes all the world-views that are pessimistic in their interpretation of life and the world, with varying ethical applications to human conduct. . . . A second set includes those philosophies of life-affirmation and action which hold the mass of humanity in low esteem, are ethicless, and glorify the will-to-power in supermen, at any cost in human suffering. . . . The third set of world-views embraces all the philosophies of optimism, life-affirmation, and activism that proclaim the ethical will to overcome suffering and other evils and make the good or the better prevail in individual behavior and in social arrangements.[30]

Historical Relativism and Reality [31]

In a sense Beard's many-sided concern regarding the nature of social reality came to a focus in his thinking and writing about

[29] "America in Midpassage," in Progressive Education Association, *John Dewey and the Promise of America* (Columbus, Ohio: American Education Press, 1939), p. 19.

[30] *The American Spirit,* with Mary R. Beard (New York: Macmillan Co., 1942), p. 3; cf. "things deemed desirable" in *The Nature of the Social Sciences in Relation to Objectives of Instruction,* p. 181.

[31] For a recent perceptive commentary on Beard's historical relativism, see Cushing Strout, *The Pragmatic Revolt in American History* (New Haven,

historiography in the thirties and forties. Long before this, of course, he had taken notice of some of the methodological and epistemological aspects of the historian's attempt to study and describe the past. In 1908 he had contended that historians, like other students of human affairs, had no business mixing ethics with an objective presentation of their data.[32] As a partner of James Harvey Robinson he, too, had revolted against traditional historical approaches which he felt did not sufficiently stress the recent past and which omitted much of the relevant data, particularly economic. For many years he had been intrigued by the possible patterns to be found in history. At a 1931 regional meeting of history teachers in Annapolis, speaking of "A Historian's Quest for Light," he had complained that social scientists, including historians, seldom interested themselves in "clues to the larger whole. . . . They would rather be right about something of no importance than wrong in

Conn.: Yale University Press, 1958), pp. 50–61. Also see Elias Berg, *The Historical Thinking of Charles A. Beard* (Stockholm: Almqvist & Wiksell, 1957), pp. 57–68; Howard K. Beale, "The Professional Historian: His Theory and His Practice," *Pacific Historical Review*, XLVII (July–September, 1939), 330–41; Henry S. Commager, *The American Mind* (New Haven, Conn.: Yale University Press, 1950), pp. 303–9 and *passim;* Whitaker T. Deininger, "Skepticism and the Historical Faith of Charles Beard," *Journal of the History of Ideas*, XV (October, 1954), 573–88; Chester M. Destler, "Some Observations on Contemporary Historical Theory," *American Historical Review*, LV (April, 1950), 503–29; Harry J. Marks, "Ground under Our Feet: Beard's Relativism," *Journal of the History of Ideas*, XIV (October, 1953), 628–33; Samuel E. Morison, "Faith of a Historian," *American Historical Review*, LVI (January, 1951), 261–75; Ferdinand Schevill, "Ranke: Rise, Decline, and Persistence of a Reputation," *Journal of Modern History*, XXIV (September, 1952), 219–34; Theodore C. Smith, "The Writing of American History in America, from 1884 to 1934," *American Historical Review*, XL (April, 1935), 439–49; Lloyd R. Sorenson, "Charles A. Beard and German Historiographical Thought," *Mississippi Valley Historical Review*, XLII (September, 1955), 274–87; Morton G. White, *Social Thought in America: The Revolt against Formalism* (New York: Viking Press, 1949), pp. 204 f., 220–35; Burleigh T. Wilkins, "Frederick York Powell and Charles A. Beard: A Study in Anglo-American Historiography and Social Thought," *American Quarterly*, XI (Spring, 1959), 21–39; William A. Williams, "A Note on Charles Austin Beard's Search for a General Theory of Causation," *American Historical Review*, LXII (October, 1956), 59–80; Esmond Wright, "History: The 'New' and the Newer," *Sewanee Review*, XLIX (October–December, 1941), 479–91. More recently, Lee Benson has published a penetrating study of Beard's earlier historical methodology, as well as that of some of his later critics: *Turner and Beard: Historical Writing Reconsidered* (Glencoe: The Free Press, 1960).

[32] *Politics* (New York: Columbia University Press, 1908), p. 14.

speculations about the ultimate nature of things."[33] In Beard's attention to the problems of historians, he had continued to probe for some "philosophy of inclusion." Then in 1933 the drift of his thinking toward historical relativism became suddenly noticeable to all his colleagues in his controversial address: "Written History as an Act of Faith."[34]

One may speculate as to the factors behind Beard's renewed surge of interest in the state of historiography from the early 1930's onward. Growing disillusionment with the older Rankean "scientific history," combined with perplexity over pressing social problems and issues, doubtless played a part. In 1932 Karl Heussi's *Die Krisis des Historismus* was published, and this may have helped turn Beard's attention to the Continent. Alfred Vagts, too, brought to Beard's notice certain German writings which he might otherwise have overlooked.[35] Beard had, of course, been aware of Benedetto Croce and some of the Germans for years, but it was not until this period that a number of their conceptions, and perhaps misconceptions, seemed to enter fundamentally into his thinking. In his doubting, questioning state of mind as to American historiographical thought he was apparently ready to lend a sympathetic ear to the antipositivist notions from Europe.

Although Beard did not accept everything the Europeans offered him, he took up enough to make some of their ideas and attitudes of considerable relevance to the direction of his own thinking.[36] It is suggestive that Croce, for example, who had had little interest in or grasp of modern science, in his youth had joined the revolt against positivism and realism and had embraced subjectivism, impressionism, and relativism. Croce had stressed the present, avoided the notion of causation in history, and tended to identify philosophy and historiography.[37]

In any event, Beard, on the occasion of his 1933 presidential address, not only in effect opened a new chapter in his own thought

[33] *Proceedings of the Association of History Teachers of the Middle States and Maryland,* XXIX (1931), 12.
[34] "Written History as an Act of Faith," pp. 219–29.
[35] Personal conversation with Vagts, July 4, 1953.
[36] See, for example, Sorenson's essay, "Charles A. Beard and German Historiographical Thought," pp. 277 f.
[37] Cf. Destler, "Some Observations on Contemporary Historical Theory," pp. 504 f.

on historiography, but also signalized the start of an intensified period of self-appraisal and controversy among other American historians. His exposition seemed to mark his final break with the traditionalists of the discipline.

Reminding his fellows that the writer of history inevitably reflects his own time and cultural setting, Beard contended that written history was actually present thought about the past. From the staggering mass of facts available—even if these represented only a fraction of the events that had occurred without leaving a trace—the historian had to select and arrange in order to present his written history.

And the selection and arrangement of facts—a combined and complex intellectual operation—is an act of choice, conviction, and interpretation respecting values, is an act of thought. Facts, multitudinous and beyond calculation, are known, but they do not select themselves or force themselves automatically into any fixed scheme of arrangement in the mind of the historian. They are selected and ordered by him as he thinks.[38]

This manipulation of data, Beard explained, inevitably proceeded according to some scheme of values, explicit or assumed. It was "an act of faith" on the part of the historian as to the order and movement of history itself inasmuch as certainty and objective knowledge were not to be had regarding these matters.

Yet there was a certain ambiguity in Beard's formulation, a looseness of terms, which not only suggested the inconclusiveness of his own thinking but also added to the warmth of the discussions generated by his essay. Thus, it was easy enough for some critics to understand Beard to mean that, since history writing was after all merely a subjective operation, the historian was as justified in selecting and passing along one set of partial facts as another. A few of his bitterest critics even accused him of insulting historical scholarship by suggesting that it was a form of "propagandizing," based ultimately on the subjective whim of the historian and, what was more ominous, open to subservience to official state policy. It should be pointed out that Beard himself seems not to have thought out some of the implications of his pronouncements. Had he done so to a greater degree, he might have seen the inappropriateness of implying that the rigorous intellectual activities connected with scholarly history writing were somehow unreliable and "unscientific," and might have chosen instead to suggest that ultimately a "philosophy

---

[38] "Written History as an Act of Faith," p. 220.

of history" could not be "proved." He might have weakened much of the criticism directed at his position had he dealt more gently with Ranke and emphasized that present thought about the past could not be merely fanciful but must still bow to the dictates of logic and scientific evidence.[39]

Further incensing his opponents, while adding to the delight of his partisans, Beard went on to claim that the historian was in the position of the statesman dealing with public affairs in that he, too, would achieve immortality to the degree that he correctly sensed the path of history yet to come. The historian's choices, like the statesman's, were a "subjective decision, not a purely objective discovery."[40] Then Beard interposed a dictum that was to invite further caustic comment, namely, his "own guess" as to the direction the world was moving. Would it be toward "a capitalist dictatorship, a proletarian dictatorship, or a collectivist democracy?" His surmise, "founded on a study of long trends and on a faith in the indomitable spirit of mankind," was that collectivist democracy lay in store. His decision that the concept of directional movement best described the totality of history was his own "act of faith" as to the three possible conceptions of history: meaningless chaos, cyclical change, or directional development.[41]

Notable among the counterattacks against Beard's broadside was Theodore C. Smith's paper, "The Writing of American History in America, from 1884 to 1934," presented at the following year's meeting of the American Historical Association.[42] The "certain tendencies" that especially drew Smith's fire were the assaults, such as Beard's, on the "whole ideal of impersonality and impartiality" in historical writing, tendencies that paid "scant attention to any of the canons of historical accuracy." Singling out Beard's earlier economic interpretation, Smith admitted that, although it had been presented with "skill and plausibility," it nonetheless eliminated "the possibility of more than one interpretation" and excluded "anything like impartiality." Defending "the Ranke conception of impersonal search for truth," Smith referred scathingly to Beard's faith in "the forward movement of society toward a collectivist democ-

---

[39] Cf. Deininger, "Skepticism and the Historical Faith of Charles Beard," pp. 579 f.; also see Schevill, "Ranke: Rise, Decline, and Persistence of a Reputation," pp. 220 f.
[40] "Written History as an Act of Faith," p. 226.
[41] Ibid., p. 228.
[42] American Historical Review, XL (April, 1935), 439–49.

racy." Historians who discarded impartiality were inviting dictatorial control of scholarship as in some European countries, Smith warned. History writing should not become a political tool. If the present age were to mark the end of the impartial search for the truth, the "final extinction of a noble dream," it was his hope, Smith stoutly concluded, that his own kind of historian would "go down with our flags flying." [43]

Beard's rejoinder was not long in coming, and shortly thereafter the *American Historical Review* carried his essay, "That Noble Dream." [44] After again assailing the notion that historians could ever hope to reproduce the past exactly as it had been, Beard discussed various interpretations of history, including the economic. Freely acknowledging that the economic interpretation was partial, he insisted that every version of written history was partial, and that all were in fact interpretations. One interpretation did not exclude other interpretations. "Neither it nor any other historical hypothesis can be regarded as valid and final, on the ground that in the nature of things—documentation and the human mind—the past as it actually was cannot be known." [45] The task before historians, Beard urged, was to keep trying to make written history as complete and objective as possible, without expecting that this could ever be finally accomplished. Moreover, historians must greatly broaden their interests to include fields previously neglected in their writings.

The effort to grasp at the totality of history must and will be continued, even though the dream of bringing it to earth must be abandoned. This means a widening of the range of search beyond politics to include interests hitherto neglected—economic, racial, sex, and cultural in the most general sense of the term. Certainly by this broadening process the scholar will come nearer to the actuality of history as it has been. [46]

In 1936 Beard published *The Discussion of Human Affairs,* which was strongly suggestive of his reading of such writers as Croce, Karl Heussi, and Kurt Riezler. [47] In this book Beard further elaborated the notions previously sketched in his recent historiographical

[43] *Ibid.,* pp. 447–49.
[44] *American Historical Review,* XLI (October, 1935), 74–87.
[45] *Ibid.,* p. 84.
[46] *Ibid.,* pp. 86 f.
[47] See Sorenson, "Charles A. Beard and German Historiographical Thought," pp. 278 f., 284 f.

articles, particularly the idea that the historian can only select and organize fragments from a vast totality according to some scheme of posited values. Discussing the frame of reference concept, Beard hedged against extreme relativism by claiming such frames to be "relatively few in number." [48] He argued against the theory that history is cyclical, that it repeats itself. Instead he claimed that "realistic dialectics," the broad and rather hazy formulation previously referred to, was the "only tenable method for taking in all relevancies and giving order to them." Events in history were not determined. Historiography, he claimed, could describe the conditions that had made possible the developments of the past, but it could not show their inevitability. It could examine, for example, the conditions surrounding the emergence of the United States as a republic in 1787, without proving this outcome to have been unavoidable.[49]

In a 1937 article, "Currents of Thought in Historiography," Beard and Vagts undertook to appraise some of the recent Continental thinking in this field, including "the new and profound work done by German scholars between 1919 and 1933." [50] This European historiographical speculation, they complained, had produced little effect in America. However, the "latest Continental contribution to the subject," the work of Friedrich Meinecke, received no sympathy from the authors, who saw Meinecke as "the historian of State Reason," the apparent epitome of "the bureaucratization of German intelligence." Referring again to the several broad conceptions open to the thinker, they asserted that "the historian may, if he can, decide whether he desires to be a maker of history after the style of the Enlightenment or a victim of it in the manner of Ranke and Meinecke." If this was Beard's statement, it indicated that he was still ambiguously tending to intermingle in his mind the notion of a philosophy of history—or possibly even the advocacy of a cause— with the more prosaic labors of historical research and scholarship.

After rejecting Meinecke's "historism," Beard and Vagts also attacked the tendency of American historians to make farfetched analogies with the organisms of biology and the substances and forces of physics. "Historiography must abandon such assumptions and procedures and return to its own subject matter—personalities,

[48] *The Discussion of Human Affairs*, p. 111.
[49] *Ibid.*, pp. 116–18.
[50] *American Historical Review*, XLII (April, 1937), 464 ff.

events, human institutions, ideas, and interests in the time span."[51]
Here Riezler and Croce could help:

Kurt Riezler seems to come near the truth in conceiving history as ideas
and interests ever evolving in time. Ideas change in the minds of thinkers
through inner examination and under the impacts of interests, psychological and material. Interests, both psychological and material, change
under the impacts of ideas. All this occurs in time and history as actuality.
Akin to Riezler's formulation and lending support to it is Croce's exposition of the relation of theory and practice—a theme that has so far received scant attention by American historians. Theory tends to conform
to practice, even though it may appear to be flatly opposed to practice.
Practice tends to conform to theory, however wide the divergence.[52]

Regardless of whether Beard had or had not captured the essence
of Riezler's conception of the dynamic interaction of "idea" and
"interest"—and footnoted doubts have been expressed on this score [53]
—Beard and Vagts did go on to make clear that they were not en-
dorsing an unlimited relativism. The fact that only a limited number of frames of reference existed showed that the range of subjective choice for the historian was narrowed sharply. There were
fewer "distinct schemes of reference" than there were historians
because "the number of social orders," such as "liberal, fascist, and
communist," was limited. This, then, was "a limited relativity, not a
chaos." Although the old illusion that one could possibly know the
totality had been disposed of, "intuitionalism" had not been restored.
The careful methods of scholarship were still necessary.[54]

After this 1937 blast against certain Continental tendencies while
welcoming others, combined with an attempt to reassure American
historians that his relativism was reasonable and limited, Beard for
a number of years was primarily occupied in other subjects and only
incidentally alluded to his historiographical position as such. In
1939 *America in Midpassage* appeared, with one chapter devoted to
"Frames of Social Thought." [55] Here, again, it was pointed out that
thinkers in every area of human affairs, as well as practical men in
such fields as politics and economics, engaged in a value-based selecting process and in effect made interpretations as to the "nature of

[51] *Ibid.*, p. 478.

[52] *Ibid.*, p. 479.

[53] Sorenson, "Charles A. Beard and German Historiographical Thought,"
pp. 284 f.

[54] "Currents of Thought in Historiography," pp. 480 ff.

[55] *America in Midpassage,* with Mary R. Beard (New York: Macmillan Co.,
1939); see especially p. 919.

history as actuality." Reviewing several of Toynbee's volumes in 1940, Beard charged the author with not having "made up his own mind on the point of the ultimate design of the universe about which he is speaking at great length." [56]

In 1943 Beard displayed a reawakened interest in Brooks and Henry Adams. Not only did he write the introduction for a new edition of Brooks's *The Law of Civilization and Decay,*[57] but he also published an *Atlantic Monthly* article on "Historians at Work: Brooks and Henry Adams." [58]

It is appropriate to recall [Beard reminded his readers] that all great human causes turn on theories of history, that all the modern revolutions which have shaken the world have been inspired and justified by theories of history. Every piece of philosophic, economic, or political writing either presents such a theory or rests on assumptions, articulate or tacit, derived from it.[59]

He had high praise for the Adamses as historians and for their keen understanding of the course of history, an understanding which he believed had been verified by subsequent events. From this time onward, through the remaining years of his life, Beard seemed to find new inspiration in the Adams' theories.

Beard's final writing in the field of historiography, other than incidental references or book reviews, was his contribution to the 1946 *Report of the Committee on Historiography.*[60] One of the grounds for reconsidering historiography, he argued, was the existing inconsistency in attitudes regarding the relation between history and practical affairs. "History can scarcely be at the same time a useless old almanac and the ultimate source of knowledge and 'laws' for demonstrating the invincible validity of policies proposed or already in practice." [61] Brooks and Henry Adams again won special praise for their "comprehension of events" and their insight into coming history.[62] Greater precision in the terminology of historical writing was needed, Beard insisted. In a signed footnote, Beard and Vagts indicated their dislike of the terms "cause" and "causality" in written history:

[56] Review of Toynbee, *A Study of History,* IV–VI, p. 593.
[57] Brooks Adams, *The Law of Civilization and Decay* (New York: Alfred A. Knopf, 1943).
[58] *Atlantic Monthly,* CLXXI (April, 1943), 87–93.
[59] *Ibid.,* p. 88.
[60] *Theory and Practice in Historical Study.*
[61] *Ibid.,* p. 5.
[62] *Ibid.,* p. 13.

Any definition of a complicated aggregation of events, conditions, and personalities in history-as-actuality, such as the French Revolution or the American Revolution, is an arbitrary delimitation in time and space—an isolation of the "data" in the mind or the imagination, not outside the mind or the imagination (as in chemistry, for example); and the assignment of cause or causes to anything that cannot be accurately defined and isolated in fact is at best a highly dubious intellectual operation. In any case, if Event A is assigned as the cause of Event B, the act is wholly arbitrary as far as time is concerned, and any person who does not arbitrarily stop at Event A will ask: "What is the cause of Event A and so on backward into the darkness of prehistory?" Where historians are concerned, as they should be, with consequential and coexisting relations between events and personalities and interests, which are intimate in nature and have the appearance of necessity, they can describe such relations in terms more precise than those of causality. . . .[63]

Beard apparently felt that unless causal relationships could be traced back *ad infinitum* to some dim first cause the notion of causality was of little utility. The footnote was not entirely lucid as to whether he believed that causal relationships among the complicated events of human history, aside from their infinitely greater complexity, differed from *causal relationships as such* in other areas or parts of reality—"as in chemistry, for example." Yet obviously— Beard to the contrary notwithstanding—the relationships among antecedent and consequent chemical events and conditions, whatever the terminology adopted to describe the relationships, have been rewardingly studied without tracing a preceding chain of chemical events "backward into the darkness of prehistory."

Taken as a whole, Beard's historical relativism as developed in the final decade and a half of his life was an unfinished product. It is impossible to say exactly what his full and undivided intellectual effort might have yielded. As it was, he imperfectly distinguished between the interpretive activity entailed in the selecting and organizing of historical data, and the broader concept of a philosophy of history. As Deininger has succinctly put it: "Confusions resulted in part from Beard's tendency to lump together a variety of historiographical problems, epistemological, psychological, and methodological. . . . He seemed to imply at times that epistemological incompleteness meant selective arbitrariness."[64] Still, Beard's historiographical writings did help to stimulate other American thinkers into critical self-analysis. This in itself was no mean achievement.

[63] *Ibid.*, pp. 136 f.
[64] Deininger, "Skepticism and the Historical Faith of Charles Beard," p. 575.

Revised Realities of Politics [65]

Concomitantly with his labors in the field of historiography, Beard during this final period of his intellectual career also continued revising and "correcting" his earlier thought as to the underlying factors in politics, and particularly as to the relationship between economics and politics. Near the beginning of the period he reissued his *Economic Basis of Politics* (1934) with a newly written preface, followed shortly thereafter by another printing of his 1913 volume, *An Economic Interpretation of the Constitution of the United States* (1935), with a new introduction. The other main effort along these lines was a final edition, toward the close of his life, of his *Economic Basis of Politics* (1945), with substantial amendment in the form of an added chapter. Interspersed with these three works dealing specifically with the subject, and reflecting their modified ideas, were, of course, various other writings touching incidentally on it, such as brief book reviews and passages in history or foreign policy volumes. The combined effect, although not previously unheralded, was a considerable further revision of Beard's former thought.

The 1934 reissue of Beard's *Economic Basis of Politics,* coming twelve years after the first edition of the book and eighteen years after he had delivered the Amherst lectures on which it had originally been based, was in effect his commentary on his own political theorizing as it had evolved since World War I days. In answer to criticisms of "vagueness" directed at his formulation, Beard's defense, in his new preface, was that vagueness was inescapable "in any interpretation of history and politics, for the reason that, in dealing with human affairs, the student is not dealing with problems in physics or, to speak still more concretely, with problems in hydraulics." Just as the student of human affairs must not pretend that his subject matter is something it is not, he must also not omit obviously relevant factors. Since omission of economics made political science "an unreal and ghostly formalism," the realistic student of politics had to take fullest possible account of "the known economic relevancies." [66]

With this opening, Beard was enabled to soften his earlier empha-

[65] Cf. Strout, *The Pragmatic Revolt in American History,* pp. 105–11; also see Berg, *The Historical Thinking of Charles A. Beard,* pp. 18–56.

[66] *The Economic Basis of Politics* (new ed.; Alfred A. Knopf, 1934), pp. ii–v.

sis, perhaps already having in his mind his subsequently adopted threefold Machiavellian formula as to things necessary, possible, and desirable in human affairs. He still believed there were "immense areas of necessity in the world of human occurrences—biological and economic necessity." Yet, "in the philosophical sense," he had never been a "convinced determinist, in the all-embracing sense of the term." However, neither Bolshevism in Russia, Fascism in Italy, Hitlerism in Germany, nor the New Deal in America could be explained "without fundamental reference to preceding economic conditions and to economic objectives." Citing figures to show security holdings among various groups in modern Russia, much as he had once used statistics on the security holdings of the American founding fathers, Beard claimed that his Russian figures upheld the contention that even in a supposedly "classless society" there were economic groups based on occupations and possessions. Here he seemed once more to be revising the "grand conclusion" of *Federalist* No. 10 in a fundamental point, namely, the point he had made in the 1922 edition to the effect that ownership of property was irrelevant to possession of political power.[67] Now again he was implying that Madison helped explain "the old problem of the distribution of wealth" even in a noncapitalist society, although Beard qualified this by saying that "the distribution of wealth remains a matter, if not an issue, of politics."[68]

In 1935 Beard took occasion to reprint his 1913 work on the economic interpretation of the Constitution. Endeavoring now, more than twenty years after its initial appearance, to explain some of his reasons for originally publishing the book, he claimed that the economic conflict in connection with the adoption of the Constitution "had been so long disregarded, I sought to redress the balance by emphasis, 'naturally' perhaps."[69] He had aimed, he explained in his newly penned introduction, to re-emphasize those "realistic features of economic conflict, stress, and strain, which my masters had, for some reason, left out of it, or thrust far into the background as incidental rather than fundamental." Acknowledging that he had been familiar with the ideas of various political thinkers including Aristotle, the founding fathers, and Karl Marx, Beard nonetheless

---

[67] *Ibid.* (1st ed.; 1922), p. 99.
[68] *Ibid.* (new ed.; 1934), p. vii.
[69] *An Economic Interpretation of the Constitution of the United States* (2nd ed.; New York: Macmillan Co., 1935), pp. vii f.

now edged away from this former stress on economics as the prime mover in politics and contented himself with pointing instead to the "callings, occupations, professions, and interests" in which the framers had been engaged. "I have never been able to discover an all-pervading determinism in history," he declared. "In that field of study I find what Machiavelli found, *virtù, fortuna,* and *necessità* [*sic*], although the boundaries between them cannot be sharply delimited." [70]

Following and accompanying this republication of his two earlier works, Beard in widely scattered comments, sometimes in connection with his writings on historical relativism, attempted to defend or further define his position. Rejecting allegations that his ideas had been Marxian in origin, he claimed in the *American Historical Review* that they had rested on much earlier documentation, namely, on *Federalist* No. 10.[71] In *The Open Door at Home* he specifically criticized the Marxian concept of class for ignoring many other relevant bonds of unity among men, such as race, language, culture, and patriotism.[72] In the *New Republic* he insisted that his economic interpretation could most accurately be called a "positive and realistic interpretation of history." [73] Moreover, as he made clear in *Public Policy and the General Welfare* (1941), in his belief economic conflicts and acquisitive instincts would enter as fully into political processes and power struggles under one economic and social system as under another.[74] But certainly, as he declared in *The Republic* (1943), he did not believe that economics wholly determined politics. "I sometimes think," he added, "that politics is more of a determining force in history than economics." [75]

Perhaps the most notable statement of Beard's latter-day thinking on the fundamental realities of politics was his 1945, and last, version of *The Economic Basis of Politics,* particularly the newly added chapter. By this date his position had moved so far from its progressive era beginning that use of the word "economic" to describe it is scarcely justified. Reverting to a usage he had once seemed to shun, he claimed that the "economic man," as a result of

[70] *Ibid.,* pp. xiv, xvi.
[71] "That Noble Dream," p. 85.
[72] *The Open Door at Home,* p. 169.
[73] "That Promise of American Life," *New Republic,* LXXXI (February 6, 1935), 351.
[74] (New York: Farrar & Rinehart, 1941), pp. 157 f.
[75] (New York: Viking Press, 1943), p. 316.

recent vast changes in the functions of government, had been losing much of his old influence and power to the "political man." [76] But further, because of the cataclysmic effects and ramifications of global wars, both of these fictional characters were now being brusquely pushed and shoved by the "military man."

In ways utterly immeasurable and indescribable, two world wars have also altered the social, intellectual, and moral setting in which the theory of the economic basis of politics was discussed prior to 1914. From Aristotle's time down through the centuries the theory had been limited by the condition that economic forces operate freely only in the absence of military force . . . but during the long period between the close of the Napoleonic wars in 1815 and the opening of the first World War in 1914, the conditional clause, which severely limited the theory, had been regarded as largely academic, particularly in the United States. Now a single generation has experienced the shattering impacts of military force around the globe on a scale beyond all precedents. Not an aspect of life— economic, political, intellectual or emotional—has escaped its actions and devastations. During the momentous years since 1914 "the military man" has again entered into full competition with "the economic man" and "the political man" for power over the state and its fortunes.[77]

In its altered emphasis this statement virtually obliterated Beard's earlier notions on the subject. He now read in a new light Daniel Webster's old axiom to the effect that economics determines politics only "in the absence of the sword." The years of unprecedented violence in the world had apparently convinced Beard once and for all that the "rough stuff of reality" was more than economics. The element of military force was now admitted to a major place in his concept of social reality. Not only on the world scene but in domestic politics as well—particularly in dictatorships such as Russia and Fascist Italy—he saw an expanded role for naked force in human affairs.[78]

In addition to this greatly increased emphasis on military factors, Beard in his 1945 presentation drew new attention to the other noneconomic bases of politics as well. It was the same conceptual broadening process that had been going on in his mind since the 1920's (as noted above in chapter 6). He had little patience now with "oversimplified economic interpretations" that held economic interests to be the sole or even main "causes" of political phenomena

[76] *The Economic Basis of Politics* (3rd rev. ed.; 1945), p. 72.
[77] *Ibid.*, p. 75.
[78] *Ibid.*, pp. 85–90.

in peace or war. Among the factors which, according to Beard, realistic students must not omit from consideration were ambitious leaders, feelings of popular resentment over real or alleged wrongs, a passion for revenge, irrational doctrines of race, antidemocratic sentiments, and other elements.[79]

Moreover, because of developments within the United States since World War I, *Federalist* No. 10, he now seemed to suggest, no longer applied. For example, by means of the large-scale regulatory, fiscal, and other economic tasks undertaken by government in the preceding quarter of a century, various economic interests *"once treated as primarily private and as forming the chief economic basis of politics, were made dependent upon politics to an extent which in this respect signalized a breach with the past."* No longer standing "outside the government," these great interests were now so closely linked to the fortunes of politics that they themselves "assumed a semi-political and semi-official character." [80]

Exactly how, then, was economics still a basis of politics, according to Beard's final theoretical formulation of the matter? "Politics," he asserted, "including military aspects, must have an economic basis or perish. People must have food, clothing, and shelter before and while they engage in politics and fighting." Yet this way of putting it, rather than portraying politics as being fundamentally imbedded in, and an integral part of, the very processes of getting food and fighting, tended, except for the logistical connection, to divorce politics from them. Regardless of the nature of economic institutions, and regardless of whether the political system was democracy or dictatorship, the state must have "an economic underwriting sufficient to sustain it" so that it would not "wither away." [81] In effect the logistical basis of politics had replaced Beard's "economic basis of politics." Where once he had maintained that economic interests and motives comprised the real stuff of political dynamics, he now was saying little more than that men must eat before they can engage in any human activities.

Beard ended his 1945 book in a series of "formulas" purporting to be a restatement of "the theory of the economic basis of politics." Some of his formulas appeared to be simple and straightforward: "In the absence of military force, economic interests will come to

[79] *Ibid.*, pp. 90 f.
[80] *Ibid.*, pp. 94–97.
[81] *Ibid.*, p. 107.

expression in political power." Some sounded truistic or insignificant: "If historical experience is any guide, drastic changes in economy will find expressions in politics; and, on the other hand, changes in the functions of government will be followed by repercussions in economy." Others seemed ambiguous or vague: "If private economic interests, having achieved political power, cannot provide an efficient economic underpinning of society in the long run, they will lose their sovereignty to politics or military force." [82] In any event, the formulas covered a miscellaneous assortment of propositions, suggesting that Beard was fearful lest he omit any conceivably relevant factor. His statement concluded:

The realities to which the above formulas refer come within the sweep of total history in time. They are not self-contained and independent "tracts of matter and force." They are enmeshed in other human characteristics and events—biological, mental, moral, artistic, and religious—that also appear in total history. The origins of total history, like that of the physical universe, are shrouded in the darkness of pre-history, and the law or laws of total history, if there be any, have not been discovered. Given the fragmentary evidences available, these origins and law or laws cannot be discovered by the human mind. Hence the above formulas of economics and politics are not "laws of history" but are in the nature of conditioned and conditional axioms respecting probabilities of high degree, subject to modifications by the acquisition of new knowledge and by the experiences of a future that cannot be forecast with any mathematical or descriptive certainty worthy of the name.[83]

Thus, Beard's final revised thought respecting the "bases of politics," merging with his notions of historical relativism, resulted in a greatly qualified and hedged-in formulation to describe his conception of the nature of social reality. To the end of his life he emphasized that "thinking and writing about government or any aspect thereof" were necessarily controlled and directed by the same kind of built-in mental framework that guided the historian's labors.[84] The succeeding stages in his "interpretation" of politics and history, had he lived to publish further works on the subject, would doubtless have been interesting to follow.[85]

[82] *Ibid.*, pp. 112 f.

[83] *Ibid.*, p. 114; cf. Williams, "A Note on Charles Austin Beard's Search for a General Theory of Causation," pp. 73, 80.

[84] "Neglected Aspects of Political Science," *American Political Science Review*, XLII (April, 1948), 212.

[85] Cf. William Beard's comments on his father's "unfinished business," in *The Economic Basis of Politics and Related Writings* (New York: Vintage Books, 1957), pp. ix f.

CHAPTER X
THE RESTORATION OF IDEAS AND ETHICS

The Power of Ideas

As Beard's multifaceted conception of social reality thus continued developing through the years of depression, New Deal, and war, one of the characteristic accompaniments was the growing importance he placed on "ideas," using the term in a broad sense. This was, of course, no sudden shift on his part. In the 1920's he had already tended to acknowledge the significance of ideas as factors in social life.[1] Yet in comparison with the earlier days there was a considerable difference. During the progressive era he had typically considered the ideational elements to be only a pale reflection of the rough stuff of reality. In those years he had intended no compliment in characterizing a writer's work as dealing largely in "theory," "abstractions," "philosophy," "spiritual factors," or "metaphysics." These aspects, in his mind, had been more or less equated with "the Ouija board" and "myth." Certainly they were not to be taken very seriously by the realistic student.

In the light of these earlier views, therefore, Beard's later attitude concerning the relationship between mental constructs and external reality represented, if not almost a reversal, at least a great evolution. In a 1939 book review, for example, he could speak in sober appraisal of "the great schemes of thought" with which the author dealt, whereas eighteen years earlier, with tongue in cheek, he had characterized the political ideas accompanying "the world of reality" as "a great deal of talk." [2] Now he insisted on the need for exploring "the assumptions, philosophy, and methodology of the history of ideas," as well as closer attention to "the relations of ideas and

[1] See above, pp. 125 ff.
[2] Review of Bingham, *Man's Estate, Common Sense*, VIII (June, 1939), 24; but cf. review of Merriam, *American Political Ideas, 1865–1917, New Republic*, XXV (January 19, 1921), 236.

interests." [3] Now his complaint was that "the study of the history of ideas" was being unduly neglected in this country.[4] By 1944 he could remark with satisfaction that such study was "beginning to receive in the United States some of the thoughtful attention it deserves." [5]

Beard's own study was apparently convincing him that, as he pointed out in *The Open Door at Home* (1934), economic crises and emergencies did not exist solely outside the human mind. They could not be entirely "separated from the operation of thinking." Even the hardest-headed practical man who scorned theoretical abstraction could scarcely admit that he had "no *idea*" of what he was about.[6] Sometimes Beard indicated that ideas were important in history "with or without relation to the world of external events." [7] But usually he related ideas intimately to external reality. Their actual function, however, was not always spelled out. He often spoke figuratively when alluding to the role of ideas. At times his writings suggested that ideas lagged behind objective social phenomena, whereas at other times he indicated that they preceded them.

At various stages in history, explained Beard in the *Virginia Quarterly Review* in 1935, "a conflict in ideas" develops. Men become aware of the fact that ideas appropriate to a former age are no longer appropriate to "the changed order of things." Some leaders, sensing this maladjustment, may propose corrective action, and "at that point in history an adjustment of some kind takes place— compromise, surrender, or open conflict." [8] In *America in Midpassage* (1939), however, Beard declared that, "as in physical nature the flash of lightning always precedes the roll of thunder, so in human affairs the flame of thought has always gone before a transformation in the social arrangements of mankind." [9]

[3] Review of Gabriel, *The Course of American Democratic Thought: An Intellectual History since 1815, American Historical Review,* XLVI (October, 1940), 165.

[4] *The Republic* (New York: Viking Press, 1943), p. 28.

[5] Foreword, Don Marion Wolfe (ed.), *Leveller Manifestoes of the Puritan Revolution* (New York: T. Nelson & Sons, 1944), p. vii.

[6] *The Open Door at Home,* with G. H. E. Smith (New York: Macmillan Co., 1934), pp. 2 f.

[7] "Currents of Thought in Historiography" (with Alfred Vagts), *American Historical Review,* XLII (April, 1937), 461.

[8] "Constitution and States' Rights," *Virginia Quarterly Review,* XI (October, 1935), 495.

[9] *America in Midpassage,* with Mary R. Beard (New York: Macmillan Co., 1939), p. 860.

In any event, there was little doubt in Beard's mind during his later years that ideas in numerous ways were a great force and influence in human affairs. Their power to set in train substantial achievements was shown in practical politics, where so often the schemes and dreams of obscure cranks and "third parties" in one age became the great programs and institutions of a succeeding age.[10] Their influence might be adverse, too. Beard in *The Republic* (1943) expressed the opinion that "Greek metaphysics," for example, had done damage rather than good "to the Western world and to Christian thought and practice." Elsewhere he indicated that Adam Smith's thought had entered powerfully "into the shaping of history." Likewise, the concepts of such men as Locke and Rousseau, even if the ideas were impractical or defective, had exercised "enormous" influence in the Western world.[11]

The relation of ideas to concrete reality, and especially their connection to its political and economic aspects, was a topic that often engaged Beard during the years of depression and war toward the close of his life. He wondered not only about the linkage between mental constructs and the external world, but also about the correspondence or lack of correspondence between such concepts and the language and symbols that human beings manipulated so dexterously. This is not to say that he was suddenly preoccupying himself with philosophical systems such as nominalism, conceptualism, realism, or idealism. But he did feel that lack of semantic precision often underlay the failure to understand the real world and occasioned much of the cloudy thinking about economic and political problems. In the early thirties, when discussion of economic issues and depression waxed hot, he wrote:

Among the new spooks introduced into the discussion of American politics is "the profit system." Along with the Constitution, freedom of contract, private property and manifest destiny, the profit system is to be fought for and died for. . . . If we turn, however, to the works of economists who have given most thought to the subject in its theoretical and realistic bearings, we find that the term is as elusive as moonshine.

[10] "Are Third Parties Futile?" *Today,* III (December 22, 1934), 24; cf. also Beard's references to "the force of ideas in history," *The Republic,* p. 1.

[11] *The Enduring Federalist* (ed.) (New York: Doubleday & Co., 1948), p. 20; see also *The Republic,* p. 301, and "Grounds for a Reconsideration of Historiography," in Merle E. Curti (ed.), *Theory and Practice in Historical Study: A Report of the Committee on Historiography* (Social Science Research Council Bulletin, No. 54, 1946), p. 8.

. . . The thrice-blessed words "profit system". . . do not exactly describe anything that intelligent persons should fight and die for. On the contrary, it would seem that each political and economic prestidigitator who thrusts this spook into our affrighted gaze should get down to brass tacks and tell us *just what he means* when he performs the miracle.[12]

Here Beard appeared to be objecting primarily to the fallacy of confusing vague symbols with precise concepts. Puzzled in his own mind as to exactly how changing social reality could be grasped by the human intellect and effectively dealt with, he tended to overdraw the difficulty of communicating meanings among intelligent discussants of economic and political issues. At this point, too, Croce and the German philosophers of history may have been impressing him with the obstacles to meaningful thought.

Further reading and reflection, however, seemed to make Beard draw back from extreme relativism. Recognizing that time and circumstance conditioned all discussions of human affairs, he nonetheless decided that this need not make men helpless victims of their age and surroundings, trapped in a "Serbonian bog of relativity and total impotence." The insights of Croce, the "profound and courageous Italian scholar," need not lead one into a frustrating subjectivism. "If not permitted to climb Mount Olympus, we may perhaps stand a little bit outside ourselves and look at ourselves. That is one of the profound discoveries of modern psychology, especially social psychology."[13] By the early forties Beard was ready to grant that a considerable degree of semantic precision was, after all, possible:

Words carefully chosen do convey ideas, with more or less precision, to persons competent out of study and knowledge to reproduce these ideas in their minds. Yet the exactness is not the kind of exactness that appears when a three-foot model of a hundred-foot machine is made with mechanical conformity to the original. This is another way of saying that no book on government tells the whole truth and nothing but the truth about any system of government, for government is life, not mechanics.[14]

---

[12] "Blessed Profit System," *New Republic*, LXXXI (December 26, 1934), 188 f.

[13] "Historiography and the Constitution," in Conyers Read (ed.), *The Constitution Reconsidered* (New York: Columbia University Press, 1938), p. 161; also see Beard's remarks in *Virginia Quarterly Review*, XVII (Autumn, 1941), 600, and in "Grounds for a Reconsideration of Historiography," p. 9.

[14] *Public Policy and the General Welfare* (New York: Farrar & Rinehart, 1941), p. 171.

Moreover, with Locke, Beard saw that the "internal operations of our minds," as well as external phenomena, were a valid source of that experience which supplied "the materials of thinking." That is, both introspection and the perception of external objects were "real forces" in human affairs. He acknowledged that there was "a great deal of sense" in Locke's position in his *Essay on Human Understanding,* even if the statement was "by no means the whole truth of the business." [15] As Beard viewed the matter, "the mind does things with experiences. Ideas received by discussion and reading are as much a part of experience as sticks and stones seen and felt, and by reflection ideas are 'turned over in the mind.' Ideas are 'forces' in history, in the making of events." [16]

Searching further for "light on men's thinking," Beard examined other aspects of the relation between ideas and concrete reality. How did ideas relate to "interests"—a term Beard for decades had been fond of using in realistic vein? Whereas in the earlier days he had tended to divorce "interests" from "ideas," emphasizing the former while discounting the latter, he now habitually linked them, both in usage and in meaning:

In a strict sense there are no material interests outside the human spirit. A mountain full of iron standing in an empty world is not an interest. It becomes such only when human attention and affection are turned to the use of it and the apportionment of benefits. There are, to repeat again and again, no ideas without interests, and no interests without ideas.[17]

In this dual conception of ideas and interests Beard's latter-day "economic interpretation" found its place, and this conception in turn was assimilated into the even broader notion of "realistic dialects" which was supposed to take in "all relevancies." [18] Here, again, the Continental thinkers came into the picture. "The answer most satisfactory to me," wrote Beard in 1938, "is the one formulated by Kurt Riezler: History is a manifestation of ideas and interests, evolving and involving in time." [19]

Thus in the last period of his life, Beard—regardless of the general validity or clarity of his thought—had definitely discarded his

---

[15] Prefatory note, Samuel J. Konefsky, *Chief Justice Stone and the Supreme Court* (New York: Macmillan Co., 1945), p. xiv.

[16] "The Interpretation of Events," *Events,* II (December, 1937), 445.

[17] *The Open Door at Home,* pp. 157 f.

[18] See pp. 147 f., above.

[19] "Historiography and the Constitution," p. 160.

earlier disdain for "ideas." If he had not gone all the way to an implicit philosophical idealism, at least he had come to acknowledge the power of ideas in the real world. He had come to believe that, if ideas could not literally transform physical nature, at least they could move men, and men could move mountains.

The Ideal and the Real

Still, as Beard had long been convinced, mental perception of an objective reality did not automatically dictate a particular course of human action relative to that reality. At some point in such cases of more or less intentional action, value judgments not necessarily entailed in the objective phenomena entered the picture and set the course.

Although in his earlier years he had felt "ethics" to be outside the proper scope of the scientific-minded student of politics and history, in middle life he had tended to acknowledge that realistic social inquiry had to take account of men's values as well as of the more tangible data. In the late 1920's he had begun sensing the need for a new twentieth-century social philosophy built around an "ethical center." [20] By the thirties and forties, he had become greatly concerned over the neglect of "ethics" and over "the crisis in thought" running deeper than objective phenomena such as idle factories or the realities of war:

This crisis lies in the discovery that science, facts, and the scientific method do not, and in the nature of things, cannot provide inescapable and irrefutable policies. No scientific finding of fact dictates any policy of action respecting the facts. The possibilities of carrying out policies, and ways and means of executing them, may be more or less successfully disclosed by science. But policies themselves are moral decisions—the assertions of moral values (one way or another)—and the roots of moral decisions lie deep in the human spirit. [21]

Beard in this period of his life had come to feel strongly that cherished human values—such as peace, civil liberties, and economic justice—were being unduly frustrated or frittered away through ignorance and blindness on the part of intellectual and political leaders. He feared that preoccupation with external symptoms was distracting attention from the fundamental questions of ends and

[20] See pp. 130 ff., above.

[21] Review of Lindeman, *Wealth and Culture, Saturday Review of Literature,* XIII (March 14, 1936), 21.

means. The nature and source of ends had long been ignored. In his view, such considerations were of deepest significance in relation to public policy and to the guidance of human action generally.

When, on the eve of the New Deal, the President's Research Committee on Social Trends issued its book-length report, Beard sharply questioned the contention that its "findings" were purely factual. Even if the committee had presented objectively verifiable facts concerning social trends, did "the conclusions inevitably flow from the facts admitted to court?" Obviously not, he claimed. The study not only contained selected facts, but it also expressed opinions, judgments, and values. And, despite long-standing illusions to the contrary among American social thinkers, values did not flow from "exhaustive surveys of facts." [22]

Writing early in 1933, at the outset of the New Deal, Beard paid tribute to empirical method but claimed that too much had been expected of it. Empiricism was "absolutely indispensable to disclosing the realities which condition action," but it was no "substitute for thought, for purpose, for will." Scientific method was, after all, "only a method." He felt that a profound intellectual revolution was at hand: "The subjection of science to ethical and esthetic purpose." [23]

In *The Open Door at Home*, Beard dwelt further on the crisis in thought and its relation to ideal ends and practical policy. "The predicament in which the nations of the earth are now floundering," he asserted, "is a crisis in thought as well as economy." He explained that each dilemma and emergency was involved in the other, and neither could be resolved by itself. The essence of the economic crisis was that the present economic situation did not accord with men's "hopes, aspirations, and values." On the other hand, the crisis in thought had grown out of the ethical void resulting from the secularization of the nation-state in past centuries. After "theological supremacy and assurance" had been disrupted, science of itself had been incapable of providing "certainty, understanding, and unequivocal direction to policy and practice." [24]

In the face of these crises, why were economists, political scientists, and other students of human affairs seemingly so unable to

[22] Review of President's Research Committee on Social Trends, *Recent Social Trends in the United States, Yale Review*, XXII (March, 1933), 596 f.

[23] "Limitations to the Application of Social Science Implied in Recent Social Trends," *Social Forces*, XI (May, 1933), 506, 510.

[24] *The Open Door at Home*, pp. 1, 4.

furnish practical guidance? The root of their apparent helplessness, he felt, lay in the fact that the students seeking to understand man had so long ignored the moral and ethical side of man, as well as other relevant realities. Economists, for example, had fallen victim to their own fictional economic man whose greed produced general good only because they had stretched logic and evaded moral issues by inventing a preposterous "invisible hand." Political scientists, in their seeming realism, had busied themselves with descriptions of institutions and minute facts, "without much reference to any ends, purposes, or expectations." Thus, economists confronted by economic breakdown suddenly found their medicine useless, and political scientists in the presence of imperialism and the wreckage of democracy were as confused as the economists. Accordingly, "no positive commands to policy and statecraft" were forthcoming, and the wisdom of great thinkers of the past had fallen into neglect.[25]

Looking back at this intellectual heritage of Western civilization, Beard now tended to emphasize its ethical foundations. Where once he had marveled at past insights into the economic "realities," he now especially noticed the "assertions of values" by great leaders of thought. The teachings of men such as Socrates, Plato, Christ, and Confucius had not presumed to rest on so-called realities but in essence had been "assertions of good submitted to the judgment of mankind." At the center of these systems of thought had lain "a conception of the good life . . . on this earth." It was a conception, he suggested, which had gained the support of mounting historical evidence "in the sifting that accompanies relativity."[26]

Thus Beard's position in *The Open Door at Home* was that the points of reference for "the triangulation of policy" were not inherent in the objective data or the facts. They were ethical and esthetic standards that could not be "proved." The ideal elements residing in such standards were simply "posited and asserted." Human affairs, then, comprised a great many aspects, including the idealistic and ethical, and did not consist merely of matter and motion endlessly fulfilling a predetermined fate. A crisis existed because of "the assumption that something better or more satisfactory than the present disarray of things is possible, as well as desirable.

[25] *Ibid.,* pp. 11 f.; cf. Beard's comments on Adam Smith's economics in "Grounds for a Reconsideration of Historiography," p. 8.
[26] *The Open Door at Home,* p. 146.

. . . A crash among stars is no crisis but a fulfillment of predetermined relations." [27]

In these depression-era pronouncements regarding "the ideal and the real," Beard's relativist historiography and the notions associated with it were frequently implied. When addressing himself to what he conceived to be political and economic realities, he was simultaneously shedding light on his views regarding the methodological shortcomings in the social sciences. When urging that realism on the part of thinkers and policy makers required greater attention to ethics, he was likewise discoursing on the built-in mental frame of reference guiding every human being:

> Every thinker, large or small, even when using the scientific method in dealing with human affairs, has in his own mind a scheme of ethical and esthetic values, or frame of reference, which controls more or less his selection of problems to be studied, facts to be gathered, and policies of action to be determined upon. Thus the assertion of ethical and esthetic values . . . is made in humble life, in scientific life, in business and economy, and in the field of statecraft. The conscious, living mind inquires what is possible and what is desirable, and applies ethical and esthetic canons to the consideration of actions.[28]

Characteristically, Beard undiscriminatingly tended to lump together different meanings of "frame of reference." He made little distinction between choosing a scientific problem for study and choosing a public policy from possible alternatives, or between selection of facts by the scholar and assumption of ethical norms by a moral agent. Yet, rigorous investigation of a hypothesis is not identical with moral advocacy, no matter how earnestly the scholar or scientist as a man may prefer one outcome to another. Beard's loose terminology and vague concepts frequently resulted in considerable ambiguity in meaning.

Toward the close of his life, in his contribution to the 1946 *Report of the Committee on Historiography,* Beard was still analyzing the nature of the multiple crisis he envisaged in human affairs, "the most widespread and tumultuous crisis of the kind since the beginning of recorded history." Compounded of economic maladjustments, the inability to conceive remedies, defects in knowledge, and other elements, the crisis, he believed, was of immense practical significance with respect to "bringing about an ideal or better state

[27] *Ibid.,* pp. 15, 32.
[28] *Ibid.,* p. 31.

of things." All students of the "humanistic sciences," he felt, should be concerned with the great intellectual challenge thus presented.[29]

Science, Relativism, and Social Reality

In the same 1946 *Report of the Committee on Historiography* to which Beard contributed, Sidney Hook wrote a brief but suggestive essay on frames of reference.[30] If, a number of years earlier, Beard could have stopped to work out the implications of some of the same points Hook was now making, Beard's subsequent thought as it touched on such matters as the relationship between scientific method and value judgments might have gained greatly in clarity and consistency.

Beard's failure to discriminate sufficiently among interrelated though distinguishable intellectual operations, as well as his loose usage of terms such as "frame of reference," resulted in a certain amount of confusion and ambiguity. Among the general kinds of *intellectual operation* he variously alluded to in his writings, four may be usefully distinguished:

1. *Posing a hypothesis or making an allegation of fact.* The scholar or scientist, whether dealing with human affairs or with physics, can frame a certain hypothesis whose validity tends to be confirmed or denied by means of empirical methods. When Beard during the early and middle periods of his life dealt specifically with hypotheses as such, or with other phases of the acquisition of verifiable knowledge in limited areas, his treatment included little that the strictest scholar could basically object to. He realized that tentative initial conclusions or hypotheses are necessary to guide research and are quite different from mere hopes or desires reminiscent of what Francis Bacon criticized in warning against the error of "anticipating nature." He knew that hypotheses do not necessarily survive the test of subsequent scientific investigation. They may be confirmed, modified, or completely shattered.

---

[29] "Grounds for a Reconsideration of Historiography," pp. 5 f.

[30] Sidney Hook, "Frame of Reference," in Curti, *Theory and Practice in Historical Study,* pp. 125–27. Even though Hook's statement was directed primarily at history writing, it had wider methodological and epistemological ramifications. Some of the ideas expressed below are adaptations of certain of Hook's conceptions, somewhat differently categorized. For related comments, cf. also Elias Berg, *The Historical Thinking of Charles A. Beard* (Stockholm: Almqvist & Wiksell, 1957), pp. 57–68, and Cushing Strout, *The Pragmatic Revolt in American History: Carl Becker and Charles Beard* (New Haven, Conn.: Yale University Press, 1958), pp. 50–61.

But in his later years Beard at times slipped into the fallacy of assuming that in the study of human affairs such hypothesizing is indistinguishable from imposing prior value judgments. His relativism on occasion led him to doubt the possibility of valid knowledge of more than insignificant fragments of social reality.[31]

2. *Defining the scope of an investigation or study.* The resulting delineated area of interest might in certain contexts be designated a "frame of reference." Quite appropriately, of course, such problems or investigative areas vary widely among different scholars or scientists. Several investigators may attack different segments of a general field, or they may approach the same problem from different angles. Yet the findings of all, if these have been scientifically validated, must necessarily be compatible with one another.[32] Beard acknowledged that "an interpretation" of history or politics was a partial treatment that did not exclude other equally valid partial treatments or interpretations.[33] This seemed to imply that as far back as 1913 he saw no particularly adverse epistemological implications in this unavoidable operation of drawing explicit or implicit intellectual boundaries.

His later historiography, however, put a different face on the matter. Now the implication was that selecting one aspect of social reality for study rather than another was an arbitrary and subjective operation damaging to epistemological soundness. Furthermore, the implication was that knowledge of only a part of social reality must be epistemologically unsound because this partial knowledge would probably bear little resemblance to hypothetical knowledge of the whole. He implied, for example, that, precisely because the historian could not tell "the whole truth" about the past or describe it "in miniature as it actually was," it was peculiarly difficult for historians to be objective or to acquire exact knowledge. Yet, when Beard admitted that verifiable knowledge of limited areas of social reality was possible, he tended to refute some of his own relativist inferences. As Harry J. Marks has indicated, history, like the natural sciences, cannot tell " 'the whole truth' about the whole of its subject matter," but in neither case need this "limiting condition"

<hr />

[31] Cf. Morton G. White, *Social Thought in America: The Revolt against Formalism* (New York: Viking Press, 1949), p. 234.

[32] Cf. Hook's third meaning of "Frame of Reference," p. 126.

[33] See Beard's discussion, for example, in "That Noble Dream," *American Historical Review*, XLI (October, 1935), 84.

lead to overly pessimistic conclusions as to the acquisition of reliable knowledge.[34]

3. *Applying rigorous scientific or scholarly methods to the matter under investigation or study.* The expressed or implied objective
in this kind of intellectual operation is to increase reliable knowledge. Facts and relationships are discovered and probed. Hypotheses
are empirically tested. The results achieved by one investigator are
subject to verification, refinement, or correction by other investigators. All separately derived results, to the extent that they are actually
valid, must be compatible with one another. The cumulative outcome is to arrive at conclusions that are probable or relatively true,
but seldom, if ever, absolutely certain. The actual validity of the
results of this kind of intellectual operation is quite without relevance
to a preconceived "frame of reference" or prior value commitment.
Such preconceptions may properly be exposed and faced in an attempt to minimize their distorting influence, or in some cases they
may themselves be formulated as hypotheses to be tested. In no case
are they a proper part of scientific or scholarly validation as such.

When Beard recognized that "objective truth" could be told about
tiny fragments of past social reality, even if "the whole truth" was
beyond reach, he thereby admitted a standard of objectivity or validation. Numerous small accretions of truth tend to approach "the
whole truth" even if the latter can never be fully reached. In a sense
this is the method of increasing reliable knowledge generally.[35]
Beard sometimes forgot that "the latest and best hypotheses," despite
the great differences in their degrees of validation, must be the
pragmatic definition of "truth" at a given time in any field.

Part of his difficulty grew out of his notions about causality and
other relations among phenomena. Often he appeared to assume
that relationships dealt with in physical science were necessary and
objective facts that inhered in the reality outside the mind, whereas
the relationships of social science were subjective creations of a
quite different order.[36] Frequently he indicated that human affairs

[34] Harry J. Marks, "Ground under Our Feet: Beard's Relativism," *Journal of
the History of Ideas,* XIV (October, 1953), 633.

[35] Cf. *ibid.,* pp. 628–33.

[36] Cf. William A. Glaser, Critique of Two Economic Interpretations of Politics: Charles A. Beard and A. M. Simons (Unpublished Ph.D. dissertation,
Harvard University, 1952), p. 49: "One fallacy was the assumption held by
Beard . . . that a statement of causality is a mere recording of a necessary fact
which inheres in objective reality."

consisted of a unique chain of events that did not repeat itself.[37] He felt that in order to comprehend present social reality, to be really scientific, one would have to trace this chain "backward into the darkness of prehistory"—an obvious impossibility.[38]

In turn, his conception of future history, of unfolding social reality, was also uncertainly intermingled in his mind with assumptions respecting the nature of science and scientific predictability. He assumed that a science concerning "the great history" must remain an impossibility, inasmuch as "unforeseen consequences" were always occurring.[39] He often slipped into the assumption that scientific predictability meant the ability to forecast consequent events with certainty and unerring accuracy. He was fond of using words such as "fate" in a figurative sense, and at times he appeared to become a victim of his own terminology. Erroneously he tended to equate scientific predictability in the social sciences with fate and predestination:

If a science of history were achieved, it would, like the science of celestial mechanics, make possible the calculable prediction of the future in history. It would bring the totality of historical occurrences within a single field and reveal the unfolding future to its last end, including all the apparent choices made and to be made. It would be omniscience. . . . The future once revealed, humanity would have nothing to do except to await its doom.[40]

Beard's notions as to causality, the nature of scientific predictability, and the results to be expected from application of rigorous methods also had a bearing on his final vague position regarding economic determinism. He felt that a posited formula, such as "economics comes first and determines politics," was arbitrary. And

---

[37] For example, Beard asserted that "history is irreversible and never repeats itself" (Introduction, Franklin Watts (ed.), *Voices of History: Great Speeches and Papers of the Year 1941* [New York: Franklin Watts, 1942], p. ix).

[38] "Signed Footnote" (with Alfred Vagts), in Curti, *Theory and Practice in Historical Study*, p. 137; cf. a similar notion expressed by Esmond Wright, *Sewanee Review*, XLIX (October–December, 1941), 490; on this point, also see Merle Curti's comments in Howard K. Beale (ed.), *Charles A. Beard* (Lexington: University of Kentucky Press, 1954), p. 206.

[39] As expressed, for example, in his testimony of February 4, 1941 ("Statement of Charles A. Beard, New Milford, Conn.," February 4, 1941, *To Promote the Defense of the United States: Hearings before the Committee on Foreign Relations United States Senate on Senate [Bill] 275*, 77 Cong., 1 Sess., p. 308).

[40] "Written History as an Act of Faith," *American Historical Review*, XXXIX (January, 1934), 224.

yet economics and politics had always been "inextricably entangled" in the real world. "Human beings had to eat in order to live and they began eating before they established great societies and states; but human beings were more than mere eating-animals even in the most primitive times of which we have knowledge." [41] The question of "which precedes which," he decided, could not be settled. Neither "freedom" nor "determinism" ruled completely in human affairs, inasmuch as there were always large areas of freedom even though some things were "fated." [42]

4. *Applying value judgments.* This operation, though irrelevant to the actual validity of knowledge, may nonetheless be explicitly or implicitly performed with respect to matters dealt with by science and scholarship. Value judgments underlie the scholar's pronouncements of good and bad, as they do those of other men. When the scholar or scientist views with alarm or heaps with praise, he is revealing his own scheme of values rather than expounding something entailed in his findings alone. [43]

Thus a physicist may have an impelling ethical urge to stop atomic bomb testing on the ground that the accumulating fallout may be harming the human race. Nonetheless, within the capabilities of his scientific instruments and techniques, he can still make careful measurements of the actual levels of radiation in given areas, as his colleagues in other fields can continue to apply rigorous scientific methods in studying the actual effects of exposure on human beings.

Similarly in the social sciences, applying value judgments may be usefully distinguished from the operation of validating knowledge through application of scientific or scholarly methods. Clear thinking would seem to require an attempt to disentangle, at least in thought, ethical and ideal elements from the factual and causal aspects. The student of human affairs, like the physicist, can appreciate that what does happen is not necessarily what he hopes will happen.

Beard's writings in the last period of his life displayed inconsistencies in his thought regarding the effects of value commitments on intellectual processes. At times he erroneously implied that the

---

[41] *The Economic Basis of Politics* (3rd rev. ed.; New York: Alfred A. Knopf, 1945), p. 108.
[42] See, for example, Beard's discussion in *The Republic,* pp. 274, 276.
[43] Cf. Hook's fourth meaning of "Frame of Reference," pp. 126 f.

attempt to acquire knowledge in human affairs was scarcely distinguishable in principle from the operation of applying value judgments. At other times his earlier attitude reasserted itself. Near the end of 1933, for example, he insisted that "the assumption that any historian can be a disembodied spirit as coldly neutral to human affairs as the engineer to an automobile" was no longer acceptable. But in 1935 he wrote that "an economic analysis may be coldly neutral" and indicated that the question of judgments of praise or blame must be referred "to moralists and philosophers, not to students of history as such." [44]

On some occasions Beard equated the conception, "things deemed desirable," with a thinker's value scheme, whereas on other occasions he implied that a thinker's value-based frame of reference comprised the threefold conception, *necessità-fortuna-virtù* (things "deemed" necessary, possible, and desirable). Elsewhere Beard claimed that every individual carried around in his head an apparently culture-oriented "world-view" to which all his ideas were referred, but Beard did not make entirely clear whether this world-view was essentially a subjective value scheme, or how it might affect the individual's apprehension of an objective reality. [45]

Thus, as we have seen, Beard in the thirties and forties variously alluded to, and tended to blur the distinctions among, four general kinds of intellectual operations: (1) posing a hypothesis or making an allegation of fact, (2) defining the scope of an investigation or study, (3) applying rigorous scientific or scholarly methods to the matter under investigation or study, and (4) applying value judgments.

But, further, when he employed linguistic forms such as "scheme of reference," "frame of reference," "conception of the ultimate design of the universe," and similar terminology, his meaning was frequently ambiguous. The precise relationship between such concepts and the previously mentioned intellectual operations was generally not indicated. At times the intellectual operations themselves seemed to be equated with "what lay behind" these operations. Sharper distinctions might have helped to clarify some of the methodological, epistemological, and valuational problems that Beard pondered over. He used *frame of reference,* or similar terminology, to refer to

[44] As pointed out by White, *Social Thought in America*, p. 229.
[45] See *The American Spirit*, with Mary R. Beard (New York: Macmillan Co., 1942), pp. 1 ff.

two general kinds of concept which it may be useful to attempt to differentiate.

1. *The personal inclination or propensity of an individual.* Naturally scientists and scholars, like other human beings, have such propensities. The personal bent of a scientist or scholar—various factors "in his biography"—may impel him to select a particular hypothesis or problem for investigation. However, his reasons for selecting a problem do not govern the validity of its answer. Even a strong inclination on his part to glorify an institution, reduce human suffering, or influence events, need not lead him to distort his findings. Indeed, the more aware he is of his frame of reference in this sense, as Hook has indicated, the less likely he is to let it interfere with his application of rigorous scientific or scholarly methods in his work.[46] Beard made frequent mention of this kind of reference frame, with varying implications as to its epistemological effects. He acknowledged that the scheme of reference that had been imposed on a scholar by the social order in which he lived did not necessarily prevent him from achieving "a degree of scientific exactness."[47]

2. *A more or less systematically organized guidance pattern, philosophy, or set of beliefs.* Although it is scarcely possible to separate completely a frame of reference in this sense from a frame of reference in the preceding sense, nevertheless the two may differ considerably in degree. Guidance patterns in this second sense may have marked influence in various directions: personal conduct, religion, values.[48] Although the ethical and valuational elements in this kind of reference frame are not susceptible of validation in the usual scientific sense, the frame itself can nevertheless be scientifically studied, analyzed, and clarified. Again, such a guidance pattern—"what lies behind" a person's value judgments, for example —is itself irrelevant to the actual scientific validity of knowledge.

Beard's writings on historical relativism contained numerous statements alluding to broad frames of reference in this second sense. For example, the general conception of history which a thinker accepted through an "act of faith" appeared to be such a guidance pattern. Beard implied that it was proper for the historian

[46] Hook, "Frame of Reference," p. 126.
[47] Cf. Beard's and Vagts's exposition in "Currents of Thought in Historiography," pp. 480 ff.
[48] See "Applying value judgments," p. 178, above.

to select, more or less deliberately, a suitable guiding conception and then decide whether he desired "to be a maker of history after the style of the Enlightenment or a victim of it in the manner of Ranke and Meinecke." [49] If the thinker happened to envisage history as directional movement, either backward or forward, another act of faith was apparently involved in conceiving the goal or end toward which the movement pointed.

However, in opposition to Beard's apparent position, it may be pointed out that the fact that a historian, or any other scholar or scientist, is convinced of some ultimate pattern or design in history or in the universe is itself irrelevant to the actual validity of his findings. His work must submit to the usual rigorous standards. Regardless of the purposes behind his intellectual labor, its scientific validity is independent of them. [50]

Beard's latter-day relativist historiography was in a sense reminiscent of his early economic interpretation of history. In the earlier period he had put so much emphasis on the motives of past political actors that he had often slighted the substantive and lasting results of their action. In his later historiography he seemed so preoccupied with the subjective elements involved in the historian's attempt, with only fragmentary evidence, to comprehend the past that he unduly discounted the validity of the product of historical scholarship. [51]

Consequently, Beard, maintaining that what the social scientist produced was not a reconstruction of social reality but only "thought," came to the conclusion that this in itself made the social scientist's product uniquely defective. But the conclusion was unwarranted. The failing, if it is a failing, is one shared with scholars and scientists in every field of human inquiry. [52]

[49] "Currents of Thought in Historiography," p. 478.

[50] Cf. White, *Social Thought in America*, pp. 232 ff.

[51] Cf. Henry S. Commager, *The American Mind: An Interpretation of American Thought and Character since the 1880's* (New Haven, Conn.: Yale University Press, 1950), p. 309.

[52] Also see Chester M. Destler, "Some Observations on Contemporary Historical Theory," *American Historical Review*, LV (April, 1950), 511; and Whitaker T. Deininger, "Skepticism and the Historical Faith of Charles Beard," *Journal of the History of Ideas*, XV (October, 1954), 586 f.

CHAPTER XI
POLITICS IN LIBERAL DEMOCRACY

The Human Factor

With due allowance for the impact of critical times, Beard's political thought in the thirties and forties was in one respect, at least, continuous with notions he had expressed many years earlier in his 1908 public lecture, *Politics,* at Columbia University. In his thinking the central factor in politics remained human nature itself. As before, he continued to believe that the study of politics was but an aspect of the study of the "whole man," of human affairs in general. Political science, he explained in *The Nature of the Social Sciences* (1934), was concerned with "those aspects of human nature and human activity which pertain to government." A great state, like a great economy, rested in the last analysis on "the habits, ideals, morals, and capacities" of persons high and low.[1] "The central problem of historiography and philosophy," he wrote in his 1945 version of *The Economic Basis of Politics,* was "the origin, nature, dynamics, and capacities of human beings in relation to one another and their environment."[2]

Moreover, human nature, he felt, was relatively a constant compared to the other more changeable phenomena of politics. Though states, institutions, and other edifices built by man kept changing in form and characteristics, the basic "facets and propensities" of man's nature remained comparatively stable. Man, as if convinced of his own continuity and survival power, "insisted on conceiving history as a tragedy, as divine comedy, as progress toward a golden day, or as melodrama, with heroes, heroines, and villains."[3] Explain-

[1] *The Nature of the Social Sciences in Relation to Objectives of Instruction* (New York: Charles Scribner's Sons, 1934), pp. 73, 120; cf. *Politics* (New York: Columbia University Press, 1908), p. 6.

[2] *The Economic Basis of Politics* (3rd rev. ed.; New York: Alfred A. Knopf, 1945), p. 108.

[3] *America in Midpassage,* with Mary R. Beard (New York: Macmillan Co., 1939), p. 664.

182

ing near the close of his life that the human race had already "traveled a long and hard road," Beard expressed his own faith that, even if atomic catastrophe should set mankind back two thousand years, it would nonetheless survive.[4]

Beard believed that, in spite of the complex group structure of modern society, human beings retained a considerable degree of individuality. They were not swallowed up in a social organism. "The relations existing between the members of a society," he asserted, "are not the relations existing between the members of a living body."[5] He considered the organic conception not only false but misleading. Furthermore, there was no absolute opposition between "the individual and society, collectivism and individualism."[6] American frontier life, for example, had demonstrated the compatibility of a rugged spirit of individualism with friendly cooperation.[7] The human individual was more than a "Darwinian man" or a "purely economic man" who struggled and competed blindly for "survival of the fittest."[8]

Mankind, Beard continued to believe, possessed a basic rationality. This did not mean, however, that "wisdom, judgment, and good sense" automatically accompanied "an extensive knowledge of ideas and words."[9] Nevertheless, reason was a power in human affairs, including politics. Even when conflict of ideas and interests in American history had "burst the bounds of argument" and led to the Civil War, the participants and onlookers in that bloody struggle had not regarded its results as better or more effectively achieved than if the conflict had been settled peaceably and by resort to reason.[10] Reason moved men, despite appearances at times that they were moved solely by irrational urges. The fact that all people were "in

[4] See George S. Counts in Howard K. Beale (ed.), *Charles A. Beard* (Lexington: University of Kentucky Press, 1954), p. 252.

[5] *The Discussion of Human Affairs* (New York: Macmillan Co., 1936), p. 98.

[6] Review of Robson, *Public Enterprise, American Political Science Review*, XXXI (December, 1937), 1159.

[7] Letters to the *New York Times*, January 23 and 28, 1938.

[8] See Beard's remarks in "America in Midpassage," in Progressive Education Association, *John Dewey and the Promise of America* (Columbus, Ohio: American Education Press, 1939), p. 24.

[9] "Ideas: An Inquiry," *Journal of Adult Education*, IX (April, 1937), 122; cf. *The Nature of the Social Sciences in Relation to Objectives of Instruction*, p. 80.

[10] *American Government and Politics* (8th ed.; New York: Macmillan Co., 1939), p. 4.

the broad sense" moved by interest did not mean they were being irrational. "No one does anything about a matter that is of no concern to him, that does not attract his attention, that does not affect in any way his sense of values," wrote Beard in *The Open Door at Home* (1934). "This is true of both 'material' and 'spiritual' interests. . . . Hence to say that mankind is not moved by interest is false; the opposite is a truism." [11]

Closely associated with man's basic rationality were other latent capacities which could be further developed by education. Indeed, popular education, Beard had always felt, was a fundamental pillar of liberal democracy. Education, he told a meeting of the American Association for Adult Education in 1936, had the task of expounding and upholding the humane ideals on which democracy rested. Youth should be instructed not only in these moral values but also in the realities of politics and economic processes and in "letters, the arts, the sciences and all other splendid manifestations of the human spirit." [12] Beard retained a conviction that the people could be trusted to make sound decisions if they had access to the relevant information. Recalling an incident in which a visiting European lecturer had expressed amusement at the "frenzy for current events" and other things "democratic" in America, Beard in 1937 wrote:

In fact democracy itself is rather amusing—from one point of view. It assumes that Tom, Dick, Harry, and Will, accompanied by Bridget, Susan, Harriet, and Jane, should have the right to govern themselves and to pass upon all the great matters of state. The fallibility of the idea and shortcomings in practice have formed the subjects of learned or contemptuous reflections ever since the days of Socrates and Aristotle. Most of the subsequent reflections on the business by such sages as John Adams and Alexander Hamilton, have been copies of older arguments. When the preposterous character of democracy has been demonstrated to the complete satisfaction of the demonstrators, a question equally old arises: Who is to judge the judges? . . . If democracy engaged in discussing current events and making decisions on current affairs is rather amusing, what and who are to be substituted for it? [13]

[11] *The Open Door at Home*, with G. H. E. Smith (New York: Macmillan Co., 1934), p. 155.
[12] "Democracy and Education in the United States," *Social Research*, IV (September, 1937), 397; cf. Beard's remarks in "What Is This Democracy?" in *Adult Education and Democracy* (New York: American Association for Adult Education, 1936), p. 5.
[13] "The Interpretation of Events," *Events*, II (December, 1937), 441.

Even in parts of the world in which democracy's roots were shallow or still nonexistent, the interests and desires of ordinary people had to be taken increasingly into account in the decisions of political and military leaders. In 1942 Beard wrote that "the masses of humanity" were now "on the move." People by the hundreds of millions had learned to read. No longer could leaders ignore "the tumult from below." [14] The implication was that common humanity everywhere possessed the potential to guide its own destinies.

But Beard's primary focus in his references to man's nature during these years was on America. Among his favorite targets were "thinkers" and public officials who implied that man was a creature of severely limited abilities:

We are told that man is a poor kind of creature, incapable of action on a grand scale, unfitted to control the leviathan which he has created. Man is at bottom a forty-acre farmer, a general-store manager, a selectman, a justice of the peace, a fence viewer, a hog reeve. He cannot run a transcontinental railway or wield an instrument of government as huge and complicated as that established at Washington. When this little man attempts some grand enterprise on a national scale, he is, we are told, a waster, a fumbler, a weakling, perhaps a chiseler. In his smithy, corner store or cow lot he is good and efficient. While he remains there liberty and democracy flourish. If he leaves his parish the pillars of American society will fall. At most he should stick within state boundaries and cling to states' rights.[15]

Thus, included in Beard's political thought, as in his social thought in general, during this last period of his life, was the notion that social reality could be adequately grasped by the mind only if the actual nature and capabilities of its central factor, man, were realistically viewed. Prejudices and erroneous ideas respecting human nature could only cause further distortion of the social scientist's already limited vision.

Realism also required due notice of the moral and ethical aspects of human affairs. As Beard had been noting since the late 1920's, there was urgent need for an adequate twentieth-century "social philosophy" in which ethics should be central. At least implicitly, he had accordingly come to appreciate more keenly than ever that values were a part of the relevant data to be considered by the

[14] Introduction, Franklin Watts (ed.), *Voices of History: Great Speeches and Papers of the Year 1941* (New York: Franklin Watts, 1942), p. xiii.
[15] "America Must Stay Big," *Today,* IV (September 14, 1935), 3.

realistic student of democratic politics. In a 1936 address devoted to the subject of democracy, he called attention to the "moral ideals, legal institutions, and economic foundations" of democracy. "Our democracy," he wrote subsequently, "rests upon the assumption that all human beings have a moral worth in themselves and cannot be used for ends alien to humanity. This is an assumption and cannot be proved, but it underlies democratic conceptions." [16] In his 1948 *American Government and Politics,* published shortly after his death, he reminded students that "human hopes and aspirations of many kinds" were an important part of the story of government.[17]

If the essence of democratic politics was a "conflict of parties and ideas," this conflict, thought Beard, was meaningless apart from the values and ends sought. The observer of political activity who ignored the latter saw only a part of the total picture. Requisite new political policy, as in the case of a broader social philosophy, must necessarily contain "ideal elements of ethics and esthetics" which were "at bottom assertions of values, not demonstrations of mathematics." [18]

To Beard's mind, the source of the values through which American democracy must renew itself was obvious. These values must spring from our "cultural heritage." Our literature was full of assertions of such values, and from time to time some of them had been realized in practice. Thus, the ethical foundations of liberal democracy derived from "a few commonsense aphorisms, fables, and maxims evolved by ordinary humanity in its varied efforts to grapple with the stuff of life." [19] The implication was that value postulates were ultimately a form of adaptation to the total environment in which the human mind found itself. Great ethical philosophies, he believed, rested finally "on a few simple propositions— usually obvious propositions if they are any good." [20]

In a sense Beard in his old age was reaffirming the position of young Beard the Oxford student. The end of politics was, after all,

---

[16] "Democracy and Education in the United States," p. 394; cf. "What Is This Democracy?" p. 4.

[17] *American Government and Politics* (10th ed.; 1948), p. 388.

[18] *The Open Door at Home,* p. 152.

[19] Review of Sandburg, *Abraham Lincoln: The War Years, Virginia Quarterly Review,* XVI (January, 1940), 116; cf. *The Open Door at Home,* p. 152.

[20] "Talking into the Wind," *Harper's Magazine,* CLXXXV (November, 1942), 607.

man. In final analysis, *human* goals and purposes underlay and pervaded social reality.[21]

The Question of Progress

At about the time Hitler's move on Poland was igniting World
War II, Beard strongly attacked a statement to the effect that mankind's progress had been "a pageant that moves before us from
primitive times down to our own day." The tone of his attack was
vastly different from the tenderness with which he himself had
penned similar phrases in his earlier years. The profoundest students, he now sharply reminded his readers, disagreed as to whether
history exhibited any pattern at all or was merely senseless chaos.[22]

This reaction was rather characteristic of Beard during his later
years. Moods of pessimism and optimism seemed to contend for
mastery as he successively qualified and modified his thinking on
the question of progress, including application of the concept to the
fortunes of liberal democracy. Darwinism, he now acknowledged,
had been one of the great misconceptions or at least "overemphasized conceptions." [23] He was inclined to subject the idea of
progress to much closer analysis than formerly. Progress, he noted,
had little meaning except in terms of the goals sought. A man
traveling from one point to another was literally making progress
toward his objective, but the American people were not necessarily
making progress in general and in all realms. He appeared to have
little use for the notion that "we are fated to make progress," although he implied that progress in a particular sphere was possible
"if we work hard at the enterprise." [24]

Yet, almost in spite of himself and the times, Beard's lifelong faith
in ultimate human progress kept reasserting itself. Many features
of civilization, he suggested, outlived the rise and decline of particular institutions. Regardless of setbacks, certain aspects of culture
were cumulative. Accordingly, he could not lead himself to believe
that human affairs amounted merely to "drifting temporarily

[21] For one of Beard's later discussions on this matter, see his essay, "Freedom
in Political Thought," in R. N. Anshen (ed.), *Freedom: Its Meaning* (New
York: Harcourt, Brace & Co., 1940), pp. 290, 298.

[22] Review of Neurath, *Modern Man in the Making, Saturday Review of Literature,* XX (September 30, 1939), 11.

[23] "America in Midpassage," p. 21.

[24] "America—Yesterday and Today," with Clay Coss, *Weekly News Review,*
XVIII (September 11, 1939), 6.

between original chaos and future ruin." But, even if reason pointed to retrogression or chaos, Beard's final line of defense was sentiment. In his view it seemed "nobler in mind to co-operate with forces that move toward order and mastery than to cultivate the barren field of negation. But I admit that this may be a matter of temperament rather than of metaphysics."[25] The idea of civilization itself, he maintained, "embraces a conception of history as a struggle of human beings in the world for individual and social perfection—for the good, the true, the beautiful—against ignorance, disease, the harshness of physical nature, the forces of barbarism in individuals and in society. . . ."[26]

In his 1943 introduction to *The Law of Civilization and Decay,* Beard rejected Adams' cyclical theory of history because he could not accept the notion that "there is nothing new under the sun." Men could learn from history, Beard felt, without committing themselves to a "pleasing theory of straight-line and ever-lasting progress" of the kind Brooks Adams had attacked as invalid.[27]

Nevertheless, Beard in the 1930's was virtually compelled by events to re-examine his conception of human progress as this applied to the preservation and spread of political democracy. With despotism riding high, he could scarcely repeat his claim of the twenties that democracy was at the moment "holding its ground." He now called it a "mistaken impression" that democracy had been succeeding admirably in central Europe, only to be wrecked by evil leaders who had suddenly come along to stir up the worst passions of the people and "upset the fair pageant established by the good."[28] But, despite his antipathy toward the rising dictatorships of Europe and Asia, he was not particularly alarmed at the possible external threat to American democracy at this time.

[25] *Public Policy and the General Welfare* (New York: Farrar & Rinehart, 1941), p. 160; see also Beard's remarks in *The Discussion of Human Affairs* (New York: Macmillan Co., 1936), p. 97, and in "Freedom in Political Thought," pp. 303 f.

[26] *The American Spirit,* with Mary R. Beard (New York: Macmillan Co., 1942), p. 672; cf. "Freedom in Political Thought," pp. 298 f.

[27] Introduction, Brooks Adams, *The Law of Civilization and Decay* (New York: Alfred A. Knopf, 1943), pp. 51 f.

[28] Review of Rauschenbush, *The March of Fascism, Yale Review,* XXIX (September, 1939), 167; but cf. Beard's attitude in "The Rise of the Democratic Idea in the United States," *Survey Graphic,* XXVI (April, 1937), 201-3. Also see his essay, "Essentials of Democracy," *School and Society,* L (August 19, 1939), 229–34.

It is possible that America may maintain a democratic process of government if all Europe goes fascist. It is well to remember that when this republic was created all of Europe, with some minor exceptions, was under despotic forms of government. This was a republic with democratic features in an age when despotism dominated the Old World, and we may conceivably preserve some forms and processes of our democracy if despotism again dominates the Old World. As for myself, I don't propose to enjoy the prospect of having smallpox because my neighbors have it.[29]

Beard's concern with the preservation of American democracy centered, rather, in what he conceived to be the internal threats and weaknesses. He was concerned, for example, with the great concentration of income in a relatively small number of families, although he recognized that some of the class differences were due to "psychological elements" which showed little correspondence to statistics of wealth distribution, and that "these psychological features seemed to become more conspicuous as the depression deepened." Yet he particularly decried, in language worthy of John Taylor, the special rights and property of "a few hundred artificial persons" as against those of the millions of real persons in the United States.[30]

We confront a number of questions as fundamental and imperative as those with which the founders of the Republic wrestled. . . . Will "popular power," as Webster foretold, "break in upon the rights" of property held in mortmain by deathless corporations? Or will some Prince, pursuing the strategy recommended by Machiavelli, intervene by an appeal to the *ultima ratio* and seek to hold a balance of interests? If he does, how long can his system of balance be maintained? [31]

Thus it was neither a domestic dictatorship of the proletariat nor fascist aggression from abroad that Beard especially feared. Rather, he was alarmed at the possibility that American democracy, because of some weakness in our economic and social system, might be gradually sapped from within. Here, again, he looked to education as one of the mainstays of democracy in the long run. If education, as in central Europe, might be permitted to prepare people for tyranny, it could also be used in America to make democracy more

[29] "Democracy and Education in the United States," p. 393; also cf. "War with Japan?" *Events*, VIII (November, 1940), 322.

[30] "Corporations and Natural Rights," *Virginia Quarterly Review*, XII (July, 1936), 353; cf. Beard's similar discussion in *America in Midpassage*, pp. 556 f. See also George S. Counts's remarks on this point in Howard K. Beale (ed.), *Charles A. Beard* (Lexington: University of Kentucky Press, 1954), p. 238.

[31] "Corporations and Natural Rights," p. 353.

secure. But, to do so, it had to deal "resolutely and realistically with the processes of democracy, with questions of sustaining economy and culture and with the protection of civil rights." [32] As he wrote in *The National Elementary Principal* in 1938:

The future of American democracy depends upon popular education. If we are to overcome the stresses and strains of our civilization by democratic processes rather than by the sword then the foundations must be laid by the front-line teachers. If we are to widen the civilization of the people, as distinguished from the culture of an elite, teachers must be advance-guards. [33]

But there was another internal threat to American democracy, which was also related to the question of human progress in general. Inaction was dangerous. In Beard's opinion, failure to take forceful and positive action to deal effectively with grave economic and social problems would undermine democracy as surely as any "prince":

Unless we can effectively apply our psychological and other "techniques" to the business of bringing our economic plant into something like full use and provide a far wider distribution of employment and income, no noble theories on the dignity of man and the perfectability [*sic*] of the species (however necessary to democracy) will save us from some kind of new despotism. [34]

Positive Democracy

Beard's deep concern over the human degradation and economic problems associated with the depression had, even before the New Deal, put him in a mood to favor vigorous action by the national government. The dilemma of hunger beside food surpluses, of idle men and factories in the face of gnawing want, seemed to him to present a threat and a challenge to democratic society and its political machinery. In the early and middle 1930's he was more than ever convinced that the role of government in modern life must be a great and expanding one. He believed that a vast and interdependent national economy particularly required a powerful national government to make it function effectively for the general welfare.

It logically seemed to follow that planning was the only way out

[32] "Essentials of Democracy," *School and Society*, L (August 19, 1939), 234.

[33] "Education Enriched by Living," *National Elementary Principal*, XVII (February, 1938), 106.

[34] Review of Merriam, *The New Democracy and the New Despotism, American Political Science Review*, XXXIII (October, 1939), 885 f.

of depression. If the American people could apply their technical skills and organizing genius to their economic needs, Beard felt, the despair and suffering might be quickly and astonishingly relieved. In 1935 he warmly welcomed Harold Loeb's volume *The Chart of Plenty:*

Mr. Loeb's book represents the first attempt, on a scale commensurate with the issues involved, to apply the rationality of engineering and accountancy to the central problem of American life and economy, namely, the capacity of American technology, the technical arts, labor and management as applied to American resources, to provide a decent standard of living for all the people in the United States.[35]

Warmly denouncing the conception of "rugged American individualism" as "myth," Beard, as always, kept up his attacks on laissez faire. The idea that the state must keep strictly aloof from the economic activities of its citizens was a notion imported from abroad and propagandized here largely by professors of political economy, he charged. So deeply had the fallacious assumptions of the laissez-faire thesis of classical economics penetrated into American thinking that even official advisers of the national government were unconsciously affected by them. Monopoly investigations and trust busting were pursued in the vain belief that so-called flexible prices and free competition would automatically result in economic adjustments, utmost efficiency, and high prosperity. Federal judges apparently still under the influence of the ideas of Herbert Spencer and William Graham Sumner persisted in negating measures aimed at effective guidance of the nation's economic life. Yet elimination of a few abuses would not bring about an automatic regeneration of capitalist economy. Unemployment as "a malignant social disease" would not vanish by itself.[36]

In view of Beard's attitude toward laissez faire, it is not hard to imagine his reaction to Friedrich von Hayek's *The Road to Serfdom* (1944) [37] when it appeared. He disagreed vigorously with Hayek's thesis that fascist and Nazi dictatorships resulted from abandonment of individualism and consequent expansion of the functions of modern government. It was by no means a foregone

[35] *New Republic,* LXXXII (March 20, 1935), 164.
[36] "Going Ahead with Roosevelt," *Events,* I (January, 1937), 9; see also "Idea of Let Us Alone," *Virginia Quarterly Review,* XV (October, 1939), 501, and "Monopoly in Fact and Fiction," *Events,* IV (November, 1938), 383 f.
[37] (Chicago: University of Chicago Press, 1944).

conclusion, he argued, that state intervention in the economy was necessarily "the road to serfdom." Rather, just the opposite was more apt to be true. Hayek's thesis was fallacious, Beard contended, because it made no distinction between "state intervention by despotisms and state intervention by constitutional governments under popular mandates." [38] To Beard's mind democratic government was accountable to the people and autocracy was not; whether government engaged in many or few functions was in itself largely irrelevant to this question.

What in his view was important, however, was the manner in which modern democracy handled its necessarily growing tasks. Although years had passed since his more active days in the public administration movement, he continued to stress the significance of the techniques and organizational structure through which the public business was administered. The high efficiency of the World War I German General Staff still impressed him, and he apparently felt that democracy would do well to aim at somewhat similar effectiveness. In 1937 he urged more exactness and precision in federal administration. More exact units of cost and of performance were particularly needed, he felt, in order that accounting and other administrative controls might become more effective. "The future of civilized government, and even, I think, of civilization itself," he declared, "rests upon our ability to develop a science and a philosophy and a practice of administration competent to discharge the public functions of civilized society." [39]

When Beard in 1947 was called on to speak at a banquet celebrating the fortieth anniversary of the founding of the New York Bureau of Municipal Research, his remarks demonstrated not only a continuing interest in public administration problems but also his feeling that the old progressive era formulas must be continuously re-examined. The beliefs he appeared to delight in challenging included the following: that administrative streamlining, once accomplished, remains permanently done; that the chief executive of a unit of government is necessarily a good administrator or better informed on administrative problems than all of its legislators; that all administrative agencies are in the executive department or should be; that either legal or actual separation of powers exists; that

[38] *The Economic Basis of Politics* (3rd rev. ed.; 1945), pp. 89 f.
[39] "The Role of Administration in Government," *The Work Unit in Federal Administration* (Chicago: Public Administration Service, 1937), No. 56, p. 3.

complete functional departmentalization at a high level makes for good administration; that administrative centralization is always desirable; that management principles of business are always applicable in government; that the spirit of self-government is permanently ingrained in the American people; that civil servants will perform their duties efficiently despite continuous unjust public criticism. Such formulas, Beard acknowledged, had a limited validity, but administrative researchers and reformers were cautioned to keep always in mind "the extent to which our operating principles are true and applicable in practice." [40]

Leviathan democracy, he pointed out, did not necessarily mean the advent of a cold and impersonal bureaucracy. "As a dairy farmer," he himself could testify to the helpfulness and cooperative spirit of federal agricultural officials and employees. In their Washington headquarters as in the rural countryside, these agents of big government had shown themselves to be efficient yet understanding human beings.[41]

He also attacked advocates of minimal government who maintained that private property rights were independent of public authority, or that economics and politics should be kept separated. In a 1934 essay on "Property and Democracy," he pounced on a college president's contention that private property and freedom of contract were fixed features of American life. All history showed the changing nature of private property, argued Beard. "The objects of property and the servitudes to be imposed upon it by government" were forever being altered. In the mutual interaction of property and politics, even forms of government underwent change. The danger to be faced was not an imaginary threat to a mythical unchanging entity, but the growing concentration of wealth.[42] Moreover, it was not a fact that property was something independent of politics, for "this Leviathan, the state," he declared, "defines property." [43]

Despite Beard's general dilution of his former economic interpretation of politics, he nonetheless during later life frequently brought qualified versions of the thesis into his writings on the functioning of American democracy. Noting the vast increase in gov-

[40] See Luther Gulick's account in Beale, *Charles A. Beard,* pp. 58 f.
[41] Preface, Milburn L. Wilson, *Democracy Has Roots* (New York: Carrick & Evans, 1939), p. 13.
[42] *Social Frontier,* I (October, 1934), 13.
[43] "Blessed Profit System," *New Republic,* LXXXI (December 26, 1934), 189.

ernmental responsibilities since Andrew Jackson's day, he pointed
out that it was the motive power of the multiplying private economic, social, and political associations that lay behind the complicated governmental machinery.[44] On occasion Beard seemed to put
the old thesis to new use by suggesting the economic basis of democracy:

The founders of the republic *and the promoters of democracy* recognized
the role of property—its forms and distribution—in the establishment and
maintenance of government. It is true that for a time, roughly speaking
from 1865 to the end of the nineteenth century, our political philosophers
ran to abstractions and in general ignored *the relation of democracy to the
ownership and distribution of wealth.* But more recently a deep awareness
of the relation of wealth and its distribution to democracy has been restored to our political thought, and we now witness immense efforts,
blundering no doubt, to employ democratic processes in effecting a wide,
if not universal, diffusion of wealth and security.[45]

Thus he could portray New Deal reforms as essentially a continuation of an old tradition of economic realism in American thought
and statesmanship. His "new economic interpretation" could embrace both the individualist assumptions of Rousseau and the group
contentions of the realist philosophers. New Deal programs for the
general welfare could be supported on the implicit ground of the
moral worth of human individuals and at the same time could be
pictured as rediscovered realism concerning the group basis of politics. "The fundamental idea of the New Deal," he claimed, "is the
coordination of classes and the maintenance of balance by regulation
and by a certain control over the distribution of wealth." Although
by the early twentieth century it had become "almost indecent" to
mention it in our preoccupation with the notion of free and equal
citizens, the idea that society is "a congeries of particular interests,"
Beard explained, was an old one, running back to Madison and even
Aristotle.[46]

In *The Idea of National Interest* (1934) Beard analyzed the New
Deal in more critical detail. A new idea of national interest, he suggested, appeared to be evolving out of older Jeffersonian and Hamil-

[44] "Sign of the Times," *National Municipal Review*, XXII (December,
1933), 581 f.
[45] "Democracy and Education in the United States," p. 396 (italics supplied).
[46] "Behind the New Deal," *Saturday Review of Literature*, XI (December 22,
1934), 381 f.

tonian conceptions. Whereas the Jeffersonian concept had emphasized an agricultural economy, a low-tariff policy of seeking foreign
outlets for farm products, and a small military establishment, the
Hamiltonian concept had favored encouragement for industry, emphasis on government-aided foreign trade, and a strong navy. Inasmuch as foreign outlets for "surpluses" had seemed to vanish after
1929, the New Deal now aimed to keep the domestic economy running in high gear with internal markets. Yet, despite the abandonment of dependence on foreign trade, no corresponding change had
been made in foreign policy, and huge funds continued to pour into
naval construction. Consequently, a new conception of national interest awaited "formulation at the hands of a statesman as competent
and powerful as Hamilton or Jefferson." [47]

Beard did not claim to know precisely what this new ideal for
America would be. But he was convinced that the matter must be
boldly confronted so that a more clearly defined ideal could emerge
to keep policy and practice from drifting haphazardly. His own
suggested utopia was a "workers' republic," using the term "worker"
in a broad sense to include all persons engaged in productive or
socially necessary activity. It was an ideal clearly indicating his warm
acceptance of positive democracy:

My vision for America . . . is a workers' republic—a republic in which
industry is carried on in ways conducive to virtue and the fruits thereof
are distributed in ways calculated to favor the good life for all—that is,
without the degradation of poverty and unemployment on the one side or
the degradation of luxury, rivalry, and conspicuous waste on the other.
. . . Industry will be widely decentralized. . . . The people will be de-
cently and beautifully housed. . . . Immense productive energies now
wasted in competitive duplications of effort will be devoted to the production of non-competitive and non-consumable goods of beauty and taste.
. . . Education will naturally assume a place of prime importance.[48]

Presently, however, Beard's views respecting the New Deal became
mixed, and in time they underwent a considerable change. At first
he saw the national government's efforts to grapple with the depression and to effect social reforms as a more or less logical continuation of historical trends. America was witnessing a further replacement of the earlier laissez-faire democracy by positive democracy.
Although he appeared to have some doubts initially as to the efficacy

[47] *The Idea of National Interest*, with G. H. E. Smith (New York: Macmillan Co., 1934), pp. 548 f.
[48] "World as I Want It," *Forum and Century*, XCI (June, 1934), 333.

of public works "pump priming," he nevertheless did not rejoice at the Supreme Court's apparent predilection for laissez faire in denying the national government powers he considered requisite to deal with the economy.[49] Seeking in 1937 to assess the immediate "future of democracy" in this country, he foresaw socialization of "whole sectors of the capitalist system" in the advent of a severe new economic collapse. Moreover, "democratic processes would be employed in the socialization."[50] And yet Beard was perplexed by the fact that so many domestic problems remained basically unsolved despite New Deal efforts. The dread possibility of a "foreign venture" to divert attention from domestic troubles increasingly disturbed and preoccupied him. By the end of the decade of the 1930's he was looking with greater skepticism on the idea of "ever-expanding outlets abroad to absorb the ever-expanding potentials of manufacturing industry."[51]

As Beard's sharp concern with foreign policy came to overshadow his early admiration for the New Deal, he increasingly tended to emphasize the strains and crushing burdens which greater participation in world affairs would impose on the national government. In his testimony against the Lend-Lease bill early in 1941, for example, he reminded Congressional committee members of the massive national debt already built up after nearly ten years of wrestling with the depression to bring about the "present false prosperity" at home, and of the untold billions that would be added by assuming further foreign responsibilities.[52] When the United States had fully entered World War II, he warned of the heavy responsibilities for this country in the postwar years ahead.[53] After the conflict had subsided, he spoke, in his final edition of *American Government and Politics* (1948), of the incalculable consequences for domestic policy and

[49] "America Must Stay Big," *Today*, IV (September 14, 1935), 3; for a discussion of the New Deal as a continuation of former tendencies, see *America in Midpassage*, pp. 941 ff.

[50] "Future of Democracy in the United States," *Political Quarterly*, VIII (October, 1937), 504.

[51] *Democracy Has Roots*, p. 10; see also Beard's comments on the New Deal in "Going Ahead with Roosevelt," pp. 9–12, and "Our Choice in Foreign Policy," *Events*, I (March, 1937), 161.

[52] "Statement of Charles A. Beard, New Milford, Conn.," February 4, 1941, *To Promote the Defense of the United States: Hearings before the Committee on Foreign Relations United States Senate on Senate [Bill] 275*, 77 Cong., 1 Sess., pp. 312, 316 f.

[53] Introduction, Watts, *Voices of History*, p. xix.

economy brought about by an unprecedented war debt, controls over business and agriculture, and massive foreign commitments.[54]

Blessings of Liberty

As the school year in America drew to a close in the spring of 1938, not long after Hitler had taken over Austria, the columns of the *Weekly News Review* carried a brief essay by Beard and Coss on "What Democracy Means." Democratic government, the student readers were told, meant rule by an enlightened majority freely formed in an atmosphere of freedom of opinion and expression. It included minority rights. In a democratic society the government helped the people to realize objectives such as equal opportunity for all, economic security, and the general welfare.[55] In essence, this was Beard's conception of liberal democracy. His emphasis was clearly on broad human freedom. His grounds for upholding freedom were equally clear:

In every society that is not frozen and on the way to death, there must be some freedom of inquiry, and some freedom for criticism. Unless it is assumed that any particular order is perfect, that abuses cannot exist in it, that those in power at the moment represent the last word in economy, science, art, scholarship and government, then there will be criticism. Without it abuses will go uncorrected and possible improvement in the lot of humanity will go unachieved.[56]

Central to Beard's liberalism, as always, was intellectual freedom. Fullest freedom of the mind, he was convinced, underlay and insured all other human freedoms. It was an integral aspect of the dynamics of democracy, as well as essential to that human dignity which was democracy's continuing goal. To enable citizens to have informed opinions and to make intelligent judgment on public matters, the differing sides of every question, he contended, must have opportunity for full airing. The notion of dangerous ideas, he felt, was virtually a contradiction in terms in a liberal democracy.[57]

[54] *American Government and Politics* (10th ed.; 1948), pp. v, 400.

[55] *Weekly News Review*, XVI (May 16, 1938), 8.

[56] "Beard on Liberalism," letter to the editor, *New Republic*, LXXXI (January 30, 1935), 334.

[57] It was in this vein that Beard, as he recalled shortly before his death, had helped further a Senate bill in 1930 to regulate the " 'censorship of imported literature' then freely and wonderfully exercised by customs agents" (Introduction, John P. Frank, *Mr. Justice Black: The Man and His Opinions* [New

Freedom of teaching, Beard believed, was simply a basically vital part of freedom in general. Students had a right to hear. He thought that, as long as appropriate language was chosen, teachers should be free to express themselves regardless of the subject matter. He could not comprehend, for example, how American government could be taught without bringing in "controversy." Discussion of issues was an essential of democracy in the real world. "Even if it were possible to keep every other controversial issue out of the schoolroom, it would be impossible to teach the American system of government without discussing this process of American government." [58] Beard's advocacy of academic liberty remained strong throughout his life. In 1937, twenty years after he himself had resigned from Columbia University over the same principle, he vigorously protested the action of the regents of the University of Wisconsin in dismissing President Glenn Frank without consulting the faculty. Such cases, he felt, "endanger freedom of the spirit to inquire and expound." [59]

Beard recognized that intellectual freedom had ramifications throughout the whole pattern of political and civil rights underlying liberal democracy. Even before American newspapers had begun giving Senator Joseph R. McCarthy lavish front-page space to spread his accusations, Beard became alarmed at the illiberal implications of "guilt by association." In the 1944 edition of *American Government and Politics,* he implied sharp criticism of certain Congressional commitees for "hunting down employees and officials of the Federal Government who were charged with entertaining radical theories or even merely associating with organizations more or less tinged with radicalism." [60] Although he agreed that perhaps, as an abstract principle, those who would destroy freedom should not be given freedom to work for their destructive ends, "practically speaking, it would be difficult to draw a line to that effect which in administra-

York: Alfred A. Knopf, 1948], p. xii). It was also the spirit in which he struck a blow for freedom of discussion and criticism when he figuratively demolished a Hearst offensive on the schools during an education meeting in Atlantic City in 1935 (*New Republic,* LXXXII [March 6, 1935], 86). Beard himself, after deliberately exposing his mind to "dangerous ideas" by rereading Marx and Engels in the middle 1930's, apparently was only strengthened in his anti-Marxism (see Beale, *Charles A. Beard,* pp. 70, 121, 236).

[58] "Freedom of Teaching," *Social Frontier,* I (March, 1935), 18.

[59] "The Case of Glenn Frank," letter to the editor, *New Republic,* LXXXIX (February 3, 1937), 413.

[60] *American Government and Politics* (9th ed.; 1944), p. 23.

tion would not open the door to persecution." [61] To his last years, he opposed government-sponsored spying on the people, and all forms of "witch burning." In 1944 he still had praise for Chief Justice Harlan Fiske Stone who, as attorney general twenty years earlier, had abolished the "prying General Intelligence Division" and put a halt to the activities of the "volunteer corps of sniffers and snoopers who had aided department officials in terrorizing citizens and aliens of unorthodox opinions for about seven years." [62]

In a word, throughout his life Beard's espousal of broadest human freedom never ceased. If anything, his desire to conserve the cherished freedoms and other values of democratic society deepened with the passing years. In his view, regardless of the disconcerting relativism of man's history and the growing perplexities of politics in the atomic age, unfettered scholarship and free inquiry remained supremely worthwhile: "Insistence on opening archives and on critical research and writing is among the firmest guarantees that the night of despotism will not close over the world." [63]

[61] *The Republic* (New York: Viking Press, 1943), p. 133.
[62] Prefatory note, Samuel J. Konefsky, *Chief Justice Stone and the Supreme Court* (New York: Macmillan Co., 1945), p. xviii.
[63] Review of Collingwood, *The Idea of History, American Historical Review*, LII (July, 1947), 708.

CHAPTER XII
A NEW FEDERALISM

The Problem of Power and Liberty

Contributing to a symposium on the "Future of Democracy" in 1937, twenty years after America had entered the war that was to have made the world safe for democracy, Beard looked back and tried to project historical trends. The high tide of popular self-government, he felt, had occurred about 1920. But, since that time, democracy, both in practice and aspiration, had been on the decline among the world's peoples. Although the reaction had been most severe in countries that had known little or no popular control or liberty before 1920, counterdemocratic currents had become increasingly noticeable even in the older democracies.[1] In this age of crisis, what would be the future of liberal democratic government—with its associated humane values and institutions—in America? This, of course, was Beard's primary concern.

As he often formulated the matter, there was a difficult practical problem involved in governance, especially in democratic governance. Abstractly phrased, it was the problem or dilemma of balancing authority and freedom, power and liberty. If in some ways there appeared to have been a recent "decline in civil liberty" and in other ways a "gain," Beard's contemplation of the subject did not stop with the generalization that "the battle between liberty and authority apparently is eternal."[2] The specific ramifications of this "battle," interwoven as they were with his various other intellectual interests, continued to concern him to the end. The great problem, although never finally to be settled, could be simply put: "How to maintain a government strong enough to defend society against external and internal foes and yet so organized as to protect, by supreme law and

[1] *New Republic,* XCI (May 12, 1937), 13 f.
[2] *The Republic* (New York: Viking Press, 1943), p. 160.

its administration, the liberties of the people against oppressive actions by public agents or popular tumults." [3]

In addition, Beard had long recognized that the greatest threats to human freedom did not necessarily spring from governmental actions. Sometimes governmental inaction was worse, especially in modern times. Despite the tradition, leading back to the period of English classical liberalism, that a laissez-faire policy on the part of government was the best assurance of popular liberty, it was patently not true that the less the government did the more the people could do. The great depression itself demonstrated that, if government kept its hands off too many things, millions of people would have only the empty liberty of being hungry, cold, and unemployed.[4] Modern democracy, Beard was convinced, must be positively acting democracy.

Another kind of threat to liberty in modern times was the danger that democratic government "as now constituted" might prove unable to "deal effectively with the general functions common to all governments." These functions had mushroomed as technology and science created new instruments and new needs, and had continued broadening in depression and prosperity, war and peace. As Beard well knew, the expression of the people's wishes was only the prelude to the far-flung operations of government and administration. Welfare activities, defense preparations, economic undertakings, regulation of corporations and labor unions, aid to agriculture, conservation of resources, relief of unemployment, and numerous other tasks and problems now burdened government. If democracy broke down under these mountainous burdens, would some form of decisively acting, but liberty-killing, despotism result? [5]

Thus the dangers to liberty and democracy seemed to threaten from opposite quarters. If the government did too little, meaningful freedom for most people would shrink. Yet, if the necessary reversal of laissez faire were carried too far in too many realms of human life, the freedom of the individual would be endangered by the measures

[3] Introduction, John P. Frank, *Mr. Justice Black: The Man and His Opinions* (New York: Alfred A. Knopf, 1948), p. v.

[4] Cf. *Public Policy and the General Welfare* (New York: Farrar & Rinehart, 1941), p. 146.

[5] See Beard's discussion in "Essentials of Democracy," *School and Society,* L (August 19, 1939), 230 f.

of excessively strong leadership. In either direction lay undesirable consequences.

Beard displayed distrust of powerful leadership more frequently in his last years than in former periods of his life. His feeling on this score was magnified by the coming of World War II and his conviction that President Roosevelt had been instrumental in bringing this country needlessly into the conflict. But, aside from his anger at what he considered to be the duplicity of particular leaders, he was concerned about the general shift of power from legislature to executive. Extreme centralization and concentration of power, he feared, might seriously undermine responsibility in government. In the 1944 edition of *American Government and Politics,* he disagreed with those who sought to present theoretical justification for the power shift, claiming that "in sum and substance this theory savors of the fascist 'leadership principle.' " The fact that various democratic controls, such as popular elections and legislative checks, might temper the demands of leadership apparently did not entirely relieve his anxiety.[6]

Beard's misgivings respecting unrestrained leadership rose drastically as World War II began in Europe during Roosevelt's second term. There was a marked contrast between his remarks on presidential power in a 1937 article in *Social Research* and his statement to a Congressional committee four years later regarding a proposed grant of presidential power. In the article he had written approvingly of "the theory of a necessary dictatorship in times of great social crisis," as exemplified in the thought of the *Federalist*. Hamilton, he noted, had vigorously defended a strong executive because historic experience had shown "great concentration of power" to be necessary "in times of domestic crisis and foreign war." In Beard's opinion, our presidential system provided governmental strength and unity against the internal diversities and conflicts that might otherwise disrupt society. He appeared to find comfort in the thought that, since the presidency was elective, great concentration of power in some periods of our history had alternated with dissipation of power in other periods.[7]

But, in his Lend-Lease testimony in early 1941, Beard made vigor-

[6] *American Government and Politics* (9th ed.; New York: Macmillan Co., 1944), pp. 214 f.

[7] "Democracy and Education in the United States," *Social Research,* IV (September, 1937), 395 f.

ous and detailed objection to the proposed delegation of power to the President. Because of the "sweeping language" of the bill, he felt that it was inappropriate to entitle it an act to "promote the defense of the United States." In his view the title should read as follows:

All provisions of law and the Constitution to the contrary notwithstanding, an Act to place all the wealth and all the men and women of the United States at the free disposal of the President, to permit him to transfer or carry goods to any foreign government he may be pleased to designate, anywhere in the world, to authorize him to wage undeclared wars for anybody, anywhere in the world, until the affairs of the world are ordered to suit his policies, and for any other purpose he may have in mind now or at any time in the future, which may be remotely related to the contingencies contemplated in the title of this Act.[8]

Beard's concern for the future of liberal democracy in America led him into continuing re-examination of the actual processes of government. In his later years he tended to place more emphasis than formerly on the conception of politics as power, as the wielding of various kinds of influence and sanctions over human action. In 1924 he had pointed out how the concept of government had been changing through the years: *in the past* the prevalent conception had been that the essence of government was power, whereas in the modern day acts of state had come to comprise "acts of service" rather than of force. "Today we have reached a point where government is no longer defended or justified on the ground of mere power."[9] But by the thirties and forties Beard himself appeared to have acquired a new appreciation of the old conception centering around power.

Thus, in *The Open Door at Home* (1934), he asserted that in final analysis the essence of government was compulsion, even though this necessarily involved a large degree of passive acquiescence, active consent, and willing cooperation on the part of the people. Although practitioners of politics, he acknowledged in 1935, *gained* power in democracy by acting as brokers of opinion, once they had won power they bent all efforts and used virtually any device to retain it. In 1936, when Nazi troops illegally reoccupied the demilitarized Rhineland, he pointed to the Hitler regime as an example of power that was little

[8] "Statement of Charles A. Beard, New Milford, Conn.," February 4, 1941, *To Promote the Defense of the United States: Hearings before the Committee on Foreign Relations United States Senate on Senate [Bill]* 275, 77 Cong., 1 Sess., p. 309.

[9] *American Government and Politics* (4th ed.; New York: Macmillan Co., 1924), pp. 5 f.

restrained by established rules or the desires of its subjects, in contrast to power in other governments in which officials were under the restraints of law even while necessarily exercising a great degree of discretion. Yet, ultimately, in every government, he reiterated in 1943, physical power lay behind all other forms of power, even though simple naked force was certainly not the sole characteristic of government.[10]

In *The Republic* (1943) Beard explained that historically rule over large areas had originated in military conquest, and down to the present time "physical power to compel action or obedience" had remained vital to the existence of government. But the modern complex of political power was far from simple. It included such imponderable realities as human will, fear, gratitude, affection, loyalty, avarice, and ambition. Yet, for all Beard's analysis, his fear of the dangers inherent in political power did not thereby diminish. An appreciation of the vital need for power in modern society, combined with a fear of power, seemed only to sharpen his concern. Human liberty and democracy depended on maintaining the correct precarious relationship between power and the restraint on power:

This composite power which we call political may be concentrated in the hands of one person and his clique, or it may be widely diffused among many persons. If the dispersion is wide enough, you have a democracy. Too much concentration is despotism. Too much diffusion approaches anarchy and dissolution. Despotism and anarchy are both mortal foes of human liberty.[11]

Many years earlier, in the so-called flag incident of 1916, Beard's theoretical and practical position on the balance of authority and liberty had been revealed in a letter to the *New Republic* by fifty-three of his graduate students. Beard believed, his students had written, "that we could not expect to have liberty without some abuse of it, and that as between having too much authority or too much liberty, he preferred the latter."[12] If this preference in later life re-

[10] See *The Open Door at Home,* with G. H. E. Smith (New York: Macmillan Co., 1934), p. 309; "Peace Loads the Guns," *Today,* IV (June 29, 1935), 3; "Living Constitution," *Annals of the American Academy of Political and Social Science,* CLXXXV (May, 1936), 29; *The Republic* (New York: Viking Press, 1943), p. 180. Cf. also Max Lerner's comments on Beard as "a theorist of power," in Howard K. Beale (ed.), *Charles A. Beard* (Lexington: University of Kentucky Press, 1954), p. 45.

[11] *The Republic,* pp. 180 f.

[12] "What Professor Beard Said about the Flag," *New Republic,* VII (May 6, 1916), 18.

mained generally the same, he nonetheless seemed to reopen his position to further examination. His continued explorations led back, as often in his lifetime of history writing, to the wisdom of the American founding fathers. Like them, he feared too much flux and too much tyranny.

Return to the Fathers

In 1943 Beard admitted that his more recent studies had given him a changed view of the formative period of the American Constitution. Whereas in his progressive era writings he had seen the early struggle over the Constitution as a conflict between populists and federalists, or between the small farmers and propertyless on one side against planters and personalty interests on the other, he now claimed to have discovered that a third force had also been involved. "On the extreme right of the conservatives" had been an incipient movement favoring military dictatorship of some kind. Beard's new view was in keeping with an apparently general change in liberal attitude toward America's past, an attitude more appreciative and less critical of the legacy left by the founders. The fact that the founding fathers had been republicans now impressed him more than the fact that they had not been democrats. He admired General Washington's courage in handing back, over the opposition of the militarists, the dictatorial powers that had been granted him: "His firm resistance to every proposal for the seizure of power showed his unfailing devotion to constitutional methods, even in a revolutionary war." [13]

Thus, paying less attention to the motives and more to the lasting political achievements of the fathers, Beard now re-examined their insights and views for possible light on present problems. Something of their spirit of realism, he felt, was again needed. With the spread of dictatorships in Europe and the growth of antidemocratic sentiments in America, perhaps "a re-exploration of power politics, based on ferocity and ambition," would be fruitful. In the same spirit that had been exhibited by Machiavelli, by the founding fathers, and by other

[13] *The Republic*, pp. 24, 45; cf. also George S. Counts's remarks on this changed attitude on Beard's part, in Beale, *Charles A. Beard*, p. 250. It may also be pointed out that a number of recent scholars, despite their impressive researches on Beard's earlier writings and ideas, have tended to overlook the fact that Beard himself (whether validly or not) in later life revised his former contentions.

political realists, it was necessary to take into account the seamy side of human nature as well as the pleasing side. Fully recognizing the "ambitions, passions, ferocities, and lusts of men," the founding fathers had built soundly so as to preserve "the sacred fire of liberty and the destiny of the republican model of government."[14]

Recognizing the factious propensities of human nature, the founders, Beard emphasized, had conceived of government as power, and according to their philosophy human liberty was best sustained by pitting power against power. Montesquieu's teachings had held a high place in their thinking. Power, they had believed, must be controlled, limited, and separated. Government must rest on stable economic and legal foundations, or the ends of government would be defeated.[15] Their realistic philosophy of government, Beard felt, was clearly and admirably set forth in the *Federalist* papers. However else his attitude toward the work of the founding fathers might have changed throughout his life, Beard's admiration for the *Federalist* continued unabated. In 1946 he called it "the one powerful work on political science produced in the United States" and praised its authors for avoiding foggy abstractions and for grappling with concrete problems. At the close of his life he published selected numbers of the *Federalist* in book form, suggesting that "with the world just emerging from one global war and trembling on the verge of another" the federalism of the American founding fathers might be a useful model for the world.[16]

The framers of the Constitution, Beard noted, had foreseen future emergencies in which strong leadership would be required for safety and stability. They had intended their work, as Marshall had phrased it, "to endure for ages to come, and, consequently to be adapted to the various crises of human affairs." Yet the framers, also understanding that "government in action is power," had provided safeguards against undue concentration of power in any one branch or agency of government. Realizing that "balance and movement are

[14] *America in Midpassage*, with Mary R. Beard (New York: Macmillan Co., 1939), p. 893; *American Government and Politics* (9th ed.; 1944), p. 7.

[15] Cf. *American Government and Politics* (9th ed.; 1944), p. 13; also see "What Is This Democracy?" in *Adult Education and Democracy* (New York: American Association for Adult Education, 1936), pp. 2 f.

[16] *The Enduring Federalist* (ed.) (New York: Doubleday & Co., 1948), p. 4; also cf. Beard's remarks in "Grounds for a Reconsideration of Historiography," in Merle E. Curti (ed.), *Theory and Practice in Historical Study: A Report of the Committee on Historiography* (Social Science Research Council Bulletin, No. 54, 1946), p. 9.

compatible," they had set up a government that was under restraint and yet could act. To the fathers, restraint had meant neither paralysis in the face of emergencies nor inability to carry out necessary functions. Furthermore, capacity to act had also not meant excessive and arbitrary power in official hands.[17]

Beard denied that a return to the wisdom of the fathers meant blindness to all later developments in our history. The present needs and wants of the people must be given fullest weight. If necessary, the powers of government as embodied in the fundamental law would have to be amended.[18] Moreover, it was not true that "we must merely go back to the Fathers in a quest for knowledge of the Constitution." [19] It was necessary also to examine its *development* down to the present day.

Nevertheless, Beard's later writings did reflect a marked change in attitude toward the political accomplishments of the founding fathers. Richard Hofstadter has shown, for example, an interesting contrast between the treatment of the Constitution-making period in *The Rise of American Civilization* in 1927, and that appearing in *A Basic History of the United States* in 1944. In 1927 the Beards labeled the period in question "Populism and Reaction," but in 1944 they entitled it "Constitutional Government for the United States." In 1927 the constitutional system of checks and balances was described as "dissolving the energy of the democratic majority," whereas seventeen years later the same checks and balances were characterized as a system to prevent "accumulation of despotic power in any hands." The 1927 book mentioned the fear of democracy on the part of the fathers, their substantial personalty interests, and their appreciation of the economic basis of politics as expounded by *Federalist* No. 10. The 1944 book, in contrast, pointed out how the balanced nature of the government prevented the "snap judgment" of a temporary majority from prevailing generally. It described the conservative nature of the assembled delegates and, without reference to the Madisonian thesis, praised their achievement as follows: "Without drawing the sword in civil war, without shedding a drop

[17] *The Republic*, p. 190; see also Franklin Watts (ed.), *Voices of History: Great Speeches and Papers of the Year 1941* (New York: Franklin Watts, 1942), p. xii; cf. *American Government and Politics* (9th ed.; 1944), p. 214.

[18] "Great Constitutional Issues before the Nation," with Clay Coss, *Weekly News Review*, XIV (September 9, 1935), 8.

[19] "The Living Constitution," letter to the editor, *New Republic*, LXXXVIII (August 26, 1936), 77.

of blood, a new plan of government had been proposed, framed, discussed, and adopted." [20]

Constitutionalism and Old Bill Walters

At one point in the dialogue of *The Republic,* Beard had "Dr. Smyth" fulminating against the frailties and general ineptitude of ordinary mortals. This led Beard to mention "that old bum, Bill Walters, who was found drunk and half-frozen on the edge of town two years ago," but who, none the less, had regained his health, reformed, and taken a steady job. Conceding that the people have many faults, even if not to the extent of old Bill Walters, Beard maintained that, "in spite of everything, the people composed of many nationalities have kept the Republic going for more than a hundred and fifty years, and . . . it has taken an immense amount of virtue to perform this single feat." [21]

How had the American people managed to harness ability and energy in such a way as to keep the republic going for so long despite the obvious shortcomings and disruptive tendencies of human nature? An important key to this achievement, Beard came increasingly to think, consisted of those instruments and devices wisely fashioned by the founding fathers. Even with the growing democratization of the republic in later generations, to an extent the fathers would probably not have approved, its continued survival had been made possible by constitutional principles which, as Beard remarked in *School and Society,* fastened "restraints upon the regular operations of majorities and upon the irregular insolence of mobs." As he pondered the stresses and strains on the republic in his last years, his admiration for "the refuge established by the Constitution against the passions of rulers and multitudes" rose even higher.[22]

Yet the American political system, he conceded, had not been intended as an absolute restraint on the wants and desires of the masses of the people. As conflicting groups and individuals had asserted and attempted to implement their respective demands, compromises had been worked out. Successfully established claims had evolved into "rights," as these had come finally to rest on "the moral standards of the community and the nation." [23] In the historic interplay

[20] As quoted by Richard Hofstadter, in Beale, *Charles A. Beard,* pp. 91 f.

[21] *The Republic,* pp. 11 f.

[22] Frank, *Mr. Justice Black,* p. xiv; "Essentials of Democracy," *School and Society,* L (August 19, 1939), 233.

[23] *The Republic,* pp. 38 f.

of contending groups, constitutional principles had evolved along with the idea of democracy. Nonetheless a realistic student of the American political system could not consider it simply as democracy:

Democracy is only one element in the American system and we must consider other essentials. Two of the essentials are authority and liberty—power and freedom. The Constitution of the United States provides for both; indeed, the very word "constitution" itself implies limited government. Hence it is useful to consider the Constitution as a system of power and as a system of liberty.[24]

Beard did not imagine, however, that the republic, as founded by the fathers and as it had evolved through our history, was a wholly automatic or self-correcting machine. Notwithstanding all its brakes and built-in stabilizers to offset human frailties, human beings still manned the controls. His studies of both democracy and constitutionalism as features of the American system led him to the same ultimate sanction for government, namely, the people. The final reliance, after all, was on old Bill Walters and the other millions of individuals, good, bad, and indifferent. As he stated in 1943 in *The Republic*:

Political science involves human beings, and human beings are moral beings. Note that I do not say righteous beings. If for decency, progress, order, and liberty in the community and the nation, we cannot rely upon the character, sentiments, allegiances, and moral habits of the people, upon what, in heaven's name, can we rely? [25]

Beard's emphasis, of course, varied from time to time. On some occasions he seemed unimpressed by the fact that "the people" were not in closer direct control of the political machinery. On other occasions he rose up in vigorous defense of the people's capacity for self-government. Thus in the *American Mercury* in 1936, in discussing "minority rule" under our system, he doubted that anyone was "likely to get excited about free and equal heads and absolute majority rule—at least, excited enough to move the mountain of constitutional barrier." In his view, "nothing short of a long-time obstruction of some clear majority resolve" could alter present arrangements.[26] Six years later in the same magazine he decried the widespread habit of reviling Congress, declaring that, if all the

[24] *Public Policy and the General Welfare*, p. ix.
[25] *The Republic*, p. 39.
[26] "Minority Rule in America," *American Mercury*, XXXVII (February, 1936), 196.

charges were true, "representative government is dead in the United States and merely waits the kind of funeral that Hitler provided for the German Reichstag." Even more ominous, since the American people who elected Congress were "incapable of self-government," only tyranny lay in store. His point was that the wholesale indictment was not true.[27]

The American system of power and liberty, as Beard knew, was characterized by the mutal interaction of human discretion and impersonal imperatives. The operation of the judiciary was an illustration of this interaction. Although the "social and economic views of the judges" were finally determining when vague constitutional provisions were being interpreted, nevertheless the courts were a significant protection of human freedom against arbitrary power.[28] Beard thought the court controversy of 1937 revealed something deeply significant for American constitutionalism. That is, regardless of the precise outcome of the battle, all antagonists were agreed on the need for retaining the principle of checks and balances in American political practice. The "sense for the limitation of power" which had guided the founders was still very much a part of American tradition, and it was not on the verge of being destroyed.[29] To the end of his life, he saw in "judicial resistance to governmental encroachments" one of the prime examples of constitutionalism.[30]

But, if constitutionalism limited the exercise of arbitrary power, it also specifically placed limits on the decision-making processes of democratic majorities. When the Supreme Court, for example, decided whether the Congressional majority that passed a bill had the constitutional power to do so, it was guided in part by the judges' views "as to what Congress *should* do."[31] To Beard's mind, the

[27] "In Defense of Congress," *American Mercury,* LV (November, 1942), 529 f.

[28] "Advocates of Constitutional Change Do Not Aim to Destroy State Powers," with Clay Coss, *Weekly News Review,* XIV (September 30, 1935), 8; cf. also *American Government and Politics* (8th ed.; 1939), pp. 38 f.; "Living Constitution," p. 31; review of White, *Essays in Honor of Charles E. Merriam: The Future of Government in the United States, American Political Science Review,* XXXVI (October, 1942), 953.

[29] "Court and Constitution," *Events,* I (June, 1937), 407–11.

[30] Frank, *Mr. Justice Black,* p. xiii; cf. "Origin of Supreme Court's Power to Overrule Congressional Laws," with Clay Coss, *Weekly News Review,* XIV (December 9, 1935), 8; *American Government and Politics* (8th ed.; 1939), p. 193.

[31] "TVA Raises Issue over Power of Congress to Control Navigation," with Clay Coss, *Weekly News Review,* XIV (October 21, 1935), 8.

constitutional limitations on the exercise of majority power were
not, however, an absolute veto or final block to action. Rather, they
were intended as a kind of suspensive veto to help insure that the
majority judgment would be matured and was not the snap decision
of the moment. Prevention of hasty and ill-considered action
through the operation of the brakes and frictions of the system
would allow time for second thoughts and cooler reflection. Presumably more humane and reasonable government would result.
Beard indicated something of this feeling when he commented in
1936 that he found himself unwilling to "entrust everything I hold
dear to a mere majority of Congress." [32] A system that provided for
"some delay, popular discussion, and popular judgment" held more
appeal for him.

Democracy requires that the judgment of the people must prevail, but
American institutions are designed to assure that in matters fundamental
the popular judgment be matured. In other words, they do not place all
rights and obligations of life, liberty, and economy at the disposal of the
majority or plurality which carries a single election for political officers.
. . . Legal safeguards, tenure, and independence, of whatever kind or degree, are intended to serve, not to block, the deliberative processes of
democracy and to guarantee the competent discharge of its primary functions. The principle . . . is so fundamental to the future of democratic
society that it must be respected, maintained, and defended, if a way is to
be steered between government by plebiscite and government by privi-
lege.[33]

In his later years Beard closely associated constitutionalism with
the kind of democracy he felt had developed in the United States.
Although he insisted that democracy, in strict theory, was not
identical with constitutionalism, he sometimes used the terms almost
interchangeably. In *The Republic,* for example, he explained that
the American system of constitutional government included such
elements as "the process of proposal, discussion, and popular decision at the polls," restraints on officials, reservation of rights to the
people, direct or indirect choice of officials by the voters, limited
powers and terms, and periodic elections. Constitutionalism was in

[32] "Rendezvous with the Supreme Court," *New Republic,* LXXXVIII (September 2, 1936), 93.
[33] *The Unique Function of Education in American Democracy* (Washington, D.C.: Educational Policies Commission, National Education Association
of the United States and the Department of Superintendence, 1937), pp.
111 f.

contradiction to despotic government, which denied that "the people are fit to govern themselves." [34]

As a result of his latter-day reflections on American government, Beard concluded that the basic pattern was sound, and his concern was to preserve the heritage of the fathers as gradually modified in practice. He felt that the system was democratic to a significant degree because "in the long run the sustained and matured will of the duly constituted majority is allowed to prevail." But he also found comfort in the fact that "no mere majority" could make basic alterations hurriedly. It was a system of majority rule in a "time span," a system that prevented "the snap judgment" of the moment from determining fundamental matters. [35] It was an ideal of delayed-reaction democracy, however, which represented a considerable evolution in Beard's attitude toward the built-in frictions he used to criticize as a "tripartite scheme of negation."

The Theory of Neofederalism

In theory, as Beard made clear in 1943, he did not equate constitutional government with democracy. Democracy meant "majority or plurality rule." On the other hand, government being power, constitutional government meant "restraint on power," or "civilian and limited government" which made provision for maintaining human rights. Thus, constitutional government included the notion of "fundamental rights reserved to the people," the necessity of extraordinary majorities to amend constitutional provisions, and certain arrangements in the "organization of the government itself." Beard claimed that constitutionalism, however, necessarily implied "a degree of democracy," thereby suggesting that constitutional government required that the rights and wishes of the majority must be to some degree maintained. He felt that beyond question we had to link democracy in our thinking with "constitutionalism with its guarantees of individual rights." [36]

Applying his theoretical distinction to practice, Beard showed how "democracy under the mechanical theory" might grossly violate the canons of constitutionalism. Through "the majority principle," a minority might be forced into acquiescence even if this meant endangering or destroying individual rights. But constitutional

[34] *The Republic,* p. 16.
[35] "Essentials of Democracy," *School and Society,* L (August 19, 1939), 230.
[36] *The Republic,* pp. 37 f.

government entailed restraints on power, "even the power of democracy." Therefore constitutionalism and democracy could actually be "at war with each other."[37]

The heart of the theoretical matter engaging Beard was thus not the distinction between democracy and autocracy. If, abstractly, modern democracy means government in which rulers are responsible to "the people," and autocracy (or despotism) means government in which they are not, Beard clearly favored the former. But what if "the people" to whom the rulers are to be responsible are fundamentally at odds among themselves? Beard's deep conviction was that, in such a case, a "mere majority" should not ruthlessly trample over the opposition. It was not the fact that great numbers might support a prevalent view, but the deliberative method of arriving at and implementing basic social decisions, which Beard cherished. The "method or manner of rule" could be as significant for human rights as whether or not the government was effectively responsible.[38]

Beard's theoretical problem, accordingly, might be said to concern not democracy and autocracy, but constitutionalism and dictatorship. He cherished the method of constitutionalism, the method or manner of rule in which "due process of law" prevails, with wide discussion and the presentation of opposing viewpoints by important leaders before final decision of great public issues. What he feared was any inclination toward dictatorship, the method or manner of rule in which little attention is actually paid to due process of law, and in which important decisions are made by a leader or leaders in advance of the public discussion stage. He was anxious to preserve a system of constitutionalism under which the great social decisions tend to represent a compromise among the diverse interests affected by them, and under which rights are generally protected. He was concerned to resist, on the other hand, any tendency toward a system of dictation under which conformity is imposed with little reference to particular interests, and under which rights are insecure.

More than a century and a half earlier, John Adams, the "philosopher of federalism," had pondered similar problems of government.

[37] *Ibid.*
[38] The theoretical relationship of the "method or manner of rule" to constitutionalism and dictatorship (as distinguished from democracy and autocracy) is ably discussed by G. Lowell Field in his volume, *Governments in Modern Society* (New York: McGraw-Hill Book Co., 1951), pp. 38 f., 526–32.

Holding that neither the masses nor the classes were really trustworthy, he had thought that the power drives of the two strata could
be channeled and neutralized through political arrangements designed to safeguard the larger welfare of the whole community. The
American founding fathers, well acquainted with this Adams
federalism, had presumably sought to implement it to some extent in
the instrument fashioned at Philadelphia in 1787. If their federalism
had been pervaded by a feeling for the limitation of power and did
not exactly coincide with democratic accountability, so Beard's neofederalism, even though he trusted popular controls more than
they did, was also not exactly identical with majoritarian democracy.

In the later years of his life Beard had come to feel more keenly
than before, even if only implicitly, that majority rule was but one
human value among several others. Granting—as he had done all his
life—that the ultimate ideal, the highest priority value, was to treat
human individuals as ends in themselves, he had come to recognize
a broader range of subsidiary values (or "intermediate ideals" [39]).
These subsidiary values were *instrumental* in relation to the highest
priority value. By and large they usually served and furthered the
ultimate ideal. In the political realm, such subsidiary values might
include majority rule, stable and orderly government, internal peace
and order, national unity, attention to various shades of popular
opinion, and so on. Roughly, to further these subsidiary values was
to further the ultimate value, the human individual himself.

But what if one subsidiary value conflicted with another? In order
to serve the ultimate value most effectively in the long run, how
should conflicting subsidiary values be weighed? What if strict
majority rule could be had only at the cost of internal disorder and
chaos? What if, in another global war, human survival itself temporarily took precedence over all else? In short, although Beard
cherished majority rule, he wanted it exercised in moderation, with
safeguards to prevent the destruction of other values. Majority rule,
which he defined as democracy, was not the supreme value in the
priority of human values. Majority rule might on occasion be "at
war" with other values. Thus one faced a difficult matter of judgment among intangibles and imponderables rather than a nicely
calculable "problem in hydraulics."

Constitutionalism, then, represented for Beard the method of

[39] Arnold S. Kaufman, "The Nature and Function of Political Theory,"
Journal of Philosophy, LI (January 7, 1954), 5–22.

moderation and reason in human affairs. Doctrinairism and extremism of all kinds—including liberty, authority, or radical democracy carried too far—were incompatible with constitutionalism.[40] He saw constitutionalism as a defense of human liberty against even democracy if need be. Yet, accountability to the majority, in turn, was a shield for human values which despotism might otherwise destroy. Beard felt that the United States Constitution, embodying the wisdom of the fathers, struck an admirable balance among potentially diverse purposes. As he declared in the 1948 edition of his *American Government and Politics:*

The very essence of government, everywhere and always, is power—the power of persons called officials to make and enforce laws affecting the life, liberty, and property of the people. Such power is necessary in any great society to prevent it from dissolving into warring elements or utter chaos. If vested in a moderate and competent government held responsible to the people under supreme law, power may be so wielded in the public interest as to promote domestic tranquility, measured liberty, and the general welfare. If it becomes unrestrained in the hands of ruthless leaders, power may be employed to arouse violent hatreds and destroy cherished liberties; through the launching of extravagant wars of conquest, such power may produce disaster at home and devastation abroad. . . . The founders of the United States . . . created a system of government and liberty, so framed in terms of power and so checked by concrete devices as to avoid, at least up to the present, both the extremes of anarchy and despotism.[41]

Thus Beard's political philosophy had evolved into a theory of neofederalism. It is true that in the progressive era his ideas had already been somewhat reminiscent of the federalism of John Adams in that he had placed great confidence in political machinery, properly reformed. But then his main goal, in contrast to that of Adams, had been democracy and efficiency. Structural arrangements had seemed important to Beard because sometimes they hampered the democratic political process. He had complained of the "friction" of governmental machinery, and his reformist inclinations had been on the side of oiling the machinery and minimizing the frictions to permit democracy to roll more smoothly.

In the 1920's the distinction between "politics" and "administration" had seemed significant to Beard and other public administration scholars. Keeping the two processes separated had appeared to

[40] Cf. "Future of Democracy: V," *New Republic,* XCI (May 12, 1937), 14; *The Republic,* p. 35.
[41] *American Government and Politics* (10th ed.; 1948), p. 3.

be a basic prerequisite for reconciling democracy and efficiency. Considerable attention had also been given to the problem of modernizing and streamlining the instruments of popular representation. By and large the emphasis on democracy had continued. It had been felt that what the people wanted the people should have, with frictions minimized.

Beard's subsequently developed neofederalism, however, exemplified a renewed reliance on political forms and mechanisms which seemed to place him closer to the position of the founding fathers. It was a theoretical system meant not only to give scope to the constructive potentialities of human nature, but also to curb its destructive and authoritarian propensities. It was "democracy in a time span." Reason would rule action, but reason was to be allowed to operate effectively before action took place. It was an ideal permeated by a "sense for the limitation of power," even the power of democracy.[42]

[42] Cf. also Beard's discussion and remarks in *The Republic,* pp. 254 f.; *Enduring Federalist,* pp. 6, 8 f.; prefatory note, Samuel J. Konefsky, *Chief Justice Stone and the Supreme Court* (New York: Macmillan Co., 1945), p. xiii.

CHAPTER XIII
AN AMERICAN GARDEN

The Unity of Politics

Domestic and world politics, Beard often reiterated, were one and inseparable. Spokesmen of various nations might assert with emotion that their tariffs and armaments were purely domestic issues, yet their assertions did not lessen the repercussions throughout the world. Tariffs and armaments were "outward thrusts of power," as much so as the display of naked force against another nation, stimulation of foreign investment, or trade promotion.[1] With international tensions again rising in the 1930's, Beard took a renewed interest in this unity of politics, with its implied danger of American involvement in another general war.

He had, of course, long underscored the tightening economic unity of the world, and before World War I he had especially noted the close relationship between economics and international politics. Despite his changing views respecting the economic undergirding of politics generally, in 1934 he still claimed that "there is no emotional outburst in international affairs on a large scale which is not accompanied and stimulated by economic interests of some kind."[2]

Accordingly, with questions of war and peace so closely tied to domestic political and economic developments, Beard's enthusiasm for New Deal recovery efforts was tempered by a constant concern for their effect on international politics. In like manner, he was vitally interested in the repercussions of foreign crises on America's politics and economy. He realized that the activities of private eco-

[1] *The Idea of National Interest*, with G. H. E. Smith (New York: Macmillan Co., 1934), pp. 311, 357; see also review of Lenin, *The Revolution of 1917* and *Toward the Seizure of Power, New Republic*, LXXV (May 17, 1933), 24.

[2] *The Open Door at Home*, with G. H. E. Smith (New York: Macmillan Co., 1934), p. 172.

nomic interests, if completely unregulated by the government, could produce serious international complications. Excess anarchy in the world's economy contributed to anarchy and war in the world political realm. Yet, on the other hand, it would be unheard of to sever completely American economic and commercial ties with the rest of the world. The welfare of America had long been closely related to economic developments elsewhere, and economic intercourse with other nations had contributed considerably to America's industrialization.[3] Therefore the nation's economic well-being, as well as the goal of peace, seemed to Beard to call for skillful and dedicated statesmanship which would steer a successful course between the extremes of aloofness and intimacy toward the rest of the world.

The policies of any nation, Beard pointed out, were supposedly based on something termed the "national interest." Yet, the concept was a changing one, and over the years American national interest had meant different things. Moreover, at the present time it could be taken to include our interests throughout the world, or merely within this hemisphere. But, regardless of variable content or name, throughout history national interest had been closely associated with the wars nations fought.

Beard undertook a thorough exploration of this subject in *The Idea of National Interest* (1934), written in collaboration with G. H. E. Smith. The idea, he found, had been developed to serve the nation-state system, just as previous formulas had served the dynasties and princes of earlier centuries. The formula of national interest was now used to cover the objectives of diplomacy and had become the center around which international relations seemed to revolve. In recent times the concept had taken on a considerable economic content. Indeed, the principal national interests pursued in the years leading up to the war of 1914 had been the imperialistic activities of the great powers as to territory and trade.[4] The clash of rival economic imperialisms had therefore been largely instrumental in bringing on war. Similarly, thought Beard, economic factors would weigh heavily in bringing on a future war:

[3] For related comments, see Thomas I. Cook and Malcolm Moos, *Power through Purpose* (Baltimore, Md.: Johns Hopkins Press, 1954), pp. 163–65.

[4] *The Idea of National Interest,* pp. v-vii, 21 f.; also see *The Devil Theory of War* (New York: Vanguard Press, 1936), p. 116; Beard develops a similar theme in "War Springs from Peace," *Scholastic,* XXV (November 10, 1934), 12, 29.

The degree of probability that the United States will become involved in any war arising anywhere in Europe or Asia bears a direct relation to the extent of the economic interests possessed by American nationals in the affected area, and in the fortunes of the respective belligerents.[5]

Beard did not deny that moral and ethical considerations played a possible part in national interest, even though it was difficult to judge the relevance of such factors from official statements alone. President Taft had made fewer official references to these noneconomic factors than had Theodore Roosevelt before him. But President Wilson's foreign policy declarations had usually purported to rest on moral values rather than on national interest conceived in commercial terms. It was impossible to know for certain whether moral obligation or estimates of material advantage had been weightier considerations for American leaders making free use of the term "national interest." With precision therefore lacking, it seemed to Beard that the most important national interest was to preserve peace. Like the statesmen he discussed, he put into the formula what his own value scheme dictated. Avoidance of war seemed to him of the highest priority.[6]

Analyzing the origins of war, Beard saw it as "the transfer to the battlefield of policies pursued in time of peace." War was not, therefore, a "phenomenon of nature" or an "absolute law of history" against which man was helpless. As a social phenomenon, a man-made catastrophe, war was the outgrowth of interests asserted against other states, objectives to be attained "by violence if necessary." War could not be avoided by reconstructing the peaceful world of the pre-1914 era. It was a delusion to think that we could "recover a hypothetical world system from the past." Moreover, it had been that era of "peace" which had produced war, an era embracing laissez faire, protectionism, imperialism, colonialism, and a host of other factors and conditions. Out of this complex had come war. "The World War did not come as a *Deus ex machina* to disrupt the system; it was one of the fruits of the system."[7]

Beard reasoned that if war flowed from policy, and if policy in turn was intimately connected to domestic economic factors, it followed that efforts to minimize the chances of war should begin at

[5] *The Open Door at Home,* p. 269.
[6] *The Idea of National Interest,* pp. 375, 377, 399.
[7] *The Open Door at Home,* p. 127; see also *Today,* IV (June 29, 1935), 3; "War Springs from Peace," pp. 12, 29.

home. Our peacetime policy must be based on defense of "the American nation in its continental domain." On the other hand, if our policy were based on defense of private interests all over the world, the probabilities of war would be immeasurably increased, and its scope would be magnified if it came.[8] The assumption that seemed to creep into Beard's reasoning was that problems are more amenable to sound solution on a smaller than on a larger scale. It could be pointed out, however, that, at least on the level of logic, exactly the reverse might be equally valid. Conceivably, if domestic and world politics are a continuum, the problem of war might be as logically attacked on a world scale as on the national scale.

In 1936 Beard extended his analysis of the origins of war in a small volume entitled *The Devil Theory of War*. It was entirely fallacious, he insisted, to think that wicked men or wicked forces made war, and that, if only the peace-loving masses were left undisturbed in their "peaceful" pursuits, tranquility would reign forever. In place of this idyllic and childish notion, the hard fact was that war sprang from peace. Beard's attack on the devil theory was thus in a sense a re-echo, in the mid-thirties, of his old contention that *impersonal* forces rather than great men tend to make history.

In the pursuit of peace, people are doing things that have a direct bearing on war. They are producing goods and offering them for sale. . . . War is not made by a *deus ex machina,* but comes out of ideas, interests and activities cherished and followed in the preceding months and years of peace. . . . War is not the work of a demon. It is our very own work, for which we prepare, wittingly or not, in ways of peace. But most of us sit blind-folded at the preparation.[9]

Thus Beard seemed to be pulled in opposite directions: on the one hand he implied that a hardheaded realist should recognize that impersonal forces largely shape human events, and on the other hand he was troubled by the lurking suspicion that some people might be *wittingly* working to bring on war. Indeed, as early as 1934 he was suggesting that, with reference to the New Deal, the unity of domestic and world politics might be exemplified in a way decidedly opposed to the *real* national interest (i.e., avoidance of war). Failure to solve problems at home might lead to an attention-diverting foreign venture. In *The Idea of National Interest* he broadly hinted that the Roosevelt administration, frustrated by

[8] "War Springs from Peace," p. 29.
[9] *The Devil Theory of War,* pp. 21, 28 f.

seemingly insoluble domestic problems, might lead the country into war. The New Deal's emphasis on domestic recovery did not mean, he warned, that "outward thrusts in every direction" had ceased. The navy building program was going ahead on the official ground that it aided economic recovery despite the fact that the money could have been used in the domestic program. As a result, the Japanese and the British felt justified in pushing their naval expansion as well. Hope of gaining foreign markets for domestic "surpluses," although waning, was not altogether dead. "A grand diversion," Beard suggested ominously, "might not be unwelcome, should the domestic recovery program fall far short of its aims." [10]

Although warmly supporting the New Deal's program for domestic recovery, he continued to be troubled by the fact that Roosevelt had "not yet brought the foreign policy of the United States entirely into line with his domestic theory." In early 1935 Beard made explicit his previous hints, openly asserting in a *Scribner's Magazine* article on "National Policies and War" that Roosevelt would choose foreign war, or "stumble into" it, in preference to facing deepening domestic problems. "The Jeffersonian party gave the nation the War of 1812, the Mexican War, and its participation in the World War. The Pacific War awaits." [11] Thus, nearly seven years before Pearl Harbor, Beard was formulating his theme regarding "the Pacific war" and its origins.

When presently he was further aroused by Roosevelt's foreign policy pronouncements, he argued vigorously that we must attend to affairs at home *before* meddling with matters abroad. "If we cannot solve even the problem of putting 10,000,000 of our own citizens to work on the lavish resources right at hand, or have collective security at home," he asked in the *New Republic* in 1938, "how can we have the effrontery to assume that we can solve the problems of Asia and Europe, encrusted in the blood-rust of fifty centuries?" [12] Here, again, was the assumption that problems are more easily solvable on a

---

[10] *The Idea of National Interest*, pp. 546–48.

[11] *Scribner's Magazine*, XCVII (February, 1935), 70; cf. also "Peace Loads the Guns," *Today*, IV (June 29, 1935), 4; review of Curti, *Peace or War: The American Struggle, 1636–1936, New Republic*, LXXXVI (April 15, 1936), 289; "What I Expect of Roosevelt," with Others, *Nation*, CXLIII (November 14, 1936), 572; "Going Ahead with Roosevelt," *Events*, I (January, 1937), 9–12; *America in Midpassage*, with Mary R. Beard (New York: Macmillan Co., 1939), pp. 481 ff.

[12] "Collective Security," *New Republic*, XCIII (February 2, 1938), 359; cf. *The Open Door at Home*, p. 130.

smaller scale than on a larger. A different assumption, however, had also crept in, namely, that domestic and foreign policies are easily separated. Whereas typically he maintained that the unity of politics was such that changes in domestic politics always affected world politics, he was now in effect arguing for separation.

In Beard's view, World War II, whatever else he thought about it, was a catastrophic demonstration of the relationship of domestic and world politics. During and after it, as before, he repeatedly alluded to this relationship. Thus, in early 1941, when France had already gone under and Nazi power was continuing to expand, he protested strongly against the proposed Lend-Lease bill on the ground that it would have a ruinous effect on the domestic economy. He feared that the postwar strains imposed by this additional foreign commitment would be beyond our powers, and that it would magnify subsequent unemployment, debt, unrest, and depression.[13] When American troops and their allies were reinvading the European continent, he reminded his readers, in the *Basic History of the United States* (1944), of the disastrous connection between domestic politics and foreign war which had developed in the prewar years.[14] In the final edition of his *American Government and Politics* he described how international problems had come to dominate domestic politics in postwar America.[15]

The Historic Alternatives

Probing the roots of American foreign policy, Beard sought to analyze its various historical phases and the schools of thought that had accompanied these developments. Such analyses sometimes revealed as much about his own position respecting current controversies as they did about past history.

The earliest phase of American foreign policy, he explained in 1937, had been "political isolation, with such commercial relations as circumstances made possible." This had continued from Washington's administration to about 1890. Thereupon, imperialism,

[13] "Statement of Charles A. Beard, New Milford, Conn.," February 4, 1941, *To Promote the Defense of the United States: Hearings before the Committee on Foreign Relations United States Senate on Senate [Bill] 275*, 77 Cong., 1 Sess., p. 312.

[14] *A Basic History of the United States,* with Mary R. Beard (New York: Doubleday & Co., 1944), pp. 457 f., 462, 464.

[15] *American Government and Politics* (10th ed.; New York: Macmillan Co., 1948), p. 400.

which meant the use of force to obtain economic advantages in various parts of the world, had become the dominant policy. Sponsored by such men as Alfred Thayer Mahan and John Hay, the policy of imperialism had, by the turn of the century, pushed American power across the Pacific. The "open door" formula, Beard felt, had simply been a camouflage for economic imperialism. It had not in actuality been merely a policy of "trading equality, disinterestedness, and magnanimity." Yet, despite the economic imperialism motivating it, the "great American adventure in the Philippines and other distant places" did not "pay." Consequently, such enterprises had come to be described in terms of heavenly missions and moral obligation.[16]

Previous to the outbreak of the Great War, he pointed out, a new American policy had arisen. This had featured the Wilsonian vision of world-wide democracy, arbitration, and justice, "to the advantage of British and French imperialism." Now the Wilsonian dream had long since been exploded, and old-style imperialism was outmoded, even though a few Americans still entertained delusions of grandeur. Therefore the present choices, thought Beard, were narrowed to three: a return to imperial activities, a resumption of the attempt to make "peace and democracy" prevail everywhere, or "tending our own garden."[17]

In *America in Midpassage* (1939) Beard extended and refined his analysis of the historical roots of American foreign policy. He strongly hinted that unsound past policies had led to current domestic difficulties:

Was it possible then that the widespread crisis in town and country could be attributed, in substantial measure, to the foreign policies that had been pursued by the Government of the United States, to the false hopes that they had raised? Certainly neither the imperialism of 1900 nor the moral crusade of 1917 nor the feverish money lending of 1928 had led to the haven of prosperity and security.[18]

This was the converse of Beard's usual suggestion that domestic troubles might be the motive for foreign adventurism: here foreign policy helped bring on domestic difficulties.

Furthermore, he believed, past American policy had defeated its own purposes by producing undesirable effects abroad. The open

[16] Preface, Melvin M. Knight, *Morocco as a French Economic Venture*, pp. vi f.; see also Beard's description in *Events*, I (March, 1937), 164 f.

[17] "Our Choice in Foreign Policy," *Events*, I (March, 1937), 164 f.

[18] *America in Midpassage*, p. 435.

door in China, as a cloak for imperialism by various powers, had contributed to that Chinese weakness which gave way before a militant Japan. Thus American policy had in effect encouraged Japanese aggression.[19]

In 1939, Beard distinguished *four* historic schools of thought which had been associated with American foreign policy. Of these, "isolationism pure and simple" was the oldest. Stemming back to Washington's administration, by the end of the nineteenth century it had developed into "imperial isolationism." Its aim had been to avoid all entangling alliances and to remain insulated from the troubles of Europe. With the advent of McKinley and John Hay, this tradition had been deflected into an imperialist expansionist course. It had been appealed to in support of the policy of fostering loans, stimulating foreign trade, and advancing "the national interest" generally. In the Republican administrations preceding the depression it had been identical in practice with so-called dollar diplomacy. Under it, the United States had refused to join the League of Nations or to submit vital disputes to international tribunals. In recent practice it had come to mean political isolation combined with "deepening economic entanglements through commerce and investments." Beard himself felt this "imperialist capitalism of the Lodge-Mahan fraternity" merited no further support.[20]

A second school of American foreign policy was "collective internationalism," which had utterly failed in its attempt to get French and British cooperation in halting the Japanese aggression in Manchuria in 1937. Roosevelt's 1937 quarantine speech in Chicago had seemed to put the President in the camp of the collective internationalists, Beard suggested, but the "popular counterblast" greeting his proposals had apparently induced him to abandon them temporarily. Yet this internationalist school persisted, Beard complained, despite its fallacious assumptions. Resting on an invalid world image from the era of Cobden and Bright, it worked for the ideal of free trade and ever expanding capitalism. But attempting to implement these "free trade theories of the Cobden-Wilson-Hull school" could only lead to American involvement in new foreign wars.[21]

[19] *Ibid.*, pp. 441 f.
[20] *Ibid.*, pp. 442–46; see also *American Government and Politics* (8th ed.; 1939), p. 266.
[21] *America in Midpassage,* pp. 446–48.

The third school of foreign policy for America was that related to current doctrines of international communism. Based on a defective concept of history, it had little influence in the United States. The facts of recent years had belied its theories. In Russia, believers in this kind of world brotherhood through world revolution had been expelled, shot down, and generally persecuted. Russia's rulers had turned to "building socialism in one country," and consequently a policy aiming at "the universal brotherhood of Marxism" was now of little actual significance anywhere in the world.[22]

Having examined and rejected the tenets of the imperialists, the internationalists, and the communists as guides to American foreign policy, Beard set forth the principles and objectives of a more recently emerging fourth school: continentalism. "Its theories and sentiments were enclosed in such phrases as: let us keep out of the next world war; mind our own business; till our own garden." This continental or "American civilization" school disavowed all imperialist schemes camouflaged under such phrases as the white man's burden. It did not feel called upon to settle the centuries-old controversies of Europe. Despite charges by critics that the school was nationalistic or that it subscribed to an outworn isolationism, the continentalists, Beard explained, welcomed international cooperation, arbitration, conciliation, and even collective action on certain matters. Proponents of continentalism acknowledged that its central ideas were not necessarily universally applicable in a pluralistic world. The real interests and needs of this country were unique and unlike those of other nations. The continentalists particularly denied that foreign policy should, or in reality could, solve domestic American economic problems.[23]

Obviously, the continental school was close to Beard's heart. It represented the cumulative result of his perplexed thinking on foreign policy through the years since World War I. Soon forsaking his own idealism of the Wilsonian period, he had become disillusioned in the 1920's and increasingly critical respecting the first World War's professed aims, the thesis of war guilt, and the peace settlements. Although his growing fear of American involvement in another general war had seemed to subside temporarily in the early days of the New Deal, his apprehension had mounted rapidly as domestic recovery faltered. On the eve of World War II, the con-

---

[22] *Ibid.*, p. 451.
[23] *Ibid.*, pp. 452 ff.

tinental school represented for him the sensible notion of "tilling our own American garden."

But in 1944 Beard basically modified his classification of the schools of foreign policy. This reclassification had the effect of making his own position a continuation of a much older American tradition, rather than connected to a recent development. The principal schools, Beard claimed, were:

Continentalism, originating in Washington's administration. *Hemispheric Security,* the Monroe Doctrine of 1823 added to continentalism. *Imperialism,* put into effect at the close of the nineteenth century. *Collective Security,* announced by President Wilson, temporarily rejected; reaffirmed in a general way by President Franklin D. Roosevelt (1937–44) and by resolutions of the House of Representatives and Senate in 1943.[24]

Aside from the reshuffling of labels which now placed Beard within the school of hemispheric security, this revised analysis revealed further refinements in his thought. Most noticeably, he had severed imperialism from the tradition leading back to early American isolationism, and instead had made his own school of thought a continuation of this tradition going back to President Washington. Imperialism thus became a more recent development, starting near the end of the nineteenth century and extending to the pre-New Deal dollar diplomacy of recent Republican administrations. In terms of advocates, Beard had now in effect expelled the imperialistic Mahan group from Washington's company and had taken up his own position there escorted by Monroe. Woodrow Wilson and Franklin D. Roosevelt, as advocates of collective security, were now made to represent internationalism. A further effect of Beard's reclassification was to sharpen current foreign policy controversy into something of a bipolar affair. With Washington as well as the Mahan imperialists gone and their disciples largely out of the picture, the debate had tended to narrow, in Beard's mind, to a struggle between two contending schools typified by President Roosevelt and Beard himself.

Beard and other proponents of his school of hemisphere security —frequently called continentalism or isolationism by its friends and enemies, respectively—thus sought to convince themselves that they were restoring an earlier realistic tradition in American foreign policy. Were they not, like Washington and Monroe, advocating the

[24] *American Government and Politics* (9th ed.; 1944), p. 303.

self-sufficiency of this hemisphere and the avoidance of entangling alliances? Their position appeared to be a kind of laissez faire in foreign policy which implicitly assumed a beneficent state of nature composed of fortunate geography and sagacious forefathers who had wisely settled in the New World. Yet, in their supposed realism the continentalists sometimes forgot that the earlier American statesmen whose realism they aimed to emulate had engaged in active policies designed to resist European imperialism in this hemisphere, and that the success of their policies had been assured by European preoccupation with other matters as well as by British naval protection against outside adventurers.[25]

It is true that in a sense Beard's school of hemispheric security was a continuation of a long tradition in American history, but not in the sense Beard implied. Alexander DeConde has recently analyzed various elements in this tradition, from Washington's day to present times.[26] According to DeConde, among the factors supporting and giving rise to separatist feelings and policies throughout our history have been the British naval policing of the world in the nineteenth century, long-standing American hatred of militarism and war, distrust of foreigners, American-Catholic sentiment aroused by the Spanish Civil War, Irish-American prejudice against Britain, the liberal isolationism of nationalist reformers, the America First movement, pacifist doctrines, the fortress America theory of defense, and anticommunism. Thus, with respect to his foreign policy views, Beard was a part of that larger company of Americans who throughout our history, for diverse reasons, have advocated various kinds and degrees of isolation from the world.

Beard's Vision for America

The darker the clouds on the world political horizon, the more tenaciously Beard clung to his vision of an insulated American garden. It was an ideal that had started forming in faint outline shortly after World War I. Before that time he had felt that "no political doctrines with regard to our independence from the rest of the world" were strong enough "to overcome those material and moral forces which are linking our destinies to those of the world at

[25] Cf. Hans J. Morgenthau, *In Defense of the National Interest* (New York: Alfred A. Knopf, 1951), pp. 28 f.

[26] Alexander DeConde, *Isolation and Security* (Durham, N.C.: Duke University Press, 1957), pp. 3–32 *passim*.

large." [27] But, as his disillusionment with America's participation in the war had deepened through the 1920's, he had begun speaking kindly of "Little Americanism," expressing "a prejudice for the land of my birth" as it had existed before the era of imperialism and colonialism. More and more openly he had advocated a policy of self-defense of America only and had spoken up sharply against "the big navy boys." [28] His vision was thus no sudden makeshift, but a slowly maturing ideal which in his later years he had come to define and defend with some warmth.

The American garden, Beard argued, was well worth tending and improving, and consequently it was entirely unnecessary to look abroad in the manner of the old-fashioned "Hay-Roosevelt-Mahan type" of imperialism. The proper purpose of the navy and army was not to serve such an outmoded "capitalist racket," but to protect America. So-called surpluses which caused tremendous selling pressures were not absolute surpluses. Our appalling slums and our unemployment showed how desperately these goods were needed at home. In any case, there appeared to be no workable way by which they could be sold abroad. Therefore, he insisted, it behooved us to make whatever drastic modification was necessary in the American economic system. Let the domestic economy absorb the "overproduction" rather than permit the terrific pressures for selling it abroad involve us in war. "If we go to war," he exclaimed in 1936, "let us go to war for some grand national and human advantage openly discussed and deliberately arrived at, and not to bail out farmers, bankers and capitalists or to save politicians from the pain of dealing with a domestic crisis." [29]

In defense of his ideal for America, Beard was prepared to marshal almost every conceivable argument. Thus, even if it were possible to dispose of our surplus products abroad, it was not desirable. To do so, he claimed, would encourage an undesirable degree of in-dustrialization in America. Thomas Jefferson himself could well have nodded approval at Beard's warning of the dreaded conse-quences of expanding industrialization engendered by the un-checked growth of foreign markets:

[27] *American Government and Politics* (1st ed.; 1910), p. 333.
[28] See above, pp. 116 f., 119.
[29] *The Devil Theory of War,* pp. 121, 124; cf. *A Foreign Policy for America* (New York: Alfred A. Knopf, 1940), pp. 9 ff.; *The Republic* (New York: Viking Press, 1943), p. 307.

It means, if experience is a guide, the increasing predominance of manufacturing over agriculture and the urban way of life over the rural way
of life. It means an ever-larger proportion of talents concentrated on the
manipulations of business as distinguished from agriculture and an ever-
increasing proportion of working people transformed into urban proletariat—"asphalt flowers," as they are known in Europe—toolless, homeless,
and propertyless, dependent upon the sale of bare labor power—proletari-
ans trained, if trained at all, in narrow mechanical specialties likely to be
destroyed at any time by new invention. It means also the increasing accumulation of wealth in the hands of the directing classes, with the manners,
standards, and artificialities which undermine the very qualities of courage and leadership requisite to the successful operations of those classes.
If possible in practice, the policy is to be condemned as undesirable in
terms of consequences.[30]

In addition to indicating a Jeffersonian fear of proletarian "sores
on the body politic," Beard also maintained that advocates of ever
expanding world trade based their arguments on fallacious economic assumptions. Their frame of reference was none other than
that of old-style classical economics. Indeed, the dislocations from
which the world suffered could be largely attributed to precisely
their kind of faulty economics. Such outworn theories, he suggested, not only underestimated the force of nationalism and the
variations in culture among peoples, but overemphasized the notion
of economic man motivated exclusively by rational self-interest.
Consequently, "the idea of world economy," he wrote in *The Open
Door at Home* (1934), was "dissolving in contemporary thought." [31]
It should be pointed out that this was a contention in some contrast
to his often expressed notion of the world as a tightening economic
unity.

Beard claimed further that proponents of increasing world trade
were wrong in unconsciously assuming government to be a kind of
strong man to implement the acquisitive urges of selfish interests.
Unbounded economic freedom on the world stage did not necessarily mean equal opportunity among nations, but instead might
result in unfair advantages for economically advanced nations and
greater difficulties for the others. Too often the arguments of the
trade promoters were merely a rationalizing ideology for aggressive
nationalism. As far as Beard was concerned, he thought that neither
the outmoded ideas of Cobden and Bright nor the modern notion of

[30] *The Open Door at Home,* p. 69.
[31] *Ibid.,* pp. 123–25.

seeking outlets for industrialism and agrarianism could furnish a realistic guide for America.[32]

An insulated America, he argued in 1939, should remain aloof from general war because, among other reasons, the United States in any case would not be permitted to assume a position of responsibility and leadership. Instead, the probabilities were that America would "merely become a tail to the coalition kite, would receive lip praise, would have to supply more and more men and materials to the bitter end." [33]

Nor could the United States hope to assume world leadership by virtue of a superior navy. Even if "Mahan's scheme" of world hegemony through sea power might once have had a trace of validity, the notion was now entirely fallacious. It had become a dangerous fiction to suppose that sea power alone could be the deciding factor in national strength or destiny, claimed Beard in 1940. Despite our great increase in naval strength, we were unjustified in seeking to operate outside our own continental waters.[34]

In 1943 Beard maintained in *The Republic* that, regardless of America's growing power and the greater role of leadership which this was said to entail, some degree of isolation from the rest of the world was still nevertheless essential. Exactly what responsibilities did America have? "To whom, where, when, and in what form—intellectual, spiritual, and material?" Did the principle of world leadership and responsibility mean, for example, that we should admit millions of immigrants from every country of the world? [35] Asserting that the United States should aim neither at participation in clashes of interest everywhere nor at bringing peace to all nations on earth, Beard insisted that the wisest course would be to concentrate "on the continental domain and on building here a civilization in many respects peculiar to American life and the potentialities of the American heritage." [36]

As to the desirability of universal military training in his American garden, Beard apparently had a change of heart. In 1931, outlining his "Five-Year Plan for America," he had urged that instead

[32] *Ibid.*, pp. 134, 261, 273 f.

[33] "We're Blundering into War," *American Mercury*, XLVI (April, 1939), 398.

[34] Review of Davis, *A Navy Second to None*, *New Republic*, CII (February 26, 1940), 283 f.

[35] *The Republic*, p. 324.

[36] *A Foreign Policy for America*, p. 12.

of trying to dominate the world America should concentrate on "defense of the land and people of the United States—by universal military service, if Europe stubbornly refuses to come to terms on disarmament." [37] But near the close of his life, appearing before the Senate Armed Services Committee, he protested against universal military training on the ground that it would implant in America the curse of militarism from the Old World, degrade our society, create a monstrous military bureaucracy, and tend to overthrow "the first principles upon which the Constitution of the United States is based." [38]

Although his vision for America was not the ideal of strict national isolation, he did envision a nation isolated to a greater degree than that contemplated by Roosevelt and the internationalists. How much greater? Beard wanted enough isolation to keep the country out of world war, but not so much as to forfeit most of the advantages of economic and cultural interchange with the rest of the world. It was not an easy goal.

"Foreign Policy in the Making"

But assuming the goal, and given the main alternatives that he believed he saw in American foreign policy, he felt impelled to urge a course that, in his view, would achieve the desired objective. He was concerned with questionable procedures and influences which might enter into existing policy making, and with the relationship between the execution of policy and its formation. His main concern, however, was to press the continentalist case against the arch enemy, internationalism, and against the stubborn remnants of what he took to be an outdated imperialism.

Beard's frequent target in his attacks on alleged imperialists were the proponents of a bigger navy. He felt not only that their conceptions were anachronistic and mistaken, but also that some of these interests had no business attempting to influence policy in the first place. The job of admirals, for example, was to carry out policy and not to try to make it. Moreover, naval technologists had no special competence in formulating the goals of United States policy. Distrustful of navy intrigues, he attacked every evidence of what he

[37] *Forum and Century,* LXXXVI (July, 1931), 10.
[38] Quoted by George R. Leighton in Howard K. Beale (ed.), *Charles A. Beard* (Lexington: University of Kentucky Press, 1954), pp. 161 f.

took to be a re-emergence of the old Mahan doctrines. The proper size of the navy, he asserted in *Asia* magazine in 1935, was not for the admirals to decide but depended entirely on the foreign policy which the nation intended to pursue. The navy should not be used to protect and promote trade, spheres of influence, imperialism, or colonialism of any sort. "The fundamental purposes of American foreign policy," he declared, "should be to provide utmost security for the American nation in its continental home." [39]

   In Beard's eyes the main enemy, of course, increasingly became internationalism, as epitomized in the late 1930's and thereafter by Franklin D. Roosevelt. In 1935 he urged that there was still time for Americans to clarify their conceptions respecting our foreign policy, the military strength appropriate to sustain it, and the relation of these to the measures necessary for domestic recovery. "Some President of the United States," he broadly hinted, "may need the aid of such clarification as he pauses upon the brink of an abyss." [40]

   Beard himself was a frequent visitor in the nation's capital, consulting with Congressmen, testifying before committees, and watching foreign policy developments. He spent the winter of 1936–37 in Washington, and shortly thereafter *Events* magazine recorded an indirect interchange between Beard and the White House. According to this account, the magazine's editor, Spencer Brodney, had sent excerpts of two Beard essays to President Roosevelt, requesting comment. Stephen Early, secretary to the President, had replied in a letter of acknowledgment, enclosing marked copies of two recent Roosevelt speeches. "Dr. Beard's Rejoinder," however, made clear that Beard remained unconvinced that Roosevelt, despite his expressed desire for peace, would keep us out of war. Present policies, Beard was convinced, would surely lead to war. [41]

   He particularly opposed Roosevelt's stand on neutrality legislation. For Beard, neutrality "in the exact sense" meant a status that could not be changed by the executive to favor one side *"after war starts,"* even though neutrality as such always favored one side more than another. To make policy changes on behalf of one belligerent as against another after hostilities were under way was to take a step toward involvement in war. The American people, Beard

[39] "What Is This Sea Power?" *Asia,* XXXV (January, 1935), 5.
[40] "Peace Loads the Guns," p. 23.
[41] " 'Will Roosevelt Keep Us out of War?' Dr. Beard's Rejoinder," *Events,* II (September, 1937), 163 f.

charged, were now being propagandized into believing that the government must take sides in European and Asian wars. In 1914 the people had not been so prepared, and "hence it took time for Woodrow Wilson to manoeuvre the nation into war." This time, despite the desire of the American people to resist such propaganda, Roosevelt's actions showed his plain intent to follow the creed that "the United States must do good all around the world." [42]

Roosevelt's Chicago quarantine speech of October, 1937, especially aroused Beard because it appeared to place the President squarely in the camp of the internationalists. "The American people surely want to stay out of the next world war," he exclaimed in the *New Republic* after the Chicago speech. "That Roosevelt would take them in swiftly if it comes is highly probable, but they certainly are not longing for another preposterous crusade for democracy on the battlefields of Europe." [43] The quarantine speech was particularly amazing, thought Beard, coming so soon after an election campaign in which Roosevelt had counseled the American people against being drawn into another foreign war. From this time on he took every occasion to attack presidential proposals that seemed to violate continentalist principles. In the ensuing 1938 session of Congress, he appeared before the House Naval Affairs Committee to argue against Roosevelt's "new armament program," on the ground that the foreign policy these arms were intended to support had not been explicitly spelled out.[44] In April of the same year, he charged in *Events* that the administration wanted collective action against any powers who tried to disturb "the present distribution of imperial spoils" in Europe or Asia. It was perfectly proper, he contended, for the American people to discuss openly the question of collective security, but such a policy should not be secretly foisted on them "under the guise of armament legislation." [45]

In 1939, as excitement mounted with Franco's victory, dissolution of Czechoslovakia, and Hitler's aggression in Poland, Beard fought more vigorously than ever against American entanglement. The President, he charged, was maneuvering the country into war in order to avoid domestic problems.[46] By this time every move to give

---

[42] *Ibid.*, pp. 163 f.
[43] "Collective Security," pp. 358 f.; cf. also *America in Midpassage*, p. 476.
[44] *Congressional Digest,* XVII (March, 1938), 90.
[45] "The Supreme Issue for America," *Events,* III (April, 1938), 275.
[46] See also George R. Leighton in Beale, *Charles A. Beard,* pp. 179–82.

the President more discretionary power to deal with domestic or foreign affairs seemed to Beard to be a transparent attempt by the internationalists to implement their designs.

As the 1940 election campaign drew to a close, Beard indicated that, although the American people were opposed to getting into the European war, a war against Japan "would doubtless encounter less opposition" because of long-standing hatred against the Japanese. "Authorities in Washington eager to get into the war could scarcely overlook this roundabout way of accomplishing their designs." In the event of such an Asiatic war, sincere and well-meaning Americans would talk much of saving democracy despite the fact that "economic and military and naval interests of high potency in large circles of American life" would have other considerations in mind.[47] Thus, Beard appeared to be in something of a dilemma as to how the people in a war-threatened democracy could be depended on to make the right decisions, especially if they were not kept fully informed.

It is in the midst of such quivering uncertainties that the fortunes of the United States are now being decided. Our fate, in this respect, is no longer in the hands of the people or of Congress, despite the provision in the Constitution that vests in Congress the power to declare war. In fact wars are no longer declared. Situations exist or are created. Actions are taken by authorities in a position to act. The people wait for their portion.[48]

When the people had re-elected Roosevelt in November of 1940 to an unprecedented third term, Beard came to Washington to battle the proposed Lend-Lease bill then before Congress. The bill would give the President virtually life and death powers over the lives and fortunes of the American people, he warned, and would hand over the policy-making power of Congress to "experts in war and diplomacy." It was plainly "a bill for waging an undeclared war." In any event the projected measure was futile, he felt, because Americans could not possibly recast Europe and Asia in the image of democracy with full economic security for all their people. Moreover, the lessons of World War I were too plain to be ignored. Although the American people then had been propagandized by European war leaders, this should not be allowed to happen again. United States

[47] "War with Japan?" *Events*, VIII (November, 1940), 321 f.
[48] *Ibid.*, p. 323.

participation in World War I, he insisted, had been contrary to the national interest.[49]

When all of his continentalist arguments seemed to have failed, and Pearl Harbor had plunged America fully into World War II, Beard busied himself gathering materials and data as to how the war had come about. Part of his answer came in 1946 with the publication of *American Foreign Policy in the Making, 1932–1940,* in which he laid out the history of New Deal foreign policy leading up to the fateful year. He recounted how Roosevelt before 1937 had been disposed against foreign entanglements of a political and economic nature. But a change had apparently taken place in 1937, claimed Beard, as suggested by various unpublicized moves and decisions which had now come to light. Faced with continuing economic collapse, the administration in midpassage had been forced to look for desperate solutions for its ills. Consequently, in the October quarantine speech Roosevelt had "discarded the doctrine of neutrality for the United States and espoused the idea of collective security—the cardinal principle of internationalism." When a storm of popular protest greeted the speech, Roosevelt had seemed to back down, and during the next two years he had even reaffirmed his former nonentanglement position. In the 1940 election campaign he had taken a similar stand. The President had not "found" a state of war existing in Manchuria. But various other actions and unpublicized decisions, contended Beard, showed that Roosevelt had not exactly been working for peace despite his repeated assurances to the American people and to Congress.[50]

[49] "Statement of Charles A. Beard . . . ," February 4, 1941, *Hearings before the Committee on Foreign Relations,* pp. 307 ff.

[50] *American Foreign Policy in the Making, 1932–1940* (New Haven, Conn.: Yale University Press, 1946), p. 184 and *passim;* for a somewhat different appraisal of this period, see, for example, Julius W. Pratt, *A History of United States Foreign Policy* (Englewood Cliffs, N.J.: Prentice-Hall, 1955), pp. 778 f.

CHAPTER XIV
"A NEW AND DANGEROUS AGE"

Aggression and Neutrality

At about the time President Roosevelt was suggesting in Chicago that aggressor nations ought to be "quarantined," Beard published an essay on the "Future of Democracy in the United States" wherein he clearly set forth the grounds of his continentalism in contrast to Roosevelt's internationalism. Many people, Beard pointed out, were supporting neutrality legislation because of their fear that democratic institutions might not survive another general war. As for himself, he had no doubts on the matter:

It is my firm conviction that the United States cannot prevent war in Europe and that if it participates in another general European war, no matter what the alleged pretexts or the alignment of powers may be, that participation will mark the end of democratic institutions in the United States. Some forms may survive, as of the Roman Republic, but the spirit and substance will be destroyed.[1]

Admitting, not long after this, that our participation in a new war might bring temporary "recovery" to the domestic economy, he predicted that such a boom would be followed by inevitable collapse. But, immeasurably worse, universal democracy would probably give way to some variety of universal fascism. If communist or socialist upheavals occurred in the defeated Axis countries, the likely result of American, British, and French military efforts to quell the uprisings would be as futile as similar intervention had been in Russia in 1917.[2]

Twenty years earlier Beard had agreed with many of his countrymen that American participation in general war was necessary in order to help save democracy. Now he was as firmly convinced that democracy, at least in the United States, could be saved only by our avoidance of general war. Despite reversal of means his purpose

[1] *Political Quarterly*, VIII (October, 1937), 505.
[2] "Collective Security," *New Republic*, XCIII (February 2, 1938), 358.

236

remained constant—to safeguard democracy. Then our interest, he had believed, lay in helping to crush German militarism. What should now be our attitude toward the militaristic tendencies of European dictatorships, and toward aggression outside our continental domain?

With Hitler's accession to power, Beard immediately recognized the Nazi regime as an expansionist autocracy. But, precisely because he realized that such a regime meant war, he felt that an American attitude of aloofness toward Europe would be least likely to involve us in the conflict. Again European powers were finding it useful, he noted, to cultivate a favorable public opinion in America, as they had done prior to 1914. Again they were feverishly rearming, this time presumably against the specter of revolutionary Russia. Posing as the champion of peace against the danger from the east, Hitler had raised the "Communist spook." By pointing to the threat of tyranny from Moscow, he sought to divert attention from his tyranny at home.[3] As early as 1936, Beard was convinced that sooner or later Nazi Germany would launch an aggressive attack.

Turned in upon themselves, nourishing deep resentments, and lashed to fury by a militant system of education, the German people are conditioned for that day when Hitler, his technicians, and the army, are ready and are reasonably sure of the prospects of success in a sudden and devastating attack, East or West. To cherish any other conception of Hitler's State or of the aims of German education is to cherish a delusion.[4]

Nonetheless, thought Beard, this did not particularly concern America. The business of resisting aggression in Europe belonged to Europeans. In any event, the "war guilt" farce after World War I should have taught us the virtual impossibility of determining who was an aggressor and who was not in the real world. Moreover, even if we recognized the aggressor, we could not prevent war by throwing the weight of the United States on one side or the other in foreign quarrels. Therefore the only wise course for this country was the path of strict neutrality.[5]

Strict neutrality, as far as Beard was concerned, apparently meant not only carefully refraining from taking sides in disputes among

---

[3] "Spooks, Made in Germany," *New Republic,* LXXVII (December 6, 1933), 97 f.
[4] "Education under the Nazis," *Foreign Affairs,* XIV (April, 1936), 452.
[5] Cf. "Heat and Light on Neutrality," *New Republic,* LXXXVI (February 12, 1936), 8 f.

foreign nations outside this hemisphere, but also meticulous observance of international custom as regards trade with belligerents. But, whether our neutrality was expressed in customary observance or by national legislation, he strongly felt that its application should be mandatory and not dependent on the President's discretion, nor should it be altered in favor of one belligerent as against another after hostilities had started. However, in actual cases Beard appeared to vacillate somewhat on the question of whether neutrality should consist merely of passive avoidance of foreign troubles or should be an active expression of American foreign policy.

Writing of the Spanish Civil War in mid-1937, he complained that President Roosevelt, under pressure, had "found" an international war existing in Spain, thereby imposing an arms embargo whose actual effect was to hurt the Loyalists. Representing the legal Madrid government, they, like other governments, had been entitled under international law to buy arms and supplies in the United States. But, partly because of pressure from Insurgent sympathizers in Congress, our neutrality law had been applied to a civil war "without any justification in terms of peril to American interests." Beard's implication seemed to be that peril to American interest might be sufficient in some cases to justify violation of customary international law principles. Objecting to the discretionary power which the neutrality legislation lodged in the President, he warned that "the American people may well prepare themselves to see President Roosevelt plunge the country into the European war, when it comes, far more quickly than did President Wilson." [6]

On the other hand in 1939, when the Nazis were rushing their war build-up to completion, Beard argued in the *American Mercury* that the flow of American materials to Germany should be cut off by application of our antidumping laws. The administration, he declared, "could have stopped the sale of war materials to Germany long ago by applying pre-existing law and without resorting to any hostile acts under the laws of war." Beard's somewhat legalistic contention that stopping the "life-stream" flowing to Germany would not have been "committing any acts of hostility" suggests that he was not adverse to "unneutrality" respecting potential aggression if the danger to the United States did not appear great. His continuing purpose was to prevent American participation in

[6] "Will Roosevelt Keep Us out of War?" *Events*, II (July, 1937), 2–6.

European or Asian war, regardless, apparently, of whether this involved strict observance of international custom or not, and whether it meant discretionary "neutrality" or not. He clearly opposed American armed intervention in Europe in an attempt to restrain aggression there. It was "certainly not the business of the United States to take on the job" if the other countries of Europe did not want to prevent German and Italian domination.[7]

> The European powers whose immediate business is to stop Hitler and Mussolini dead in their tracks should get down to their business, without expecting to muddle around and then fall back on the United States. . . . After they have stopped the saber-rattlers by a show of force, then let the aforesaid powers try to work out some decent plan for easing the tension in Europe.[8]

In Beard's view there appeared to be almost no justifiable reasons for the United States to engage in war outside our continental zone. The assumption was that we would be undisturbed if we let other nations alone. He felt that the reasons for American participation in most past wars had been largely illusory, and that, profiting by this experience, we could avoid virtually all future wars. When arguing in this vein, Beard sometimes tended to overstate and oversimplify the reasons for American participation in past wars. In 1936, speaking of proposals for keeping out of war, he noted: "One view, stated baldly, holds that the United States, in the interest of democracy and humanity, should sustain Great Britain, France and Russia against the fascism and despotism of Germany, Italy and Japan." Telling much about his own position in an earlier day, he added: "It is a case, once more, of 'saving civilization,' as some of us thought and honestly believed in 1914."[9] His attitude was that wars, even those supposedly against aggression, accomplished little that was worthwhile.

Beard implied that American participation in general war could almost never be in the real interest of the United States. Early in 1937 he declared in the *Forum* that, "if our efforts to right historic wrongs and bring peace and reason to Europe in 1917–1919 have not taught American citizens anything, no words of mine can add to

---

[7] "We're Blundering into War," *American Mercury,* XLVI (April, 1939), 394–96.

[8] "America and the Next War," with Others, *New Republic,* XCIX (June 14, 1939), 148.

[9] *The Devil Theory of War* (New York: Vanguard Press, 1936), p. 115.

their education." His own program with respect to Asiatic and European tensions was "to preserve neutrality and to preserve it by drastic limitations on selling munitions and lending money to all belligerents." [10] There was no room in his conception of war for the possibility of fighting for self-defense or survival outside continentalist limits. He saw little reason to suppose that resistance to the Axis could have much to do with "saving civilization" or democracy this time. It would only be a futile repetition of 1917.

In contrast to his almost immediate suspicion of Hitler's ultimate intentions, Beard took the position that the probability of Russian aggression was not particularly great. The Russian "spook" which Hitler had been conjuring up to frighten democratic nations was mainly diversionary propaganda intended to hide his own designs. Beard did not believe that Russia was an aggressive and warlike troublemaker who had to be fenced in. She seemed inclined to mind her own business of socialism in one country, although, as he admitted, appearances might be deceptive. All the great powers had been pursuing their national interest in the traditional ways, and it was likely that the pivot of Russian policy, as in the case of other powers, was the usual national interest and sovereignty.[11]

In view of the distempers and wrangling prevalent on the world political scene, Beard was typically inclined to oppose what he took to be unneutral activities and pronouncements on the part of American leaders. Every violation of international principles should not be the occasion for a gratuitous lecture on morals by the President or some military leader. If aggression occurred it was not our place to taunt members of the League of Nations with the charge that the organization was not doing its duty. In 1935 he urged that, if naval disarmament failed, the United States should enact a complete body of neutrality legislation. Its strict enforcement would "serve notice on future belligerents that they are to receive no aid or comfort from the United States when they start on the headlong course of war, destruction and defeat." [12]

President Roosevelt's speech in Buenos Aires in early 1937 drew Beard's criticism because of its alleged hints to foreign nations that

[10] "How to Stay out of War," with Others, *Forum*, XCVII (February, 1937), 90.
[11] *The Open Door at Home,* with G. H. E. Smith (New York: Macmillan Co., 1934), p. 152; *The Devil Theory of War,* p. 117.
[12] "What Is This Sea Power?" *Asia,* XXXV (January, 1935), 9.

the United States might take a hand in helping them solve their problems. Despite the firm resolve of the American people to "keep out of war," the President had suggested calling an international conference "for some undefined purpose." Beard suspected the President of thinking of "acting as arbiter in the imminent conflict of nations," although this was not America's concern.[13] He continued to be wary of "the insatiate desire of the Roosevelt administration to issue discourses on the virtues of peace-loving democracies and the wickedness of the three great disturbers of harmony— Japan, Italy, and Germany."[14]

Thus, an underlying assumption of Beard's thinking on foreign policy in the last period of his life was that events and conditions outside this hemisphere posed no great threat to the security of the United States. He consistently tended to minimize rather than emphasize the possible dependence of American security on non-American phenomena. For example, he admitted in 1937 that Hitler might plunge out to the seacoast of western Europe and become an Atlantic power. Although acknowledging that such a contingency would be of some concern to the United States, he did not profess to feel the concern very deeply. Americans, he intimated, would be "inclined to await the event rather than to anticipate it" as they watched Britain trying to preserve her interests in Europe and the Mediterranean.[15]

Similarly, in testimony before the House Naval Affairs Committee in March of 1938, Beard clearly indicated that he saw little actual danger to this country from a foreign aggressor. He stressed, rather, the wisdom of keeping out of European and Asian quarrels and of limiting our defense to continental America and its neighboring waters. To his mind there was little validity in the frightening stories of "Fascist goblins" about to devour the Western Hemisphere or even a part of it. Such talk was merely "the new racket created to herd the American people into President Roosevelt's quarantine camp." In the light of America's existing defenses, he believed it impossible for either Hitler or the Mikado to perform a "water-crossing miracle" to invade America or its environs.[16]

[13] "Our Choice in Foreign Policy," *Events*, I (March, 1937), 163.
[14] *America in Midpassage*, with Mary R. Beard (New York: Macmillan Co., 1939), p. 497.
[15] "Future of Democracy in the United States," p. 506.
[16] As reported in *Christian Science Monitor Weekly Magazine Section*, March 9, 1938.

A logical concomitant of Beard's assumption that political phenomena in other parts of the world had little real effect on America was, of course, his contention that the United States could avoid future war. As he pointed out in 1939, several months before the German attack on Poland, in his opinion this country should and could *"stay out of the next war in Europe and the wars that follow the next war."* [17]

He showed little inclination to pursue the theoretical ramifications of the question of what America's interest would be if it turned out that the European or Asian countries "immediately and directly concerned" lacked the power to prevent Axis domination. What would *our* real interest be if the currently democratic near neighbors of Axis states decided that *their* long-range interest lay in not resisting such domination? Beard, prior to the outbreak of World War II in Europe, appeared to be more concerned with making forcefully known to Old World democratic nations that they must not "shirk their own responsibilities" than with making sure that potential aggressors would feel deterred from attacking the democracies.

In fact, he claimed to put slight credence in suggestions that European dictatorships were seeking to dominate more than Europe itself. It was foolish to commit ourselves in advance with respect to Britain and France "on the remote contingency of a German and Italian domination in the Atlantic." [18] He was convinced that, inasmuch as peace and security in our hemisphere were clearly possible for us, we would be wiser to confine our attention to our part of the world and to remain neutral respecting alleged aggressions in other parts of it.

Apparently Beard's views on these matters remained fundamentally unmodified after the United States became fully engaged in World War II. Characterizing the Axis leaders in 1942 as "the insatiable and ferocious seekers after power over mankind," he did seem to imply that they seriously sought world domination. Yet, after the struggle had ended, he made plain that he still disapproved of United States participation in international undertakings against future aggression. In his *American Foreign Policy in the Making* (1946) he acknowledged that, although he fully supported the promotion of good will and peace among all nations, he firmly rejected attempts to accomplish this through a collective security organiza-

[17] "We're Blundering into War," p. 395 (Beard's italics).
[18] *Ibid.*, p. 399.

tion. This country must not become entangled in any such "association of nations empowered to designate 'aggressors' and bring
engines of sanction and coercion into action against them." In short,
Beard remained clearly opposed to the use of force against aggression. Discounting the utility of the old League of Nations, he continued to his last years to oppose American military action outside
the hemisphere and insisted on "neutrality, peace, and defense for
the United States through measures appropriate to those purposes." [19]
That these three purposes might, on occasion, conceivably be inconsistent with one another did not appear to interest him. After
having lived through two world wars, he had not altered his view
that peace was divisible.

Although Beard reflected, and helped create, a wider liberal-
isolationist belief in the thirties and forties to the effect that European and Asiatic wars posed no particular threat to America's
security, apparently the great majority of American liberals of this
persuasion changed their minds under the impact of Hitler's early
World War II aggressions. Figuratively, Beard's own school of
thought packed up and left him. He seemed to imply on the eve of
the war that, if "some formidable European power comes into the
western Atlantic, breathing the fire of aggression and conquest,"
the United States must perforce extend its concern beyond this
hemisphere to Europe, but apparently nothing that happened during
the global conflict led him to believe that American security had in
fact been threatened to any serious extent.[20] Although before the
war he insisted that the European democracies were strong enough
to defend themselves against Germany and Italy, did he continue to
think, after the war started, that the Axis powers could be defeated
without United States military participation? Or, assuming our
neutrality in the war and a resulting Axis victory, was he concerned
about the security status of a possibly "encircled" United States in a
world of unfriendly Nazi-Fascist states? [21]

[19] *American Foreign Policy in the Making, 1932–1940* (New Haven, Conn.:
Yale University Press, 1946), p. 17 n.; cf. Introduction, Franklin Watts (ed.),
Voices of History: Great Speeches and Papers of the Year 1941 (New York:
Franklin Watts, 1942), p. xv.

[20] Cf. Alexander DeConde (ed.), *Isolation and Security: Ideas and Interests
in Twentieth-Century American Foreign Policy* (Durham, N.C.: Duke University Press, 1957), pp. 21–23; Eric F. Goldman, *Rendevouz with Destiny*
(New York: Alfred A. Knopf, 1952), pp. 384 f.

[21] For a succinct summary of the recent history of international relations,
and an assessment different from Beard's, see Julius W. Pratt, *A History of*

Certainly Beard had never embraced the Wilsonian notion of collective security, the notion that "nations would have to regard aggression upon one nation as aggression upon all, instead of each nation resting its security upon its independent power and the power of allies to counter only those aggressions that happened to threaten its special interests." [22] It also seems highly unlikely that he would have looked favorably on United States "entanglement" in a defensive coalition against a potential aggressor, as exemplified by the North Atlantic Treaty Organization. Indeed, the very concept of aggression, as related to the broader notion of international security, was a concept that seemingly did not interest Beard. Rather, his thought on foreign policy and international relations revolved around the concept of American neutrality in a world of warring states.

The World as Diversity

To bolster his continentalist views, Beard in his later years consciously or unconsciously carried into his thinking a somewhat altered assumption as to the nature of the human interrelationships permeating the social universe—the notion that the world is a plural realm comprising many diversities which effectively block unifying tendencies. This was not, of course, a sharp break with his previous thought. He did not suddenly deny his earlier contention that the world had become "a great economic unity." But neither did he so frequently emphasize the point that economics was drawing the world ever more closely together. Instead he insisted that it was unrealistic for Americans to underemphasize the immense political and cultural variations existing on earth, and futile to try to eliminate them. When he did refer to economic bonds, he was now as likely as not to think of them as "economic entanglements" to be guarded against in our resolve "to stay out of the next war." [23]

In the years before World War I, Beard at times had implied that tightening economic unity could help bring about a kind of social and moral commonwealth of mankind. In his 1908 lecture on *Politics* he had pointed out how the "shuttle of trade and inter-

United States Foreign Policy (Englewood Cliffs, N.J.: Prentice-Hall, 1955), pp. 778 f.

[22] As described by Robert E. Osgood in his essay, "Woodrow Wilson, Collective Security, and the Lessons of History," *Confluence*, V (Winter, 1957), 343 f.

[23] Cf. *America in Midpassage*, p. 421.

course" might be effecting "that unity of mankind which rests on the expansion of a common consciousness of rights and wrongs through the extension of identical modes of economic activity." [24] After World War I, as before, he had acknowledged the increasing inter-dependency of all peoples. The web of international relations, he had claimed, was so strong that "no sword can cut it. The East and the West have met, and they are one." [25] Although in the 1920's his scorn for the notion of "splendid isolation" on the part of the United States in a steadily shrinking world had greatly diminished, in 1929 he had suggested that the replacement of national capitalism by "the towering rise of international capitalism" might be one of the best hopes for peace.[26]

By 1934, however, Beard had apparently abandoned the idea that economic unity might bring a lessening of war. "Notwithstanding this growing interdependence," he remarked in *The Nature of the Social Sciences* (1934), "the tendency of nations to engage in armed conflicts has not disappeared." [27] In his subsequent allusions to the war-threatening troubles of Europe and Asia, and to the special responsibilities and conditions of the nations in those continents, the implication was that the East and the West, as well as the Old World and the New, were not one but quite distinct and different. European and Asian interests tended to become, in Beard's writings, less and less America's interests.

Profoundly moved as the nation was by the agonies of Europe and Asia [he wrote in 1939], it seemed inclined to the view that the peoples of those continents, deeply experienced in their own histories and possessing special interests of their own, could and would order their destinies better without extraneous and incalculable interferences from the Western Hemisphere.[28]

Even President Roosevelt's diplomatic recognition of Russia, it was suggested, had also been a recognition of "the world as diversity." [29]

In *The Republic* (1943), when the dialogue turned to the possi-bility of organizing a world federal union somewhat as the thirteen

[24] *Politics* (New York: Columbia University Press, 1908), p. 30.
[25] *Cross Currents in Europe Today* (Boston: Marshall Jones Co., 1922), p. 2.
[26] "Prospects for Peace," *Harper's Magazine*, CLVIII (February, 1929), 320.
[27] *The Nature of the Social Sciences in Relation to Objectives of Instruc-tion* (New York: Charles Scribner's Sons, 1934), p. 153.
[28] *America in Midpassage*, p. 500; cf. "We're Blundering into War," pp. 395 f.
[29] *America in Midpassage*, p. 469.

American states had once set up an American federal union, Beard
made a point of emphasizing the dissimilarities existing among the
nations of the world. In contrast to the situation in English America
in the late eighteenth century, the present nation-states, he pointed
out, were "utterly diverse in race, history, sentiments, and economy."
Then, the overwhelming majority of the people had been of British
origin. They had possessed a common language, common religion,
common legal system, common tradition. They had been united in
sentiment. Moreover, "fear of foreign aggressions against the young
Republic was a potent force in overcoming their diversities of interest." [30] And, although Beard had once talked of the growth of a
"common consciousness" of all mankind supposedly being hastened
by trade and the spread of modern industry, he now quite reversed
his former emphasis as to the relationship between economic and
other kinds of social unity.

The ancient heritages of Europe and Africa and Asia have not been
wholly uprooted by the mere adoption and use of the machines and the
gadgets of modern industrialism. Nor does a common use of machines
make men, women, and children of all nations alike in traditions, habits,
sentiments, and values. . . . There is no reason I can fathom for believing that the closer nations are drawn together by commerce and intercourse, the more alike they become intellectually, morally, and spiritu-
ally. [31]

With regard to the kind of world that was to follow World
War II, Beard was careful to avoid detailing an exact blueprint.
But he made clear that he hoped for a peaceful world in which
"highly civilized peoples *as nations*" would apply themselves toward fuller attainment of general goals such as truth, good, and
beauty. [32] International cooperation among diverse peoples, rather
than supranational guidance based on an overemphasized notion
of world community, was the implied ideal. Although in *The Enduring Federalist* (1948) he suggested that American federalism
might conceivably furnish the model for some kind of future world
union to insure peace, the assumption underlying this "second best"
political pattern for mankind was still that of a pluralistic world. [33]

[30] *The Republic* (New York: Viking Press, 1943), p. 315.
[31] *Ibid.,* p. 316.
[32] *Ibid.,* p. 327 (italics supplied).
[33] *The Enduring Federalist* (ed.) (New York: Doubleday & Co., 1948),
pp. 1, 4.

Fate, Freedom, and Global War

After Pearl Harbor, during the years the United States was actually at war, Beard did not oppose our participation in the global struggle. "Personally," he stated in 1943, "I am in favor of pushing the war against Germany, Japan and Italy to a successful conclusion. Whether it is righteous in the sight of God I leave to our theologians." [34] What was theoretically more interesting, however, was his seemingly unsettled attitude toward war in its relation to democracy and civilization. From a prewar pessimism he appeared to shift to a wartime optimism, and then in turn to be troubled anew by postwar doubts near the close of his life. When Roosevelt had made his Chicago quarantine speech in 1937, Beard had declared flatly that our participation in another general war would spell the end of democratic institutions and constitutional government in the United States. A new war, he had stated, would probably lead to universal fascism and not universal democracy. [35] But in 1941, pointing out that Americans had already had two centuries of experience with self-government, he expressed confidence that freedom and constitutionalism would survive in America, as they always had during previous crises in our history.

Efforts have been made here from period to period to apply dictatorial methods. In their desperation, Federalists tried to suppress all criticism by rushing through the Alien and Sedition Acts. The Jeffersonian upheaval of 1800 repudiated them. During the Civil War, dictatorial powers were exercised in various respects, and the permanence of despotism was predicted, but at the close of the conflict constitutional government supplanted military government. Immense powers were conferred upon President Wilson during the World War and often exercised with needless severity, but abuses of power were attacked even while the war was raging and at the conclusion of the struggle hysteria receded and constitutional processes were restored. [36]

Totalitarianism in the United States, Beard wrote in 1943, would be an unlikely product of the current world conflict. America had passed through the Revolution and through the Civil War without falling into a totalitarian system, despite predictions to the contrary

[34] *The Republic,* p. 309.
[35] "Collective Security," p. 358; "Future of Democracy in the United States," p. 505.
[36] *Public Policy and the General Welfare* (New York: Farrar & Rinehart, 1941), p. 173.

during those periods. Possibly in some unusually grave crisis, he admitted, the nation might go so far as to resort to a "straight military dictatorship under the President or a joint committee of Congress." But he thought that such a dictatorship would prove to be temporary.[37] His wartime faith in the future seemed to retain much of its earlier buoyance, even if it was now formulated in terms of "continental Americanism":

I believe that there will always be an America, an America with unique characteristics, however great the changes that will come. . . . America is not fated to repeat the history of Rome or any other nation in the world. . . . America is fated to be America, and all the pulling and hauling of the world-planners cannot alter that fact. . . . I have confidence in the tenacity of civilization, always in conflict with its foe, barbarism, and I hold to the conviction that it will not be extinguished on the earth. . . . Civilization in the United States, I believe, will continue for long centuries to come. . . . There are immense and varied opportunities in which we can work for the good, the true, the useful, and the beautiful.[38]

But as the war drew to a close Beard's mood again darkened. In July of 1945 he wrote to George S. Counts: "The sky is clear and ominous; only two mighty armed powers are on the horizon. What impends and with what portents? Day and night I wonder and tremble for the future of my country and mankind." [39] News of the dropping of the first atomic bomb led him to doubt his "little system" of philosophy and to think it imperative to "take new observations from the stars." In 1947 he remarked that, although he did not doubt that the human race would survive the unleashing of atomic energy, he acknowledged the possibility of an atomic catastrophe from which civilization might not recover for two thousand years.[40]

Reflected in these various statements were Beard's notions of history. As suggested in his numerous writings on historical relativism, his "act of faith" was that history exhibited a directional movement. Notwithstanding his recurrent doubts and pessimism, he persisted in believing that mankind, despite numerous setbacks, was moving generally forward toward greater democracy and social justice. This stubborn faith in long-term human advance sometimes emerged even in his darkest moments. "By appealing to

[37] *The Republic*, p. 253.
[38] *Ibid.*, pp. 340, 342 f.
[39] As quoted in Howard K. Beale (ed.), *Charles A. Beard* (Lexington: University of Kentucky Press, 1954), p. 235.
[40] *Ibid.*, p. 252.

myth, symbol, force, and fear, Mussolini and Hitler reversed, at least for a time," he wrote in 1936, "the long trends toward complete political democracy." [41] Even in such a statement the underlying optimism showed through the pessimism on the surface. Perhaps what added to the perplexity and poignancy of Beard's thinking amid the repeated crises and disappointments in his last years was an emerging conviction that, with regard to ultimate progress, the mills of the gods grind infinitely more slowly than he had formerly imagined.

Irrespective of his occasional assertion to the effect that "history is irreversible and never repeats itself," he nonetheless often appeared to assume that history is in fact repetitive. Thus at times his optimism was implicitly based on the dubious logic that, if an event has not happened in the past, then it will not happen in the future. During the dark days of the war, for example, he insisted in effect that because the United States had never been a totalitarian despotism in the past it would not become one in the future. He sometimes forgot the limits of historical analogy, limits which he himself at other times pointed out.

Beard's implicitly held conception of total history as directional movement was related also to an ambiguity in his thought as to the nature of scientific predictability. He had long held that a science of history would be impossible because the data on which predictability in human affairs would have to be based are too fragmentary, and that it would be undesirable on the ground that discovery of an inexorably unfolding pattern in human affairs would imprison us in an "iron web." But when arguing in this vein he had unconsciously equated modern scientific prediction with discovery of a predetermined pattern and had leaped from the realm of empirical probabilities to the realm of fate and predestination. He had tended to confuse prediction of the probable outcome of antecedent events or phenomena with positive knowledge of an outcome that was certain. With regard to America's future, he sometimes suggested that despite all our "pulling and hauling" we were helpless against that which was "fated."

Yet, practically speaking, Beard operated on the belief that we could considerably influence our future. His own writings were often eloquent appeals for some kind or degree of pulling and haul-

[41] "What I Expect of Roosevelt," with Others, *Nation*, CXLIII (November 14, 1936), 572.

ing in human affairs in order to affect the outcome. He knew that in many cases probabilities could be foreseen with sufficient precision to guide action. During World War II, for example, at the same time that he claimed history to be nonrepetitive—a unique series of events—he urged that preparations for peace must go forward even while the war was being waged because "realistic thinking" could divine at least some of the probable postwar conditions that would confront us.[42]

Despite his frequent lapses into somewhat fatalistic terminology employed variously in support of moods of pessimism or of optimism, Beard's conception of history thus allowed considerable scope for human freedom and choice. Analyzing, in *The Republic,* some of the "human ultimates in thinking about our universe and in reaching convictions about it," he insisted that his own faith in the future was not blind, but was a "calculation based on knowledge of numerous relevant facts . . . and . . . formulated with reference to the highest degree of probability that seems warranted by these facts." The real world, he pointed out, not only confronted us with fate or determinism, but also permitted us *"opportunity* to exercise our powers, intellectual and moral." [43]

Beard himself used to assert that optimism and pessimism were matters of temperament rather than of philosophy. Perhaps this is also the best explanation of his own seemingly unsettled theoretical views as to the relationship between global war and the survival of liberal democracy.

A Devil Theory Applied

As Beard's concern with foreign policy grew, the role of diplomats, statesmen, and leaders assumed magnified proportions in his thought. Diplomacy, he now stressed, might work for war or for peace. Diplomats could help shape events so as to make war inevitable, or they could help forestall the wars of the future. "If, in the long flow of time, America becomes involved in a terrible conflict and is brought face to face with ruin," wrote Beard in 1939, "that circumstance, too, will be laid at the door of diplomacy." [44]

[42] See, for example, Introduction, Watts, *Voices of History,* p. xix.

[43] *The Republic,* pp. 340, 342.

[44] *American Government and Politics* (8th ed.; New York: Macmillan Co., 1939), p. 246.

This increasing emphasis on the directing influence of leading personalities in history, accompanied by a receding emphasis on the determinism of impersonal forces, was an evolution that had been going on in Beard's thought for many years. In the 1920's he had broadened his theoretical "basis of politics" considerably beyond the narrower economic thesis of his earlier progressive era writings. In that middle period of his life he had seemed to vacillate between (1) the assumption that it is statesmen who make or prevent wars, and (2) the belief that another war would be the inevitable outcome of impersonal forces. It is likely that his later fascination with historical relativism also tended to magnify in his mind the importance of the subjective elements in human affairs and to diminish the place of impersonal determinism.

Mingled with these tendencies in his thought was a growing anti-Roosevelt feeling, which became especially noticeable after the middle thirties as he increasingly questioned the President's foreign policy intentions. At the same time, as the likelihood of a new world conflict loomed larger, bitter memories were revived in Beard's mind, memories of disillusionment at opened archives, of Wilson's internationalism, and of America's "entanglement" in World War I. Consequently, as soon as Beard heard the news of the Pearl Harbor disaster, he was certain that here was no mere accident of war, but "a culmination in more than a hundred years of American diplomatic negotiations and activities in respect of the Far East, and the opening of a new and dangerous age for the Republic."[45] What evidence of sinister machinations did the official documents hold this time? Undoubtedly he was convinced that the evidence existed —if only the appropriate documents could be made available for study—which would prove that our entry into war was indeed that "grand diversion" about which he had insistently warned.

In 1942, at the time his own digging for documents and papers relating to the war was presumably getting under way, Beard wrote the Introduction to Franklin Watts's *Voices of History: Great Speeches and Papers of the Year 1941.* "Hundreds of other sources, perhaps none so startling or official as *How War Came,* are at hand," he explained, "to provide materials for interpreting the papers included in *The Voices of History.*" He himself would resist the

[45] *President Roosevelt and the Coming of the War, 1941* (New Haven, Conn.: Yale University Press, 1948), p. 234 n.

temptation to "supplement these papers by editorial comments," pending the availability of further materials.[46] But during the next few years, including the months immediately after the war's end, he apparently came to feel that sufficient materials had become available to support the thesis of his last two foreign policy books.

The thesis of these two books, particularly of his 1948 volume on *President Roosevelt and the Coming of the War, 1941,* was in considerable contrast to certain notions he had expressed in earlier decades. The President, Beard now strongly contended, had deliberately helped push the nation into war. Despite Roosevelt's public protestations that acts of war had been committed against the United States, Beard's view was that the real war guilt rested on the President, that "in reality the said acts were secretly invited and even initiated by the armed forces of the United States under his secret direction." At this stage in our history, Beard charged, the American government had apparently come to be managed on the theory that the President had "limitless authority publicly to misrepresent and secretly to control foreign policy, foreign affairs, and the war power." [47]

Beard's 1948 book was in a sense irony compounded, for it was Beard who had scoffed at a war guilt thesis after 1918, and Beard who for many years before that had derided historians for relying too heavily on diplomatic papers and leaving out of account the "real forces." Moreover, his Roosevelt thesis diverged considerably from that developed in his little volume, *The Devil Theory of War* (1936), in which he had belittled the idea that "wicked men make war." [48] It was a thesis that also stood in considerable contrast to his earlier criticism of the so-called great man theory of history.

The particular emphasis in Beard's last foreign policy writings appeared to stem both from his anti-Rooseveltism and from the evolution that had occurred in his implicit social theory. On the one hand, his implicit theory of politics and history justified a new emphasis on personal responsibility in human affairs. On the other hand, the destruction of his dream of an insulated American garden by the plunge into foreign war seemed to underscore the crucial historical importance of the decisions of leaders. In Beard's view, Roosevelt, like Wilson before him, had dragged his country need-

---

[46] Introduction, Watts, *Voices of History,* p. xvii.
[47] *President Roosevelt and the Coming of the War, 1941,* pp. 583, 598.
[48] *The Devil Theory of War,* p. 18.

lessly into war. But far worse, Beard felt, Roosevelt had perhaps irretrievably damaged our democratic and constitutional institutions by clinging "tenaciously to the idea of intervening in the controversies of Europe." [49]

If Beard's "revisionist" thesis regarding America's entry into World War II in part reflected his implicit social theory as this had evolved up to the latter 1940's, numerous questions of possible significance for theory nonetheless remained unanswered. The United States had not been the only nation in the grip of economic depression before World War II. Had Australian leaders, for example, also connived to bring their country into the war in order to divert attention from domestic difficulties? Or had Roosevelt brought in the entire Pacific community? If so, did this mean that America and other countries could not, after all, be effectively insulated from each other? Do troubles at home tend to cause leaders to look abroad for diversionary adventures, or does a threatening world situation tend to cause leaders to shift their attention from domestic reform to problems of defense and to measures to counter the moves of potential enemies? [50]

Beard's argument, of course, did not turn simply on theoretical assumptions concerning leaders versus impersonal forces in history, any more than it was merely a disputation regarding the relative merits of continentalism and internationalism as effective means of furthering America's ultimate security. It was a particular leader, Roosevelt, who was being arraigned and found guilty of deliberately involving the United States in war. Accordingly, both emotional commitment and intellectual conviction lay behind Beard's reaction against applying the thesis of impersonal determinism to World War II:

It is needless to point out to anyone given to precision in the use of language how elusive are such phrases as "war was inevitable," "drawn into war," "compelled to take up arms," "forced into war," and "America has been wantonly attacked." They connote a determinism of events for the United States, as if President Roosevelt was a mere agent of "forces" beyond his initiation or control, not an active agent in a conjuncture of circumstances which he had helped to create by deliberate

[49] *America in Midpassage,* p. 476; cf. "Roosevelt's Place in History," *Events,* III (February, 1938), 85.
[50] For an account of the situation from the viewpoint of Australia, see F. P. Chambers, C. H. Harris, and C. C. Bayley, *This Age of Conflict* (New York: Harcourt, Brace & Co., 1950), p. 585.

actions on his own part. Of course, it may be assumed that the whole world drama has been determined from the beginning of human time and that all the men and women who have taken part in it have been mere actors, mere puppets speaking lines and acting roles assigned to them by fate or "the nature of things." If so, so-called human virtues of courage, prescience, wisdom, and moral resolve are to be reckoned as phantoms.[51]

Conclusion

Beard's lifetime of thinking and writing about human affairs not only exemplifies the evolution of one man's ideas, but also represents something of a commentary on the wider currents of American social thought since the 1890's. In the early years he had sought to correct the previous underemphasis on economic factors in politics by implying that economics was virtually the only element worth mentioning. Ever after, his thinking had continued to be affected by the problem of how heavily personal responsibility weighs against the determinism of impersonal forces.

During the middle period of his life, Beard had moved from a decided economic interpretation of politics and history to a broader and more indefinite conception of the dynamism in human affairs. Ideas and ethics had received successively greater stress. From an earlier inclination to shun theoretical formulations as meaningless abstractions, he had developed the habit of portraying idea patterns as rationalizing instruments of defense or attack. At length he had come full circle to insist on occasion that thought was the prime determinant in human existence. Yet he had given little evidence of accepting the possibility of "theory" in politics except as found in the classics devoted to "what ought to be." When he had mentally associated politics with causal theory as found in the physical sciences, his thinking had tended to leave the world of empirical science and to soar to an imaginary realm of fate and predetermination. To his mind the "grand drama of history" had come to embrace human values associated with moral choices, as well as deterministic elements.

Now, in the final decade and a half of a long life, Beard's former implicit theory of politics had become vaguer, having developed into a considerably attenuated "realistic dialectics" apparently designed to gather in all relevancies and to omit nothing. He himself had continued strongly cherishing democracy and constitutionalism, or the "civilian way of living together in a republic." In his

[51] *President Roosevelt and the Coming of the War, 1941*, p. 407.

mind, "majority rule in a time span" had become the most desirable practicable system of politics. But increasingly his thought had been dominated by intense preoccupation with one area of politics— foreign policy. Yet all the arguments he had been able to marshal in defense of his ideal of an insulated American garden had not stemmed the tide. War had come.

Now the republic had entered a "new and dangerous age," its future threatened by internal changes and by developments in the world at large. The old multipower world had given way to a world becoming dangerously polarized between two superstates. Almost unbelievable technological and scientific changes had sprung from those beginnings which Beard as a young man in England had described in his little book, *The Industrial Revolution* (1901). Now he wondered fearfully whether these changes were leading to a nobler civilization or to inevitable catastrophe. As he reminded readers of the final edition of his *American Government and Politics* (1948), we had come to a "revolutionary time in the history of our nation." With our country now in the thick of world affairs, and laboring under crushing postwar burdens, "the American system of government and liberty" faced its greatest test.[52]

Although Beard was mistaken in his prewar prediction that World War II would spell the end of democratic institutions in America, who knows *what* would survive an atomic missile conflict in the space age? If insulation from impending storms could be seriously advocated as recently as Beard's last decades, who now doubts that, internationally speaking, the era of hermits is irretrievably past? And if the new dark ages arrives tomorrow, can human civilization—in a thousand years, or in ten thousand—once more crawl out of the caves to try again?

Beard's political thought would seem to demonstrate the proposition that a vast fund of knowledge is not by itself a sure guide to policy. His lifetime of thinking indicates that operative philosophies rest ultimately on a few simple principles accepted largely on faith. This appears to be as true of a learned historian charting man's journey through time as it is of an illiterate fisherman sailing by the stars. Yet, regardless of our agreement or disagreement with particular aspects of Beard's thinking, we are in his debt for his stimulating influence on a half century of social thought.

[52] *American Government and Politics* (10th ed.; 1948), p. v.

BIBLIOGRAPHY

WRITINGS OF CHARLES A. BEARD

Articles

"Address at Meeting of Teachers at Atlantic City, February 24, 1935," *Social Frontier*, I (April, 1935), 6.

"Administration, a Foundation of Government," *American Political Science Review*, XXXIV (April, 1940), 232–35.

"Advocates of Constitutional Change Do Not Aim to Destroy State Powers," *Weekly News Review*, XIV (September 30, 1935), 8.

"Agriculture in the Nation's Economy," *Nation*, CXXV (August 17, 1927), 150–51.

"America: A Month's Record," *Current History*, XL (September, 1934), 641–50.

With Mary R. Beard. "America and the Far East: The Issues of Pacific Policy," *Survey*, LXVI (May 1, 1926), 189.

With Others. "America and the Next War," *New Republic*, XCIX (June 14, 1939), 148.

"America Debates War Plans," *Current History*, XLII (June, 1935), 290–94.

"America Must Stay Big," *Today*, IV (September 14, 1935), 3–4, 21.

"American Business Is Better," *Current History*, XLIII (November, 1935), 182–90.

"American Influence on Municipal Government in the Orient," *National Municipal Review*, XIV (January, 1925), 7–11.

"American Invasion of Europe," *Harper's Magazine*, CLVIII (March, 1929), 470–79.

With Clay Coss. "American Presidents," *Weekly News Review*, LI (November 16, 1936—May 24, 1937), 8.

"America's 'Duty' to England," *Events*, II (November, 1937), 327–31.

"America Twists and Turns," *Current History*, XLI (January, 1935), 459–66.

With Clay Coss. "America—Yesterday and Today," *Weekly News Review*, XVI (September 6, 1937—May 9, 1938), 8.

With Clay Coss. "America—Yesterday and Today," *Weekly News Review*, XVII (September 12, 1938—November 14, 1938), 7.

With Clay Coss. "America—Yesterday and Today," *Weekly News Review*, XVIII (September 11, 1939—May 27, 1940), 6.

257

"Announcement of Change in Editorial Management," *Social Studies*, XXV (January, 1934), 5–6.

"Another Job for Mr. Hoover," *Outlook*, CLIII (September 4, 1929), 17, 38.

"Anti-trust Racket," *New Republic*, XCVI (September 21, 1938), 182–84.

"Are Third Parties Futile?" *Today*, III (December 22, 1934), 6–7, 24.

With Clay Coss. "As the Parties See It," *Weekly News Review*, XV (September 7, 1936—October 26, 1936), 8.

"Awakening of Japanese Cities," *Review of Reviews*, LXIX (May, 1924), 523–27.

With Clay Coss. "Background of Today's Problems," *Weekly News Review*, XIX (September 9, 1940—February 24, 1941), 6.

"Ballot's Burden," *Political Science Quarterly*, XXIV (December, 1909), 589–614.

"Bankruptcy Fire-Sale," *American Mercury*, XI (July, 1927), 283–87.

With W. G. Carr. "Battle for Free Schools," *Journal of the National Education Association*, XXIV (March, 1935), 77–80.

"Beard's Criticism of William Randolph Hearst," *New York World Telegram*, February 25, 1935.

With W. G. Carr. "Before Schools Began," *Journal of the National Education Association*, XXIII (November, 1934), 201–3.

"Behind the New Deal," *Saturday Review of Literature*, XI (December 22, 1934), 381–83.

"Bigger and Better Armaments," *Harper's Magazine*, CLVIII (January, 1929), 133–43.

"Big Navy Boys," *New Republic*, LXIX (January 20, 27, February 3, 1932), 258–62, 287–91, 314–18.

"Big Railway Smash," *New Republic*, XCIV (March 9, 1938), 123–24.

"Blessed Profit System," *New Republic*, LXXXI (December 26, 1934), 188–90.

"Bolshevik Session of the National Municipal League Annual Conference," *National Municipal Review*, VII (September, 1918), 449–67.

"Books for Building Stones," *National Parent-Teacher*, XXX (September, 1935), 18–19.

"Budgetary Provisions of the New York Constitution," *Annals of the American Academy of Political and Social Science*, LXII (November, 1915), 64–68.

"Call upon Every Citizen," *Harper's Magazine*, CXXXVII (October, 1918), 655–66.

"Captains Uncourageous," *Virginia Quarterly Review*, VII (October, 1931), 500–506.

With William Beard. "Case for Bureaucracy," *Scribner's Magazine*, XCIII (April, 1933), 209–14.

"Challenge to the New Deal," *Current History*, XLIII (February, 1936), 513–20.

"City's Place in Civilization," *Survey*, LXI (November 15, 1928), 213–15.

"Collective Security," *New Republic*, XCIII (February 2, 1938), 356–59.

With W. G. Carr. "Colonial Schooldays," *Journal of the National Education Association*, XXIV (February, 1935), 41–44.

With Clay Coss. "Commerce Clause of Constitution Is Source of Much Debate and Friction," *Weekly News Review*, XIV (October 7, 1935), 8.

"Conditions Favorable to Creative Work in Political Science," *American Political Science Review*, XXIV Suppl. (February, 1930), 25–32.

"Conflicts in City Planning," *Yale Review*, XVII (October, 1927), 65–77.

"Confusion Rules in Washington," *Current History*, XLI (December, 1934), 333–37.

With Clay Coss. "Congress' Power of Taxation to Meet Supreme Court Test in Cotton Case," *Weekly News Review*, XIV (November 11, 1935), 8.

"Congress under Fire," *Yale Review*, XXII (September, 1932), 35–51.

"Conservatism Hits Bottom," *New Republic*, LXVIII (August 19, 1931), 7–11.

With Clay Coss. "Constitutional Issues Are Involved in New Deal's Housing and Labor Plans," *Weekly News Review*, XIV (November 4, 1935), 8.

"Constitution and States' Rights," *Virginia Quarterly Review*, XI (October, 1935), 481–95.

With Clay Coss. "Constitution, as Finally Adopted, Compromise of Opposing Forces," *Weekly News Review*, XIV (September 16, 1935), 8.

"Constitution of Oklahoma," *Political Science Quarterly*, XXIV (March, 1909), 95–114.

"Contest between Rural and Urban Economy," *Bulletin of the University of Georgia: Institute of Public Affairs and International Relations*, XXX (November, 1929), 70–78.

"Co-operation and the New Century," *Young Oxford*, II (December, 1900), 96–100.

"Corporations and Natural Rights," *Virginia Quarterly Review*, XII (July, 1936), 337–53.

Pseud. John W. Bradford. "Could Daniel Webster Teach in New York's Schools?" *Nation*, CIX (August 2, 1919), 147.

"Count Karolyi and America," *Nation*, CXX (April 1, 1925), 347–48.

"Court and Constitution," *Events*, I (June, 1937), 407–11.

"Court Issues," *Social Frontier*, III (June, 1937), 269–71.

With Clay Coss. "Court Issues Arise over Power of Congress to End Holding Companies," *Weekly News Review*, XIV (October 28, 1935), 8.

"Creating the Good Life for America," *Journal of the American Association of University Women*, XXVIII (June, 1935), 195–98.

"Crisis in Local Government and the Task Ahead," *American City*, XLIX (October, 1934), 47.

"Culture and Agriculture," *Saturday Review of Literature*, V (October 20, 1928), 272–73.

With Alfred Vagts. "Currents of Thought in Historiography," *American Historical Review*, XLII (April, 1937), 460–83.

"Danger Spots in Europe," *Bulletin of the University of Georgia: Institute of Public Affairs and International Relations*, XXX (November, 1929), 79–81.

"Dear Old Constitution," *Harper's Magazine*, CLX (February, 1930), 281–91.

"Democracy and Education in the United States," *Social Research*, IV (September, 1937), 391–98.

"Democracy Holds Its Ground: A European Survey," *Harper's Magazine*, CLVII (November, 1938), 680–91.

"Dislocated Soldier of Industry," *Journal of Adult Education*, III (January, 1931), 8–11.

"Education Enriched by Living," *National Elementary Principal*, XVII (February, 1938), 104–6.

"Education under the Nazis," *Foreign Affairs*, XIV (April, 1936), 437–52.

"The Educator in the Quest for National Security," *Social Frontier*, I (April, 1935), 13–15.

"Electric Fire of Thought," *Journal of Adult Education*, II (January, 1930), 5–7.

"Emerging Issues in America," *Current History*, XLI (November, 1934), 203–9.

"Emerson as an American Dream-er," *Social Frontier*, IV (December, 1937), 75–79.

"Essentials of Democracy," *School and Society*, L (August 19, 1939), 228–35.

With Clay Coss. "Europe—Yesterday and Today," *Weekly News Review*, XVII (October 3, 1938), 7.

"Events and Personalia" (ed.), *National Municipal Review*, I (January, April, July, October, 1912), 124–60, 284–325, 475–520, 714–43.

With Clay Coss. "Extent of Congress' Taxing Power May Soon Meet Supreme Court Test," *Weekly News Review*, XIV (October 14, 1935), 8.

With Clay Coss. "Federal Judge Takes Broad View of Commerce Clause in Coal Case," *Weekly News Review*, XIV (December 2, 1935), 8.

"Fiction of Majority Rule," *Atlantic Monthly*, CXL (December, 1927), 831–36.

With Others. "Final Report of Committee on a University Center for Research in Washington," *Annual Report of the American Historical Association,* I (1921), 74–82.

"Five Pages from Newton D. Baker," *New Republic,* LXXXVIII (October 7, 1936), 247–48.

"Five-Year Plan for America," *Forum and Century,* LXXXVI (July, 1931), 1–11.

With Clay Coss. "Flexibility of Constitution Permits Disputes over Its Real Meaning," *Weekly News Review,* XIV (September 23, 1935), 8.

"For a Greater Tokyo," *Far Eastern Review,* XIX (April, 1923), 263–66.

"Forces Making for Peace," *Bulletin of the University of Georgia: Institute of Public Affairs and International Relations,* XXX (November, 1929), 82–84.

"Freedom of Teaching," *Social Frontier,* I (March, 1925), 18–20.

"Frontier in American History," *New Republic,* XCVII (February 1, 1939), 359–62.

With G. H. E. Smith. "Future Comes," *Journal of the National Education Association,* XXIII (March, 1934), 94.

"Future of Democracy: V," *New Republic,* XCI (May 12, 1937), 13–14.

"Future of Democracy in the United States," *Political Quarterly,* VIII (October, 1937), 495–506.

"Germany Up to Her Old Tricks," *New Republic,* LXXX (October 24, 1934), 299–300.

"Going Ahead with Roosevelt," *Events,* I (January, 1937), 9–12.

"Good versus McCormick Budget Bill," *National Municipal Review,* IX (April, 1920), 222–25.

"Goto and the Rebuilding of Tokyo," *Our World,* V (April, 1924), 11–21.

"Government by Technologists," *New Republic,* LXIII (June 18, 1930), 115–20.

"Government Employment Policy," *Good Government,* XXXVI (January, 1919), 11–18.

"Great American Tradition," *Nation,* CXXIII (July 7, 1926), 7–8.

With Clay Coss. "Great Constitutional Issues before the Nation," *Weekly News Review,* XIV (September 9, 1935), 8.

"Heat and Light on Neutrality," *New Republic,* LXXXVI (February 12, 1936), 8–9.

"Heroes and Villains of the World War," *Current History,* XXIV (August, 1926), 730–35.

With George M. Wrong. "Historian and Society," *Canadian Historical Review,* XIV (March, 1933), 1–4.

"Historians at Work: Brooks and Henry Adams," *Atlantic Monthly,* CLXXI (April, 1943), 87–93.

"A Historian's Quest for Light," *Proceedings of the Association of History Teachers of the Middle States and Maryland,* XXIX (1931), 12–21.

"Historical Approach to the New Deal," *American Political Science Review,* XXVIII (February, 1934), 11–15.

"Historical Woman Suffrage," *New Republic,* IV Suppl. (October 9, 1915), 1–3.

With Mary R. Beard. "History and Culture," *Saturday Review of Literature,* VI (September 7, 1929), 101–2.

"History and Travel," *Proceedings of the Association of History Teachers of the Middle States and Maryland,* XXII (1924), 46–54.

"History as Actuality," *Progressive Education,* XV (March, 1938), 243.

"History in the Public Schools," *New Republic,* LII (November 16, 1927), 348–50.

"Hitlerism and Our Liberties" (text of address given at New School for Social Research, April 10, 1934). New York, 1934 (?).

With Others. "How to Stay out of War," *Forum,* XCVII (February, 1937), 89–95.

"Human Nature and Administration," *Nation,* CVI (April 25, 1918), 502–4.

"An Ideal Labour College," *Young Oxford,* IV (December, 1901), 79–81.

"Idea of Let Us Alone," *Virginia Quarterly Review,* XV (October, 1939), 500–514.

"Ideas: An Inquiry," *Journal of Adult Education,* IX (April, 1937), 121–25.

The Immediate Duty of an American Citizen. New York: Unpublished Essay in Columbiana Collection of Low Memorial Library of Columbia University, May, 1902.

"In Defense of Civil Liberties," *Current History,* XLIV (April, 1936), 66–72.

"In Defense of Congress," *American Mercury,* LV (November, 1942), 529–35.

"Industry's Attack on the New Deal," *Current History,* XLIII (January, 1936), 399–406.

"In Justice to Judge Lindsey," *New Republic,* III (May 15, 1915), 35–37.

"Internationalism in the United States," *New Review,* III (1915), 159–60.

"The Interpretation of Events," *Events,* II (December, 1937), 441–46.

"Is Babbitt's Case Hopeless?" *Menorah Journal,* XIV (January, 1928), 21–28.

"Is Western Civilization in Peril?" *Harper's Magazine,* CLVII (August, 1928), 265–73.

"It Is Not True," *In Review,* Governmental Research Association, 1948.

"James Harvey Robinson," *Journal of Adult Education*, VIII (June, 1936), 247–49.

"Japan's Statesman of Research," *Review of Reviews*, LXVIII (September, 1923), 296–98.

"Jefferson and the New Freedom," *New Republic*, I (November 14, 1914), 18–19.

"Jefferson in America Now," *Yale Review*, XXV (December, 1935), 241–57.

"John Purroy Mitchel," *Survey*, XL (July 13, 1918), 422, 436–37.

"Justice Oliver Wendell Holmes," *Current History*, XXXIII (March, 1931), 801–6.

"Keeping America Out of War," *Current History*, XLIII (December, 1935), 290–98.

"The Key to the Mexican Problem," *New Review*, II (June, 1914), 321–24.

"Labors of Congress," *Current History*, XLIII (October, 1935), 64–73.

"Last Years of Stephen Raditch," *Current History*, XXIX (October, 1928), 82–84.

"League and the Future," *National Municipal Review*, XXXIII (November, 1944), 503–10.

"Lesson in Civics," *Social Frontier*, IV (October, 1937), 9–10.

"Lessons from Science," *Young Oxford*, II (June, 1901), 338–41.

"Letter of Resignation from Columbia University," *School and Society*, VI (October 13, 1917), 446–47.

"Life Is Not a Table of Logarithms," *Public Management*, XI (July, 1929), 511.

"Limitations to the Application of Social Science Implied in Recent Social Trends," *Social Forces*, XI (May, 1933), 505–10.

"List of Books on Economics," *School Life*, XVIII (January, 1933), 86.

"Little Alice Looks at the Constitution," *New Republic*, LXXXVII (July 22, 1936), 315–17.

"Living Constitution," *Annals of the American Academy of Political and Social Science*, CLXXXV (May, 1936), 29–34.

"A Living Empire, I," *Young Oxford*, III (October, 1901), 24–25.

"A Living Empire, II," *Young Oxford*, IV (November, 1901), 39–43.

"Looking Backward," *New Republic*, CI (November 8, 1939), 74.

"Looking Forward to 1936," *Current History*, XLII (August, 1935), 513–21.

"Looking Forward to 1940," *Events*, V (June, 1939), 401–4.

Pseud. John W. Bradford. "Lo! the Poor Professor," *Nation*, CIX (September 20, 1919), 392–93.

With Clay Coss. "Makers of America," *Weekly News Review*, XVII (January 9, 1939—May 29, 1939), 6, 7, 8.

"Making a Bigger and Better Navy," *New Republic*, LXVIII (October 14, 1931), 223–26.

"Memorandum from an Old Worker in the Vineyard," *Social Education,* II (September, 1938), 383–85.

"A Memorandum on Social Philosophy," *Journal of Social Philosophy,* V (October, 1939), 7–15.

"Memorandum Relative to the Reconstruction of Tokyo," *Far Eastern Review,* XXI (June, 1925), 252–56.

"Men Who Have Helped Us: I. William Cobbett, Friend of Man," *Young Oxford,* II (February, 1901), 171–74.

"Men Who Have Helped Us: II. Robert Owen," *Young Oxford,* II (March, 1901), 206–9.

"Men Who Have Helped Us: III. Thomas Carlyle," *Young Oxford,* II (April, 1901), 246–48.

"Men Who Have Helped Us: IV. William Morris," *Young Oxford,* II (May, 1901), 290–93.

"Men Who Have Helped Us: VI. Mazzini," *Young Oxford,* II (July, 1901), 358–60.

"Men Who Have Helped Us: VII. Charles Darwin," *Young Oxford,* II (September, 1901), 439–41.

"Methods of Training for Public Service," *School and Society,* II (December 25, 1915), 904–11.

"Mine Eyes May Behold," *New Republic,* XCIII (January 19, 1938), 306.

"Minority Rule in America," *American Mercury,* XXXVII (February, 1936), 190–96.

With Clay Coss. "Modern Industry Raises Issue of Greater Government Regulation," *Weekly News Review,* XIV (November 18, 1935), 8.

"Money in Federal Politics," *New Republic,* LXIII (July 30, 1930), 305–7.

"Monopoly in Fact and Fiction," *Events,* IV (November, 1938), 383–87.

"The Month in America," *Current History,* XLI (March, 1935), 718–25.

"Municipal Research Abroad and at Home," *Journal of Social Forces,* III (March, 1925), 495–97.

"Municipal Research in Japan," *National Municipal Review,* XII (September, 1923), 520–23.

"The Myth of Rugged American Individualism," *Harper's Magazine,* CLXIV (December, 1931), 13–22.

"National Politics and War," *Scribner's Magazine,* XCVII (February, 1935), 65–70.

"The Nation Seeks Security," *National Education Association Department of Superintendence Official Report,* pp. 290–91. Washington, D.C.: Department of Superintendence of the National Education Association, 1935.

"Need for Direction: What Is the Adult's Goal in the Social Sciences?" *Journal of Adult Education,* V (January, 1933), 5–10.

"Neglected Aspects of Political Science," *American Political Science Review*, XLII (April, 1948), 211–22.

"Neutrality Deadlock," *Events*, VI (September, 1939), 161–64.

"Neutrality: Shall We Have Revision?" *New Republic*, XCVII (January 18, 1939), 307–8.

"New Deal's Rough Road," *Current History*, XLII (September, 1935), 625–32.

"New Morgan Thesis," *New Republic*, LXXXIX (January 20, 1937), 350–53.

"The New School for Social Research," in *Workers' Education: A Symposium*. New York, 1919 (?).

"New York Constitutional Convention," *National Municipal Review*, IV (October, 1915), 637–45.

"New York, the Metropolis of Today," *Review of Reviews*, LXIX (June, 1924), 608–24.

With Robert H. Jackson and Frank Murphy. "Next Step for the Progressives," *American Teacher*, XXIII (May, 1939), 24.

"Notes and Events" (ed.), *National Municipal Review*, II (January, April, July, October, 1913), 116–47, 284–326, 470–515, 675–720; III (January, April, 1914), 114–65, 371–407.

"On Puritans," *New Republic*, XXV (December 1, 1920), 15–17.

"On the Advantages of Censorship and Espionage," *New Republic*, XXVII (August 24, 1921), 350–51.

"On the Diplomatic Front," *Events*, II (September, 1937), 165–69.

With Clay Coss. "Origin of Supreme Court's Power to Overrule Congressional Laws," *Weekly News Review*, XIV (December 9, 1935), 8.

"Our Choice in Foreign Policy," *Events*, I (March, 1937), 161–65.

"Our Confusion over National Defense," *Harper's Magazine*, CLXIV (February, May, 1932), 257–67, 768.

"Our Foreign and Domestic Policies," *Current History*, XLI (February, 1935), 586–92.

"Outlook of City Improvements in Tokyo," *Trans-Pacific*, VIII (January, 1923), 79–81.

With Clay Coss. "Pan American Union," *Weekly News Review*, XVIII (April 8, 1940), 6.

"Peace for America," *New Republic*, LXXXVI (March 4, 11, 18, 1936), 100–102, 127–29, 156–59.

"Peace Loads the Guns," *Today*, IV (June 29, 1935), 3–4, 23.

With Clay Coss. "Personal Sketches of American Presidents," *Weekly News Review*, XV (November 9, 1936), 8.

"Planning and Chain Stores," *New Republic*, LXXIII (November 30, 1932), 66–67.

"A Plea for Greater Stress upon the Modern Period," *Minutes of the Sixth Annual Convention of the Association of History Teachers of the Middle States and Maryland* (1908), pp. 12–15.

"Political Heritage of the Twentieth Century," *Yale Review,* XVIII (March, 1929), 456–79.

"Political Parties in City Government: A Reconsideration of Old View Points," *National Municipal Review,* VI (March, 1917), 201–6.

"Political Science in the Crucible," *New Republic,* XIII Suppl. (November 17, 1917), 3–4.

"Politics and Education," *Teachers College Record,* XVII (May, 1916), 215–26.

"Politics of Our Depression," *Current History,* XLI (October, 1934), 77–83.

"Potency of Labor Education," *American Federationist,* XXIX (July, 1922), 500–502.

"Practice and Culture," *Journal of Adult Education,* VII (January, 1935), 5–9.

"Preparedness: An American Issue," *Current History,* XLII (May, 1935), 179–86.

"President and Congress," *Outlook,* CLII (May 29, 1929), 179.

"Presidential Appointments," *Nation,* CXXXIII (July 22, October 7, 1931), 82–84, 364.

"President Loses Prestige," *Current History,* XLII (April, 1935), 64–71.

With Others. "Professional and Patriotic Obligation," *School and Society,* XXXV (February 27, 1932), 296–97.

"Propaganda in Schools," *Dial,* LXVI (June 14, 1919), 598–99.

"Property and Democracy," *Social Frontier,* I (October, 1934), 13–15.

"Prospects for Peace," *Harper's Magazine,* CLVIII (February, 1929), 320–30.

With Clay Coss. "Provisions of Fifth Amendment Involved in Utility Decision," *Weekly News Review,* XIV (November 25, 1935), 8.

"Public Employment," *National Municipal Review,* VIII (January, 1919), 26–33.

"Queries from the Hills," *New Republic,* LXXXV (November 27, 1935), 71–72.

"Quest for Academic Power," *Journal of Higher Education,* III (December, 1932), 464–69.

"Rebuilding in Japan," *Review of Reviews,* LXVIII (October, 1923), 373–82.

"Recent Activities of City Clubs," *National Municipal Review,* I (July, 1912), 431–35.

"Recent Gains in Government," *World Tomorrow,* X (November, 1927), 438–42.

"Reconstructing State Government," *New Republic,* IV Suppl. (August 21, 1915), 1–16.

With K. Sawada. "Reconstruction in Tokyo," *Review of Reviews,* LXXI (March, 1925), 268–70.

With Alvin S. Johnson. "Record of Political Events," *Political Science Quarterly*, XX (June, December, 1905), 351–84, 740–76; XXII (December, 1907), 748–76; XXIII (June, December, 1908), 351–84, 746–76; XXIV (June, December, 1909), 343–76, 730–60.

"Rendezvous with the Supreme Court," *New Republic*, LXXXVIII (September 2, 1936), 92–94.

"Reply to the Secretary of the Navy C. F. Adams," *Harper's Magazine*, CLXIV (May, 1932), 772–74.

With Others. "Report of a Conference Held in Cincinnati, December 27, 1916, on the Organization of a University Center for Higher Studies in Washington," *Annual Report of the American Historical Association*, I (1916), 271–74.

With J. D. Lewis. "Representative Government in Evolution," *American Political Science Review*, XXVI (April, 1932), 223–40.

"Rise of the Democratic Idea in the United States," *Survey Graphic*, XXVI (April, 1937), 201–3.

"Roosevelt and the Judges," *Events*, I (April, 1937), 241–45.

"Roosevelt's Place in History," *Events*, III (February, 1938), 81–86.

"Rough Seas for the Super-Navy," *New Republic*, XCIV (March 30, 1938), 210.

"Rushlights in Darkness," *Scribner's Magazine*, XC (December, 1931), 571–78.

"Ruskin and the Babble of Tongues," *New Republic*, LXXXVII (August 5, 1936), 370–72.

"Ruskin Hall and Temperance Reform," *Young Oxford*, II (March, 1901), 221.

With John Dewey and Edward Weeks. "Savants Select Most Influential Volumes," *English Journal*, XXV (June, 1936), 496–98.

"Scholar in an Age of Conflicts," *School and Society*, XLIII (February 29, 1936), 278–83.

With W. G. Carr. "Schools Accept New Jobs," *Journal of the National Education Association*, XXIV (April, 1935), 117–20.

With W. G. Carr. "Schools of Cloister and Castle," *Journal of the National Education Association*, XXIV (January, 1935), 7–10.

With W. G. Carr. "Schools of Greece and Rome," *Journal of the National Education Association*, XXIII (December, 1934), 230–32.

With W. G. Carr. "Schools Weathering a Storm," *Journal of the National Education Association*, XXIV (May, 1935), 149–52.

"Search for the Centre," *Scribner's Magazine*, XCI (January, 1932), 2–7.

"Self-Education," *Young Oxford*, I (October, 1899), 17–18.

"Shooting It Out in Russia," *Events*, III (March, 1938), 161–64.

"Should Congress Be Empowered to Override Supreme Court Decisions?" *Congressional Digest*, XIV (December, 1935), 317.

"Should Congress Enact a Federal Sedition Law?" *Congressional Digest*, XIV (October, 1935), 245.

"Sign of the Times," *National Municipal Review,* XXII (December, 1933), 581–83.

"Social Change v. the Constitution," *Current History,* XLII (July, 1935), 345–52.

"Social Studies Curriculum," *Social Frontier,* II (December, 1935), 78–80.

"Some Aspects of Regional Planning," *American Political Science Review,* XX (May, 1926), 273–83.

"Some Economic Origins of Jeffersonian Democracy," *American Historical Review,* XIX (January, 1914), 282–98.

"Some Regional Realities," *Survey,* LVI (April 15, 1926), 85–87.

"Spooks, Made in Germany," *New Republic,* LXXVII (December 6, 1933), 97–98.

"Squirt-Gun Politics," *Harper's Magazine,* CLXI (July, 1930), 147–53.

"The Stream of Tendencies in American Government," *St. Louis Post-Dispatch, Sixtieth Anniversary Section,* December 11, 1938.

"Study and Teaching of Politics," *Columbia University Quarterly,* XII (June, 1910), 268–74.

"Suggested Economy for Congress," *National Municipal Review,* X (November, 1921), 541–42.

With Clay Coss. "Suggestions Made to Curb Power of Supreme Court over Congress," *Weekly News Review,* XIV (December 16, 1935), 8.

"The Supreme Court Controversy," *Events,* I (May, 1937), 341–46.

"Supreme Court—Usurper or Grantee?" *Political Science Quarterly,* XXVII (March, 1912), 1–35.

"The Supreme Issue for America," *Events,* III (April, 1938), 275–77.

With Charles Raymond Atkinson. "Syndication of the Speakership," *Political Science Quarterly,* XXVI (September, 1911), 381–414.

"Talking into the Wind," *Harper's Magazine,* CLXXXV (November, 1942), 607.

"Tariff in the Campaign," *New Republic,* LXXII (November 2, 1932), 318–19.

With William G. Carr. "Task before Us," *Social Studies,* XXV (May, 1934), 215–17.

With Mary R. Beard. "Ten Years Back," *Survey,* LVIII (April 1, 1927), 5–7, 51–61.

"Teutonic Origins of Representative Government," *American Political Science Review,* XXVI (February, 1932), 28–44.

"That Noble Dream," *American Historical Review,* XLI (October, 1935), 74–87.

"That Promise of American Life," *New Republic,* LXXXI (February 6, 1935), 350–52.

"Thomas Jefferson: A Civilized Man," *Mississippi Valley Historical Review,* XXX (September, 1943), 159–70.

"Those Old-World Quarrels," *Events*, II (October, 1937), 257–62.

"Time, Technology, and the Creative Spirit in Political Science," *American Political Science Review*, XXI (February, 1927), 1–11.

With K. Sawada. "Tokyo Reconstructed," *Trans-Pacific*, XII (May 2, 1925), 20.

"Toward Civilization," *Saturday Review of Literature*, VI (April 5, 1930), 894–95.

"Training for Efficient Public Service," *Annals of the American Academy of Political and Social Science*, LXIV (March, 1916), 215–26.

"Training the Commercial Organization Secretary," *American City*, XIII (October, 1915), 310–11.

"Trend in Social Studies," *Historical Outlook*, XX (December, 1929), 369–72.

"A Tribute to Co-operators," *Young Oxford*, II (November, 1900), 79.

"Turn of the Century," *Survey Graphic*, XXVI (December, 1937), 679–82.

With Clay Coss. "TVA Raises Issue over Power of Congress to Control Navigation," *Weekly News Review*, XIV (October 21, 1935), 8.

"Twilight of Social Systems," *Living Age*, CCCLVII (January, 1940), 410–17.

With Others. "Two Documents in the Case of Jerome Davis," *New Republic*, LXXXIX (November 18, 1936), 86–92.

"The University and Democracy," *Dial*, LXIV (April 11, 1918), 335–37.

"Use of Sources in Instruction in Government and Politics," *History Teacher's Magazine*, I (November, 1909), 49–50.

"War—If, How, and When?" *Events*, II (August, 1937), 81–86.

"War Springs from Peace," *Scholastic*, XXV (November 10, 1934), 12.

"War with Japan?" *Events*, VIII (November, 1940), 321–23.

"War with Japan: What Shall We Get Out of It?" *Nation*, CXX (March 25, 1925), 311–13.

"We're Blundering into War," *American Mercury*, XLVI (April, 1939), 388–99.

"What about the Constitution?" *Nation*, CXLII (April 1, 1936), 405–6.

"What a Budget Should Be," *New Republic*, X (February 17, 1917), 66–67.

With Clay Coss. "What Democracy Means," *Weekly News Review*, XVI (May 16, 1938), 8.

"What Do We Mean by Democracy?" *Consumers' Cooperation*, XXII (October, 1936), 150–53.

With Others. "What I Expect of Roosevelt," *Nation*, CXLIII (November 14, 1936), 572.

"What Is a Statesman?" *American Mercury,* I (April, 1924), 394–96.
With Others. "What Is the Meaning of Life?" *Literary Digest,* CXIV (November 5, 1932), 20.
"What Is This Sea Power?" *Asia,* XXXV (January, 1935), 4–9.
"What Is Worth While in Education," *Young Oxford,* I (December, 1899), 16.
"Whom Does Congress Represent?" *Harper's Magazine,* CLX (January, 1930), 144–52.
"Who's to Write the History of the War?" *Saturday Evening Post,* CCXX (October 4, 1947), 172.
"Why Did We Go to War?" *New Republic,* XC (March 10, 1937), 127–29.
"Why Study Socialism?" *Intercollegiate Socialist,* I (1913), 3.
"Will Roosevelt Keep Us Out of War?" *Events,* II (July, 1937), 1–6.
"'Will Roosevelt Keep Us Out of War?' Dr. Beard's Rejoinder," *Events,* II (September, 1937), 163–64.
"Woman's Party," *New Republic,* VII (July 29, 1916), 329–31.
"The Word-Revolution Begins," *Events,* III (January, 1938), 23–26.
"World as I Want It," *Forum and Century,* XCI (June, 1934), 332–34.
"World Bureau of Municipal Research," *National Municipal Review,* XIV (January, 1925), 1–2.
"Written History as an Act of Faith," *American Historical Review,* XXXIX (January, 1934), 219–29.

Books and Contributions to Books

The Administration and Politics of Tokyo. New York: Macmillan Co., 1923.
With Mary R. Beard. "Adopting the National Constitution" and "Whom Does Congress Represent?" in A. N. Christenson and E. M. Kirkpatrick (eds.), *The People, Politics, and the Politician,* pp. 49–54, 338–49. New York: Henry Holt & Co., 1941.
America Faces the Future (ed.). Boston: Houghton Mifflin Co., 1932.
With Mary R. Beard. *America in Midpassage.* 2 vols. New York: Macmillan Co., 1939.
"America in Midpassage," in Progressive Education Association, *John Dewey and the Promise of America,* pp. 18–25. Columbus, Ohio, 1939.
With Mary R. Beard. *American Citizenship.* New York: Macmillan Co., 1914.
American City Government. New York: Century Co., 1912.
American Foreign Policy in the Making, 1932–1940. New Haven, Conn.: Yale University Press, 1946.
American Government and Politics. New York: Macmillan Co., 1910. Rev. ed., 1914; 3rd ed., 1920; 4th ed., 1924; 5th ed., 1928; 6th

ed., 1931; 7th ed., 1935; 8th ed., 1939; 9th ed., 1944; 10th ed., in collaboration with William Beard, 1948.

30 With William Beard. *The American Leviathan*. New York: Macmillan Co., 1930.

28 *The American Party Battle*. New York: Macmillan Co., 1928.

42 With Mary R. Beard. *The American Spirit*. New York: Macmillan Co., 1942.

38 With William C. Bagley and Roy F. Nichols. *America Today*. New York: Macmillan Co., 1938.

38 With William C. Bagley and Roy F. Nichols. *America Yesterday*. New York: Macmillan Co., 1938.

38 With William C. Bagley and Roy F. Nichols. *America Yesterday and Today*. New York: Macmillan Co., 1938.

49 "Baconian Scholar" and "Mr. Henderson's North Carolina," in Samuel S. Hood (ed.), *Archibald Henderson, the New Crichton*, pp. 71–72, 73–75. New York: Beechhurst Press, 1949.

29 With George Radin. *The Balkan Pivot: Yugoslavia*. New York: Macmillan Co., 1929.

44 With Mary R. Beard. *A Basic History of the United States*. New York: Doubleday & Co., 1944.

33 *A Century of Progress* (ed.). New York: Harper & Bros., 1933.

32 *A Charter for the Social Sciences in the Schools*. New York: Charles Scribner's Sons, 1932.

23 A Collection of Lectures (in Japanese). Tokyo: Shisei Chosa-kai, 1923.

34 With Commission on Social Studies in the Schools. *Conclusions and Recommendations of the Commission*. New York: Charles Scribner's Sons, 1934.

Contemporary American History, 1877–1913. New York: Macmillan Co., 1914.

22 *Cross Currents in Europe Today*. Boston: Marshall Jones Co., 1922.

36 With G. H. E. Smith (eds.). *Current Problems of Public Policy*. New York: Macmillan Co., 1936.

With James Harvey Robinson. *The Development of Modern Europe*. 2 vols. Boston: Ginn & Co., 1907, 1908. Rev. ed., 1929, 1930.

30 "The Development of Social Thought and Institutions: Individualism and Capitalism," in Edwin R. A. Seligman and Alvin Johnson (eds.), *Encyclopedia of the Social Sciences*, I, 145–63. New York: Macmillan Co., 1930.

36 *The Devil Theory of War*. New York: Vanguard Press, 1936.

36 *The Discussion of Human Affairs*. New York: Macmillan Co., 1936.

31 "Dislocated Soldier of Industry," in Morse A. Cartwright (ed.), *Unemployment and Adult Education*. New York: American Association for Adult Education, 1931.

With Birl E. Shultz. *Documents on the State-wide Initiative, Referendum and Recall*. New York: Macmillan Co., 1912.

22 *The Economic Basis of Politics.* New York: Alfred A. Knopf, 1922. New ed., 1934; 3rd rev. ed., with new chap. v entitled "Economics and Politics in Our Revolutionary Age," 1945.

13 *An Economic Interpretation of the Constitution of the United States.* New York: Macmillan Co., 1913. With new introd., 1935.

Economic Origins of Jeffersonian Democracy. New York: Macmillan Co., 1915.

32 With William C. Bagley. *Elementary World History.* New York: Macmillan Co., 1932.

48 *The Enduring Federalist* (ed.). New York: Doubleday & Co., 1948.

19 "The Evolution of Democracy: A Summary," in Frederick A. Cleveland and Joseph Schafer (eds.), *Democracy in Reconstruction,* pp. 486–91. Boston: Houghton Mifflin Co., 1919.

20 With William C. Bagley. *A First Book in American History.* New York: Macmillan Co., 1920. Rev. ed., 1924; 2nd rev. ed., 1934.

40 *A Foreign Policy for America.* New York: Alfred A. Knopf, 1940.

44 Foreword, Don Marion Wolfe (ed.), *Leveller Manifestoes of the Puritan Revolution.* New York: T. Nelson & Sons, 1944.

22 Foreword, René Brunet, *The New German Constitution.* New York: Alfred A. Knopf, 1922.

30 Foreword, Alfred Lief (ed.), *The Social and Economic Views of Mr. Justice Brandeis.* New York: Vanguard Press, 1930.

40 "Freedom in Political Thought," in R. N. Anshen (ed.), *Freedom: Its Meaning,* pp. 288–304. New York: Harcourt, Brace & Co., 1940.

36 "Freedom of Teaching," in J. E. Johnson (comp.), *Freedom of Speech,* pp. 149–52. New York: H. W. Wilson Co., 1936.

33 With George H. E. Smith. *The Future Comes.* New York: Macmillan Co., 1933.

39 *Giddy Minds and Foreign Quarrels.* New York: Macmillan Co., 1939.

46 "Grounds for a Reconsideration of Historiography," "Problems of Terminology in Historical Writing: The Need for Greater Precision in the Use of Historical Terms," "Signed Footnote" (with Alfred Vagts), in Merle E. Curti (ed.), *Theory and Practice in Historical Study: A Report of the Committee on Historiography,* pp. 1–14, 103–8, 136–37. Social Science Research Council Bulletin, No. 54, 1946.

38 "Historiography and the Constitution," in Conyers Read (ed.), *The Constitution Reconsidered,* pp. 159–66. New York: Columbia University Press, 1938.

29 With James Harvey Robinson. *History of Europe, Our Own Times.* Boston: Ginn & Co., 1921. Rev. ed., 1929.

18 With William C. Bagley. *The History of the American People.* New York: Macmillan Co., 1918. Special ed. for Army educational commission; rev. ed., 1920; rev. ed., 1923; 2nd rev. ed., 1928; with correction, 1932, 1934.

With Mary R. Beard. *History of the United States*. New York: Macmillan Co., 1921. Rev. ed., 1929; 2nd rev. ed., 1932; 3rd rev. ed., 1934.

With G. H. E. Smith. *The Idea of National Interest*. New York: Macmillan Co., 1934.

The Industrial Revolution. London: S. Sonnenschein & Co., 1901. 2nd ed., 1902.

"The Inside of Germany's War Politics," in *Essays in Intellectual History Dedicated to James Harvey Robinson*, pp. 109–24. New York: Harper & Bros., 1929.

Introduction, Walter F. McCaleb, *The Aaron Burr Conspiracy*. New York: Wilson-Erickson, 1936.

Introduction, *Ambassador Dodd's Diary*. New York: Harcourt, Brace & Co., 1941.

Introduction, René Stourm, *The Budget*. New York: D. Appleton & Co., 1917.

Introduction, Chester C. Maxey, *County Administration*. New York: Macmillan Co., 1919.

Introduction, John B. Bury, *The Idea of Progress*. New York: Macmillan Co., 1932.

Introduction, Edgar S. Maclay (ed.), *The Journal of William Maclay, United States Senator from Pennsylvania, 1789–1791*. New York: Albert and Charles Boni, 1927.

Introduction, John Paul Frank, *Mr. Justice Black: The Man and His Opinions*. New York: Alfred A. Knopf, 1948.

Introduction, Brooks Adams, *The Law of Civilization and Decay*. New York: Alfred A. Knopf, 1943.

Introduction, Paxton Hibben, *The Peerless Leader: William Jennings Bryan*. New York: Farrar & Rinehart, 1929.

Introduction, Franklin Watts (ed.), *Voices of History: Great Speeches and Papers of the Year 1941*. New York: Franklin Watts, 1942.

An Introduction to the English Historians. New York: Macmillan Co., 1906.

Jefferson, Corporations and the Constitution. Washington, D.C.: National Home Library Foundation, 1936.

Loose Leaf Digest of Short Ballot Charters (ed.). New York: Short Ballot Organization, 1911.

With Mary R. Beard. *The Making of American Civilization*. New York: Macmillan Co., 1937. Rev. ed., 1939.

With William C. Bagley. *Manual to Accompany the History of the American People*. New York: Macmillan Co., 1919.

"Method in the Study of Political Science as an Aspect of Social Science," in Brookings Institution Committee on Training, *Essays on Research in the Social Sciences*, pp. 51–63. Washington, D.C.: Brookings Institution, 1931.

With Frederic A. Ogg. *National Governments and the World War.* New York: Macmillan Co., 1919.

The Nature of the Social Sciences in Relation to Objectives of Instruction. New York: Charles Scribner's Sons, 1934.

The Navy: Defense or Portent? New York: Harper & Bros., 1932.

The Office of Justice of the Peace in England in Its Origin and Development. New York: Columbia University Press, 1904.

With G. H. E. Smith. *The Old Deal and the New.* New York: Macmillan Co., 1940.

With G. H. E. Smith. *The Open Door at Home.* New York: Macmillan Co., 1934.

With William C. Bagley. *Our Old World Background.* New York: Macmillan Co., 1922. Rev. ed., 1925.

With James Harvey Robinson, Donnal V. Smith, and Emma Peters Smith. *Our Own Age.* Boston: Ginn & Co., 1940.

With James Henry Breasted and James Harvey Robinson. *Outlines of European History.* 2 vols. Boston: Ginn & Co., 1912–14. Rev. ed., 1918; enl. and rev. ed., 1927.

Politics. New York: Columbia University Press, 1908.

Preface, *The Accounting and Reporting Methods of the State of New York.* New York: Bureau of Municipal Research, 1916.

Preface, *Budget Systems: A Discussion before the New York Constitutional Convention.* New York: Bureau of Municipal Research, 1915.

Preface, Milburn Lincoln Wilson, *Democracy Has Roots.* New York: Carrick & Evans, 1939.

Preface, Frederick E. Breithut, *The Engineer in Public Service.* New York: Bureau of Municipal Research, 1916.

Preface, Huntington Gilchrist, *The Governor's Budget in Maine, 1917.* New York: Bureau of Municipal Research, 1917.

Preface, *Japanese Administration and Finance.* New York: Bureau of Municipal Research, 1917.

Preface, Melvin M. Knight, *Morocco as a French Economic Venture: A Study of Open-Door Imperialism.* New York: Appleton-Century, 1937.

Preface, Yusuke Tsurumi, *The Mother.* New York: R. D. Henkle, 1932.

Preface, *The New York City Budget.* New York: Bureau of Municipal Research, 1917.

Preface, *The New York State Legislative Budget and Financial Measures for 1918.* New York: Bureau of Municipal Research, 1918.

Preface, Fred W. Powell, *Recent Movement for State and Government Reform, 1911–1917.* New York: Bureau of Municipal Research, 1917.

Preface, *State Administration: Discussions of Proposed Amendments for the Reorganization of the Executive Branch before the*

New York Constitutional Convention. New York: Bureau of Municipal Research, 1915.

Prefatory note, Samuel J. Konefsky, *Chief Justice Stone and the Supreme Court.* New York: Macmillan Co., 1945.

Prefatory note, Birl E. Shultz, *The History of Appropriations in the Legislative Session of 1916, New York State.* New York: Bureau of Municipal Research, 1916.

The Present Status of Civil Service Reform in the United States. Unpublished Master's essay, Columbia University, ~~1903.~~

President Roosevelt and the Coming of the War, 1941. New Haven, Conn.: Yale University Press, 1948.

The Presidents in American History. New York: J. Messner, 1935. Rev. ed., 1946.

Public Policy and the General Welfare. New York: Farrar & Rinehart, 1941.

"Political Science," in Wilson Gee (ed.), *Research in the Social Sciences,* pp. 269–91. New York: Macmillan Co., 1929.

Readings in American Government and Politics (ed.). New York: Macmillan Co., 1909. Rev. ed., 1913.

With James Harvey Robinson. *Readings in Modern European History.* 2 vols. Boston: Ginn & Co., 1908–9.

With G. H. E. Smith. *The Recovery Program (1933–1934).* New York: Macmillan Co., 1934.

The Republic. New York: Viking Press, 1943.

With Mary R. Beard. *The Rise of American Civilization.* 2 vols. New York: Macmillan Co., 1927. 1-vol. ed., 1930; new ed., 1933.

The Supreme Court and the Constitution. New York: Macmillan Co., 1912.

Toward Civilization (ed.). New York: Longmans, Green & Co., 1930.

The Unique Function of Education in American Democracy. Washington, D.C.: Educational Policies Commission, National Education Association of the United States and the Department of Superintendence, 1937.

"What Is This Democracy?" in *Adult Education and Democracy,* pp. 1–6. New York: American Association for Adult Education, 1936.

Whither Mankind (ed.). New York: Longmans, Green & Co., 1928.

Congressional Statements, Letters to the Editor, Pamphlets

In addition to the items listed below, a number of Beard's unpublished letters have been preserved. For example, the Albert J. Beveridge Papers, Library of Congress, include letters that Beard wrote to Beveridge in the 1920's; the Becker Papers in the Mann Library, Cornell University, include letters to Carl L. Becker; the Department of History Archives, University of Wisconsin, contain a letter to Frederick J. Turner, dated April 24, 1903; there are letters to

Harry Elmer Barnes in the Barnes File; the Villard Papers in the Houghton Library, Harvard University, include letters to Oswald Garrison Villard.

"An Amazing Book," *New Republic,* LXXII (October 19, 1932), 264.

"America and the Next War," *New Republic,* XCIX (June 14, 1939), 148.

"Beard on Liberalism," *New Republic,* LXXXI (January 30, 1935), 334.

"The Case of Dr. Fisher," *New Republic,* XCIX (July 12, 1939), 283.

"The Case of Glenn Frank," *New Republic,* LXXXIX (February 3, 1937), 413.

Constitution and Social Issues. New York: Council for Social Action of Congregational and Christian Churches, 1935.

A Correlated Curriculum. New York: Appleton, 1936.

Cumulative Annual Guide to American Government and Politics. New York: Macmillan Co., 1935–38.

"Defending Women as Physicians," *New York Times,* July 18, 1915, p. 10.

"The Economic Basis of Politics," *New Republic,* XXXII (September 27, 1922), 128–29.

"An Economic Interpretation of Navies," *New Republic,* LXIX (November 25, 1931), 47.

European Sobriety in the Presence of the Balkan Crisis. New York: American Branch of the Association for International Conciliation, 1908.

"Federal Reserve System and Labor," *New Republic,* XXVIII (November 16, 1921), 399.

"The Fels Plan for a Federal Trade System," *Survey Graphic,* XXII (May, 1933), 269.

"Freedom to Laugh," *New Republic,* LXXVIII (March 21, 1934), 161.

"Go Easy on the Professors," *New Republic,* XXVII (August 14, 1921), 328.

Government Research: Past, Present and Future. New York: Municipal Administration Service, 1926.

"History and Social Science," *Saturday Review of Literature,* XII (August 17, 1935), 9, 22–23.

With Others. "Homage Where Due," *New Republic,* XC (March 3, 1937), 114.

How American Citizens Govern Themselves. New York: Educational Bureau, National War Work Council of Young Men's Christian Associations, 1919.

"How They Are Voting," *New Republic*, CIII (September 23, 1940), 411.

"Invitation to a Bronx Cheer," *New Republic*, LXXVII (January 3, 1934), 227.

Issues of Domestic Policy. Chicago: University of Chicago Press, 1932.

"Killing the Intellect," *Outlook*, CLVI (October 1, 1930), 200.

"Letting Down the Bars," *New Republic*, LXXV (June 28, 1933), 183–84.

"The Living Constitution," *New Republic*, LXXXVIII (August 26, 1936), 77.

"Mr. Bingham's Intent," *New Republic*, C (September 6, 1939), 133.

"Mr. Lennes Excepts," *New Republic*, LIV (March 21, 1928), 157.

The Myth of Rugged American Individualism. New York: John Day, 1932.

My Views regarding the Reconstruction of Tokyo (in Japanese). Tokyo: Shisei Chosa-kai, 1924.

"New Light on Bryan and War Policies," *New Republic*, LXXXVII (June 17, 1936), 177–78.

"The New River Ruling," *Nation*, CXXXIII (October 7, 1931), 364–65.

"On Frontier Folk," *New York Times*, sec. 4, January 23, 1938, p. 9.

"On Japan's Problems," *New York Times*, September 17, 1923.

"On Nobel Peace Prize," *New York Times*, July 20, 1936, p. 14.

"An Opening for Idiots," *New Republic*, LXXIX (June 13, 1934), 130.

"The Perils of Diplomacy," *New Republic*, XI (June 2, 1917), 136–38.

Philosophy, Science and the Art of Public Administration. Princeton, N.J.: Governmental Research Association, 1939.

"The Problem of Training for the Public Service," in *Training for Municipal Service* (Municipal Research, No. 68), pp. 5–14. New York: Bureau of Municipal Research, 1915.

Public Service in America (Public Service Series, No. 2). Philadelphia: Municipal Court, 1919.

"Realism about Money," *New Republic*, XCIX (May 17, 1939), 48–49.

"Relative Normality," *New Republic*, LXXV (August 2, 1933), 318.

"Reply to James Truslow Adams's Letter," *New York Times*, sec. 4, February 13, 1938, p. 8.

With Robert Moses and Others. *Report of Reconstruction Commission to Governor Alfred E. Smith on Retrenchment and Reorganization in the State Government*. Albany: J. B. Lyon Co., 1919.

"The Role of Administration in Government," in *The Work Unit in Federal Administration*, No. 56, pp. 1–3. Chicago: Public Administration Service, 1937.

With William G. Carr. *Schools in the Story of Culture.* Washington, D.C.: National Education Association, 1935.

"Section Four and Suffrage," *New Republic,* I (Jan. 9, 1915), 23.

Six Years' Experience with the Direct Primary in New Jersey. N.Y., 1917.

"Statement," *Federal Licensing of Corporations: Hearings before a Subcommittee of the Committee on the Judiciary on Senate Bill No. 10* (Washington, D.C., 1937), Part I, pp. 70, 72, 79.

"A Statement by Charles A. Beard," *New Republic,* XIII (December 29, 1917), 249–51.

Statement by Charles A. Beard quoted, in Charles G. Haines and Marshall E. Dimock (eds.), *Essays on the Law and Practice of Governmental Administration,* pp. vi–vii. Baltimore, Md.: Johns Hopkins Press, 1935.

"Statement of Charles A. Beard, New Milford, Conn.," February 4, 1941, *To Promote the Defense of the United States: Hearings before the Committee on Foreign Relations United States Senate on Senate [Bill] 275,* 77 Cong., 1 Sess., pp. 307–17.

"Statement of Dr. Charles A. Beard," March 19, 1935, *To Make Better Provision for the Government of the Military and Naval Forces of the United States by the Suppression of Attempts to Incite Members Thereof to Disobedience: Hearings before the Committee of Military Affairs and Subcommittee No. 10 House of Representatives on House Resolution 5845,* 74 Cong., 1 Sess., pp. 49–54.

"Statement of Dr. Charles A. Beard, April 3, 1948," *Universal Military Training: Hearings before the Committee on Armed Services United States Senate,* 80 Cong., 2 Sess., pp. 1053–57.

"Statement of Dr. Charles A. Beard, Historian," February 10, 1938, *To Establish the Composition of the United States Navy: Hearings before the Committee on Naval Affairs, House of Representatives on House Resolution 9218 to Establish the Composition of the United States Navy, to Authorize the Construction of Certain Naval Vessels, and for Other Purposes,* 75 Cong., 3 Sess., pp. 2133–46.

"The Supreme Issue," *New Republic,* XVII (January 18, 1919), 343.

The Traction Crisis in New York. New York: Bureau of Municipal Research, 1919.

"Who Is Superior Now?" *Nation,* CXX (April 1, 1925), 356.

"Who Runs the Japanese Government?" *New Republic,* LXIX (December 16, 1931), 137.

"Why China Entered the War," *New Republic,* XXX (April 12, 1922), 201.

"Woman Suffrage and Strategy," *New Republic,* I (December 12, 1914), 22–23.

"Woodrow Wilson and Science," *New Republic,* XLVI (April 14, 1926), 226–27.

Reviews

Abbott, Frank F., and Allan C. Johnson. *Municipal Administration in the Roman Empire. National Municipal Review,* XVI (September, 1927), 587–88.

Adams, Arthur B. *National Economic Security. Social Studies,* XXVII (April, 1936), 285.

Adams, Ephraim D. *Great Britain and the American Civil War. New Republic,* XLIV (September 30, 1925), 5–6.

Adams, George B. *Political History of England. Political Science Quarterly,* XXI (September, 1906), 531–35.

Adams, Henry. *Degradation of the Democratic Dogma. New Republic,* XXII (March 31, 1920), 162–63.

Adamson, Robert. *Municipal Year Book of the City of New York. National Municipal Review,* III (April, 1914), 428–29.

Alexander, De Alva Standwood. *Political History of the State of New York. Political Science Quarterly,* XXII (March, 1907), 141–43.

Angell, Norman. *From Chaos to Control* (Halley Stewart Lectures, 1932). *Saturday Review of Literature,* IX (June 10, 1933), 637–39.

Ballard, Adolphus. *The Domesday Boroughs. Political Science Quarterly,* XX (March, 1905), 158–59.

Barnes, Harry E. *The Genesis of the World War. Current History,* XXIV (August, 1926), 730–35.

Batault, Georges. *La guerre absolue. New Republic,* XXVIII (September 21, 1921), 109–10.

Becker, Carl L. *The Heavenly City of the Eighteenth-Century Philosophers. American Historical Review,* XXXVIII (April, 1933), 590–91.

———. *The United States: An Experiment in Democracy. Nation,* CXI (October 13, 1920), 416–17.

———, J. M. Clark, and William E. Dodd. *The Spirit of '76 and Other Essays. New Republic,* LII (August 24, 1927), 23–24.

Beckerath, Herbert von. *Modern Industrial Organization. American Political Science Review,* XXVII (October, 1933), 833–35.

Bennett, Jesse L. *The Essential American Tradition. New Republic,* XLIII (July 29, 1925), 269–70.

Bentley, Arthur F. *The Process of Government: A Study of Social Pressures. Political Science Quarterly,* XXIII (December, 1908), 739–41.

Bérard, Victor. *La France et Guillaume II. American Historical Review,* XII (July, 1907), 895–97.

Bingham, Alfred. *Man's Estate. Common Sense,* VIII (June, 1939), 24–25.

Bogart, Ernest L. *The Economic History of the United States. Educational Review,* XXXVII (April, 1909), 418–19.

Bowley, A. L. *The Need and the Purpose of Measurement of Social Phenomena. National Municipal Review,* V (July, 1916), 518.

Bowman, Isaiah. *The New World. New Republic,* LVIII (April 17, 1929), 257–58.

Brady, Robert A. *Business as a System of Power. American Political Science Review,* XXXVII (April, 1943), 329–30.

Broderick, George C., and J. K. Fotheringham. *The Political History of England, 1801–1837. Political Science Quarterly,* XXII (September, 1907), 522–23.

Brooks, Robert C. (ed.). *Bryce's American Commonwealth: Fiftieth Anniversary. American Political Science Review,* XXXIV (February, 1940), 131.

California Committee on Efficiency and Economy. *Report to Governor William D. Stephens and His Message to the Legislature in Relation Thereto March 12, 1919. National Municipal Review,* VIII (December, 1919), 727–28.

Campbell, Thomas D. *Russia: Market or Menace? New Republic,* LXX (April 27, 1932), 305–6.

Carr, Albert. *America's Last Chance. American Political Science Review,* XXXV (February, 1941), 155–56.

Catlin, George, E. G. *The Science and Method of Politics. American Political Science Review,* XXI (August, 1927), 652–53.

Chafee, Zechariah. *Freedom of Speech. National Municipal Review,* X (April, 1921), 247–48.

Chamberlin, William H. *The Russian Revolution. American Political Science Review,* XXX (February, 1936), 174–75.

Channing, Edward. *A History of the United States, IV. New Republic,* XI (July 7, 1917), 282–83.

———. *A History of the United States, 1815–1846, V. New Republic,* XXIX (January 4, 1922), 160–61.

———. *A History of the United States, VI. New Republic,* XLIV (November 11, 1925), 310–11.

Chase, Stuart. *Men and Machines. Yale Review,* XIX (September, 1929), 159–61.

Chinard, Gilbert. *Thomas Jefferson: The Apostle of Americanism. Nation,* CXXIX (December 4, 1929), 686.

Chugerman, Samuel. *Lester F. Ward: The American Aristotle. New Republic,* CI (November 15, 1939), 119.

Churchill, Winston S. *Liberalism and the Social Problem. Political Science Quarterly,* XXV (September, 1910), 529–31.

Cleveland, Frederick A., and Arthur E. Buck. *The Budget and Responsible Government. Nation,* CXI (September 4, 1920), 275.

Coe, G. D. H. *A Guide through World Chaos. American Political Science Review,* XXVII (February, 1933), 118–19.

Collingwood, R. G. *The Idea of History. American Historical Review,* LII (July, 1947), 704–8.

Committee on Municipal Program of the National Municipal League. *Model City Charter and Municipal Home Rule. American Political Science Review*, X (August, 1916), 602–5.

Commons, John R. *Industrial Government. Nation*, CXIII (November 9, 1921), 543.

Cooke, Morris L. L. *Our Cities Awake: Notes on Municipal Activities and Administration. New Republic*, XVII (January 25, 1919), 381–83.

Curti, Merle. *Peace or War: The American Struggle, 1636–1936. New Republic*, LXXXVI (April 15, 1936), 289.

Davis, George T. *A Navy Second to None. New Republic*, CII (February 26, 1940), 283–84.

Dennett, Tyler. *Roosevelt and the Russo-Japanese War. New Republic*, XLIII (June 3, 1925), 52–53.

Deville, Gabriel. *Histoire socialiste: Du 9 thermidor au 18 brumaire. Political Science Quarterly*, XXI (March, 1906), 111–20.

De Witt, Benjamin P. *The Progressive Movement. National Municipal Review*, IV (October, 1915), 682–83.

Dodd, Walter F. *Modern Constitutions*. 2 vols. *Political Science Quarterly*, XXIV (September, 1909), 524–25.

Duguit, Leon. *Traite de droit constitutionnel. Political Science Quarterly*, XXVII (September, 1912), 518–19.

———. *Les transformations du droit public. Political Science Quarterly*, XXIX (June, 1914), 340–41.

Earle, Edward M. *The Federalist. American Historical Review*, XLIII (April, 1938), 651–52.

Eckardstein, Baron von. *Ten Years at the Court of St. James. New Republic*, XXXII (September 27, 1922), 5.

Ely, Richard T. *Property and Contract in Their Relation to the Distribution of Wealth. Political Science Quarterly*, XXX (September, 1915), 510–11.

Errera, Paul. *Das Staatsrecht des Konigreichs Belgien. Political Science Quarterly*, XXV (September, 1910), 533–34.

Eyschen, Paul. *Das Staatsrecht des Gross-herzogtums Luxemburg. Political Science Quarterly*, XXV (September, 1910), 533–34.

Farrand, Max. *The Records of the Federal Convention of 1787. Political Science Quarterly*, XXVI (September, 1911), 551–53.

Fenwick, Charles G. *Political Systems in Transition: War-Time and After. Nation*, CXII (February 23, 1921), 297–98.

Fischer, Louis. *Oil Imperialism. New Republic*, XLIX (December 8, 1926), 82–83.

Fisher, H. A. L. *The Republican Tradition in Europe. Political Science Quarterly*, XXVII (September, 1912), 512–13.

Fitzpatrick, John C. (ed.). *The Diaries of George Washington 1748–1799. New Republic*, XLVI (April 21, 1926), 279.

Forbes, Russell. *Governmental Purchasing. National Municipal Review*, XVIII (September, 1929), 580.

Fox, Richard M. *The Triumphant Machine. Saturday Review of Literature,* V (June 1, 1929), 1071.

French, Allen. *The Day of Concord and Lexington. New Republic,* XLIII (July 15, 1925), 215–16.

Friedrich, Carl J. *Foreign Policy in the Making. Common Sense,* VIII (January, 1939), 25.

Gabriel, Ralph H. *The Course of American Democratic Thought: An Intellectual History since 1815. American Historical Review,* XLVI (October, 1940), 164–65.

Gaus, John M. *Great Britain: A Study of Civic Loyalty. American Political Science Review,* XXIII (November, 1929), 1005–7.

Glaser, Friedrich. *Wirtschaftspolitische Annalen. Political Science Quarterly,* XXIV (March, 1909), 165–67.

Grey, Viscount Edward. *Twenty-five Years, 1892–1916. New Republic,* XLIV (October 7, 1925), 172–75.

Grumbach, Solomon. *Das annexionistische Deutschland. New Republic,* XI (July 14, 1917), 309–10.

Guest, L. Haden. *The Struggle for Power in Europe, 1917–21. New Republic,* XXX (March 29, 1922), 144–45.

Gulick, Luther H. *The Evolution of the Budget in Massachusetts. Nation,* CXI (September 4, 1920), 275.

Gundolf, Friedrich. *Aufange deutscher Geschichtsschreibung. Political Science Quarterly,* LIV (March, 1939), 138.

Hacker, Louis M., and Benjamin B. Kendrick. *The United States since 1865. New Republic,* LXX (March 30, 1932), 187.

Halle, Ernst von. *Die Weltwirtschaft: Ein Jahrund Lesebuch. Political Science Quarterly,* XXIV (March, 1909), 165–67.

Harper, Samuel N. *Civic Training in Soviet Russia. American Political Science Review,* XXIII (November, 1929), 1005–7.

Hatschek, Julius. *Englisches Staatsrecht. Political Science Quarterly,* XXII (December, 1907), 719–23.

Haworth, Paul L. *The United States in Our Own Times, 1865–1920. Nation,* CXI (October 13, 1920), 416–17.

Hayes, Carlton J. H. *A Brief History of the Great War. New Republic,* XXV (December 22, 1920), 114–15.

Haynes, Fred E. *Third Party Movements since the Civil War. New Republic,* IX (November 18, 1916), 22–24.

Haynes, George H. *The Senate of the United States. New Republic,* XCVIII (February 8, 1939), 26.

Hazen, C. D. *Europe since 1815. Annals of the American Academy of Political and Social Science,* XXXVII (May, 1911), 777–78.

Henderson, Archibald. *North Carolina: The Old North State and the New. Virginia Quarterly Review,* XVII (Autumn, 1941), 600–603.

Hobson, J. A. *The Crisis of Liberalism. Political Science Quarterly,* XXV (September, 1910), 529–31.

Hobson, S. G. *National Guilds and the State. New Republic,* XXV (December 8, 1920), 50–51.

Hodgkin, Thomas. *The Political History of England to 1066. Political Science Quarterly,* XXI (December, 1906), 699–702.

Holland, Francis (ed.). *Constitutional History of England.* 3 vols. *New Republic,* XVI (October 19, 1918), 350–51.

Holmes, Oliver Wendell. *Collected Legal Papers. National Municipal Review,* X (April, 1921), 247–48.

Humphreys, John H. *Proportional Representation. Political Science Quarterly,* XXVII (March, 1912), 137–38.

Hunt, Gaillard. *The Department of State of the United States. Political Science Quarterly,* XXIX (December, 1914), 710–11.

Hunter, Robert. *Poverty. Political Science Quarterly,* XX (June, 1905), 341–43.

Huntington-Wilson, F. M. *Money and the Price Level. New Republic,* LXXIV (March 15, 1933), 134–35.

Ise, John. *The United States Forest Policy. Nation,* CXII (February 2, 1921), 187.

Jameson, J. Franklin. *The American Revolution Considered as a Social Movement. New Republic,* XLVII (August 11, 1926), 344.

Jaurès, Jean. *Histoire socialiste jusqu'au 9 thermidor.* 4 vols. *Political Science Quarterly,* XXI (March, 1906), 111–20.

Jellinek, George, Paul Laband, and Robert Piloty (eds.). *Jahrbuch des offentlichen Rechts. Political Science Quarterly,* XXIV (March, 1909), 165–67.

Kerney, James. *The Political Education of Woodrow Wilson. New Republic,* XLVI (May 12, 1926), 372–73.

Kirkland, Edward C. *A History of American Economic Life. Saturday Review of Literature,* IX (August 13, 1932), 42.

Kleeck, Mary van. *Miners and Management. American Political Science Review,* XXVIII (August, 1934), 699–700.

Korff, Baron S. A. *Russia's Foreign Relations during the Last Half Century. New Republic,* XXX (March 29, 1922), 144–45.

Laband, Paul. *Deutsches Reichsstaatsrecht. Political Science Quarterly,* XXV (September, 1910), 533–34.

Laidler, Harry W. *History of Socialist Thought. New Republic,* LI (July 13, 1927), 208–9.

Larson, Laurence M. *The King's Household in England before the Norman Conquest. Political Science Quarterly,* XX (December, 1905), 738–39.

Laski, Harold J. *The Foundations of Sovereignty and Other Essays. Nation,* CXIII (October 26, 1921), 482–83.

——. *A Grammar of Politics. New Republic,* XLV (December 9, 1925), 91–92.

——. *Political Thought in England from Locke to Bentham. New Republic,* XXIV (November 17, 1920), 303–4.

Laski, Harold J. *Where Do We Go from Here? American Political Science Review,* XXXV (February, 1941), 155–56.

Leacock, Stephen. *Elements of Political Science. Educational Review,* XXXV (February, 1908), 201–3.

Lebon, Andre. *Das Verfassungsrecht der französischen Republik. Political Science Quarterly,* XXV (September, 1910), 533–34.

Lenin, Vladimir I. *The Revolution of 1917* and *Toward the Seizure of Power. New Republic,* LXXV (May 17, 1933), 22–24.

Lennes, N. J. *Whither Democracy. New Republic,* LI (August 10, 1927), 314–15.

Liefmann, Robert. *Cartels, Concerns, and Trusts. Nation,* CXXXVI (May 31, 1933), 618–19.

Lindeman, Eduard C. *Wealth and Culture. Saturday Review of Literature,* XIII (March 14, 1936), 20–21.

Lodge, Henry C. (ed.). *Selections from the Correspondence of Theodore Roosevelt and Henry Cabot Lodge, 1884–1918. New Republic,* XLIII (June 17, 1925), 103–4.

Loeb, Harold, and Associates. *The Chart of Plenty. New Republic,* LXXXII (March 20, 1935), 164.

Lynd, Robert S. *Knowledge for What? American Political Science Review,* XXXIII (August, 1939), 711–12.

McCall, Samuel W. *The Life of Thomas Brackett Reed. Political Science Quarterly,* XXX (September, 1915), 530–31.

MacCunn, John. *The Political Philosophy of Burke. American Historical Review,* XIX (October, 1913), 170–71.

McLaughlin, Andrew C. *A Constitutional History of the United States. New Republic,* XCII (September 15, 1937), 162–64.

———. *The Courts, the Constitution, and Parties: Studies in Constitutional History and Politics. American Historical Review,* XVIII (January, 1913), 378–79.

McMaster, John B. *A History of the People of the United States during Lincoln's Administration. New Republic,* LI (June 29, 1927), 156–57.

Mandelbaum, Maurice. *The Problem of Historical Knowledge: An Answer to Relativism. American Historical Review,* XLIV (April, 1939), 571–72.

Marriott, J. A. R. *Second Chambers: An Inductive Study in Political Science. Political Science Quarterly,* XXV (December, 1910), 721–23.

Marsh, Benjamin C. *Taxation of Land Values in American Cities. Political Science Quarterly,* XXVI (December, 1911), 714–15.

Mathews, John M. *The Conduct of American Foreign Relations. New Republic,* XXX (March 29, 1922), 144–45.

Maurer, James H. *It Can Be Done. New Republic,* XCVIII (February 22, 1939), 81–82.

May, Sir Thomas E. *The Constitutional History of England since the Accession of George III*. Political Science Quarterly, XXVII (December, 1912), 701–3.

Megaro, Gaudens. *Mussolini in the Making*. American Historical Review, XLV (January, 1940), 393–94.

Merriam, Charles E. *American Political Ideas, 1865–1917*. New Republic, XXV (January 19, 1921), 235–36.

———. *The Making of Citizens*. American Political Science Review, XXVI (February, 1932), 150–51.

———. *The New Democracy and the New Despotism*. American Political Science Review, XXXIII (October, 1939), 884–86.

———. *Primary Elections*. Political Science Quarterly, XXIV (June, 1909), 316–17.

Michels, Robert. *Political Parties: A Sociological Study of the Oligarchical Tendencies of Modern Democracy*. Political Science Quarterly, XXXII (March, 1917), 153–55.

Millett, John D. *Federal Administrators*. New Republic, CII (May 20, 1940), 678–79.

Mims, Edwin. *The Advancing South*. New Republic, XLVII (June 23, 1926), 144–45.

Morgan, George. *James Monroe*. Nation, CXIV (April 26, 1922), 499–500.

Morison, Samuel E. *The Life and Letters of Harrison Gray Otis*. Political Science Quarterly, XXIX (December, 1914), 716–18.

———. *The Maritime History of Massachusetts, 1783–1860*. New Republic, XXIX (January 25, 1922), 253–54.

Muir, Ramsay. *How Britain Is Governed*. National Municipal Review, XIX (August, 1930), 550.

Müller-Armack, Alfred. *Entwicklungsgesetze des Kapitalismus*. Nation, CXXXVI (March 22, 1933), 323.

Murdock, Harold. *The Nineteenth of April, 1775*. New Republic, XLIII (July 15, 1925), 215–16.

Neurath, Otto. *Modern Man in the Making*. Saturday Review of Literature, XX (September 30, 1939), 10–11.

Nevins, Allan. *American Press Opinion: Washington to Coolidge*. New Republic, LVII (February 13, 1929), 354.

——— (ed.). *The Diary of John Quincy Adams*. New Republic, LVII (February 13, 1929), 354.

———. *Gateway to History*. Nation, CXLVII (September 24, 1938), 300–302.

———. *John D. Rockefeller: The Heroic Age of American Enterprise*. American Political Science Review, XXXV (October, 1941), 977–80.

Newell, Frederick H. *Water Resources: Present and Future Uses*. Nation, CXII (February 2, 1921), 187.

O'Brien, George. *An Essay on Mediaeval Economic Teaching. Nation,* CXI (October 27, 1920), 480.

Panaretoff, Stephen. *Near Eastern Affairs. New Republic,* XXX (March 29, 1922), 144–45.

Parrington, Vernon L. *Main Currents in American Thought. Nation,* CXXIV (May 18, 1927), 560–62.

Pasvolsky, Leo. *Russia in the Far East. New Republic,* XXX (March 29, 1922), 144–45.

Paul, Eden, and Cedar Paul. *Creative Revolution: A Study in Communist Ergatocracy. Nation,* CXII (March 2, 1921), 342.

——, and ——. *Proletcult. Nation,* CXIV (February 15, 1922), 196.

Pease, Edward R. *The Case for Municipal Drink. Political Science Quarterly,* XIX (December, 1904), 697–99.

Penty, Arthur J. *A Guildsman's Interpretation of History. Nation,* CXI (December 29, 1920), 783.

Pettus, Daisy C. (ed.). *The Rosalie Evans Letters from Mexico. New Republic,* XLVIII (October 13, 1926), 225–26.

Porter, Kirk. *History of Suffrage in the United States. National Municipal Review,* VIII (September, 1919), 495.

President's Research Committee on Social Trends. *Recent Social Trends in the United States. Yale Review,* XXII (March, 1933), 595–97.

Puleston, Captain W. D. *The Life and Work of Captain Alfred Thayer Mahan. New Republic,* XCIX (June 28, 1939), 221–25.

Rauch, Basil. *The History of the New Deal. American Political Science Review,* XXXIX (February, 1945), 196–97.

Rauschenbush, Stephen. *The March of Fascism. Yale Review,* XXIX (September, 1939), 167–69.

Reinsch, Paul S. *An American Diplomat in China. New Republic,* XXX (March 29, 1922), 144–45.

——. *Secret Diplomacy. New Republic,* XXX (March 29, 1922), 144–45.

Repington, Charles à Court. *After the War. New Republic,* XXX (March 29, 1922), 144–45.

Report of the Commission of Inquiry on Public Service Personnel: Better Government Personnel. American Political Science Review, XXIX (April, 1935), 296–97.

Report of the New York City Commission on Congestion of Population. Political Science Quarterly, XXVI (December, 1911), 714–15.

Rhodes, James F. *History of the United States, 1877–1896. New Republic,* XXI (December 17, 1919), 82–83.

Rightor, Chester E. *City Manager in Dayton. National Municipal Review,* IX (January, 1920), 45–46.

Ripert, Henry. *La présidence des assemblées politiques. Political Science Quarterly,* XXVI (March, 1911), 145–46.

Rippy, J. Fred. *The United States and Mexico. New Republic*, XLVIII (October 13, 1926), 225–26.

Robson, William A. (ed.). *Public Enterprise. American Political Science Review*, XXXI (December, 1937), 1157–59.

Round, J. Horace. *Peerage and Pedigree. Political Science Quarterly*, XXV (September, 1910), 527–28.

Ryan, Oswald. *Municipal Freedom. National Municipal Review*, IV (October, 1915), 681–82.

Sandburg, Carl. *Abraham Lincoln: The War Years. Virginia Quarterly Review*, XVI (January, 1940), 112–16.

Sanger, C. P. *The Place of Compensation in Temperance Reform. Political Science Quarterly*, XIX (December, 1904), 697–99.

Schlesinger, Arthur M. *The Colonial Merchants and the American Revolution, 1763–1776. New Republic*, XIV (April 6, 1918), 301–4.

———. *The Rise of the City. American Historical Review*, XXXVIII (July, 1933), 779–80.

Schneider, Herbert W. *Making the Fascist State. New Republic*, LVII (January 23, 1929), 277–78.

———, and Shepard B. Clough. *Making Fascists. American Political Science Review*, XXIV (February, 1930), 181–82.

Seasongood, Murray. *Local Government in the United States. National Municipal Review*, XXII (June, 1933), 290–91.

Seldes, George. *Freedom of the Press. Social Studies*, XXVI (December, 1935), 563–64.

Seymour, Charles (ed.). *The Intimate Papers of Colonel House, I–II. New Republic*, XLVI (March 17, 1926), 109–11.

——— (ed.). *The Intimate Papers of Colonel House, III–IV. American Political Science Review*, XXIII (February, 1929), 190–91.

Shambaugh, Benjamin F. (ed.). *Applied History. Political Science Quarterly*, XXX (March, 1915), 173–74.

Siegfried, André. *America Comes of Age. New Republic*, LI (June 8, 1927), 75–76.

Skelton, Oscar D. *The Life and Letters of Sir Wilfrid Laurier. New Republic*, XXXI (August 9, 1922), 313.

Skrine, Francis H. *The Expansion of Russia, 1815–1900. Annals of the American Academy of Political and Social Science*, XXIV (September, 1904), 391–92.

Slemp, C. Bascom. *The Mind of the President. New Republic*, XLVII (May 26, 1926), 38–39.

Small, Albion W. *Between Eras from Capitalism to Democracy. National Municipal Review*, II (October, 1913), 771–72.

Smith, J. Allen. *The Spirit of American Government. Political Science Quarterly*, XXIII (March, 1908), 136–37.

Sprout, Harold, and Margaret Sprout. *The Rise of American Naval Power. New Republic*, XCIX (June 28, 1939), 221–25.

Steffens, Lincoln. *The Autobiography of Lincoln Steffens. American Political Science Review*, XXV (August, 1931), 755–57.

Stimson, Frederic J. *The American Constitution. Political Science Quarterly*, XXIII (June, 1908), 340–43.

Taft, William H. *Popular Government. Political Science Quarterly*, XXXIII (December, 1918), 594–96.

Tout, T. F. *The Political History of England, 1216–1377. Political Science Quarterly*, XXI (December, 1906), 699–702.

Toynbee, Arnold J. *A Study of History*, I–III. *American Historical Review*, XL (January, 1935), 307–9.

———. *A Study of History*, IV–VI. *American Historical Review*, XLV (April, 1940), 593–94.

———. *Survey of International Affairs, 1924. New Republic*, XLIX (December 8, 1926), 82–83.

———. *Survey of International Affairs, 1926. New Republic*, LVIII (April 17, 1929), 257–58.

Tugwell, Rexford G. *Industrial Discipline and the Governmental Arts. American Political Science Review*, XXVII (October, 1933), 833–35.

Turner, Frederick J. *The Frontier in American History. New Republic*, XXV (February 16, 1921), 349–50.

Ulbrich, Josef. *Das österreichische Staatsrecht. Political Science Quarterly*, XXV (September, 1910), 533–34.

Van Loon, Hendrik. *The Story of Mankind. New Republic*, XXIX (December 21, 1921), 105.

Viallate, Achille (ed.). *La vie politique dans les deux mondes. Political Science Quarterly*, XXIV (March, 1909), 165–67.

Vinogradoff, P. *The Growth of the Manor. Political Science Quarterly*, XXI (March, 1906), 165–67.

Walling, W. E. *Progressivism and After. National Municipal Review* IV (January, 1915), 132–33.

Walsh, C. M. *The Political Science of John Adams: A Study in the Theory of Mixed Government and the Bicameral System. Political Science Quarterly*, XXX (September, 1915), 521–22.

Walsh, Edmund A. (ed.). *The History and Nature of International Relations. New Republic*, XXX (March 29, 1922), 144–45.

Wandell, Samuel H., and Meade Minnigerode. *Aaron Burr. Saturday Review of Literature*, II (November 28, 1925), 337.

Ward, Sir A. W., and Others. *The Cambridge Modern History. Social Studies*, XXVI (January, 1935), 59–60.

Ward, Harry F. *The New Social Order. New Republic*, XXIII (July 14, 1920), 208–9.

Ware, Caroline F. (ed.). *The Cultural Approach to History. American Historical Review*, XLVI (July, 1941), 844–46.

Waterhouse, Paul, and Raymond Unwin. *Old Towns and New Needs. National Municipal Review*, II (July, 1913), 561.

Watson, David K. *The Constitution of the United States. Political Science Quarterly*, XXVI (September, 1911), 549–51.

Webb, Sidney, and Beatrice Webb. *A Constitution for the Socialist Commonwealth of Great Britain. Nation*, CXI (December 8, 1920), 664–66.

——, and ——. *English Local Government from the Revolution to the Municipal Corporation Act: The Parish and the County. Political Science Quarterly*, XXIII (March, 1908), 144–47.

——, and ——. *The History of Liquor Licensing in England, Principally from 1700 to 1830. Political Science Quarterly*, XIX (March, 1904), 152–54.

Weber, Elizabeth A. *The Duk-Duks. American Political Science Review*, XXIII (November, 1929), 1005–7.

Wells, H. G. *Washington and the Riddle of Peace. Nation*, CXIV (March 8, 1922), 289–90.

Welschinger, Henri. *L'Alliance Franco-Russe. New Republic*, XXIX (February 22, 1922), 375–76.

Weyl, Walter. *The End of the War. New Republic*, XV (July 6, 1918), 297–99.

White, Leonard D. (ed.). *Essays in Honor of Charles E. Merriam: The Future of Government in the United States. American Political Science Review*, XXXVI (October, 1942), 953–54.

Wilcox, Delos F. *Municipal Franchises. Political Science Quarterly*, XXVII (December, 1912), 713–15.

Wilson, Woodrow. *The New Freedom. Political Science Quarterly*, XXIX (September, 1914), 506–7.

Wingfield-Stratford, Esme. *The History of British Civilization. New Republic*, LVII (February 6, 1929), 327–28.

Workers' Education Bureau. *Workers' Education in the United States. New Republic*, XXVIII (November 9, 1921), 327–28.

Works Progress Administration. *Index of Research Projects. New Republic*, XCIX (July 12, 1939), 286–87.

Young, George. *Diplomacy, Old and New. New Republic*, XXX (March 29, 1922), 144–45.

Zweig, Egon. *Die Lehre vom Pouvoir constituant. Political Science Quarterly*, XXIV (September, 1909), 522–23.

WRITINGS ABOUT BEARD AND HIS INTELLECTUAL WORLD

Adair, Douglas. "The Tenth Federalist Revisited," *William and Mary Quarterly*, VIII (January, 1951), 48–67.

Ausubel, Herman. *Historians and Their Craft: A Study of the Presidential Addresses of the American Historical Association 1884–1945.* New York: Columbia University Press, 1950.

Barnes, Harry E. *A History of Historical Writing.* Norman: University of Oklahoma Press, 1937.

Barnes, Harry E. *The New History and the Social Studies*. New York: Century Co., 1925.

Beale, Howard K. (ed.). *Charles A. Beard*. Lexington: University of Kentucky Press, 1954.

———. "The Professional Historian: His Theory and His Practice," *Pacific Historical Review*, XXII (August, 1953), 227–55.

Bean, Walton E. "Revolt among Historians," *Sewanee Review*, XLVII (July–September, 1939), 330–41.

Beard, Mary R. *The Making of Charles A. Beard*. New York: Exposition Press, 1955.

Beard, William. Introduction, *The Economic Basis of Politics and Related Writings*. New York: Vintage Books, 1957.

Beloff, Max. "Another Fallen Idol?" *Encounter*, XII (January, 1959), 73–76.

Benson, Lee. *Turner and Beard: Historical Writing Reconsidered*. Glencoe, Ill.: The Free Press, 1960.

Berg, Elias. *The Historical Thinking of Charles A. Beard*. Stockholm: Almqvist & Wiksell, 1957.

Black, Wilfred W. "Historians and American Foreign Policy," *Social Studies*, XLIV (February, 1953), 43–51.

Blinkoff, Maurice. *The Influence of Charles A. Beard upon American Historiography*. Buffalo, N.Y.: Committee on Publications on the Roswell Park Publication Fund, 1936.

Bliven, Bruce. "The Hang-back Boys," *New Republic*, CX (March 6, 1944), 305–7.

Borning, Bernard C. "The Political Philosophy of Young Charles A. Beard," *American Political Science Review*, XLIII (December, 1949), 1165–78.

Boudin, Louis. *Government by Judiciary*. New York: William Godwin, 1932.

Brown, Robert E. *Charles Beard and the Constitution*. Princeton, N.J.: Princeton University Press, 1956.

Commager, Henry S. *The American Mind: An Interpretation of American Thought and Character since the 1880's*. New Haven, Conn.: Yale University Press, 1950.

Cook, Thomas I., and Malcolm Moos. *Power through Purpose*. Baltimore, Md.: Johns Hopkins Press, 1954.

Croce, Benedetto. "Letter to Charles A. Beard" (dated June 24, 1933), *American Historical Review*, XXXIX (January, 1934), 229–31.

———. *Politics and Morals*. New York: Philosophical Library, 1945.

Curti, Merle. "Charles Austin Beard," *Year Book of the American Philosophical Society*, 1948.

———. "A Great Teacher's Teacher," *Social Education*, XIII (October, 1949), 263–67.

DeConde, Alexander (ed.). *Isolation and Security: Ideas and Interests in Twentieth-Century American Foreign Policy*. Durham, N.C.: Duke University Press, 1957.

Deininger, Whitaker T. "The Skepticism and Historical Faith of Charles Beard," *Journal of the History of Ideas,* XV (October, 1954), 573–88.

Destler, Chester McArthur. "Some Observations on Contemporary Historical Theory," *American Historical Review,* LV (April, 1950), 503–29.

Edman, Irwin. *Philosopher's Holiday.* New York: Viking Press, 1938.

Feis, Herbert. *The Road to Pearl Harbor: The Coming of the War between the United States and Japan.* Princeton, N.J.: Princeton University Press, 1950.

Freeman, Joseph. *An American Testament.* New York: Farrar & Rinehart, 1936.

Giddens, P. H. "Views of George Bancroft and Charles A. Beard on the Making of the Constitution," *Journal of American History,* XXVII (1933), 129–41.

Gideonse, H. D. "Nationalist Collectivism and Charles A. Beard," *Journal of Political Economy,* XLIII (December, 1935), 778–99.

Glaser, William A. Critique of Two Economic Interpretations of Politics: Charles A. Beard and A. M. Simons. Unpublished Ph.D. dissertation, Harvard University, 1952.

Goldman, Eric F. "Historian at Seventy," *New Republic,* CXI (November 27, 1944), 696–97.

———. "Origins of Beard's Economic Interpretations of the Constitution," *Journal of the History of Ideas,* XIII (April, 1952), 234–49.

———. *Rendezvous with Destiny.* New York: Alfred A. Knopf, 1952.

Graser, Ferdinand H. "Our Moot State Constitutional Convention," *National Municipal Review,* IX (February, 1920), 66–68.

Harrington, F. H. "Beard's Idea of National Interest and New Interpretations," *American Perspective,* IV (Fall, 1950), 335–45.

Heaton, Herbert. "The Economic Impact on History," in Joseph Strayer (ed.), *The Interpretation of History,* pp. 85–117. New York: Peter Smith, 1950.

H. E. B. "North Carolina Meeting of the American Historical Association," *American Historical Review,* XXXV (April, 1930), 481–500.

Herring, Hubert. "Charles A. Beard, Free Lance among Historians," *Harper's Magazine,* CLXXVIII (May, 1939), 641–52.

Hofstadter, Richard. "Beard and the Constitution: The History of an Idea," *American Quarterly,* II (Fall, 1950), 195–213.

———. "The Historian's Risk," *Encounter,* XII (February, 1959), 56–58.

Hook, Sidney. "Charles Beard's Political Testament," *Nation,* CLVII (October 23, 1943), 474–76.

Hoxie, R. G., and Others. *A History of the Faculty of Political Science.* New York: Columbia University Press, 1955.

Hurwitz, H. L. "Economic Interpretation of the Constitution: Live Pigeon or Dead Duck?" *Senior Scholastic*, LXXV (January 6, 1960), 13T–15T.

Johnson, Alvin. *Pioneer's Progress: An Autobiography*. New York: Viking Press, 1952.

Josephson, Matthew. "Charles A. Beard: A Memoir," *Virginia Quarterly Review*, XXV (October, 1949), 585–602.

———. "The Hat on the Roll-Top Desk," *New Yorker*, XVII (February 14, 1942), 22–26; XVIII (February 21, 1942), 21–28.

Kallen, Horace M. "In Remembrance of Charles Beard, Philosopher-Historian," *Social Research*, XVIII (June, 1951), 243–49.

Kazin, Alfred. *On Native Grounds*. New York: Reynal & Hitchcock, 1942.

Kenyon, Cecelia M. "Men of Little Faith: The Anti-Federalists on the Nature of Representative Government," *William and Mary Quarterly*, XII (January, 1955), 3–43.

Kraus, Michael. *A History of American History*. New York: Farrar & Rinehart, 1937.

———. *The Writing of American History*. Norman: University of Oklahoma Press, 1953.

Lamm, L., and D. M. Feins. "Charles A. Beard," *Social Education*, V (April, 1941), 263–68.

Lerner, Max. "Beard's Economic Interpretation," *New Republic*, XCIX (May 10, 1939), 7–11.

———. "Charles Beard: Civilization and the Devils," *New Republic*, CXIX (November 1, 1948), 21–24.

———. "Charles Beard Confronts Himself," *Nation*, CXLII (April 8, 1936), 452–54.

———. "Charles Beard's Stormy Voyage," *New Republic*, CXIX (October 25, 1948), 20–23.

———. *Ideas Are Weapons*. New York: Viking Press, 1939.

———. "The Political Theory of Charles A. Beard," *American Quarterly*, II (Winter, 1950), 303–21.

Levin, Peter R. "Charles A. Beard: Wayward Liberal," *Tomorrow*, VIII (March, 1949), 36–40.

McDonald, Forrest. *We the People: The Economic Origins of the Constitution*. Chicago: University of Chicago Press, 1958.

MacMahon, Arthur W. "Charles A. Beard," *American Political Science Review*, XLII (December, 1948), 1208–10.

———. "Charles Austin Beard as a Teacher," *Political Science Quarterly*, LXV (March, 1950), 1–19.

Main, Jackson T. "Charles A. Beard and the Constitution: A Critical Review of Forrest McDonald's *We the People*," *William and Mary Quarterly*, XVII (January, 1960), 86–110.

Manny, Frank A. "A Labor College," *New Republic*, XIV (March 9, 1918), 175.

Marks, Harry J. "Ground under Our Feet: Beard's Relativism," *Journal of the History of Ideas*, XIV (October, 1953), 628–33.

Miller, Perry. "Charles A. Beard," *Nation*, CLXVII (September 25, 1948), 344–46.

Moley, Raymond. *27 Masters of Politics*. New York: Funk & Wagnalls Co., 1949.

Morgenthau, Hans J. *In Defense of the National Interest*. New York: Alfred A. Knopf, 1951.

Morison, Samuel E. "Did Roosevelt Start the War? History through a Beard," *Atlantic Monthly*, CLXXXII (August, 1948), 91–97.

———. "Faith of a Historian," *American Historical Review*, LVI (January, 1951), 261–75.

North, Cecil C. "Class Structure, Class Consciousness, and Party Alignment," *American Sociological Review*, II (June, 1937), 365–71.

Oliver, D. W. "Selection of Content in the Social Sciences," *Harvard Educational Review*, XXVII (Fall, 1957), 271–300.

Osgood, Robert E. "Woodrow Wilson, Collective Security, and the Lessons of History," *Confluence*, V (Winter, 1957), 341–54.

Parrington, Vernon L. *Main Currents in American Thought*. New York: Harcourt, Brace & Co., 1930.

Parsons, Talcott. *The Social System*. Glencoe, Ill.: The Free Press, 1951.

Patten, Simon N. "The Present Problems in the Economic Interpretation of History," *Annals of the American Academy of Political and Social Science*, XXIV (November, 1904), 540–55.

Phillips, Harlan B. "Charles Beard: The English Lectures, 1899–1901," *Journal of the History of Ideas*, XIV (June, 1953), 451–56.

———. "Charles Beard, Walter Vrooman, and the Founding of Ruskin Hall," *South Atlantic Quarterly*, L (April, 1951), 186–91.

Pixton, John E., Jr. "The Ghost of Charles Beard," *Christian Century*, LXIX (October 1, 1952), 1120–22.

Powicke, F. M. "The Economic Motive in Politics," *Economic History Review*, XVI (1946), 85–92.

Pratt, Julius W. *A History of United States Foreign Policy*. Englewood Cliffs, N.J.: Prentice-Hall, 1955.

Radabaugh, J. "Charles A. Beard's Economic Interpretations of the Constitution: A Consensus," *Social Studies*, LI (December, 1960), 243–50.

Reed, J. J. "Economic Interpretation of the Constitution," *Social Studies*, XXXIV (January, 1943), 23–28.

Rogin, Leo. "The New Deal: A Survey of the Literature," *Quarterly Journal of Economics*, XLIX (February, 1935), 325–55.

Rudd, Augustin G. *Bending the Twig*. New York: New York Chapter, Sons of the Revolution, 1957.

Schevill, Ferdinand. "Ranke: Rise, Decline, and Persistence of a Reputation," *Journal of Modern History,* XXIV (September, 1952), 219–34.

Schuyler, R. L. "Forrest McDonald's Critique of the Beard Thesis," *Journal of Southern History,* XXVII (February, 1961), 73–80.

Seligman, E. R. A. *The Economic Interpretation of History.* New York: Columbia University Press, 1902. 2nd rev. ed., 1907.

Smith, J. Allen. *The Spirit of American Government.* New York: Chautauqua Press, 1907.

Smith, Theodore C. "The Writing of American History in America, from 1884 to 1934," *American Historical Review,* XL (April, 1935), 439–49.

Sorenson, Lloyd R. "Charles A. Beard and German Historiographical Thought," *Mississippi Valley Historical Review,* XLII (September, 1955), 274–87.

Strout, Cushing. "In Retrospect: Charles Beard's Liberalism," *New Republic,* CXXXIII (October 17, 1955), 17–18.

––––––. *The Pragmatic Revolt in American History: Carl Becker and Charles Beard.* New Haven, Conn.: Yale University Press, 1958.

––––––. "The Twentieth-Century Enlightenment," *American Political Science Review,* XLIX (June, 1955), 321–39.

Thomas, Robert E. "A Reappraisal of Charles A. Beard's Economic Interpretation of the Constitution of the United States," *American Historical Review,* LVII (January, 1952), 370–75.

––––––. "The Virginia Convention of 1788: A Criticism of Beard's *An Economic Interpretation of the Constitution,*" *Journal of Southern History,* XIX (February, 1953), 63–72.

Tocqueville, Alexis de. *Democracy in America.* New York: Alfred A. Knopf, 1945.

Trask, David F. "Historians, the Constitution, and Objectivity: A Case Study," *Antioch Review,* XX (Spring, 1960), 65–78.

Villard, Oswald G. "Charles A. Beard, Patriot," *Progressive,* XII (October, 1948), 21–22.

Ware, A. "Beards, Chroniclers of the Times," *Christian Science Monitor Weekly Magazine Section* (July 22, 1939), p. 5.

"What Professor Beard Said about the Flag," *New Republic,* VII (May 6, 1916), 18.

Whitaker, Arthur P. "Charles Austin Beard," *Revista de historia de América,* XXVI (December, 1948), 419–23.

White, Morton G. "Revolt against Formalism in American Social Thought of the Twentieth Century," *Journal of the History of Ideas,* VIII (April, 1947), 131–52.

––––––. *Social Thought in America: The Revolt against Formalism.* New York: Viking Press, 1949.

ilkins, Burleigh T. "Frederick York Powell and Charles A. Beard: A Study in Anglo-American Historiography and Social Thought," *American Quarterly*, XI (Spring, 1959), 21–39.

Williams, William A. "A Note on Charles Austin Beard's Search for a General Theory of Causation," *American Historical Review*, LXII (October, 1956), 59–80.

Wilson, Edmund. "What Do the Liberals Hope For?" *New Republic*, LXIX (February 10, 1932), 345–48.

Wright, Esmond. "History: The 'New' and the Newer," *Sewanee Review*, XLIX (October–December, 1941), 479–91.

INDEX

Absolute truth: and scientific method, 176

Abstractions: Beard on, 9, 144, 165; and the Constitution, 41; irrelevance to politics, 44

Accountable government: and elections, 31, 87; and autocracy, 192. *See also* Democracy

Acquisitive motives: in Beard's early theory, 54; in all societies, 161

Act of faith, written history as, 146, 151, 152, 153

Adams, Brooks: Beard's interest in, 157; cyclical theory of, 188

Adams, Henry, Beard's interest in, 157

Adams, John: political ideas compared to Beard's, 29, 213–14, 215; theory of, 30; political creed of, 34; on democracy, 184; on control of masses and classes, 214

Administration: public, 20, 21, 28, 80–81, 82, 192; value of science in study of, 70; assumed categories of, 82; rejection of boards for, 83

Admirals, alarmist warnings of, 112

Adult Education, American Association for: Beard's address to, 184

Africa: economic effect on heritage of, 246

Aggression: use of force against, 56, 237, 242–43; outside hemisphere, 63, 189, 237; nationalist, 229

Aggression, foreign: and young Republic, 246

Agriculture: Jefferson's concept of, 195; controls over, 196–97; aid to, 201; and foreign markets, 229–30. *See also* Farmers

Alien and Sedition laws, 68, 247

Allied intervention in Russia, 109, 122, 236. *See also* Russia

Altruism, 11. *See also* Human nature

Ambition: in power complex, 204; and political realism, 206

America: Beard's attention to, xix, xxiii, 185; ideal for, 117; modified picture of, 118; depression in, 125; international economic ties of, 217, 218; international problems of postwar, 222; foreign policy history of, 222–26; fate of, 248

America First Movement, 227

American-Catholic sentiment, 227

American civilization school of foreign policy, 225

American Civil Liberties Union: addressed by Beard, xxii, 69

American credit: to Europe, 113

American federalism: as model for world union, 246

American freedom: endangered in war, 114

American garden, an: Beard's ideal of, 228, 255

American historians: Beard's stimulation of, 151–52, 158; Riezler and Croce disregarded by, 156

American Historical Association: 121, 153; presidency of, xv, xxiii; Beard's address to, 145, 146

American military intervention: after World War II, 236

American Political Science Association: presidency of, xv, xxii; Beard's address to, 129

American political system: severest test of, 255

American politics: Beard's shift of interest to, xix; international influences on, 217

American Republic: war origin of, 67

American Revolution: and international politics, 96; "cause" and, 158

American technology: and standard of living, 191

American-Yugoslav Society: Beard invited by, xxii–xxiii

Amherst College lectures, 44, 130, 159; revision of, 73, 96–98; published in book form, 96

Amoralism, 6

Analogies: as barriers to understanding, 144; misuses of, 145, 155

Anarchy: as foe of liberty, 204; philosophy of rejected, 34, 78; and laissez faire, 79

Anticommunism: and isolationist tradition, 227

Antidemocratic sentiments, 163, 205

Antidumping laws: and aid to Nazis, 238

Anti-Federalists: and cherishment of the people, 35; and small farmers, 43